Silk *Silver* Opium

The longer you can look back,
the farther you can look forward.

Winston Churchill 1944

The great enemy of truth is very often not the lie
– deliberate, contrived and dishonest –
but the myth – persistent, persuasive and unrealistic.

John F. Kennedy 1962

Silk
Silver
Opium

The TRADE *with* CHINA *that* CHANGED HISTORY

Michael Pembroke

Hardie Grant

BOOKS

Published in 2025 by Hardie Grant Books, an imprint of Hardie Grant Publishing

Hardie Grant Books (Melbourne)
Wurundjeri Country
Level 11, 36 Wellington Street
Collingwood, Victoria 3066

Hardie Grant North America
2912 Telegraph Ave
Berkeley, California 94705

hardiegrant.com/books

Hardie Grant acknowledges the Traditional Owners of the country on which we work, the Wurundjeri people of the Kulin nation and the Gadigal people of the Eora nation, and recognises their continuing connection to the land, waters and culture. We pay our respects to their Elders past and present.

A catalogue record for this work is available from the National Library of Australia

Silk Silver Opium: The Trade with China that Changed History
ISBN 978 1 76145 198 0
ISBN 978 1 76144 335 0 (ebook)

10 9 8 7 6 5 4 3 2 1

Publishing Director: Pam Brewster
Head of Editorial: Jasmin Chua
Project Editor: Antonietta Anello
Editor: Allison Hiew
Creative Director: Kristin Thomas
Cover Design: Nada Backovic
Typesetter: Kirby Jones
Head of Production: Todd Rechner
Production Controller: Jessica Harvie

Printed in Malaysia by RR Donnelley.

The paper this book is printed on is from FSC®-certified forests and other controlled material. FSC® promotes environmentally responsible, socially beneficial and economically viable management of the world's forests.

For Gigi

CONTENTS

Preface ix
Introduction xiii
East & West Timeline xvii
Dynasties & Emperors xxi
Sources and Method xxiv

Part 1 – Prelude 1
Chapter 1: Before the Europeans 3

Part 2 – Discovering the East 15
Chapter 2: The Mongols 17
Chapter 3: The Great Ming 25
Chapter 4: Age of Discovery 34
Chapter 5: Trading Posts 40

Part 3 – Porcelain & Chinoiserie 51
Chapter 6: Porcelain's Puzzle 53
Chapter 7: Kilns of Jingdezhen 65
Chapter 8: Infiltration in Beijing 75
Chapter 9: An Idealised Orient 84
Chapter 10: Chinoiserie Mania 92

Part 4 – Tea & Silver 101
Chapter 11: Qianlong Era 103
Chapter 12: Trading Tea 115
Chapter 13: Rivers of Silver 125
Chapter 14: Manila Galleons 130
Chapter 15: Global Currents 138

Part 5 – Opium Trade **145**
Chapter 16: The Humble Plant 147
Chapter 17: A Storm Brewing 159
Chapter 18: Fire & Smoke 170

Part 6 – Opium Wars **183**
Chapter 19: First Opium War 185
Chapter 20: Second Opium War 198
Chapter 21: Plunder & Pillage 210

Part 7 – Neo-colonialism **223**
Chapter 22: America & Jesus 225
Chapter 23: Upheaval & Turmoil 238
Chapter 24: Make China Strong 251

Part 8 – Decline & Fall **265**
Chapter 25: Road to Ruin 267
Chapter 26: Road to Revolution 278
Chapter 27: End of the Road 288

Conclusion 298
Notes 300
Bibliography 318
Acknowledgements 328
Index 330
Photograph Credits 341

Preface

THIS BOOK HAS GIVEN me the privilege of re-visiting some of the places of my earlier life and learning more of others that I am yet to encounter. As a boy, I travelled by ship along the fringes of the ancient trading routes where merchants and traders from East and West, their silks and spices, incense and porcelain, and a myriad other things, once mixed and changed hands in colourful profusion. I was a product of the final decades of the colonial era, conceived in one hemisphere and born in another, accustomed to the sounds of different languages and foreign accents, familiar with turbans and saris, comfortable with constant movement and regular sea travel. The children at my first small school were Hindu, Sikh, Muslim and Christian. Their families, like mine, hailed from all over the British Commonwealth. Before I was ten years of age, I had twice crossed the world in a P&O liner, clambered up the Rock of Gibraltar, delighted in the magic of the gully-gully man, frolicked in the souk in Aden and been mesmerised by the cobras and snake charmers of Colombo.

At Gibraltar, the harbour was always crowded, full of bumboats and tenders and lighters, their occupants calling and jostling for our attention. The Rock swarmed with multitudes of precocious Barbary monkeys. Across the strait were Morocco and the mountain called Jebel Musa, the southern 'Pillar of Hercules' that once marked the western end of the known world. At the other end of the Mediterranean, as we approached

Cairo's Port Said, the historic harbour at Alexandria lay on the Egyptian coast to our south. Founded by Alexander the Great, it was an entrepôt of trade and a centre of culture throughout the Greek, Roman and Byzantine periods and long after.

In the Suez Canal, the gully-gully man clambered on board during the ship's slow progression through the narrow waterway – while just over the ship's railings, the desert landscape of the Sinai on one side and the greener low-lying delta of the Nile River on the other drifted by. For newcomers and veteran travellers, the unfathomable guile of the gully-gully man was a source of hushed wonder and bemusement. From the Suez Canal the ship moved out into the wider expanse of the Red Sea, passing Jeddah in the distance to the east, then out through the narrow Bab al-Mandab Strait, the 'Gate of Tears', to the Gulf of Aden and the Indian Ocean. Steering clear of Djibouti, we rounded the corner of the Arabian Peninsula to the safety of the harbour at Aden (Yemen), which was formed from the crater of a long-dormant volcano. It is where the ancient camel trade in frankincense and myrrh began its steady journey north to Petra and Palmyra. In the city's great covered souk, I gambolled among the stalls of the Arab merchants, trailing after my mother while she shopped for gifts and memories. Across the Indian Ocean, dockside at Colombo, I squatted, transfixed, as the ubiquitous snake charmer played a haunting melody on his *pungi*, mysteriously coaxing a king cobra out of its basket.

The years of sea travel were later followed by family life among the last dying embers of colonial Singapore. The island was undeveloped in those early days, filled with kampongs and crowded with street vendors and markets. The knockout smells of tropical fruit and rotting vegetation, food and scraps, lamp oil, spices and smoke filled the atmosphere. Our home in the oddly named Ridley Park was just a walk away from the headquarters of Far East Land Forces where my father worked as a junior officer. The house had open windows, wooden shutters and ceiling fans that rotated languorously and constantly. Voluminous mosquito nets shrouded the beds and geckos ran rampant across the walls. Tropical heat and monsoon rains became part of the ritual of our daily lives.

Ah-Nan, Sue Eng and their families lived with us. Their languages and lifestyles, customs and clothing, cooking smells and washing, clattering pots and sizzling pans, daily laughter and occasional squabbles, formed part of the backdrop to my juvenile existence. We took holidays and day trips through the rubber plantations of Johor; up the Malacca Strait to Penang; overland to a cool hill station at Fraser's Hill in Malaysia and to unspoilt beaches facing the South China Sea. Everywhere we went, the Chinese, Indonesians, Singaporeans and Malays were an indelible part of our everyday existence. To borrow a phrase from Edmund de Waal, the Orient became 'the elsewhere that I love'.

Later still as a young man passing through Tehran, I stared in awe at the snow-capped Alborz Mountains that separate the city from the Caspian Sea and pondered the surrounding history-soaked region at the geographical centre of the world: the global heartland between China and the West – more important now than ever. It was a memorable moment but it was only one of many formative experiences that shaped me. I studied French and Indian history at university but as life unfolded, my dreams of history and diplomacy were gently pushed to one side and the law tugged me in a different direction. For a long time I remained wrapped in its familiar bosom, while continuing to undertake more voyages of discovery whenever I could, and sometimes pining for the career I did not pursue.

With the passing of time, my curiosity and respect for the diversity of humanity have not dimmed. And my distrust of those who believe in the universalism of their own cultures and faiths, or the exceptionalism of their own political systems, values or ideologies, has steadily grown.

Introduction

EUROPE'S TRADING RELATIONSHIP WITH imperial China started in wonder and ended in war and bloodshed. The Europeans marvelled at shimmering silk, fragrant tea and exquisite porcelain, which were unknown in the West until their introduction through the China trade. They became indispensable items of Western culture and fashion, but to the exasperation of the Europeans the secrets of their production remained a mystery for a very long time. Silk possessed qualities not shared by any other known fabric; tea became the world's most popular beverage after water; and porcelain was second in intrigue only to the philosopher's stone until its secret was finally deciphered in a royal workshop near Meissen in Germany in the eighteenth century. This is the story of those remarkable products, and the silver and opium that were funnelled into China in exchange. It is also a story of avarice, war and imperial collapse.

The China trade first reached the Europeans during the time of the Roman emperor Augustus (27 BCE – 14 CE) when camel caravans crossed the Iranian Plateau to the eastern fringes of the Roman empire. It continued and thrived along the overland route, and later along the maritime route, during the Tang, Song and Yuan (Mongol) dynastic periods, before the Ming dynasty closed China's door to foreigners in the fifteenth century. From the early 1500s, Portuguese merchant ships ventured around the Cape of Good Hope, across the Indian Ocean and through the South China Sea to Canton (Guangzhou) in southern China. Despite official disapproval, the Cantonese merchants were not averse to profiting from trade with the Portuguese, whose vessels returned to Lisbon loaded with cargoes of oriental exotica. The Dutch and the English later followed the same route to China while the Spanish crossed the Pacific to Manila in the Philippines. The primary medium of exchange for the China trade was silver and for the next 300 years most of the world's silver came to China. Sir Isaac Newton lamented when he was Warden of the Royal Mint that China 'carries away the silver from all Europe'.

The massive inflow of silver fundamentally changed Chinese society during the Ming and Qing dynasties and made it inordinately rich, while draining the West of its reserves. In the early 1800s the British began to cultivate opium in India on an industrial scale. They smuggled it to China and peddled it at Canton. The Americans soon joined in the smuggling trade. British opium weakened and impoverished China, drained it of silver and destabilised its population. It reversed the pattern of previous centuries and was a keystone of imperial dominance. Silk, silver and opium therefore represent the highs and lows of the old China trade – and its beginning, middle and end.

The narrative finishes with the collapse of China's last imperial dynasty in 1912. The end of imperial China followed the upheaval and decline of Chinese society and the depredations of the Western powers during the nineteenth century: Britain invaded China in 1840; Britain and France jointly invaded in 1857; Japan invaded in 1895; and an eight nation 'coalition of the willing' invaded in 1900. The coalition represented the Euro-American world order of the day and consisted of almost all the same G7 nations that still represent the West: United Kingdom, United States, Germany, France, Japan, Italy, Austria-Hungary and pre-revolutionary Russia. China has neither forgotten nor quite forgiven those events. Nor is the Euro-American world order the dominant force it once was.

In the late first century CE, as Rome was increasingly exposed to trade from China, the poet Juvenal complained that Roman women were interfering in the traditional affairs of men by asking the question 'What are the intentions of the Chinese?' The West is still asking the same question. I have not attempted to provide an answer but have simply sought to tell the story of imperial China's trade with the West, and perhaps to caution that if we fail to understand China's past and the history of its trading relationship with the West, we risk miscalculation and misreading, we fuel mistrust and we invite misjudgement.

Sima Qian, the Grand Historian of the Han period, wrote: 'He who does not forget the past is master of the present'. Historians as well as informed observers know that it is impossible to ignore how the past 'is inscribed on China's mental terrain in a calligraphy so powerful that it determines most of its approaches to the present'. Prolific trade and political insecurity have been recurrent features of China's history. The insecurity has manifested in comprehensive authoritarian control, frequent censorship, reflexive defensiveness, inordinate pride, sensitivity to criticism and wariness of religious movements. Much about China's modern relationship with the West is the product of its past inter-reactions, conflicts, victories and humiliations. And many of its modern agitations have been perennial sources of anxiety. The South China Sea was the place from where the ultimately destructive European sailing ships arrived. The Ryukyu Island chain was the place from where marauding Japanese *wokou* (dwarf) pirates came to prey mercilessly on China's east coast ports. Taiwan was where anti-Qing rebels established a stronghold in the seventeenth century. Tibet has been a source of problematic relations since at least the thirteenth century when it formed part of the Yuan dynasty. The far western region of Xinjiang, the grasslands of the northern steppe and the steamy jungles of Vietnam and Myanmar have been frequent sources of unrest, rebellion and conflict. Not much has changed.

This book includes colourful stories of silk and tea, porcelain and chinoiserie, silver and opium, missionaries, mercenaries and trade, and, inevitably, war. Each story could be a book in its own right but I have ranged more widely, and inevitably in less detail than a work solely devoted to one of those subjects. I have sought to shine a light rather than unravel; to reveal rather than resolve; to explain rather than analyse. The result is a book that is written for the interested reader, not a professional sinologist. I have drawn comfort from John Julius Norwich who confessed in his *A Short History of Byzantium* that his book made no claim to academic scholarship and that it would not satisfy the professional Byzantinist, who would find little that he did not already know and many a statement with which he might disagree, but it was a tale worth telling. I too have merely skated across the surface of a long and tangled history, but in doing so I hope that I have made the story of imperial China's trading relationship with the West, and its implications for the future, a tale worth telling.

EAST & WEST

Timeline
247 BCE–1912

DATE	THE EAST	THE WEST
EARLY PERIOD		
247 BCE–224 CE	Parthian Empire (Persia)	
221 BCE	First emperor Qin ends Warring States period: unification of China	
206 BCE–220 CE	Han Dynasty	
27 BCE		Augustus – founds Roman Empire
330 CE		Constantine – founds Byzantine Empire
476		Fall of Roman Empire
5–10th CENTURIES		Dark Ages in Europe
618–907	Tang Dynasty	
632	Death of Prophet Muhammad	
634	Rise of Islam	
762	Founding of Baghdad as Islamic capital	
960–1279	Song Dynasty	
1066		Battle of Hastings, William the Conqueror
1095–1291		Christian Crusades to the Holy Land
1271–1368	Yuan (Mongol) Dynasty	Plantagenet Kings Edward I, II & III
1271–1295		Marco Polo in China
1299	Rise of Ottoman Empire	
14th CENTURY		
1330s	Black Death in China	
1347		Black Death arrives in Europe
1368–1644	Ming Dynasty	

DATE	THE EAST	THE WEST
15th CENTURY		
1405–1433	Seven Voyages of Ming 'Treasure Fleets'	
1406	Yongle Emperor commences construction of Forbidden City	
1488		Bartholomew Dias sails around Cape of Good Hope
1492		Columbus crosses Atlantic to Cuba
1498		Vasco da Gama reaches India
16th CENTURY		
1501–1736	Persian Empire (Safavid)	
1509–1547		Reign of Tudor King Henry VIII
1513		Portuguese mariners reach China
1521–1620	Reign of Chinese Emperors Jiajing and Wanli	
1526–1857	Mughal Empire	
1545		Spain discovers silver in Andes Mountains
1557		Portuguese granted right to settle on Macau
1565–1898		Spanish colonial period in Philippines
1565–1815		Manila Galleon trade
1582		Jesuit Matteo Ricci arrives at Macau
1588–1675		Dutch Golden Age
17th CENTURY		
1600		Founding of East India Company
1601		Matteo Ricci invited to Forbidden City
1602		Founding of Dutch VOC
1620s–1630s		Portuguese and Dutch traders bring tea to Europe
1644–1912	Qing dynasty	
1657		First tea for sale in England
1662–1795	Lengthy reigns of the 'Three Emperors' – Kangxi, Yongzheng & Qianlong	
1670		Louis XIV builds Le Trianon de Porcelaine
1683	Taiwan incorporated into China	
18th CENTURY		
1700		East India Company commences trading at Canton
1708		Porcelain created at Meissen

DATE	THE EAST	THE WEST
1717		Sir Isaac Newton warns that China drains all the silver of Europe
1721	Kangxi Emperor bans Christianity in China	
c.1749		House of Confucius built at Kew Gardens
1750		David Hume warns that if China were closer 'everything we use would be Chinese'
mid–1700s		Chinoiserie mania grips Europe
1759	Qing dynasty re-conquers Xinjiang	
1761		Chinese Pagoda built at Kew Gardens
1768		Porcelain created in England
1784–1785		Voyage to China of the American ship, Empress of China
1789–1799		French Revolution
1793		First British embassy to China (Lord Macartney)
19th CENTURY		
1815		Battle of Waterloo
1816		Second British embassy to China (Lord Amherst)
1817		Napoleon warns Amherst against British aggression towards China
1820		East India Company expands opium production
1832		Founding of Jardine, Matheson
1839	Appointment of Commissioner Lin to stop opium trade	
1840		Britain invades China
1842	Treaty of Nanjing	
1850–1864	Taiping Rebellion	
1853		Britain invades Crimea
1857		Britain & France invade China
1857		British general election – the 'Chinese election'
1858	Treaties of Tianjin between China and Britain, France, Russia and United States of America	
1860		British & French soldiers loot the Old Summer Palace; British then destroy it
1860	Opium legalised	
1861	Cixi becomes Empress Dowager	
1868	China appoints American, Anson Burlingame, as envoy to Treaty Powers	

DATE	THE EAST	THE WEST
1870s–1880s		Russia, Japan and France make territorial incursions in China
1894		Japan launches Sino-Japanese War
1895	Treaty of Shimonoseki	
1897–1898		Germany, Russia, Britain & France seize Chinese territory and establish bases
1898	Cixi places Guangxu Emperor under house arrest and ends the 'Hundred Days' Reform'	
20th CENTURY		
1900 –1901	Boxer Uprising	
1900		Eight-Nation Alliance invades China
1900		Foreign looting of Beijing & Summer Palace
1900 –1901		Western reprisals against Chinese
1901	Boxer Protocol	
1908	Cixi appoints heir-apparent, poisons Guangxu Emperor and dies on consecutive days	
1911	Revolution in China	
1912	Collapse of Qing dynasty	

Dynasties & Emperors

referred to in the text

Qin Dynasty
(221–206 BCE)

EMPEROR
Qin (221–210 BCE)

Han Dynasty
(206 BCE–220 CE)

EMPEROR
Wu (141–87 BCE)

Tang Dynasty
(618–907 CE)

EMPERORS
Gaozu (618–626)
Taizong (626–649)
Wu Zetian, Empress (690–705)
(but effectively) from 665–705
Xuanzong (712–756)

Song Dynasty
(960–1279 CE)

EMPERORS

Taizu (960–976)
Gaozong (1127–1162)

Yuan (Mongol) Dynasty
(1271–1368 CE)

EMPERORS

Kublai Khan (1271–1294)
Toghon Temür (1333–1368)

Ming Dynasty
(1368–1644 CE)

EMPERORS

Hongwu (1368–1398)
Yongle (1402–1424)
Hongxi (1424–1425)
Xuande (1425–1435)
Zhengtong (1435–1449)
Jingtai (1449–1457)
Jiajing (1521–1566)
Wanli (1572–1620)
Chongzhen (1627–1644)

Qing Dynasty
(1644–1912 CE)

EMPERORS

Shunzi (1644–1661)
Kangxi (1661–1722)
Yongzheng (1722–1735)
Qianlong (1735–1796)
Jiaqing (1796–1820)
Daoguang (1820–1850)
Xianfeng (1850–1861)
Tongzhi (1861–1875)
Guangxu (1875–1908)
Xuantong (1908–1912)

Sources and *Method*

IN THE PROCESS OF researching and writing this book, I have relied on primary sources in conjunction with a judicious selection from the vast array of secondary sources that address the many subjects that I have canvassed. Some secondary sources were contemporaneous with the events in question and others were historical accounts written from a later perspective. Some primary sources, including Chinese writings, were available to me in translation. The rendition of Chinese characters into written language that uses the Roman alphabet is fraught with perplexity. Chinese characters cannot be rendered letter by letter into Roman script as, for example, Arabic can be. They are not words or letters but symbols that contain information about meaning. Pinyin, the standard modern form of Chinese transliteration – which uses the letters 'q', 'x', 'y', and 'z' in confusing abundance – is unable to convey all of the subtleties of meaning and explication of Chinese characters.

I have also had recourse to a number of historical novels, especially those by authors with profound knowledge of their subject or who have clearly engaged in extensive historical research. Amitav Ghosh's three-volume Ibis trilogy about the nineteenth century opium and coolie trade is a case in point. As is the classic Chinese novel of an old official family, *Moment in Peking* by Nobel prize nominee Lin Yutang. Another is Lisa See's *Lady Tan's Circle of Women* – a contemporary study about a woman physician in fifteenth century Ming China. And another is the *Golden Lotus*, a sometimes graphic sixteenth century novel of Chinese manners by Lanling Xiaoxiao Sheng.

I have used the Pinyin system of spelling throughout except for certain names and places where personal choice and familiar Western usage have made another spelling preferable. Among many examples, I have preferred Canton for Guangzhou, Commissioner Lin for Lin Zexu and Tibet for Xijang. As for the names of emperors, I have used those names that have the widest modern Western currency, despite certain formal Chinese conventions. And as for the imperial dynasties, I have focussed only on the major ones: Qin (221–206 BCE), the first dynasty; Han (206 BCE–220 CE), coeval with the Roman republic and early Roman empire; Tang (618–907), coeval with the expansion of the Arab empire; Song (960–1279), coeval with the Crusades; Yuan (1271–1368), coeval with the Plantagenet kings Edward I, II & III; Ming (1368–1644), coeval with the early Ottoman and Mughal empires; and Qing (1644–1912), coeval with European global expansion.

An obstacle for any historian in my position is Western unfamiliarity with Chinese culture, geography and history. Most readers could name several Roman emperors but few could name, let alone spell, a single Chinese emperor. And hardly any readers could name, let alone pronounce, the 23 provinces of modern China. The lack of understanding contributes to a lack of rapport, and in turn, a lack of empathy. The corollary is often a prejudice uninformed by reason or experience. Sometimes the consequence is a lack of interest. My hope is that this book will contribute to an understanding of the historical relationship between China and the West, and perhaps correct some of the misapprehensions that I have encountered along the way.

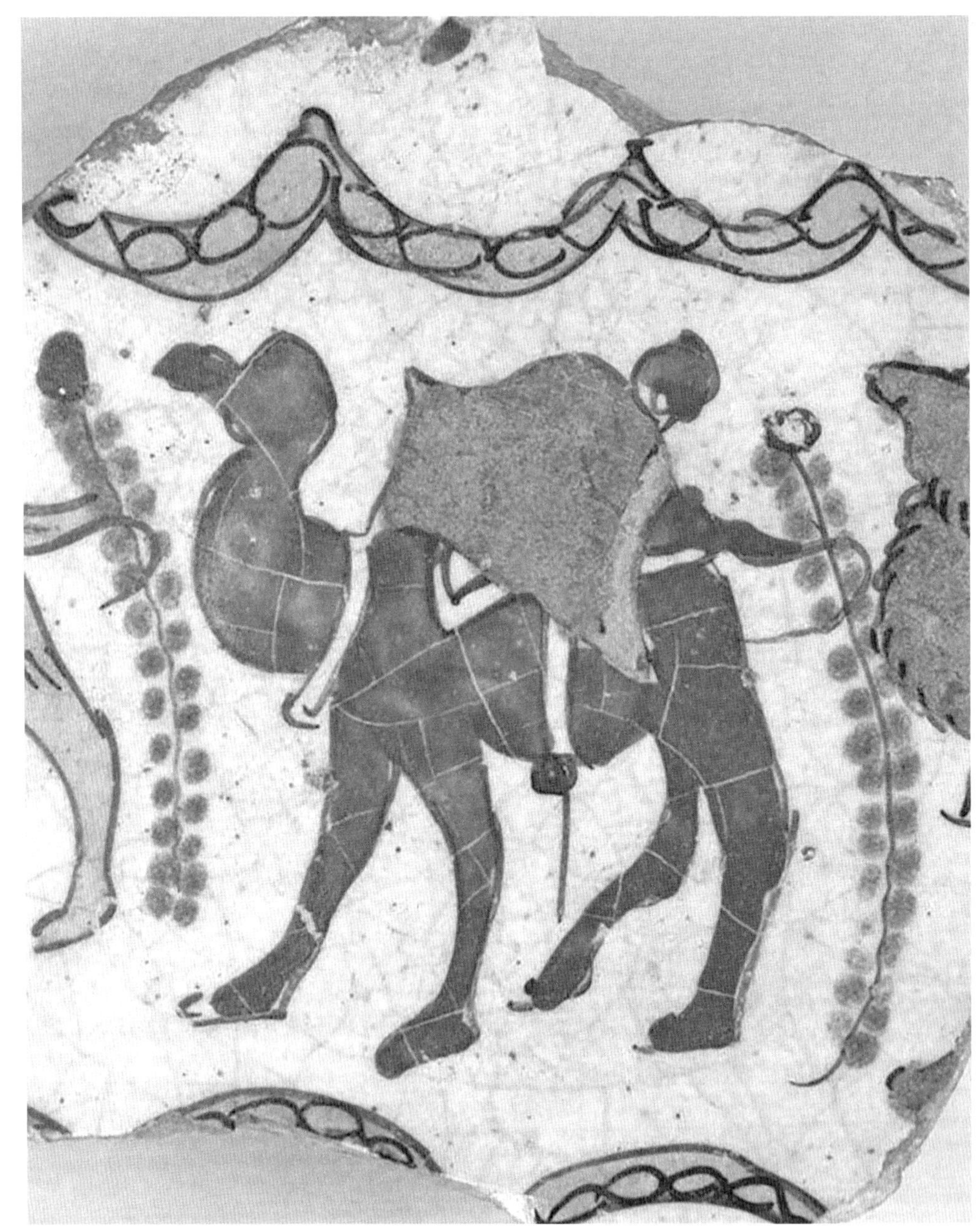

PART 1

Prelude

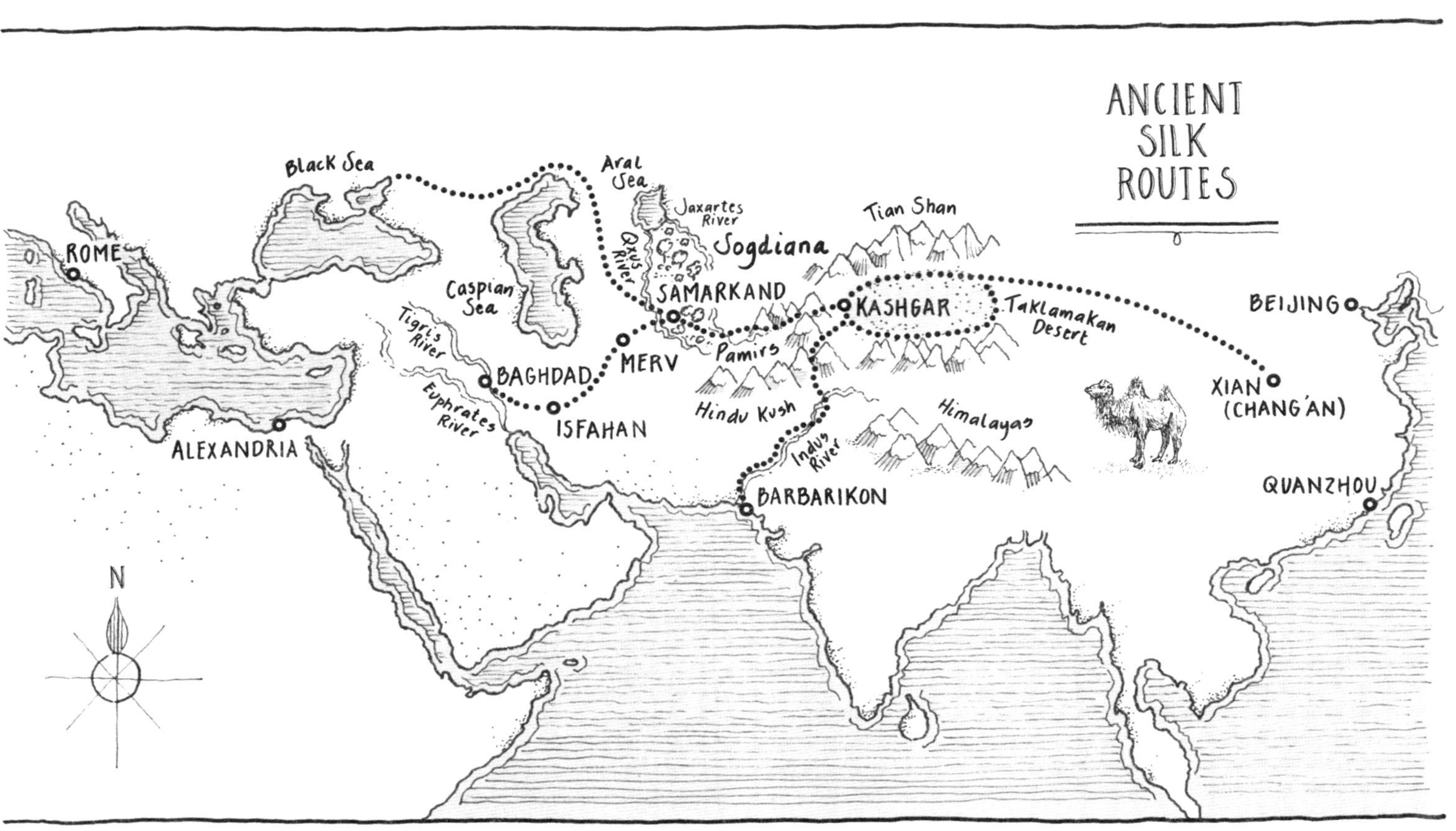
ANCIENT SILK ROUTES
Black Sea
Aral Sea
Jaxartes River
Oxus River
Sogdiana
Tian Shan
ROME
Caspian Sea
SAMARKAND
KASHGAR
Taklamakan Desert
BEIJING
Tigris River
BAGHDAD
MERV
Pamirs
XIAN (CHANG'AN)
Euphrates River
ISFAHAN
Hindu Kush
Himalayas
ALEXANDRIA
Indus River
BARBARIKON
QUANZHOU
N

CHAPTER 1

BEFORE THE EUROPEANS

221 BCE – 1271

AROUND 2000 YEARS AGO, when Britons lived in scattered settlements in round hovels made from mud, straw and wood, two superpowers coexisted at the centre of the world. The Roman empire dominated the west while imperial China under the Han dynasty dominated the east. By the second century CE, Chinese expansion and trade meant that the two empires 'almost brushed against each other'. What brought them together was trade, particularly the trade in silk, a fabric unlike any other in Europe at the time.

Silk caused a sensation when it first arrived in Rome. The Romans knew only wool and linen, or the animal skins and furs worn by rustics and barbarians. Cotton from India had not yet arrived. Affluent Roman women and some men as well went wild over Chinese silk – to the point where the balance of trade drained the Roman exchequer and invariably favoured China, just as it does with many of China's trading partners in the twenty-first century. Silk's novelty and expense made it exclusive and its physical attraction made it seductive. And silk was practical: brighter, stronger, more durable, lighter and more comfortable than any known fabric.

The Romans knew almost nothing of China and could only guess at the source of silk. To them, China was simply Serica (land of silk) or Sinae (land of the Qin), and the Chinese were the Seres. They did not know that China's imperial period began two centuries before the Roman empire when Zheng, king of the Qin state, ended the long, tumultuous chapter of China's Warring States period (475–221 BCE). He unified China around the Yellow and Yangtze rivers heartland and established the first dynasty of the Chinese imperial period. Zheng 'changed the whole course of Chinese history' and became forever known as 'First Emperor Qin', although his dynasty, the Qin (221–206 BCE), was one of the shortest. It was followed after a brief transitional period by the longest, the Han dynasty (206 BCE–220 CE), which ruled for over four centuries with a brief interruption midway through.

Qin established 'the world's oldest tradition of centralised bureaucracy' based on a meritocratic system of selection of government officials. And like his modern Chinese counterparts, he understood the importance of infrastructure and engaged in road construction on a massive scale. The first emperor exemplified the Chinese aphorism that 'if you want to get rich, build roads first'. The Qin road network is believed to have been comparable to, perhaps even longer than, the Roman system. It included a miraculous 750-kilometre north-south highway to Inner Mongolia sometimes called, with customary Chinese pride, the 'Qin Straight Road' or the 'Qin Direct Path'. Remnants remain today.

Qin's unification of the Chinese state, with a centralised national civil administration, a powerful military and a stable economy, made it possible for China to venture west. During the first and second centuries BCE, China's envoys and armies opened a grand salient into Central Asia, travelling through modern Xinjiang and the western regions, over the mountain passes and down into the rivers and valleys of Central Asia. And as the name Qin (pronounced 'Chin') passed from language to language across western Asia, it was gradually transmogrified into 'China'. The Sanskrit word was pronounced 'Chee-na'.

Far off in Rome, the Romans had no idea that the expensive silk fabrics that came from China were made from a tiny, fine and lustrous filament painstakingly unwound from the protective cocoon of a silk moth (*Bombyx mori*). Each cocoon is formed from a single strand of sticky silk fibre that the caterpillar spins around itself in figure of eight loops over a two-three-day period. The process is part of the miraculous transformation in the insect's life cycle from egg – to larva (or caterpillar) – to pupa – to moth. Extraordinarily, the fibre of one silk moth cocoon may extend for almost 1000 metres and a single silk filament is said to be 'stronger than a comparable filament of steel and more flexible than nylon'.

The closely guarded secret of Chinese sericulture was that the farmers preserved the valuable continuous filament intact by not allowing the moth to emerge from the cocoon. The process of breaking through – like a chick emerging through the shell of an egg – ruptures the silk thread surrounding the cocoon, weakens the remaining strands and leaves fibres of irregular length and inferior strength. Instead, as animal rights activists since Mahatma Ghandi have complained, the Chinese killed each pupa by immersing the cocoons in boiling water, cutting short the life cycle of many millions of silk moths and preserving the entire translucent thread. Legend has it that the inspiration for this process, and the origin of Chinese sericulture, occurred in the twenty-seventh century BCE when Empress Leizu – wife of the mythical Yellow Emperor – watched a cocoon fall from a mulberry tree into her teacup and noticed the gossamer silk thread slowly unravel.

The first Romans to see Chinese silk were the awe-struck legionnaires who were led into a fateful battle in 53 BCE at Carrhae, now Harran, a crossroads city near the Turkish border with Syria. Their opponents were soldiers from Parthia, a powerful Iranian empire in ancient Persia that blocked the Roman empire's eastward expansion. A Roman historian wrote of the battle that the Parthians appeared 'with their standards fluttering with gold and silk pennants; then without delay, the cavalry closing in on all sides, showered their weapons as thick as hail or rain upon the Romans'. As the legionnaires locked their shields and huddled together in their tightly packed testudo defensive formation, volleys of hardened steel-tipped Parthian arrows rained down mercilessly upon them. The piercing arrows punched through the shields of the Romans and tore through their chain mail chest armour. Many legionnaires had their hands pinned to their shields or their feet skewered to the ground.

The ethereal and colourful fabric that unfurled from the hundreds of long-flowing Parthian banners was Chinese silk. The Roman soldiers had never seen anything like it. Nor were they aware that the steel-tipped Parthian arrows were the product of a Chinese steel-making technology that was not yet known in the West. Within a few years of the battle at Carrhae, Roman commanders in the east began to acquire small quantities of silk for their own commercial gain and private consumption. And Julius Caesar provided a foretaste of silk to the citizens of Rome at a triumphal pageant at the Forum in 46 BCE. The crowds reacted with wonder and amazement at the colour and delicacy of the silk canopies that replaced the customary linen awnings. They were even more 'wondrous than the show of gladiators that Caesar offered'. Julius Caesar's ostentatious display ensured that silk would become an item of high fashion in Roman society, something that could not have escaped the attention of his then mistress, Cleopatra, who became intimately familiar with Chinese silk. The Roman poet Lucan described Cleopatra wearing the sheerest of silks, 'her white breasts resplendent through the Sidonian fabric', which was created 'by the skill of the Seres' and made sheer by 'the needle of the workman of the Nile' who loosened the warp and stretched the weft.

As silk began to proliferate in Rome, the old guard was critical and some disapproved on moral grounds. Seneca, who married late in life to a younger woman, fulminated that silk was a cypher for eroticism, that it neither hid the curves nor the decency of the ladies of Rome and that a 'woman who wears these silks can hardly say with a clear conscience that she is not stark naked'. More than a few venerable Roman gentlemen were also troubled by the drain on Rome's silver and gold resources. They thought the outflow of capital simply to 'enable the Roman lady to shimmer in public' was a scandal, let alone bad economic management. In the third century, the outflow of silver and the continuing imbalance of trade would contribute to the debasement of Rome's currency and ultimately its downfall. Over time, China became known as the 'graveyard of silver from the West'.

The 7000-kilometre journey of the caravans from central China to the eastern fringes of the Roman empire on the Euphrates River was long and protracted, but well trodden. The usual means of transport was the shaggy, heavy-bodied, two-humped Bactrian camel indigenous to most of the region across Persia, Central Asia and far western China – not the taller Dromedary camels of Arabia and northern Africa, with their spindly legs and thinner bodies. The sure-footed Bactrian camel excelled in the high mountains, exposed passes, cold steppes and inhospitable deserts to China's west. The breed's dense, woolly winter coat provided insulation against sub-zero conditions; its tough, flat footpads enabled it to traverse snow, ice, rock and shifting sands; its long eyelashes and sealable nostrils kept out dust and sand; and its two humps stored vital reserves of body fat. A camel caravan at the height of the silk trade might consist of hundreds of these cranky herbivorous mammals, joined nose to tail in groups of about twelve, trudging along well-worn tracks, piled high with bolts of silk fabric and other luxuries, braying and bellowing, farting and harrumphing.

Their journey took them across China for several thousand kilometres from Chang'an (Xian) to the formidable Taklamakan Desert in modern Xinjiang. The desert is a sea of shifting sand dunes, some as high as 300 metres. Aurel Stein, the famous British archaeologist of Central Asia, contended that the Saharan, Arabian and Iranian deserts were tame compared to the Taklamakan. From the Taklamakan, the caravans climbed into the jumbled fusion of mountain ranges on China's western frontier that includes the rugged Pamirs, the Hindu Kush and the celestial Tian Shan Mountains. One writer described them as a 'Mardi Gras of snow and ice'. They form a horseshoe-shaped fortress on China's west. Once over the high mountain passes, the merchant travellers and their camels descended to the fertile region in the foothills around the once-great rivers of the Oxus and Jaxartes, which flow north and north-west for over 2000 kilometres to their currently desiccated river mouths in the Aral Sea – passing through modern Tajikistan, Turkmenistan, Uzbekistan, Kyrgyzstan and Kazakhstan. The Persians called this verdant land 'Sogdiana' and the Romans called it 'Transoxiana'. It is the fabled 'Oxiana' of Robert Byron's classic travelogue, *The Road to Oxiana* (1937). The ancient capital was Samarkand.

From Sogdiana, the caravans wended their way either west across the vast Iranian Plateau to the fringes of the Roman empire or south through the Indus Valley to ancient ports such as Barbarikon at the mouth of the Indus River near modern Karachi, which connected with the Indian Ocean trade. As well as silk from China, foreign merchants could acquire 'singing boys, beautiful maidens for the harem, fine wines, thin clothing of the finest weaves and the choicest ointments'. Along its remarkable journey, the silk passed through many intermediaries and crossed multiple territories. At each stage, it 'would change hands at dramatically higher prices. It was costly enough in China; in Rome, it was yet a hundred times costlier – worth its weight in gold, so expensive that even a few ounces might consume a year of an average man's wages'.

In China by contrast, silk was such an abundant and renewable resource that Han soldiers were paid in bundles of plain silk, which circulated as currency, and 'every farming household paid a tax to the Han government in grain and silk cloth'. Han emperors lavished silk and tribute on their enemies in the hope of making them economically and culturally dependent on Chinese products. It was a time-honoured diplomatic strategy with a familiar twenty-first century ring to it. As one historian explained, 'Once this economic dependency was established, then the Chinese could exert political pressure on the [tribes] by threatening to withhold or limit their access to Han products'. As in modern times, the policy was designed to 'corrupt them with wealth' and to 'spoil them rotten to win their compliance'.

After the Han period, the early Tang dynasty (618–907) was a second golden age for the overland silk trade routes. In the eighth century, as Islamic armies were lunging forward from the Arabian Peninsula, it could be said with complete confidence that 'in terms of both commerce and culture the Silk Road was then the centre of the world'. The Tang capital city of Chang'an (Xian), a thousand kilometres south-west of modern Beijing, was 'one of the most important cities of the distant past ... nearly three times the size of Rome, nearly four times larger than Alexandria, and seventeen times bigger than Byzantium'. Its prosperity was sustained by trade, especially the trade in silk. Chang'an's location at the eastern terminus of the silk trade routes that traversed Persia and Central Asia made it a cosmopolitan gateway to the West. The immense city had twelve huge city gates and eight broad boulevards, each about 50 metres wide, divided into three lanes. The middle lane – the broadest – was reserved for the emperor. By comparison, Rome's grand Appian Way, the 'Queen of Roads' that ran for 200 kilometres from Rome to Capua and onwards to Brindisi, averaged about 6 metres wide, just enough for two chariots.

In the late Tang era, military setbacks and internal rebellions resulted in the fabled silk roads losing their pre-eminence. China forfeited control over the western regions and a permanent geopolitical line in Central Asia divided Muslim-controlled areas from Chinese western expansion. China became effectively cut off from the overland caravan trade to Central Asia, which never quite resumed its earlier importance, except during the brief Mongol era. China's foreign trade re-orientated from the camel route to the maritime route. This was the beginning of the rise and rise of China's maritime trading power, when 'merchants went by sea' and the major communication route between the Persian Gulf and China became the sea route.

The change in China's trading orientation coincided with an upswing of navigation in the Islamic world in the eighth and ninth centuries. As the Dark Ages enveloped Europe, there was 'a flowering of trade on the Monsoon Seas'. Around the year 762, the caliph al-Mansur, with his eyes set firmly on China, predicted that his newly founded and visionary capital of Baghdad – with its easy access from the Euphrates to the Persian Gulf – would be 'a waterfront for the world' and that with 'no obstacle between us and China; everything on the sea can come to us'. Like the Thames River in nineteenth-century London, Baghdad's riverbanks were lined with ships. The perilous China run – 'the 6,000-mile voyage by way of Ceylon and Southeast Asia to the fabled ports of China' – fascinated the Arabs. It was the stuff of legend, the source of tall tales and the inspiration for the adventures of Sinbad the Sailor. The names of ports along the sea route reflected China's importance to the Arabs as a trade destination: Sohar, the Arab port in Oman near the entrance to the Persian Gulf, was 'the hallway to China, the storehouse of the East'; Aden, the Arab port near the entrance to the Red Sea, was 'the gateway to China'; and the Paracel Reefs in the South China Sea were 'the Gates of China'.

By the ninth century, China's industrial-level manufacturing capacity and the depth of its export trade were unequalled. The surviving cargo of an Arab shipwreck from that period included approximately 60,000 porcelain bowls, 763 identical inkpots, 915 spice jars and 1635 ewers – all preserved in pristine condition primarily due to an intricate system of stacking them tightly in series, in helical fashion, inside large storage jars firmly packed with straw. The porcelain was made to order in Chinese kilns for the export trade and most of the bowls bear geometric designs or inscriptions from the Quran designed to appeal to the Islamic market. The serial nature of the products indicated a sophisticated supply chain of manufacturers, shippers and merchants that could coordinate massive orders and transport them 'over vast distances at considerable risk and expense, with considerable profit'. It is still the Chinese way.

The Tang dynasty was followed by the Song dynasty (960–1279), another prosperous age of maritime trade. The emperor Gaozong (r. 1127–1162) deliberately set out to take advantage of foreign trade, famously declaring that 'The profits from overseas trade are very great. If properly managed, they can be millions. Is not this revenue better than taxing the ordinary people?' Song dynasty leaders understood the intrinsic importance of economic activity – that spending and investing were better than saving and hoarding. Centuries before modern economists theorised about the velocity of circulation of money – and 600 years before English philosopher John Locke sketched out a quantity theory of money – the Song finance minister, Shen Kuo, demonstrated his own remarkably intuitive understanding:

> The utility of money derives from circulation and loan-making. A village of ten households may have 100,000 coins. If the cash is stored in the household of one individual, even after a century, the sum remains 100,000. If the coins are circulated through business transactions so that every individual of the ten households can enjoy the utility of the 100,000 coins, then the utility will amount to that of 1 million cash. If circulation continues without stop, the utility of the cash will be beyond enumeration.

The Song economic expansion was so dramatic that it resulted in – indeed it practically necessitated – the world's first introduction of paper money. And the Song maritime industry became dominated, just as European mercantile shipping would later be, by sophisticated syndicates and astute investors who financed every aspect of the trade – the cargo, the ships and the voyage – and spread their risk across multiple investments. The limited liability joint stock company, a groundbreaking vehicle for investment that is often associated with the much-later English Muscovy Company (1555) or the East India Company (1600), became a feature of Song maritime commerce. Ownership was represented by a pool of shareholders who shared profits and losses while management was in the separate hands of a class of merchants who operated the business using investors' funds.

In tandem with the exuberant growth in exports, the Song shipbuilding industry expanded at full tilt, especially at the port of Quanzhou on the Taiwan Strait. By the mid-eleventh century, a government agent could report of Quanzhou that 'the port was clogged with foreign ships, and their goods were piled like mountains'. Song shipwrights produced junks that were larger and more seaworthy than ships previously seen anywhere else in the world. They were effectively 'ocean liners, boasting staterooms, wineshops and the service of negro stewards'. Jordanus, a Spanish missionary and explorer who visited India in the thirteenth century, observed Song junks and described them as being 'very big, and have upon the ship's hull more than 100 cabins, and with a fair wind they carry ten sails, and they are very bulky, being made of three thicknesses of plank'.

In the late thirteenth century, China, like most of Eurasia before it, succumbed to the Mongols. Marco Polo thought the people of the Song dynasty were 'anything but warriors' and that 'all their delight was in women and nought but women'. He believed, as unlikely as it may seem, that the Song dynasty could have held out against the Mongols if only 'the people were a little more martial, but that is just what they were not, and so it was lost'. In truth, nothing could stop the Mongols. In 1279, as the imperial court watched the disastrous last stand of its navy from a clifftop at Yamen in southern China, the Song dynasty came to a climactic end. In shame and despair, a trusted imperial advisor scooped up the seven-year-old boy-emperor and leaped into the sea far below. In the following days, many ministers and concubines followed suit and the sea filled with floating corpses. All of China had fallen to the Mongols.

PART 2

Discovering the East

CHAPTER 2

THE MONGOLS

1271–1368

God only knows who they are and whence they came.

THE RAPIDITY OF THE Mongol expansion across Eurasia in the thirteenth century was like nothing history had ever known or would know again. It was faster than the spread of Islam and more widespread than the conquests of Alexander the Great. They 'came from nowhere and were suddenly everywhere'. An early Russian chronicler lamented: 'God only knows who they are and whence they came'. We now know they came from the disparate tribes that roamed the grassland steppe between the forests of Siberia and the barren wasteland of the Gobi Desert and that they were unified and pacified by Genghis Khan in 1206, who became the first Great Khan of the Mongol empire. The empire was the largest contiguous land empire in the history of the world – nearly five times the size of the Roman empire at its most extensive. It extended from the Korean peninsula to the banks of Russia's Dnieper River and from the Asian steppe to the Arabian Peninsula. After the death of Genghis Khan, the empire split into four separate khanates, one of which, the 'Great Khanate', encompassed the former Song dynasty China.

In battle the Mongols were ravening plunderers who acted with blood-curdling rapacity but in power they demonstrated shrewd administrative talents and an instinct for commerce.

They were not weavers and lived in a nomadic culture of furs and felt, but they treasured woven textiles and the fine silks of China, which motivated many of their conquests. Silk weavers from conquered territories were often deported to Karakorum, the Mongol capital in central Mongolia, or 'uprooted from one part of Eurasia to another'. The colour gold held symbolic value to them and sumptuous silk robes woven with gold thread became the unlikely hallmark of the Mongol court's conspicuous opulence. Visitors were dazzled by the 'spectacle of thousands of courtiers enrobed in golden robes, and the khan enthroned in a golden tent'.

The stability imposed by Mongol rule created its own form of *Pax Mongolica* linking East and West. The Mongols re-invigorated the overland silk routes, eliminated artificial trade barriers, built effective post stations and rest stops, and expanded the trade in silk and other precious goods. Openings for commerce and cultural exchange exploded from Europe through Central Asia and along the old steppe route connecting Ukraine to Mongolia and China. For more than a century in the late medieval period, Europeans were able to journey freely across Eurasia. More than ever before, the overland silk routes became an information superhighway – and a pandemic pathway – spreading, religion, ideas, commerce and disease.

Italy was Europe's gateway to the China trade then, as it has often been in modern times. Northern Italian merchants and missionaries were quick to capitalise on the opportunities for exchange with the Mongol empire. As early as 1221, Venice signed a secret trade agreement with the Mongols. By mid-thirteenth century, Chinese raw silk was appearing in the records of the silk-producing areas of northern Italy and for the next hundred years, it arrived in Europe in 'unlimited amounts'. During the thirteenth century, a 'never-ending stream of envoys' was despatched to the court of the khans including from Pope Innocent IV in 1245 and from Louis IX, King of France, who reigned from 1226–1270.

After the golden ages of China's overland silk routes during the Han and Tang dynasties, the Mongols paradoxically created a third golden age, directly connecting China for the first time to the heart of Europe. With Mongol protection from end to end, overland travel along the silk trade routes became safer than at any previous time; so safe that the contemporary Persian historian Juvayni imagined optimistically that 'a virgin with a gold dish could walk unmolested from one end of the empire to the other' and the Moroccan wanderer and legal scholar, Ibn Battuta, could assure his readers that 'China is the safest country and the best country for the traveller'.

It was not just the overland trade that mushroomed. The Mongols, a nation of horsemen, inherited the Song dynasty's shipping and maritime trading infrastructure and embraced the revenues that it generated. Marco Polo remarked of the massive shipping trade at the port of Quanzhou on the Taiwan Strait: 'I can assure you that for one shipload that goes to Alexandria destined for Christendom, there come a hundred to Zaiton [Quanzhou]'. Further south, Ibn Battuta described 'a hundred ships sailing into the Gulf of Canton, as well as innumerable smaller vessels'. In Quanzhou, diaspora communities of Persian, Arabian and Indian seamen and traders had flourished since Tang times, and many Buddhist temples and pagodas sprung up. With so much trade, multiculturalism and foreign exchange, the paper currency of the Yuan dynasty in China became for a time 'the international major currency, just like the British pound and the US dollar later'.

The Mongol rise in the East coincided with the rise of Venice as Europe's mercantile and maritime capital. The long ascent of Venice and the slow decline of Constantinople had its origin in the Fourth Crusade's sacking of Constantinople in 1204 – an unthinkable Christian betrayal that was orchestrated by the Doge of Venice. As a result, Venice became the interface between Europe and Asia while Constantinople gradually became 'economically crippled, territorially truncated, powerless to defend itself against the [later] Ottoman tide'.

For the next three centuries, until the opening of the sea route around Africa, Venice was Europe's key to world trade from China and the East. Silks, porcelain, spices and luxuries from Asia came to Venice, 'stopping over on their way to a hundred different destinations' across Europe. As the Mongols created a power shift in Asia, so did the Venetians in Europe. And the merchants of Venice, a prosperous social class to which the family of Marco Polo belonged, were well positioned to take advantage of the opportunities in China. No European visitors to China during the Mongol era became better known to history than Marco Polo, his father, Niccolò, and his uncle Maffeo, who set off overland from Venice to China in 1271. They became trusted members of Kublai Khan's foreign circle and served him as consultants, ambassadors, tax inspectors and confidants.

Marco Polo also became the first and most famous European chronicler of the wonders of China. His recollections, tantalising descriptions, iridescent stories, vast estimates and perhaps his embellishments were dictated to a novelist named Rustichello while they both languished in a Genoese prison cell during one of the periodic wars between Venice and Genoa. Some have questioned the authenticity of his account but there is little doubt that Polo was in China. And there is every reason to believe what he is alleged to have said at the end of his life: 'I did not write half the things I saw'.

European missionaries also came to China in the thirteenth century but the Mongols were initially hostile to Christian enlightenment. In 1246 Güyük Khan indignantly demanded nothing less than the submission of the Pope and a visit from all the rulers of Europe. By the time of the last Mongol emperor of the Yuan dynasty, attitudes had softened. Toghon Temür surpassed even Kublai Khan in broadmindedness and despatched an embassy to the papal court with the seemingly astonishing object of doing 'homage to the Father of Christendom' and exchanging diplomatic credentials. The Pope not only welcomed the Mongol embassy with pomp and ceremony but reciprocated with his own equally illustrious legation to China. The Pope's envoy reported that Temür received him in 1342 in a scene that was as colourful as it may now seem incredible:

> I was dressed in festive vestments and those who preceded me carried a beautiful cross and lights and incense; and singing *Credo in Unum Deum* [I believe in one God], we entered into the presence of the Great Khan who resides in a magnificent palace. And after the singing ended, I gave him a solemn blessing, which he received humbly.

The Mongol subjugation of China was not quite the blitzkrieg to which Islamic Asia and large parts of Eastern Europe and the Caucasus were subjected. The China campaign was a protracted struggle spanning six decades, much interrupted by intervening campaigns in Europe and Asia and internal Mongol succession crises at home. Genghis Khan died in 1227 and his death has been forever shrouded in mystery and salacious rumour. He led the Mongol armies into northern China in 1211 but it was another 23 years before his son Ögödei finally overcame the Jin dynasty in northern China and another 45 years before his grandson, Kublai Khan, completed the final conquest of the Song dynasty in southern China in 1279.

China became part of the wider transcontinental Mongol empire. The period of the Mongol reign in China was called the Yuan dynasty, formally declared in 1271 but without total control until 1279. The first emperor, Kublai Khan, embraced his grandfather's tolerance for foreign nationalities but exceeded him in his passionate thirst for foreign information, knowledge and trade. He opened China to a dazzling variety of outside influences and encouraged visitors from all corners. Kublai's religious tolerance may be partly explained by his mother, a Nestorian Christian, and his principal wife, Chabi, a Buddhist of the Tibetan school. Marco Polo famously attributed to Kublai Khan the diplomatically ecumenical statement that 'There are four great Prophets who are reverenced and worshipped by the different classes of mankind. The Christians regard Jesus Christ as their divinity; the Saracens, Mohammed; the Jews, Moses; and the idolaters [Buddha], the most eminent among their idols'. He then added tactfully 'I do honour and show respect to all four, so that I may be sure of invoking whichever among them is in truth supreme in Heaven'.

Marco Polo was deeply impressed by certain aspects of Kublai Khan's government and less impressed by others. He devoted a whole chapter of his book to the Mongol paper money system. At the time, Europe knew only coins. Paper currency would not be introduced until the seventeenth century. But the Mongol oppression of the ethnic Han Chinese disturbed Polo. It was heavy-handed, not altogether unlike the modern treatment of those Uyghurs alleged to be Muslim extremists in Xinjiang. Polo wrote that the Chinese 'detested the rule of the Great Khan because he set over them Tartars or still more frequently Saracens, whom they could not endure'.

The persecution of the Han Chinese was reflected in Kublai Khan's four-tier social class structure. It was a blatant exercise in positive discrimination designed to favour the minority Mongol population for office and privilege. Those of Mongol birth were at the top of the hierarchy; the second rank belonged to all the peoples of central and west Asia, mainly Muslims, Persians, Uyghurs and even Europeans; the third rank consisted of the 'northern Chinese', the subjects of the former Jin dynasty; and the lowest rank was reserved for the Han Chinese. The social engineering included more severe punishments for Han Chinese than for Mongols for the same offence and the simplification of the imperial examinations to allow the less-educated Mongols an opportunity to excel. Mongols were notionally the administrative elite but they made extensive use of foreigners – Uyghurs as civil servants and scribes; Muslims, Tibetans and Central Asians as tax collectors; and Persians as court astronomers, mathematicians and doctors. Even the Uyghur alphabet was adapted to create the first Mongol vertical written script.

The Mongols' first capital in China was Shangdu, north of Beijing in what is now the Chinese region of Inner Mongolia. Marco Polo described the city with passionate enthusiasm and the English poet Samuel Taylor Coleridge immortalised it in verse as 'Xanadu'. But Kublai Khan's triumph was his new capital to the south-east, on the site of modern Beijing, which he named Khanbaliq. Marco Polo called it 'Cambuluc'. Its construction followed meticulously the rules for city planning laid down in the Confucian classic the *Rites of Zhou*. Broad straight streets ran on a north-south axis with east-west streets perpendicular to them. The boulevards were 'wide enough for nine horsemen to gallop abreast' – sometimes translated as nine carriage tracks. Between the broad avenues there were narrow lanes called *hutongs*, some of which still exist. The Ming dynasty would later build their Forbidden City on the same site.

Kublai Khan was so pleased with Marco Polo that he was reluctant to let his Venetian visitor go and kept him in China for seventeen years, eventually releasing him in 1292 to escort a Mongol princess to Persia. The lasting achievement of Kublai's rule was the reunification of southern and northern China, which had split during the Song dynasty's early period but has remained whole ever since. In old age, he was troubled by gout and obesity and the Yuan dynasty went into decline. Misconceived foreign adventures played their part, as they do in modern geopolitics. Kublai's failed invasions of Japan, Vietnam and Java in the late thirteenth century were disastrous and costly adventures. A succession of mostly quickfire emperors followed after his death in 1294 – eight khans in seven decades – and the office of Great Khan 'bounced from brother to brother and from father to son in a flurry of assassinations, disappearances and inexplicable deaths'.

The final decades of the dynasty were marked by natural disasters from which the Mongols never recovered. From the

1330s, bubonic plague, which scientists believe originated in the Tian Shan mountains, struck hard and then recurred in a devastating second wave. Millions of Chinese died as the 'Black Death' spread west along the trade routes, arriving in the Sicilian port of Messina in 1347 and the English port of Weymouth in June 1348. Trade fanned and accelerated the flames of pestilence, just as it helped spread the Covid-19 virus from China to the rest of the world in the twenty-first century. The miseries of the plague were compounded by famine, repeated flooding of the Yellow River and government mismanagement. All manner of revolts, civil wars and consequential population decline mortally destabilised China.

Less than a century after the proclamation of the Yuan dynasty, the Mongols were forced back to the windswept steppe from which they had come. The incoming Ming dynasty, representing the native Han Chinese, severed the Mongol bridge between Europe and China. Under its Ming rulers, China became 'politically and ritually sealed into its own hermetic sphere of activity'.

CHAPTER 3

THE GREAT MING

1368–1644

How important to people are wealth and profit!

FOR THE HAN CHINESE, the Ming dynasty (1368–1644) was supposed to be an empire of great brightness in contrast to the oppression they experienced during the dark Mongol period. The founding Ming emperor Hongwu (r. 1368–1398) disappointed them. One of his first acts was to impose a dress code in which the hierarchical role of silk was central. His goal was 'to make the honoured and the mean distinct and to make status and authority explicit'. The code regulated clothing materials, colours and sleeve lengths in intricate detail. Silk was forbidden for low-ranked merchants and their families. And Mongol-style shaved foreheads and queues were punished by castration for both client and barber. But as the dynasty progressed and Ming commerce proliferated, people did not follow the rules. In the sixteenth century, a Ming scholar complained that 'All people tend to respect and admire wealth and luxury, competing for them without considering the bans of government'.

As Hongwu's 30-year reign continued, it became increasingly despotic. He felt driven to expunge evil and his cruelty was at times otherworldly. Hongwu lamented in one of his proclamations:

> In the morning I punish a few; by evening others commit the same crime. I punish these in the evening and by the next morning again there are violations. Although the corpses of the first have not been removed, already others follow in their path. The harsher the punishment, the more the violations. Day and night I cannot rest ... What a difficult situation this is!

The scholar officials, also known as the literati or the mandarins, were a special object of Hongwu's distrust. They were a sight to behold in their 'gilded sedan chairs, shaded by umbrellas', accompanied by banners proclaiming their rank, and preceded by servants who cleared a path for them. The highest scholar official in the administration was the chancellor. Hongwu not only had him executed, but he also abolished the office and the whole upper echelon of the central bureaucracy, concentrating power in himself. Over the next fourteen years, he executed over 30,000 subjects connected to the former chancellor. As one historian remarked: 'The return of native [Han] rule to China had become a nightmare for the literati'.

Hongwu was briefly succeeded by his grandson who, like the nearly contemporaneous nephews of England's Richard III, vanished and was probably murdered at the instigation of his uncle. The murderous uncle, who became the Yongle emperor (r. 1402–1424) by virtue of his long-suspected nepoticide, was an overlooked son of Hongwu. Yongle became one of the Ming dynasty's most significant emperors but he was immensely ruthless and not reluctant to invoke the punishment of slow slicing or 'death by a thousand cuts' for serious offenders. It was a method of execution similar in principle and effect, but not method, to the contemporaneous English practice of hanging, drawing and quartering, except that the Chinese went a step further – executing the accused's families 'to the ninth degree', including grandparents, parents, uncles and aunts, siblings, children, nephews and nieces, grandchildren and cohabitants.

Yongle was a tyrant but under his guiding hand, a considerable part of the built cultural and social heritage of

Chinese civilisation was established. The Chinese capital was transferred to Beijing, where it has continued ever since. The Forbidden City, which became home to fourteen Ming and ten Qing emperors, was constructed in its familiar form of painted red timber and yellow ceramic roof tiles surrounded by high walls. The Grand Canal from Hangzhou to Beijing was deepened and restored. And the countryside around Beijing was cultivated for crops – something to which the flesh-eating Mongols had not been well adapted. The Great Wall was rebuilt and strengthened in the recognisable form that exists today – less rammed earth and more brick and stone. The Yongle encyclopedia, a compendium of all knowledge contained in 11,099 volumes – the largest encyclopedia in human history – was undertaken. And the White Porcelain Pagoda of Nanjing was begun. It was a thing of beauty, a joy forever, and one of the wonders of the world, until destroyed during the turbulent nineteenth century.

Yongle's greatest achievement was the commissioning of huge junks – the Chinese 'treasure fleets' – on fantastic voyages to the ends of the known world. The word 'junk' refers to the nature of the sail rig – where rigid battens span the full width of the sail, keeping the sail cloth fixed, unlike the billowing sails that prevailed on Arab dhows and Western sailing ships. These junks were leviathans of the seas – larger than those created during the Tang and Song dynasties – with three to four decks, multiple cabins, staterooms for merchants and dignitaries, up to nine masts and plenty of bulkheads. Their length remains a matter of conjecture among modern naval architects, but 60–70 metres is sometimes suggested as 'a more reasonable if possibly conservative estimate for the largest ships'.

The object of Yongle's treasure fleets was to project China's wealth and cultural superiority to foreign civilisations. It was, in a sense, an earlier version of the Belt and Road Initiative. The Chinese then, like the Chinese now, were more interested in extending influence to foreign nations and creating wealth than in waging war and draining resources. The treasure fleet voyages ranged across Southeast Asia and around the Indian Ocean as far as the east coast of Africa. Some suggest that the voyages reached the Americas before Christopher Columbus. The world map attributed to the Italian Jesuit missionary in China Matteo Ricci – to which I turn in Chapter 8 – appears to lend support for this contentious view.

Yongle's chosen commander for the ambitious voyages was a Muslim eunuch and admiral named Zheng He, whose father and grandfather were *hajis* who had made the pilgrimage to Mecca. Eunuchs had been a part of Chinese culture since at least Qin times. They were a class of men who sought advancement in the imperial court by submitting to castration and service. Their origins were usually lowly; they often had privileged access to the emperor, the royal family and the concubines; and they were sometimes privately derided by the women at court as 'spoutless teapots'. Many became close personal advisors and trusted confidants of the emperor. Unlike the scholar officials who were appointed after succeeding in the imperial examinations, eunuchs were dependent on patronage and thrived on intrigue. They exhibited, thought one writer, 'a sucking need for power and an appetite for corruption'. The first treasure fleet expedition in 1405 'carried 17 imperial eunuch ambassadors and assistant ambassadors [and] 63 eunuch officials and chamberlains'. Ming emperors made extensive use of this social institution – appointing eunuchs to many significant posts in the secret service, the military, government trading concerns, the maritime trade superintendencies, the royal estates and as envoys to tributary states.

At times during the Ming period, the eunuchs were in control of both the throne and the administration of the empire and undermined the scholar-officials who were dedicated to preserving Confucian morality and virtue. The factional struggles between the eunuchs and the scholar-officials erupted during the reign of Yongle's grandson, the youthful Zhengtong emperor (r. 1435–1449). His tutor and head of security was a eunuch named Wang Zhen, one of a 'succession of powerful eunuchs who dominated the political scene'. Wang's royal influence was inordinate and malevolent; so great that he exercised control 'over the promotion or dismissal of even Grand Secretaries'. In 1449 the 21-year-old emperor, encouraged by Wang but against all advice, led his unwitting soldiers into a humiliating military catastrophe known as the Tumu Crisis. A Chinese army said to be a half-million strong was crushed by a minor Mongol cavalry force. Hundreds of thousands of men were lost as casualties, captives or defectors. The young emperor was led off into Mongol captivity while Wang Zhen died on the battlefield – 'probably at the hands of his own officers'.

The emperor's capture shook the empire to its core. Disenchanted Confucian mandarins representing the cream of Ming officialdom were outraged at the baneful influence of the eunuchs and gathered in the Forbidden City in a riot of recrimination. Using bare hands, shoes and anything within reach, they attacked the eunuchs. The number of deaths was low but the 'palace floor was steeped in blood'. It made no difference. After the debacle, Ming emperors retreated deeper into the Forbidden City and gave ever-growing power to their eunuchs to conduct imperial affairs.

The feebleness and inwardness of the emperors after Yongle partly explains why China's global naval dominance crumbled so abruptly after Yongle's seven extraordinary treasure fleet voyages between 1405 and 1433. The treasure fleets were the culmination of three centuries of prodigious Song and Mongol progress in expanding maritime trade, naval power and shipbuilding. China had dominated the maritime commerce of the East but suddenly, seemingly unaccountably, the government-sponsored voyages stopped. No more official expeditions were despatched and shipbuilding for overseas voyages was forbidden. It was an opportunity squandered and one of the most perplexing mysteries of history. By default, China opened the way for the subsequent European intrusion in the East.

The reversal of policy was attributable to multiple factors including the vast expense, the need to prioritise the defence of the northern frontier and a general Confucian anti-commercialism. There had long been opposition to the 'vanity and waste' of Zheng He's expeditions. A common explanation is that the expeditions were 'compromised from the start by their connection with palace eunuchs, who were associated with extravagance and imperial caprice'. The most prominent critic was Xia Yuanji, a government official who was imprisoned by Yongle and later advised Yongle's son, the Hongxi emperor (r. 1424–1425). Hongxi banned the expeditions at the first opportunity – on the very day of his coronation.

Despite Hongxi's ban, his own son, the emperor Xuande (r. 1425–1435), allowed one final expedition to Hormuz between 1430 and 1433. But the argosies finally ended in 1435 when officials 'manipulated the child-emperor Zhengtong into aborting the state-sponsored voyages permanently'. It was one of those huge policy reversals on which China sometimes unexpectedly embarked, and still does. China's maritime decline gathered a momentum that became irreversible. Naval units suffered curtailment; shipyards fell into disuse; vessels were scrapped; ship workers were retrenched; storm-damaged ships were not repaired; sea defences were allowed to deteriorate; and offshore bases were withdrawn. The Ming navy, which had approximately 3800 vessels in 1420, all but disappeared. By 1500, 'death was, at least in theory, the penalty for building a three-masted sea-going junk' in China. And in a reversal of the trend during the Song epoch when Chinese flocked to the maritime industry on the coast, households migrated away from the coastal ports to seek employment in the hinterland.

In subsequent years there was even a cover-up of the phenomenon of the treasure fleets – not unlike modern attempts to remove the Tiananmen Square crackdown from collective memory. The official records of treasure fleets disappeared and were said to be 'lost'. More probably, they were hidden – supposedly because they were 'deceitful exaggerations of bizarre things far removed from the testimony of people's eyes and ears'. The memory of faraway ports in the Persian Gulf, the Red Sea and along the East African coast faded; the construction by shipwrights of huge nine-masted junks became a lost art; and the Confucian literati turned their backs to the sea, setting China on a Sinocentric path from which it has rarely substantially deviated. In contrast to the cultural efflorescence of the Song dynasty, the official desire to learn about distant lands and foreign peoples faded, then utterly vanished. The best bureaucratic minds of the Ming dynasty devoted themselves to moral cultivation and metaphysical speculation while ordinary people were told to accept their destiny as decreed by Heaven and to suppress their desires for worldly things.

But the desire for worldly things was not suppressed and the imperial and scholarly contempt for commerce had little practical effect. The official disdain reflected the traditional Confucian bias against lowly merchants and traders who were motivated by profit rather than human benevolence. The philosopher Mencius, the second most important Confucian scholar after Confucius himself, famously asked 'Why must you speak of profit? There is only humanity and righteousness, and nothing else'. But Mencius was wrong. Voracious profit, flourishing commercialisation and unrelenting trade were unstoppable features of society, but not of government, in the Ming dynasty.

The dominant influence of Chinese merchants and traders shaped the prosperity of the later Ming era, despite the inwardness of the imperial court. Although the Ming navy was depleted, the ban on foreign trade by merchants was never particularly effective. Businesses devoted to export and maritime trade thrived, aided by disinterest and non-interference from Beijing. In the 1500s, the country was so wealthy that its emperors barely needed to rule, hardly consulted their ministers and relied almost solely on their eunuchs. Among many commercial hubs, the city of Jingdezhen in south-east China was the global centre of porcelain production, boasting 3000–4000 factories using high-capacity, large-scale dragon or 'climbing' kilns to fire ceramic objects in the hundreds of thousands.

The imperial court's approach to economic control left 'most of the wealth generated by its productive people in the regions where that wealth was produced' – as in modern China's system of economic decentralisation to cities and provinces. The wealth and stimulation of private industry created its own powerful internal growth, contributing to one of the most prosperous periods in Chinese history. The Ming economy – like the earlier Song economy – was the largest and wealthiest in the world. In the late sixteenth century, it was 'the cog running the wheel of global trade', entirely integrated into the world trading system. Even in 1820, when China was at the end of its almost two-millennia-long run as a global economic powerhouse, its gross domestic product was six times that of Great Britain.

One former senior Ming official, who was also a member of a prominent merchant family, wrote frankly about the Chinese people's love of money:

> How important to people are wealth and profit! Human disposition is such that people pursue what is profitable to them, and with this profit in mind they will even face harm. They gallop in pursuit of it day and night, never satisfied with what they have, though it wears down their spirits and exhausts them physically. Profit is what people covet. Since all covet it, they rush after it like torrents pouring into a valley.

For many people, adherence to Confucian hierarchy became secondary to the pursuit of wealth. Social mobility increased and wealth and money ruled, as they so often do almost everywhere. Another contemporary Chinese philosopher provided a flavour of the cultural transformation:

> Those who went out as merchants became numerous ... Those who enriched themselves through trade became the majority ... The rich became richer and the poor poorer ... The lord of silver rules heaven and the god of copper cash reigns over the earth.

Population, production and consumption flourished in union. And thriving agriculture resulted in a healthier and more numerous society. The Ming dynasty heralded the beginning of major population growth in China. The number of Chinese doubled during the Ming period and may have tripled between 1500 and 1800. But as the merchants prospered, the scholars and officials of the imperial court remained fixed in their outlook, stuck in their ancient rituals – just at a time when Europe was galloping ahead, energised by the Renaissance.

China existed in a state of incongruity, where the Confucian scorn for commerce and the inclination to remain introspective existed in conjunction with an unquenchable economic dynamism. Ming society became extravagantly monetised, commodified and commercialised. And powerful groups of wealthy merchant families – not unlike modern Korean chaebols – practically replaced the state as the dominant force behind Chinese industry. Merchant clans in south-east and coastal China became semi-autonomous polities, controlling their own overseas trade empires, conducting their own commercial networks and amassing vast wealth. Some Chinese merchants engaged in transactions in which they exchanged silk and other goods for silver valued at millions of *taels* – a scale beyond the comprehension of the soon-to-arrive European traders.

CHAPTER 4

AGE OF DISCOVERY

1500s

It was a very great deed Sire,
well fought and well accomplished.

THE MING EMPERORS AND court officials of the 1500s neither knew of Europe nor had any reason to think that the advent of European traders might be a watershed moment in history. No one knew then that in the next four centuries the Europeans would 'alter the course of China's strand of history more drastically than anything that came before, with the possible exception of the original Qin unification in 221 BC'. China, which had for so long surpassed the West, would almost succumb to it. And as the two civilisations 'came crashing into each other ... they quickly became entangled and would never again be unwound'.

European overland trade in the East had long been blocked by the three great Islamic 'gunpowder empires' of the Middle Ages – Ottoman, Persian and Mughal – whose power came largely from Chinese cannon invented during the late Song period. The Mughals, whose empire encompassed most of the Indian subcontinent and Afghanistan, were descendants of both Genghis Khan and the Turkic-Mongol conqueror Tamerlane. The Persian empire of the Safavids, the last great Persian dynasty, occupied the centre ground between the Mughals in the east and the Ottomans in the west. While the Ottoman empire, which replaced the Byzantines, ruled from Mecca to Vienna and from Baghdad to Algiers at its height.

The Ottomans were also a naval power, blocking the sea routes to India, China and the East. The Red Sea and the Persian Gulf were exclusive Ottoman domains. And in the eastern Mediterranean, Ottoman fleets competed fiercely with Venice and occasionally went to war over trade and territory. Periods of peace in the Mediterranean were interspersed by bloody conflicts in a continuation of the long and bitter Christian response to the rise of Islam. In the marketplace, the Venetian gold ducat and the Ottoman gold dinar became rivals for monetary primacy.

Further west, at the Atlantic end of the Mediterranean, after the last of the Moors were expelled in 1492, the new kingdom of Spain and the old kingdom of Portugal embarked on their respective empire-building missions. They would eventually break the Venetian and Ottoman monopolisation of the trade in spices from the East. The much sought-after spices grew luxuriantly in southern India and on the Indonesian Moluccas, a small group of islands of which Ambon, Ternate and Tidore are the most prominent. They were known as the 'Spice Islands'. The spices were shipped to the ports of the Persian Gulf and the Red Sea and then overland to Damascus or Cairo, from where they were funnelled to Venice or Constantinople and distributed throughout Europe. The Portuguese court in Lisbon and the Spanish court in Toledo aspired to a direct sea route that would cut out the Muslim merchants who supplied the Venetian middlemen. In Lisbon it was hoped that 'Cairo and Mecca will be completely lost and no spices will go to the Venetians except those that they go to Portugal to buy.'

The Spanish navigators sailed for what they thought was China by heading west across the Atlantic but unwittingly found themselves in the unknown and undiscovered Americas. A common belief at the time was that 'China was only five thousand miles west of Portugal'. It was an epic miscalculation. Christopher Columbus was so sure of reaching China that he carried with him a copy of Marco Polo's *Travels* in Latin. The book is preserved in Seville Cathedral and contains 366 marginal annotations by him. His plan was for a westward voyage to 'the land of India ... and the realms of the Grand Khan'. In fact, on his first voyage Columbus only reached the south-east shore of the island of Cuba. But as far as he or anyone else was concerned, the expedition 'had reached the outskirts of Cipangu (Japan) and China' – a belief that Columbus continued to assert until his death.

The Portuguese sailed in more familiar territory down the west coast of Africa where they had been progressively exploring since early in the fifteenth century seeking gold and peoples to enslave. Their breakthrough occurred in 1488 when Bartolomeu Dias sailed in a wide arc around the southernmost tip of the African continent, enabling him to avoid the notoriously turbulent seas off what he called the 'Cape of Storms' – where the cold waters of the Atlantic meet the tropical waters of the Indian Ocean. No European had gone so far south. As Dias's men left the equator behind, they watched with apprehension as the North Star dropped out of sight behind them. To the south there appeared 'six [unknown] stars low down over the sea, clear, bright and large'. This was the constellation of Crux, or the Southern Cross, which served the same navigational function in the southern hemisphere as the North Star did in the north.

The Portuguese King John II was so pleased that he ignored Dias's apt name for the cape and christened it the 'Cape of Good Hope', reflecting his optimism that the spice trade of the East was finally within reach. A decade later in 1498, Vasco da Gama completed the task when he doubled the Cape and hugged the east African coast as far as Kenya. From there, he coerced local pilots to guide his vessels on the monsoon winds across the Indian Ocean to Calicut in the modern Indian state of Kerala – then and now the spice garden of India.

The tiny Portuguese and Spanish ships of Dias, Columbus and Vasco da Gama constituted the vanguard of the European Age of Discovery but they were Lilliputian compared to the largest Chinese junks of the Song and Mongol periods, let alone the massive vessels of the Yongle emperor's treasure fleets. Columbus's largest ship, *Santa Maria*, was only about 20 metres long. But what the European vessels lacked in size, they made up for in shipboard cannon and the singleness of purpose of their masters, who combined the pursuit of trade with a fierce medieval zeal to bring the true faith to heathens, heretics and infidels – the Christian dream of universal imperium. Even the sails of Columbus's ships, like those of the Portuguese, had large red Christian crosses emblazoned on them. When Vasco da Gama was asked by the local Zamorin why he had come to India, he announced that he came 'in search of Christians and spices'. The Portuguese 'obsession with Moors and mosques' was understandable perhaps as the Iberian *Reconquista* had been going on ever since the eighth century and did not end until the last Muslims were driven out at the end of the fifteenth century.

The most famous Portuguese 'warrior of the cross' was Afonso de Albuquerque, an early viceroy of India. Like a modern-day white supremacist with designs on Baghdad, he saw his mission as threefold – combat Islam, spread Christianity and secure trade. The trade he sought was spices, which were as valuable and as important then as oil was in the early twenty-first century. Albuquerque's vivid report to the king after capturing Goa on the west coast of India exemplified the brutal Portuguese method:

> Then I burned the city and put everyone to the sword and for four days your men shed blood continuously. No matter where we found them, we did not spare the life of a single Moslem; we filled the mosques with them and then set them on fire. The peasants and the Hindu priests I ordered to be spared ... It was a very great deed, Sire, well fought and well accomplished.

Portugal's aspirations in the East met no opposition from Spain because their mutual Treaty of Tordesillas (1494) divided the known and unknown world between them. It came about when Columbus's historic passage across the Atlantic caused the Portuguese to assert that the Spanish claim to the islands discovered by Columbus amounted to a breach of a prior agreement that gave Portugal hegemony in the Atlantic Ocean south of the Canary Islands. Columbus contended that his discoveries 'were in the same latitude as the Canaries – that they were in effect a remote extension of the archipelago'. Yet 'patently they were not'. The Spanish monarchs, Ferdinand and Isabella, sought the intervention of the Pope – a Spaniard at that time – and lobbied him to uphold their claim but Portugal distrusted the Pope's partiality and preferred a government-to-government negotiation. The two nations agreed on a dividing line that was not in any sense a 'papal line' but it was sanctioned by a later Pope.

The treaty dictated the colonial shape of Asia and the Americas for centuries to come and ensured that Portuguese mariners would be the first Europeans to reach China. It established a longitudinal line of demarcation through the Atlantic that was considered to be about halfway between the Portuguese Cape Verde islands and the lands newly discovered by Columbus, namely Cuba and Hispaniola. But given the prevailing belief that Columbus had reached Japan or an extension of the Asian mainland, confusion piled on misconception. The treaty was geographically misconceived. It meant that Portugal and Spain were dividing the world on a false premise, believing that their line of demarcation was the mid-point between Asia and the Cape Verde islands.

On the other side of the world, the location of the antemeridian of the line of Tordesillas meant that China was clearly within Portugal's sphere of influence. In quick succession Portugal conquered and colonised almost all the strategic ports along the old Arab sailing route between the Persian Gulf, India and China, building massive fortresses at the strategic ports of Goa (1509), Malacca (1511) and Hormuz (1515). Only the Ottoman strongholds in the Red Sea and at Aden withstood them. From Goa on the west coast of India, Portuguese ships could patrol the sea-lanes between India and the Arabian Peninsula. From Hormuz, at the entrance to the Persian Gulf, they could interdict shipping from India and the East Indies. And from Malacca on the Malay Peninsula – strategically placed 'at the end of one monsoon and the beginning of others' – the Portuguese could command the maritime choke point known as the Strait of Malacca through which most of the shipping traffic to and from the South China Sea passed, and still does. It was said at the time that 'Whoever is lord of Malacca has his hand on the throat of Venice'. The strait remains the most significant maritime choke point in the world, particularly for China.

Malacca was close to the Spice Islands where the Portuguese acquired prodigious quantities of nutmeg, mace, cinnamon, vanilla and cloves from the local peoples and shipped them to Lisbon. It was good business for the Portuguese: the cost was minimal, the quantities were considerable, and the profits were immense. Lisbon became for a time Europe's most important entrepôt, bypassing Venice and the Ottomans. The Portuguese disruption caused the European economic centre to shift from the Venice–Ottoman dominated eastern Mediterranean to western Europe. Portugal became the controlling state for most of the European trade from the East. King Manuel styled himself 'Lord of the Conquest, Navigation and Commerce of Ethiopia, Arabia, Persia and India' and, to keep the secret to Portugal, issued a royal decree requiring the routine destruction of logbooks and maritime charts describing Asian waters. The strategic location of Ethiopia, Iran (Persia), India and Saudi Arabia in connection with maritime trade routes remains just as important today. It explains why the first three are part of the BRICS bloc, of which China and India are founding members, and Saudi Arabia has been invited.

CHAPTER 5

TRADING POSTS

1500s–1600s

It is lawful for any nation to go to any other and to trade.

IT IS NO SURPRISE that Portuguese mariners were the first to reach China. In 1513 several vessels led by Jorge Alvarez arrived at an unknown island in the Pearl River delta near Canton in southern China – where the estuarine waters of the river meet the deep ocean waters of the South China Sea. Canton was nestled safely upriver in the labyrinth of the delta, through which the huge Pearl River system discharged. It had been a maritime trading hub for well over a thousand years. Macau, the gateway to Canton, was about 100 kilometres away on a small narrow peninsula that projects from the mainland. The Chinese called it the Water Lily peninsula. Hong Kong was about 70 kilometres from Macau on the opposite side of the estuary. The islands of Lintin and Lantau lay between them. The whole area is now better known as the Greater Bay Area.

The river delta was Canton's protection zone; only skilled pilots and experienced mariners knew the way through. In those days, it was a treacherous hotchpot of sandbars, small islands, variable shoals and shifting channels, constantly moving as time and tide and the forces of nature dictated. Sandbars shifted, channels narrowed and once-navigable waters became impassably shallow. At the entrance to the delta, where the main channel of the river discharges into the estuary, a notorious tidal basin called the Tiger's Mouth presented the first of a series of impediments.

Some distance upriver from the Tiger's Mouth was the safe anchorage of Whampoa – the roadstead or 'roads' of Canton – which was as far as foreign ships were allowed to proceed. Pilots escorted visiting vessels to Whampoa and river boats took their merchandise and passengers the further 20 kilometres to the waterfront at Canton. The process of arriving at Canton was an age-old ritual of protocol and tradition designed to bolster its strategic defence; but the arrival of an official Portuguese delegation led by Captain de Andrade in 1517 was a harbinger of troubled times ahead. On board was Tomé Pires, King Manuel's proposed envoy to the Ming court. Manuel instructed Pires that he wished to 'be informed of China and the Chinese ... whether the Chinese were weak or warlike, whether they had weapons or artillery, whether they had more than one king among them, toward what place their country extended, and upon whom they bordered and all other information about them'. The mission was more intelligence gathering than diplomacy.

The Portuguese delegation was kept waiting in the estuary for a month pending official permission from authorities to travel to Canton. Permission never came but the local Chinese commander relented under duress when de Andrade threatened to sail upriver with or without consent. The Portuguese ships arrived with flags flying and guns roaring. It was meant to be a form of salute but the unexpected thundering of foreign cannon stupefied the Chinese. The provincial treasurer expressed astonishment 'at the improper conduct of the Portuguese' and a direction was issued that they be taken to an ancient temple in Canton and 'instructed for three days in the appropriate ceremonies'. It did not do much good. On the night of the Chinese Lantern Festival, while the residents were celebrating, de Andrade's men went secretly into various sections of the city to carry out espionage. One of the men 'climbed up its wall, ran around on the top of it, and counted 90 defence towers'.

The Chinese had never seen anything like these barbarians, whom they called *folangji* – derived from the Arab word *ferengi* for foreigners who hailed from the distant west. Their ships were puny by the standards of the early Ming dynasty, but the bellicosity and impertinence of those on board were something else. The Chinese were accustomed to foreign visitors – Sogdian, Indian, Persian, Arab, Japanese, even Mongol, as well as tributaries from Burma, Malacca, Siam and other maritime kingdoms of Southeast Asia. All these foreigners generally accepted Chinese cultural practices and the rules and norms of the Chinese world order. But the Portuguese – and their European successors – were convinced that their own civilisations were superior. From Beijing's perspective, the behaviour of the Portuguese was intolerable; their culture entirely unfamiliar; their impropriety, insensitivity and violence unbearable.

De Andrade departed in 1518 and his brother Simao arrived the next year. Simao was a man so unpleasant that one historical account characterised him as an 'inhuman, wanton marplot'. Simao soon committed a series of outrages that completely destroyed any prospect of friendly relations between the Portuguese and the Chinese. Worst of all – almost inconceivably – he 'kidnapped and bought a large number of Chinese children, many of them stolen from respectable families' for use as servants and for trade as slaves. Many of the children were never seen again and the Cantonese rumour mill suggested that the Portuguese had roasted them for dinner. The official history of the Ming dynasty solemnly recorded that the Portuguese went 'so far as to seize the children for food'. Portugal much later passed laws banning the buying and selling of Chinese people for slavery.

After two years, Tomé Pires went to Nanjing, hoping for an imperial audience during one of the provincial perambulations of the young libertine Emperor Zhengde. Zhengde was curious about Pires but his court officials clearly were not and sent the group on to Beijing to await the emperor's return. Officials in Beijing counselled the emperor to send the Portuguese away. They had never been heard of as a race; there was no mention in official records of any previous visit by them; no one knew where they came from and there was no report concerning them from Admiral Zheng He, whose far-ranging treasure ships of the previous century were thought to have visited the ends of the earth.

Chinese distrust was heightened by reports that the Portuguese had overthrown the tributary state of Malacca. One official urged that 'We must not receive their ambassador [and] we must order them to restore the territory of Malacca'. He continued, 'Should they remain obstinately fixed in their delusion ... punitive expeditions must be sent against them'. Another noted presciently that the foreigners are 'cruel and crafty ... if we allow them to come and go, and to carry on their trade, it will inevitably lead to fighting and bloodshed'. When the emperor died in April 1521 after apparently falling drunk from a boat into the Yellow River, the court officials got their wish. The baffled Portuguese were commanded to leave Beijing the next day. And orders were issued requiring all foreign ships – except recognised tribute-bearing vessels – to leave Chinese waters. It was one of the political reversals that frequently occurred after an imperial demise. Pires and his retinue were hustled out and returned to Canton.

In August, the new emperor – yet another youth – was advised by his officials that the Portuguese 'are untamed and disregard our law ... The governor should be ordered to expel them immediately.' Recurring naval skirmishes now occurred in the Pearl River estuary and continued for the next twelve months until, in the summer of 1522, two Portuguese ships were sunk, 'forty-two of their men were captured and thirty-five heads taken', one captain was killed and another taken prisoner. In Canton, the members of the embassy led by Pires were arrested, sentenced to death and publicly executed.

The first European foray into the China trade had ended disastrously but it was not entirely over. The Portuguese continued unofficially for the next 30 years, engaged in the shadows in smuggling transactions along the Fujian coastline. Their business was too lucrative for local Chinese to ignore. Eventually in about 1554, a deal was done that laid the foundation for the Portuguese to remain at Macau. Two enterprising Portuguese merchants, wisely eschewing the 'absurd bellicosity of the first generations of Portuguese in Asia' and recognising that 'profitable trade with China would require accommodation with Chinese interests and authorities', offered a bribe. They agreed to give 500 *taels* of silver per year personally to a senior official in return for halving the duty on Portuguese trade and allowing the Portuguese to settle on Macau.

It was a pragmatic move. From 1557 – and for the next 450 years – Portugal was permitted to administer Macau under Chinese sovereignty. There was no legal formality until the late nineteenth century but the 500-*tael* bribe was euphemistically referred to as a 'ground rent'. The pious Portuguese named their settlement the 'City of the Name of God' and installed a notice threatening all comers: 'Dread our greatness and respect our virtue'. Macau, a mere 33 square kilometres, nonetheless remained 'completely at the mercy of the Chinese state'. At the isthmus joining Macau to the mainland, there was a barrier and a gate through which food supplies and wares from the mainland passed.

The settlement was soon dotted with Catholic churches, prominent crucifixes and buildings in the Portuguese vernacular style. The ubiquitous ringing of church bells and the fervent processions of the faithful transformed Macau's culture and appearance. It was a Chinese anomaly but it was controllable: tolerated because its existence profited the economic interests of local Chinese merchant oligarchs and officials. The strange situation subsisted until Portugal returned Macau to China at the end of the twentieth century, two years after the British returned Hong Kong.

Spain followed the Portuguese to China a half century later. After founding Manila in 1571, the Spanish developed an economic bridge to China through the Ming merchants who sailed their junks from the Fujian coast and brought silks and other wares for sale to Spanish traders in Manila, from where they were shipped across the Pacific to Mexico and Europe. In 1598 some Spanish opportunists cast their envious eyes south to Canton, where officials allowed them to establish a short-lived trading post in the estuary. The Portuguese were so alarmed by the Spanish visitors that they took matters into their own hands, blockading and attacking the Spanish ships and informing the Chinese that the Spaniards were 'robbers and insurrectionaries who raise revolts in the kingdoms they enter'. In 1600 the Spaniards gave up the troublesome trading post and returned to their Manila trade.

The Dutch, whom the Chinese called the 'red hairs', were not far behind and first appeared off Macau in 1601. When they saw Macau, they remarked on 'a great town spread out before us ... on the hill a Portuguese church and on top of it a large blue cross'. But they were not welcome. Twenty men were sent ashore to negotiate but the Portuguese were so exasperated by another possible European threat to their commerce with China that they executed all but three of the visiting party. In 1602 the Dutch East India Company, the VOC (Verenigde Oostindische Compagnie), was established to trade in East. It was both a trading entity and an instrument of state with the power to wage war, contract treaties and establish forts. The leading Dutch statesman of the day boasted that he had helped establish the VOC 'in order to inflict damage on the Spanish and Portuguese'.

Dutch–Portuguese relations worsened in February 1603 when three VOC ships attacked a solitary Portuguese carrack, the *Santa Catarina*, sitting at anchor at the mouth of the

Johor River near Singapore. She was en route from Macau to Malacca laden with stupendous quantities of porcelain, silk and other precious goods – just as the Dutch had hoped. The booty was so fantastic that when auctioned in Amsterdam, the proceeds more than doubled the VOC's capital. Portugal's vigorous protests over the *Santa Catarina* affair resulted in a controversy that would change the international maritime world – and portended the great debates of the future about 'free trade' and 'freedom of the seas'.

To counter the Portuguese protests, the VOC commissioned Hugo Grotius, then a precocious 21-year-old Dutch lawyer, to draft a legal opinion to justify the actions of the ship's captain, Jacob van Heemskerck. The fact that Grotius and Heemskerck were cousins did not seem to matter. Grotius produced an opinion called *The Spoils of War* which was later expanded into his seminal work *Mare Liberum* (*The Free Sea*). His opinion was just what the Dutch wanted, and for that matter the English as well. Grotius pronounced that 'it is lawful for any nation to go to any other and to trade with it'; that Portugal's claim to a monopoly of trade in the East Indies was groundless, whether because of a treaty with Spain or any other reason; and that the Pope had no business apportioning land among secular sovereigns. The English adopted the same reasoning to defend Francis Drake's notorious piracy of Spanish galleons. The foremost English proponent of colonisation, Richard Hakluyt, fulminated that it is 'not lawful for the Pope, nor is it lawful for the Spaniard, to prohibit other nations' from the freedom of sea and trade. Freedom of the seas became a principle of international law, as it has been ever since. The Treaty of Tordesillas was trumped.

The Chinese liked the Dutch even less than the Portuguese and refused to allow them to trade. Court officials regarded them as European pirates. Their reservations were confirmed when in 1622 a small Dutch invasion fleet from Batavia arrived in the Pearl River estuary intent on taking Macau. Most of the Chinese residents of Macau fled ahead of the Dutch landing and many of the settlement's European citizens were away in Canton on trade. Macau was vulnerable, undermanned and poorly fortified. But with good fortune, a ragtag group consisting of Portuguese defenders, local citizens, Dominican friars, Jesuit priests and enslaved Africans forced the Dutch to retreat. It was said that the charge of 'drunken negro slaves' sparing no one as they beheaded Dutchmen in the name of John the Baptist 'greatly demoralised the Hollanders'. Equally propitious – or miraculous – was the cannon shot fired by a Jesuit priest that landed on a barrel of gunpowder in the midst of a Dutch formation, causing many casualties.

The Dutch fled Macau, never to return. But they redirected their efforts to the Pescadores islands further to the north in the Taiwan Strait, from where they raided the Fujian coast for several years. In 1624, Chinese warships expelled the bumptious Dutch from the Pescadores, effectively pushing them to the large island of Taiwan, a further 50 kilometres to the east. Taiwan was home to an indigenous population of Austronesian-speaking people whose predilection for headhunting had dampened past Chinese enthusiasm for settlement. The VOC built a considerable fortress in the south-west of the island that they named Casteel Zeelandia, but it survived only 38 years before the Dutch were expelled again during the turbulent mid-seventeenth century when the Ming dynasty fell and was replaced by the Qing.

Contributing to China's political turbulence at this time was a series of social and climate-related convulsions, including a disastrous sequence of repeated El Nino events, failed harvests, famine and popular uprisings. In the decades before the Qing takeover, Ming China was on the edge of political and social disintegration. From the height of its prosperity when the Wanli emperor assumed power in 1572, the country descended with frightening speed to the edge of political oblivion 50 years later. In 1644, a rebel army took Beijing and the last Ming emperor, Chongzhen (r. 1627–1644), hanged himself from a Pagoda tree in the imperial garden of Jingshan Park – but not before ordering his wife, Empress Zhou, to commit suicide, which she duly did. He then used his sword to slay Consort Yuan and his daughter Princess Zhaoren. The fourteen-year-old Princess Changping survived but without her left arm, which was severed by the emperor's slashing sword.

A Ming general then invited the foreign Manchus, who had recently established their own Qing dynasty in Manchuria and Inner Mongolia, to assist in the recapture of Beijing from the rebels. The Manchus provided assistance and recaptured Beijing but did not feel obliged to return the capital to Ming control. Instead, they extended their own Qing dynasty into China proper and announced that the Mandate of Heaven had come to them. Ming loyalists fled south to safety to continue the fight against the Manchus.

The most persistent Ming loyalist leader was the mentally unstable Koxinga, a merchant-prince of the powerful Zheng family, one of the coastal overlord clans who thrived in south-east China during the late Ming period. He mounted a huge rebel fleet consisting of 'more than a thousand ships and 150,000 sailors that had declared open rebellion against the Manchus'. So great was the alarm that the Qing court determined to take drastic defensive action. Its ensuing edicts were known collectively as the 'Great Clearance'. From 1661 onwards, the entire population of China's south-east coast was evacuated to create a 32-kilometre-wide corridor of desolation along the shoreline from Guangdong to Jiangsu province, a distance of about 2400 kilometres. Farms were dug up and fishing boats and villages burned. Millions of people were made to abandon their homes and villages at spearpoint in a cruel exodus to unfamiliar places where they had no right to land and no employment. An unknown writer at the time wrote that 'There was wailing everywhere. The sight was too painful to watch'. As an additional precaution, Beijing re-imposed the early Ming ban on maritime trade, which had been lifted in 1567. The harsh measures succeeded in depriving the rebels of food and materials but the result was woeful humanitarian hardship in the coastal regions and the ruin of China's overseas trade for the next two decades.

As an example of comprehensive authoritarian control, the clearances were effective – just as modern China's heavy-handed Covid-19 citywide lockdowns initially appeared to be. The Ming rebels retreated to Taiwan, where the Dutch had retreated in 1624 and where Chiang Kai-shek and his Nationalists would later retreat in 1949. In Taiwan, Koxinga announced to the Dutch that:

> Hitherto this island had always belonged to China ... [who] did not require it for themselves; but requiring it now, it was only fair that Dutch strangers ... should give way to the masters of the island.

When the Dutch resisted, the ensuing military campaign involved unspeakable horrors on both sides including mass executions by crucifixion and decapitation. Many indigenous tribal people joined the Chinese forces against the hated Dutch who surrendered to Koxinga on 1 February 1662. One writer ambitiously described it as China's first great victory over the West but it was no more than a rebel victory against an outpost of the VOC.

The decisive final step occurred 21 years later in 1683 when the emperor despatched a massive invasion force across the Taiwan Strait. The invasion was the seventeenth century's version of the 'million-man swim', the feared modern-day cross-strait invasion. It swiftly annexed the island and made it a prefecture of Fujian province. Life and trade along the coast normalised, the Dutch were seen off, and Taiwan became unarguably Chinese sovereign territory and remained so for the next two centuries until Japan annexed the island in 1895 and returned it in 1945.

PART 3

Porcelain & Chinoiserie

CHAPTER 6

PORCELAIN'S PUZZLE

1500s–1700s

Your Majesty has never had such an important creature as me in his hands.

ONCE THEY WERE SETTLED on Macau in the mid-sixteenth century, the Portuguese began to send shiploads of porcelain to Lisbon. For the Europeans, porcelain was a strange and unprecedented substance and one of the most coveted rarities of the Orient. The secret of its manufacture was unfathomable to them, as it had been to the Arabs before them. Alchemy had long been regarded as the Arcanum and porcelain was equally baffling. Porcelain's allure was compounded by its 'seemingly improbable combination of extraordinary fragility, coupled with glittering hardness ... so hard that ordinary steel cannot cut it'. As long ago as the mid-ninth century, the Arab traveller and merchant Sulaiman wrote of a very fine clay in China 'with which they make vases which are as transparent as glass; water is seen through them'. The riddle of silk had long ago passed out of Chinese hands – first to the Arab world and Byzantium, then to northern Italy and the Moorish cities of Spain – but porcelain continued to confound Europeans. It exercised the minds of scientists and alchemists, and excited the imaginations of popes, kings and merchant princes. It was second only to the philosopher's stone in its enigmatic appeal.

At a time when most tableware was heavy and clunky, porcelain was exquisitely fine and impossibly thin. Glass shattered, earthenware and stoneware cracked and pewter was dull, but porcelain was otherworldly in its beauty, strength and luminosity. It was as hard as flint, rang clear when tapped and was so translucent as to allow the sunlight to shine through. And despite its delicate appearance, porcelain's scientific properties of high density and low porosity, low permeability and high elasticity, ensured an unexpectedly high level of durability and resistance to damage. The earthenware pottery of the Etruscans, Greeks, Romans and Persians did not compare.

For hundreds of years after Marco Polo brought the first sample of porcelain to the West, it remained a mystery. An Italian astrologer wrote in 1550 that porcelain was 'made from a certain juice which coalesces underground and is brought from the East'. A few years later, a French missionary fantasised that 'eggshells and the shells of umbilical fish' were 'pounded into dust ... mingled with water ... shaped into vases ... hidden underground ... dug up a hundred years later ... [and] put up for sale'. Others thought that the maturation process took '80 or 100 years' and was undertaken by 'one selflessly far-sighted generation for the benefit of their descendants'. And in the seventeenth century, the Englishman Francis Bacon – philosopher, lawyer and Lord High Chancellor – prolonged the underground theory, contending that porcelain was 'artificial cement' that underwent a process of 'induration' when 'buried in the Earth a long time'.

Marco Polo gave it the name *porcellana*, a nickname for cowry shells whose shiny white surface porcelain resembled. He was poetic in describing the porcelain of incomparable beauty that he saw in the city he named Tinju, which was probably Jingdezhen. In Polo's words, 'nothing lovelier could be imagined' than these bowls, which were 'made nowhere else except in this city and ... are exported all over the world'. Porcelain's mystery was as much a part of its attraction as its beauty. Its physical transformation from crumbly earth to the most exquisite tableware seemed to exist in the realm of miracles, generating an air of magic and mystique.

The Jesuit missionary Matteo Ricci was another who could not escape a note of awe, recording in his diary:

> There is nothing like it in European pottery either from the standpoint of the material itself or its thin and fragile construction ... [it is] highly prized by those who appreciate elegance at their banquets rather than pompous display ... [and it] will bear the heat of hot foods without cracking.

Some even believed that porcelain bestowed upon any food or liquid contained within it an immunity against poison, which would have been a significant advantage in Renaissance Italy. Porcelain first began to appear in Portuguese royal collections after Vasco da Gama presented King Manuel with a dozen pieces on returning from his historic voyage. The only earlier exceptions were the sample brought back by Marco Polo and a celadon vase known as the Fonthill Vase, which a Mongol emissary presented to Louis the Great of Hungary in 1338 on his way to visit Pope Benedict XII. Half a century after Vasco da Gama's return, a Portuguese cleric commended the tableware to Pope Pius IV during a dinner at the Vatican, telling His Holiness that:

> I would counsel all princes to use it in preference to any other service and to banish silver from their tables. In Portugal, we call it porcelain. It comes from India and is made in China. The clay is so fine and transparent that the whites outshine crystal and alabaster.

By the last decades of the sixteenth century, Philip II, the Habsburg King of Spain and Portugal, possessed the largest collection of porcelain in Europe, more than 3000 pieces. In Florence, the Renaissance Medici family was also an early adopter. There were over 300 pieces of porcelain in the inventories of Francesco I de' Medici at his death in 1587. During his life, he maintained an alchemy workshop in the Uffizi where his loyal alchemists struggled in vain to solve the secret of porcelain. A few years later, Francesco's successor, his brother Ferdinando de' Medici, gave a modest gift of sixteen pieces of Ming dynasty porcelain to Christian I, Elector of Saxony. In England, by the time of her death in 1603, Elizabeth I possessed more than 1500 pieces of porcelain, thanks to the plunderings of Francis Drake and Walter Raleigh. An affliction known as *la maladie de porcelain* became a noticeable disorder among some of the rich and the royal of Europe who could not get enough of the exquisitely fine Chinese tableware.

The spread of porcelain did not reach ordinary Europeans until the seventeenth century – when the Dutch began to pillage the Portuguese carracks returning from Macau laden with porcelain. They called porcelain 'kraak ware' after the three-masted Portuguese ships that were rigged with a combination of square and lateen sails. The Dutch were following a business model of officially sanctioned piracy set by the English. Walter Raleigh had become infamous in 1592 when he captured the seven-deck Portuguese *Madre de Deus* (Mother of God) whose riches were said to be worth nearly half of England's treasury.

In 1604, the sensational auction in Amsterdam of the cargo of the captured Portuguese *Santa Catarina* delivered 'about 3.5 million guilders or 35,000 kilograms of silver' to the VOC. The proceeds were almost beyond comprehension. In an age when a Dutch labourer earned 350 guilders a year, a first-rate house in Amsterdam cost about 5,000 guilders and 100,000 guilders could buy a carrack capable of sailing to China, the bounty was 'enough to buy some 750 houses in the most exclusive district of the city' and sufficient 'to build a fleet of thirty-five carracks'. Its value represented 'fully 54 percent of the value of the VOC's entire stock'. As Hugo Grotius enthused, 'who did not marvel at the wealth revealed?'

The size of the bounty opened the eyes of European merchants to the scale of profits that could be reaped from the

China trade. And when profit calls, trade follows. This was the height of the Dutch Golden Age, when the Netherlands was the most dynamic economic region in Europe, with the wealthiest society, the world's first stock exchange and the most luxurious homes. The dominance of the Dutch VOC in the East throughout the 1600s is the reason why the Dutch developed a taste for tea and porcelain from China and tulips from Türkiye before other northern European nations. The French, English, Danish and Swedish East India companies were at least 100 years behind the Portuguese and the Dutch in the China trade.

Porcelain soon became 'a common presence in Dutch households'. By 1614, a wealthy resident of Amsterdam sniffed that Chinese porcelain was 'in daily use with the common people'. By the 1630s, Dutch imports were exceeding 200,000 pieces a year. Eventually, porcelain was everywhere, transforming 'the everyday life of a large part of the European population', first in the Netherlands and then throughout Europe. For Dutch still-life painters such as Johannes Vermeer and Jan Steen, porcelain became a subject of its own, decorating tables, display cabinets and mantles, draped with fruits, blanketed by flowers and paired with silver and glassware. By 1640, an Englishman visiting Amsterdam could remark that 'any house of indifferent quality' was well supplied with Chinese porcelain. Amsterdam was so moneyed from the China trade – as London would become two centuries later – that it was a place of wealth and dreams. The French philosopher René Descartes called Amsterdam 'an inventory of the possible' and the English writer John Evelyn said the city was 'certainely the most busie concourse of mortall men now upon the face of the earth and the most addicted to commerce'.

Fuelling the demand for porcelain and other products of the China trade was a constantly expanding supply. Europe's many East India companies were the multinational corporations and influencers of the age, generating their own demand, creating their own market and proving the truth of the economic law that 'supply creates its own demand'. The China trade helped create a defining feature of Western modernity – a society driven by consumption and fashion, 'a consuming society enthralled with novel products and pleasures ... as measures of social standing and self-esteem'. This shift 'preceded and stimulated movement toward machine production in Great Britain'. For the first time, consumption, fashion and freedom of trade became articles of faith. It is still the modern Western template – epitomised in the endless global demand for luxury products and familiar prestige brands.

The seventeenth century royal who became the greatest enthusiast for porcelain in his time was Louis XIV of France. Accounts of the beauty of the white porcelain pagoda in Nanjing inspired him to build his extraordinary *Trianon de Porcelaine* on the site of the little village of Trianon near Versailles in 1670. The fantasy pavilion was a diversion for his celebrated official mistress Madame de Montespan who, the historical writer Antonia Fraser assures us, was curvaceous and voluptuous and expensive and glorious. The elegant villa was designed as 'a place that they can escape to for intimate dinners, for music, for making love in a Chinese bed below a ceiling painted with Chinese birds'. The building was made of soft-paste faience, which mimicked Chinese porcelain but was porous and could not withstand exposure to rain and ice. No one in Europe had yet unravelled the secret of true porcelain. By 1687, the *Trianon de Porcelaine* with its 'Chambre des Amours' and its 'Appartement de Diane', had fallen apart, like the king's affair, and both mistress and pavilion were duly replaced.

In its short lifetime, the fantastic trianon inspired royal visitors from all over Europe and especially among the German-speaking states. Porcelain became an object of social emulation among European royalty, who competed to create the greatest splendour. Elaborate porcelain rooms with mirrored walls and dazzling porcelain collections appeared in baroque German pleasure palaces at Charlottenburg, Oranienburg, Nymphenburg, Ansbach and Wurzburg. In Russia, Tsar Peter the Great set up a porcelain chamber in his country palace of

Monplaisir, near Peterhof outside St Petersburg. In England, Queen Mary of Orange designed the furnishings at Hampton Court Palace to evoke Louis XIV's Trianon de Porcelaine. Daniel Defoe complained that Mary had introduced the execrable Dutch habit of

> piling their china upon the tops of cabinets, scrutores, and every chimneypiece, to the tops of ceilings ... till it became a grievance in the expense of it, and even injurious to their families and estates.

By the eighteenth century, no European royal was more ardent about porcelain than the Dresden-born Augustus the Strong, who became Elector of Saxony and King of Poland. As a teenage youth, he was sent away on a *wanderjahr* (gap year) to learn princely virtues and end his liaison with a lady-in-waiting. For three months he stayed at Versailles where the French king's *Trianon*, even in its disrepair, filled him with wonder. When he became elector, he was seized by a compulsive desire to acquire as much porcelain as possible and admitted that he had the porcelain sickness. Augustus wrote to a friend:

> Are you not aware that the same is true for oranges as for porcelain, that once one has the sickness of one or the other, one can never get enough of the things and wishes to have more and more?

But Augustus wanted more than imported porcelain from China. He wanted to create his own porcelain, manufactured in his own pottery in Saxony. He wanted to crack the code. In Dresden in 1708, Augustus, or rather his arcanist, eventually succeeded in doing just that. The arcanist was Johann Friedrich Böttger. Rumours first started to swirl about him in 1701 in Berlin. Böttger was a nineteen-year-old apothecary's apprentice, a bright lad from the country whose master swore blind that the boy created gold in front of his eyes. The German polymath

Gottfried Leibniz, who knew 'everything about everything', wrote to Sophie, the wife of the Prince Elector of Hanover, to say that:

> the philosopher's stone has suddenly appeared here in Berlin and then disappeared in the blink of an eye ... I am extraordinarily curious to see what will develop because I hesitate to believe it, but don't quite dare to neglect so many witnesses.

When King Frederick of Prussia sent soldiers to find him, Böttger fled to Saxony where Augustus had him arrested and kept under close confinement. Berlin wanted Böttger back but Augustus was determined to keep the goldmaker for himself and ordered that he be brought to Dresden. Sophie wrote back to Leibniz to say 'I pity the poor goldmaker. More people are fighting over him than fought over the beautiful Helen of Troy'.

In custody Böttger behaved strangely: he was manic, disturbed, fearful, depressed. He would not dress and plunged his arms into cold water in mid-winter. He wrote to Augustus 'Your Majesty has never had such an important creature as me in his hands'. He pledged never to leave Saxony and promised that:

> all my knowledge that might be useful ... especially my knowledge of the Arcanum, will be given to you in writing, truthfully and uprightly, without any fault or evil intent.

Augustus sent him to the Goldhaus in Dresden to work under the supervision of the mathematician Herr von Tschirnhaus. The Goldhaus was an experimental laboratory for the king, a testing ground for research, a place of alchemy and competing ideas and possibilities. It was where Tschirnhaus thought he was on his way to making porcelain, but he had had no success. Böttger ran away, was caught, brought back, kept under supervision. He had no real sense of empirical method.

He made wild promises to the king – 'I can happily recognise that we expect within eight days to have the sum of two tons of gold if God gives us luck'. But it was preposterous. So gold making was put to one side and porcelain became the focus.

In 1705 Augustus sent Böttger under guard to Meissen, 25 kilometres from Dresden, to a secret laboratory at Albrechtsburg Castle high above the Elbe River, where multiple kilns were kept running day and night. Guards were outside the doors and more guards were outside the castle. Böttger spiralled back into manic behaviour. He wore no shoes. He talked about Daniel and the lion's den, about St Paul the Apostle and how Job was punished by Jehovah. In September, Böttger was moved again to a fortress at Königstein nearer to Dresden to continue his experiments. In June 1707, Böttger implored Augustus:

> I need to see you. Things of great importance. It is my great hope that with the help of Herr von Tschirnhaus, I can within two months present something great.

Böttger was given a meeting and promised to replicate the Chinese product, to make true translucent porcelain. Three months later he was transferred under guard to a new laboratory in the vaults of the Jungfern bastion beneath the walls of the old Dresden fortress.

In that underground bastion on 15 January 1708, Böttger's trials finally bore fruit. He replicated a form of Chinese porcelain using a white kaolin clay from Colditz and a local alabaster. It was not perfect and it was still early days but Böttger had cracked the mystery of the Arcanum – more than 200 years after Vasco da Gama had brought porcelain to the court in Lisbon. In 1710, Augustus signed a decree establishing the first European porcelain factory at Meissen. In October, the first few pieces of true porcelain were fired. Two days later, Tschirnhaus mysteriously died and his papers went missing. Böttger was kept in custody in the Meissen factory and not given his freedom until 1714, upon which he 'apparently burst into hysterical laughter'. He was already ill and died a few years later.

Despite tight security, the secret of the manufacturing process for porcelain was not long confined to Meissen. It was so sought after that its monopoly was constantly threatened by infiltrators, secret agents and tricksters who lured away Meissen's key staff. Aggrieved and poorly paid skilled employees defected – some to Vienna and others to Venice – where porcelain factories opened in 1718 and 1720 respectively. Around 1750, the English gentleman traveller Thomas Nugent wrote of Vienna that – with its porcelain, Baroque palaces, glorious music and sophisticated theatre and opera –'There is no place in the world where people live more luxuriously'. England and France were a long way behind. France did not begin production of true Chinese porcelain at its national factory at Sèvres until after kaolin clay was found near Limoges in 1768. And the first English piece of porcelain – a rather drab beer tankard – was created in the same year from kaolin clay found in the hills of Cornwall. The story of the English creator of porcelain, William Cookworthy, is as sad as that of Johann Böttger.

Cookworthy was another boy, a charity case whose family lost everything in the South Sea Bubble when a much-hyped and widely-held joint stock company with a monopoly to trade enslaved Africans to the 'South Seas' collapsed in 1720. Cookworthy walked from Devon to London to work in an apothecary's shop in Lombard Street where he learned to grind and mix. Six years later, after opening his own apothecary shop in Plymouth, he became mesmerised by the mystery of the ingredients of porcelain that were 'looked for across Europe, theorised over by mineralogists and doubted by alchemists'. He read the published letters on porcelain of the French Jesuit Father d'Entrecolles, whose superiors had 'sent him to Jingdezhen on a mission of industrial espionage' to learn the secret of porcelain manufacture. Cookworthy roamed the hillsides of Devon, Cornwall and Exmoor on horseback in search of English materials similar to those used in the production of porcelain in China. As he learned the geology of the area, he started to experiment – mixing, grinding, calcining. Porcelain became his obsession.

At the time, the British pottery industry was dominated by earthenware but Cookworthy had a contrarian vision to create porcelain as true as that of the Chinese. After more than 20 years, he discovered an English kaolin clay at Tregonning Hill in west Cornwall and in 1768 he succeeded in firing a porcelain tankard. He was the first Englishman to discover how to make true porcelain, which he worked out entirely on his own, without the generous patronage of a king or the concentrated focus of imprisonment. The royal patent declared that Cookworthy had

> by a Series of Experiments, discovered that Materials of the same Nature with those of which the Asiatick porcelain is made, are to be found in immense quantities in Our Island of Great Britain.

Flushed with success, Cookworthy proudly established the grandly named Plymouth New Invented Patent Porcelain Manufactory with high hopes. But he was not a successful businessman, and Plymouth was no Meissen. The money ran out. In 1772, at the age of 67, Cookworthy walked away from the business and transferred his patent to a Richard Champion, who sought to have it extended. But Champion did not count on the opposition of Josiah Wedgwood, Fellow of the Royal Society, member of the Lunar Society, friend of Erasmus Darwin, grandfather of Charles Darwin, and one of the wealthiest industrialists of the eighteenth century.

Wedgwood occupied centre stage in English pottery. With oodles of money and platoons of attorneys, Wedgwood petitioned the House of Lords, alleging that the original Cookworthy patent was a restriction on free trade and that Champion was seeking 'a monopoly of stones and earth ... to interrupt the progress of other men's improvements'. Wedgwood won, the patent was crushed and Champion was ruined. Cookworthy's dream was in tatters. Wedgwood celebrated his victory by grandly taking a carriage to Cornwall to examine the clay and stone that Cookworthy had first found in its hills.

The final chapter was sadly predictable. Wedgwood 'got a firm and secure hold of these raw materials upon reasonable terms' from local landowners. By 1791, the white clay from the moors of Cornwall was being loaded on to boats owned by Wedgwood's eponymous firm – the Wedgwood Cornish Clay Company – and sent down the Trent and Mersey Canal to the potteries of Stoke-on-Trent. Champion died that year at the age of 48, leaving seven children and never recovering his financial position. Cookworthy was already dead. The Wedgwood firm, hitherto a manufacturer of earthenware, was now able to produce true porcelain.

The secret of China's ancient porcelain manufacture had passed to the West, as the secret of silk had already done, and the secret of tea would follow in the next century. Meissen, Sèvres and Wedgwood became famous but they owed their origins to China. By the twentieth century, some had forgotten and others never knew that porcelain was a Chinese invention. In 1972, the irony of President Richard Nixon's gift to Mao Zedong of a pair of porcelain swans made in the United States seemed to go unnoticed.

CHAPTER 7

KILNS OF JINGDEZHEN

1500s–1700s

The noise of tens of thousands of pestles thundering in the ground.

THE CENTRE OF CHINESE porcelain production was the densely crowded and bustling pottery city of Jingdezhen, which was named in 1004 after the Song emperor Zhenzong, whose era name was Jingde. The city is about 900 kilometres north of Canton on a broad swerve of the Yangtze River and only a few hundred kilometres from the best tea-growing districts in the Wuyi Mountains of neighbouring Fujian province. In its time, Jingdezhen was the largest industrial complex in the world – like the modern Zhengzhou, the 'iPhone City' in Henan province, where as many as 200,000 workers crank out tens of millions of smart phones to meet the global demand. It was a place of fire and noise, around the clock production and 'year-round thunder and lightning', where thousands of kilns operated day and night, constantly burning, firing, hardening.

A Ming imperial official who travelled to Jingdezhen in 1576 could not sleep because of 'the noise of tens of thousands of pestles thundering in the ground and the heavens alight with the glare from the fires [that] kept me awake all night'. As a Chinese poet put it, 'Ten thousand chimneys smoke to fill ten thousand mouths'. Jingdezhen looked like a city swept by conflagration – scarred by smoke and flame billowing from its many thousands of large-scale kilns that burned endlessly and fired an incalculable number of ceramic objects. Each kiln was built on a slope, with multiple chambers, each chamber higher up the slope than the other, enabling the intense heat to climb upwards at temperatures up to 1400 degrees Celsius. They were called 'dragon kilns' because their long, tunnel-like shape resembled a dragon.

To the first European visitors, the scene must have appeared like the depictions of Hell in the contemporaneous paintings of Hieronymus Bosch and Pieter Bruegel the Elder. The French Jesuit Father d'Entrecolles wrote of Jingdezhen that 'one thinks that the whole city is on fire, or that it is one large furnace with many vent holes'. His lengthy letters in 1712 and 1722 were the first accurate and comprehensive account of the process of porcelain manufacturing ever sent to the West. Cookworthy read the letters and Josiah Wedgwood made notes of them, which he copied into his Commonplace Book - a term then used to describe a journal that is a repository of thoughts and ideas.

The teeming, heaving, bustling and tumultuous activity of Jingdezhen dazzled d'Entrecolles who remarked of the smoky, polluted city that 'one seems to be in the midst of a carnival' – all noise, chaos and strangeness. Merchants from every quarter of the empire thronged alleys and warehouses and mingled with traders, incessantly doing their business. Porters jostled noisily through the crowds, trying to make passage. Couriers were coming and going day and night. Officials were arriving from everywhere and carriers strode through the streets with planks on their shoulders precariously balancing piles of fragile porcelain. All the while, the factories and furnaces of Jingdezhen operated around the clock.

The mass production of porcelain in the city was a marvel of scale and organisation. It had no parallel in the world until the centuries-later European Industrial Age of machine power and assembly line. So much porcelain was being made in Jingdezhen and exported from Canton that in 1600 a Florentine merchant at Macau expressed astonishment, saying: 'The quantity of it is so great that whole fleets, let alone single ships, could be laden with it'. The volume of trade continued to spiral ever upwards. In the years between 1600 and 1700, the VOC carried 'more than 600,000 ceramics from China every year' or 'at least 43 million pieces of porcelain to Europe' over the century; in 1710 an English vessel 'took away forty tons (or some 500,000 pieces)'; and in 1732 a Swedish ship carried home 'precisely 499,061 porcelains'.

The production process involved many hands in scores of coordinated steps that had been refined by trial and error over centuries. Such a carefully systematised process was necessary because, as d'Entrecolles explained, 'Jingdezhen alone has the honour of sending porcelain to all parts of the world'. It was the centre of the global export market for porcelain. The only way that Jingdezhen could fill the ever-growing orders for porcelain demanded in Europe and Asia, let alone in the domestic market, was by 'coordinated effort, specialised skills and standardised replication of wares'. It was just as Scottish economist Adam Smith would later write in the *Wealth of Nations*, namely that the division of labour in production increases as the market for merchandise expands.

The largest dragon kilns held as many as 100,000 pieces whose firing could take as long as a week. The firing required constant oversight and the crews worked in shifts day and night. Men known as kiln fillers loaded the wares while the kiln stokers stoked the furnaces. Furnace tenders sprinkled water and directed the blaze where needed. Kiln stokers were divided into 'the hot fire men, the slow fire men and circulating fire men' since different wares required a range of temperatures and baking times. Large pots required a slow firing to allow the great vessels to temper to the increasing heat, building over several days. The fillers, stokers and tenders were supervised by the kiln master who was regularly compelled to peer into the furnace to determine when the firing had reached perfection. His task involved a complicated balance of considerations:

> Unless the fire is hot and strong, the pieces will not get cooked evenly. Unless the fire is small and low, the moisture will not dry by degrees, with the result that the colour after baking will not be sleek and glossy. Unless the fire circulates freely, the middle and the rear, the left and right, cannot get thoroughly baked, and raw patches are bound to occur.

Chinese porcelain was made from two kinds of local mineral: the fine, dense, white silicate kaolin or 'China clay' and a type of weathered igneous rock containing a high content of mica and feldspar known as petunse. The former is native to the large mountain to the north of Jingdezhen – known as Kaoling, meaning 'High Ridge' – from which the valuable clay takes its name. The latter is otherwise known as 'China stone' or 'porcelain stone'. Kaolin gives porcelain its plasticity and white purity while petunse supplies its hardness and translucency. When the materials are ground into powder, purified and mixed in precisely the right proportion, the mixture can be fused together at an extraordinarily high heat to create a translucent, pure white, nonporous body with a glassy quality that defines true porcelain.

Kaolin broke down without difficulty but the harder petunse required more strenuous work. After quarrying, it was carried down from the hills in baskets to the river's edge where waterwheels powered iron trip hammers that crushed the rock into small pieces. The pieces were then placed in large mortars where they were manually pounded into powder. During Jingdezhen's heyday, 'a never-ending line' of boats loaded with raw petunse and kaolin came downriver to the city. Father d'Entrecolles wrote of the congestion of 'up to three rows of boats, one behind the other'. Workers cleansed and purified the kaolin clay by passing it through a series of suspension ponds and 'skimmed off the creamy residue from which organic impurities had been eliminated'. Great care was required in this task because 'one hair or one grain of sand could ruin all the work' and cause the porcelain to crack or warp when heated. After this procedure, the clay was refined and kneaded, a process that included beating the clay with wooden spatulas day and night.

When the kaolin and petunse material had been refined and prepared, a small army of workers in many separate categories combined to produce the porcelain. There were compounders for clay, grinders for oxides, glaze mixers, clay throwers and stampers, wheel spinners, mould-makers, carpenters, wood choppers, basket-makers, ash-men, experts in how to place pots in their protective fireclay boxes or saggars, others to place the saggars inside the kiln, packers, porters, boatmen and the couriers who balanced boards of stacked porcelain on their shoulders while navigating congested streets in often wet and slippery conditions.

Among the most important workers were the 'six categories of decorator, as well as the specialists in packing kilns and experts in firing kilns'. The decorators separated their roles into minute degrees of specialisation:

> One workman draws only the first colour line on the rim of the porcelain; another traces flowers, which a third one paints; this man is painting water and mountains, that one either birds or other animals.

Twenty artists could work in sequence on a single piece of porcelain before it was put into a kiln. And 'at least seventy craftsmen worked on polishing, decorating and glazing the fired porcelain before it was returned to the oven for a second firing'.

Almost the entire population of Jingdezhen was consumed with the production of porcelain, leaving room for little else. All of the necessities of sustenance and daily life had to be brought in. Father d'Entrecolles wrote that 'everything that is consumed there has to come from somewhere else'. He estimated that Jingdezhen held 18,000 families or 100,000 persons but it is commonly believed that as many as a million souls lived and worked there. On d'Entrecolles' calculations, the population needed 10,000 loads of rice or corn and 1000 pigs every day. All of it came by boat or barge along the river. And by the early eighteenth century, after the nearby hills had been deforested by centuries of pottery production, the firewood also came by river. Fir and pine were the preferred timbers for the kilns as they were light and resinous and produced the best flames. The appetite of the furnaces was voracious. An average kiln consumed about 11,000 kilograms of wood in a firing, while a large kiln used 64 tons a day.

The detritus of centuries of pottery-making piled up on the riverbank, in the river bed and at sites all over the town, where hundreds of thousands of shards, broken and discarded porcelain, saggars, kiln bricks and tiles accumulated. The force of the fire could result in beautiful, bizarre or repugnant effects. Precious objects shattered, warped or fractured. Poorly made saggars disintegrated. Colours frequently went awry. Repellent shades made the firing a waste. Potters routinely doubled the quantity ordered because half the pieces could turn out 'knock-kneed, flattened or otherwise injured and spoilt'. The extensive debris served as filler for brick walls, as masonry material and as the foundation for streets. It was a reminder of the high price of porcelain perfection.

All of this meticulous labour, this unremitting effort, was to meet the voracious demands of the domestic, imperial and export markets. The requirements of the emperor's household fluctuated according to the emperor's lifestyle but they were often considerable. The Ming emperor Jiajing, who reigned for more than 40 years in the sixteenth century, was extravagant in every sense. In 1554, he sent an order for '26,350 bowls with dragons on them in blue, 30,500 plates of the same design, 6,900 cups, white inside and blue outside decorated with blue flowers, 680 large fish bowls' and much, much more.

But his wide-ranging tastes were not limited to tableware. Jiajing's promiscuity and cruelty were so great that a group of his concubines and palace maids tried in vain to kill him in a bizarre imperial assassination attempt. The women jumped on the emperor during an unsuspecting moment and held him down while one tried to strangle him with the ribbons from her hair. Unfortunately for them, they failed and all were executed.

The pottery artists in Jingdezhen – and in Canton where they also flourished – learned to adapt their designs and their skills to meet the demands of their foreign customers. Foreign clients often wanted their own designs, not necessarily traditional Chinese imagery. Blue and white Ming porcelain, for example, had long been produced in unfamiliar shapes with geometric designs and Arab script for export to the Persian Gulf. During the Qing period, the Europeans introduced their own entirely different dimension. They brought engravings, drawings and pictures by the best Dutch, English, French and Italian artists so that Chinese pottery artists could reproduce them. A stream of commissions came for multi-coloured scenes that were entirely unfamiliar to the artists: European classical mythology and stories from the Bible; depictions of Western sailing ships and worthy nautical subjects; bravura scenes of European gallantry and heroism; armorial bearings for the newly ennobled; tantalising depictions of amours that evoked the spice and grace of eighteenth century European social mores; and of course, Western hunting scenes with their customary horses and foxes and hounds.

The commissions were never-ending but almost nothing was too difficult for the pottery artists in a land where 'copying is a valued pathway to respect'. Naturally there were mistakes – humorous in retrospect but not so for the furious owners – 'such as superimposing one coat of arms on another, facing crests in the wrong direction, muddling the colouring, appending feathers to a wolf, mistaking dolphins for birds'. George Washington's friend Samuel Shaw was frustrated in his attempt to have an ambitious composition painted on a dinner service that he had commissioned. He complained that:

> I procured two separate engravings of the goddess, an elegant figure of a military man, and furnished the painter with a copy of the emblems ... He was allowed to be the most eminent of his profession but after repeated trials [he] was unable to combine the figures with the least propriety.

But the mistakes were relatively few considering the immense quantity and variety of designs involved.

Inevitably, some cargoes were lost to the perils of the sea and the eighteenth century became the formative period for modern international marine insurance centred on the City of London. English law reports are full of cases of shipwrecks and cargo losses from this period. A noteworthy case occurred following a major maritime casualty in 1752 when the VOC ship *Geldermalsen* sank en route from Canton to Batavia carrying '162,000 porcelains including 27,531 dinner utensils, 63,623 teacups and saucers, 578 teapots, 19,535 coffee cups and saucers, 821 beer tankards and 606 vomit pots'. All ended happily, however, because after sitting at the bottom of the South China Sea for two centuries, the porcelain, including the vomit pots, eventually reached the market in the 1980s and was sold at auction in London for £10 million.

There were perils on land as well as at sea. Jingdezhen was hemmed in by mountains behind the town and the river at its front. And Canton was far away to the south. The transport presented a logistical challenge but the ancient route was well-trodden. Water transport was the only solution given the volume, weight and fragility of the porcelain cargoes. Travel by barge and boat was one of China's wonders. Adam Smith observed that the rivers and canals of eastern China 'afford an inland navigation much more extensive than that of the Nile or the Ganges, or perhaps than both of them put together'. And the Jesuit missionary Matteo Ricci remarked that 'This country is so thoroughly covered by an intersecting network of rivers and canals that it is possible to travel almost anywhere by water'. For most of the route to Canton, the porcelain made its way along regional rivers, lakes and canals south of Jingdezhen. But there was one arduous and unavoidable day of porterage at the end of the Gan River, where the only way south was over the mountains and across the Meiling Pass to connect with the Pearl River system running down to Canton.

The Meiling Pass was the most celebrated mountain pass in the whole kingdom and was the main route north to Beijing for European missionaries and diplomatic missions setting off from Canton. It was also the export route to Canton for both the porcelain trade from Jingdezhen and the tea coming down out of the mountains of Fujian. The pass is said to have been opened in 713 CE during the Tang dynasty. It was common for bearers to trundle thousands of barrows over the pass before continuing the journey onwards to Canton by river. A laden man took eight or nine hours to cross the pass and an almost continuous line of bearers snaked over the pass at all times of the year in all weathers.

In Jingdezhen, most of the landlocked residents had never seen the sea. Those who worshipped at the temple of the Taoist Queen of Heaven, the patron saint of fishermen and sailors, prayed that she would guide their porcelain to the coast. The temple surpassed in magnificence all the other temples in the city and testified to the significance of water transportation for Jingdezhen's prosperity. Matteo Ricci was shameless in his Christian aspirations for the Taoist temple and told his would-be converts in Jingdezhen that he looked forward to the day when 'this temple in fact will become a basilica dedicated to the true Queen of Heaven', by which he meant the Virgin Mary.

Jingdezhen's temple to the Queen of Heaven never became a Catholic basilica but in the late eighteenth century, England's North Staffordshire pottery towns in the conurbation of Stoke-on-Trent became a metaphorical Jingdezhen. More than 173 potteries, with their furnaces, factories and workshops, belched fumes and flames in close proximity to each other. The air was almost permanently dark from the smoke of the chimneys and a dense pall hung over the towns, choking out the sunlight. In a reverse of what had happened in Jingdezhen, English artists in the factories of Wedgwood, Derby, Coalport and Spode replicated iconic Chinese imagery, first on English earthenware and later, when they discovered its secret of manufacture, on porcelain. By the 1830s, the scale of Britain's North Staffordshire pottery towns almost rivalled that of Jingdezhen. After centuries of supremacy, Jingdezhen had 'finally encountered an adversary it could not defeat'. It was sign of the times: an indication of how Britain's industrial age would overwhelm China in the nineteenth century.

CHAPTER 8

INFILTRATION IN BEIJING

1600s–1700s

I have concluded that the Westerners are petty indeed.

THE PORTUGUESE SETTLEMENT OF Macau was not just a trading post; it was also a citadel of Christian missionary activity. The Jesuit order, which was founded in 1540 to counter the Protestant Reformation, arrived in Macau in 1560. The extent of their subsequent infiltration into the imperial court in Beijing became a phenomenon. According to Joseph Needham, the acclaimed but eccentric Cambridge sinologist, 'In the history of intercourse between civilisations, there seems no parallel'. For Edmund de Waal, renowned modern English potter, writer and lover of the East, 'The encounter between the Jesuits and China has been firmly and repeatedly shaken down by historians of science ... It is a terrific story'.

The unusual relationship began in the late Ming period and continued into the Qing. Over time, many hundreds of young white European men of the cloth from the Jesuit order achieved positions of trust and confidence at the imperial court in Beijing. Some of them had the ear of the emperor; some became trusted friends; some occupied positions of authority and influence. And as there were few, if any, competing Protestant missionaries until the nineteenth century, some enthusiasts occasionally refer to the two centuries in China from 1600 to 1800 as 'China's Catholic centuries'.

The early European traders along the coast were coarse, untrustworthy and rapacious but the missionaries who followed in their footsteps, led by Jesuit priests, were more diplomatic and less adversarial. They built success on a policy of 'accommodation' designed to encourage respect and foster rapport, starting from the top. They impressed the Chinese with their intellect, respected their customs and followed their ways. Many, perhaps most, spent the whole of their adult lives in China and never returned home. Their grasp of mathematics, physics and astronomy, and their knowledge of Western classics, history, theology, philosophy and logic struck a chord with the literati, whose own unique high status derived from their intellectual talents and success in examinations.

Several emperors embraced the Jesuits and the first Qing emperor in China, Shunzhi (r. 1644–1661), even came close to being baptised. Shunzhi's relationship with the German Jesuit astronomer Johann Adam Schall von Bell was so intimate that he consulted Schall on affairs of state as well as religious matters at all hours of the day and night and sometimes visited him at the mission residence where he would sit 'cross-legged on Schall's bed ... asking about Christianity and life in Europe'. Over time, many others within or close to the imperial court converted to Christianity. They included the sister-in-law of the last Ming emperor, who continued to harbour imperial pretensions for her husband even after the Qing takeover. She was so taken by Christianity that she changed her name to 'Helena' and wrote belatedly to the Pope beseeching him for help in resisting the Qing. Among other emperors, Shunzhi's scholarly son Kangxi was also favourably disposed for most of his long reign until losing patience with Rome in the early eighteenth century.

As the Portuguese found, the road to the imperial court was torturous. With the exception of Macau, foreigners were not allowed to reside in the country and visits were confined to envoys and tributaries. Several Spanish priests who entered illegally from Manila were imprisoned and treated so harshly that one died during his incarceration. The ensuing diplomatic brouhaha led to dangerous talk – with familiar Christian supremacist overtones – of assembling a European invasion force to conquer China. Spanish Manila-based priests were irrepressible advocates of 'military conquest as a tool of Christian mission'.

Alessandro Valignano, the Italian Jesuit leader, deplored this 'conquistador' mentality. The policy of accommodation was his brainchild. Valignano considered the sophisticated but different societies of China and Japan to be on a cultural level with that of Europe and rejected the dominant Eurocentric understanding of religion, culture and history – the belief, to which some still adhere, that Western civilisation is 'definitive for all humanity'. Valignano's foremost requirement was that his men learn to read and write Chinese. One of the first to do so was Matteo Ricci, who waited nineteen years before he was permitted to enter the Forbidden City in 1601.

While he waited, Ricci learned Mandarin and wrote a comprehensive report describing the peoples, customs, institutions and government of China. It was the first serious and reasonably accurate account by a European in China since the quixotic ramblings and sensational descriptions of Marco Polo 300 years earlier. Until Ricci, no one in Europe quite understood that Marco Polo's 'Cathay' was actually China, that his 'Khanbalic' was Beijing or that the Ming dynasty was a successor to that of Kublai Khan.

Ricci was amazed by the complexities of learning Mandarin – an ideo-phonographic language having no sounds or word identifications with an equivalence in European languages. It is said that learning to speak Chinese is 20 per cent more difficult for the English speaker than learning to speak French, while learning to read and write the language is 'five hundred per cent more difficult'. Ricci wrote to Valignano:

> I can assure you that it is totally different from Greek or German. Oral Chinese is always ambiguous. The same pronunciation may produce numerous meanings. Sometimes, when you raise your voice or lower your voice, with four tones, you will produce different meanings ... there are more than 6,000 words, which are totally different but very confusing ... All the words are monosyllable ... no inflexion is found in tense, case, sex, and singular and plural forms.

Once he had mastered the language, Ricci threw himself into the task of studying the Chinese Classics and acquiring Confucian learning. As he became immersed, he dressed in the distinctive ensemble of the literati and performed the kowtow, kneeling and bowing so that his forehead touched the ground. In the less tolerant Victorian era of the nineteenth century, English and Americans in China regarded the kowtow as 'something utterly incompatible with the dignity of the white race'. Two centuries earlier, Ricci was unencumbered by Western pride or prejudice. He translated into Latin the 'Four Books' – the staple of Confucian philosophy that were the basis of the imperial examinations; he translated into Chinese the Holy Commandments; he compiled a Chinese Character Table to facilitate the learning of Mandarin by Europeans; he translated the first six books of Euclid's *Elements* into Chinese; and he published in Chinese his own influential work entitled *On Friendship* (1595), which made a profound impression on Chinese scholars.

As Ricci progressed with his studies, his Confucian scholarship sent him in an unlikely direction that attempted to establish the parallels between Christianity and Confucianism. In Ricci's view, a unique synthesis existed between Christianity and Confucianism. He contended that the five Confucian relationships of respect – between ruler and subject, father and son, husband and wife, brother and brother, friend and friend – together with the associated virtues of benevolence, morality, propriety, wisdom and trust, were entirely consonant with core

Christian principles. His most famous book, titled *On the True Meaning of the Lord of Heaven* (1603), set out to show that Christ and Confucius could be just 'as compatible as Christ and Cicero'. Improbably, the Jesuit argument made inroads among many of the Confucian literati during the seventeenth century. It was boosted by the early conversion of a number of high-profile officials of the late Ming dynasty, especially three influential scholars immortalised as the 'Three Pillars'.

By the time of the imperial transition from Ming to Qing in the mid-seventeenth century, 'almost two hundred courtiers of the Ming court', including eunuchs and palace women, had converted to Christianity. One of the Three Pillars even held office as a grand secretary, one of the highest political offices in the empire. All of them had to give up their household concubines, an alien concept with which two of them struggled keenly. And one of them – influenced by Christian principles – contentiously queried long-cherished ideas about the distinctiveness of Chinese culture and speculated that the human race was all the same despite environmental and historical differences.

These views and practices provoked considerable hostility among conservative Chinese scholars. The fact that the first two Qing emperors in China wholeheartedly embraced the Jesuits and appointed many of them to senior scientific and advisory posts fuelled more resentment. At the same time, critics in Rome complained that the Jesuits were tolerating heresy by allowing Chinese Christian converts to continue the practice of ancestor worship. Religious doctrinal zealots – of which there is never a shortage – contended that the practice was incompatible with true Christian principles. The Jesuits thought otherwise, contending that ancestor worship was merely a secular practice. The controversy raged for almost a century but ultimately proved to be the undoing of the Jesuits in China.

In 1692, the long-reigning Kangxi emperor (r. 1661–1722), who valued the Jesuits because of their important contributions to astronomy, diplomacy and artillery technology, issued an Edict of Toleration, elevating Christianity to the same level of acceptance in China as Buddhism and Taoism. The fact that Kangxi recovered from a bout of ill-health with Spanish wine administered by a Jesuit after 'Chinese medicine did not manage to heal him' may have influenced his decision. Two of Kangxi's most important Jesuit advisors, Schall and his successor Ferdinand Verbiest, were not only astronomers and mathematicians but also engineers who made major contributions to the science of casting cannon in China. Verbiest was also a diplomat and translator who was instrumental in the negotiations that eventually settled the China–Russia border in the north-east. The resulting Treaty of Nerchinsk in 1689 – written in Latin and incomprehensible to both parties – was the first treaty between China and Russia.

This was the high point of the Jesuit mission in China, from which it began to descend. From 1704, the Pope issued a series of decrees and papal bulls condemning and banning the practice of ancestor worship by Christian converts in China. For him, their behaviour was idolatrous, barbaric, pagan. When he sent a personal envoy to Kangxi to communicate the prohibition, he only angered the emperor. In 1715, he issued an even more strongly worded proclamation, pompously announcing that its purpose was to ensure that the facts are 'permanently known to all the peoples of the world'.

Kangxi was so resolutely unimpressed by European narrow-mindedness that he decided that tolerating Christianity was no longer worth the candle. In 1721, responding to another papal proclamation, he stated in words that echo into the present:

> I have concluded that the Westerners are petty indeed. It is impossible to reason with them because they do not understand larger issues as we understand them in China. There is not a single Westerner versed in Chinese works, and their remarks are often incredible and ridiculous. To judge from this proclamation, their religion is no different from other small, bigoted sects

> of Buddhism or Taoism. I have never seen a document which contains so much nonsense. From now on, Westerners should not be allowed to preach in China, to avoid further trouble.

In 1724, two years after Kangxi's death, his son, the Yongzheng emperor (r. 1722–1735), a practising Buddhist, continued the ban on Christianity in China and ordered the removal of foreign missionaries. Christian churches were shut down and re-used as local public offices. Yongzheng's son, the long-reigning Qianlong (r. 1735–1796), carried on with the proscription of Christianity but allowed some Jesuits to remain in privileged positions at the imperial court in Beijing. They were forbidden to proselytise but Qianlong, like Kangxi, utilised their valuable talents for his own benefit – as scientists, astronomers, artists and interpreters.

In science, the Jesuit contribution was transformative. After the brilliant Song period and the whirlwind of the Mongols, scientific enquiry in Ming China had stagnated as a result of the cultural triumphalism and conservatism of Confucian elites. In centuries past, the Chinese had studied and absorbed the work of the great Arabic astronomers but in recent times they had fallen well behind the West. The Jesuits brought with them modern European celestial instruments, mechanical clocks, the triple prism, the microscope, quadrants, micrometers, telescopes, barometers, thermometers and the most recent astronomical tables. Louis XIV of France, the Sun King, reinforced their efforts in 1685 by sending fifteen of the King's Mathematicians from the Royal Academy of Sciences in Paris to aid scientific enquiry in China. Throughout the eighteenth century until as late as 1805, emperors routinely appointed Jesuit astronomers as presidents of China's all-important Board of Astronomy. The venerable board was established during the Han period and shaped daily life and imperial decision-making, setting and sometimes correcting the critical Chinese calendar.

Despite not being able to practise and preach Christianity, eighteenth-century Jesuits held diverse and important responsibilities. Giuseppe Castiglione, an artist at the imperial court of three Qing emperors, helped design the European-style palaces and gardens of the Old Summer Palace. And Michel Benoist created the palace's elaborate fountains and waterworks, including the famous water clock fountain surrounded by twelve statues depicting animals of the Chinese zodiac. The statues discharged water from the mouths of each animal for twelve consecutive hours, one hour and one statue at a time, powered by a hydraulic system that harnessed gravity and water pressure.

It is often said that, of all the Jesuit scientific legacies in China, the huge map of the world, a *mappamondo* created for the Wanli emperor in 1602 and grandiloquently described as the *Map of the Ten Thousand Countries of the Earth*, was one of the most significant. The map is entirely in Chinese and contains over a thousand place names, many accounts of the world's diverse peoples and numerous cosmographical and astronomical descriptions. It is usually attributed to Matteo Ricci but Chinese imperial scholars collaborated with Ricci and may have been its real authors.

The map presents such a challenge to conventional world history that its nickname is the 'impossible black tulip of cartography'. By 1602, the latest European world maps available to Ricci were those of Mercator (1569) and Ortelius (1570). Ricci's mappamondo is considerably superior, with more accurate and detailed information than was known to contemporaneous European mapmakers and explorers. Apart from placing China at the centre of the world, the map contains over 500 place names in Chinese, including many in the Americas that had no equivalent in any prior European map. In addition, and strangely for a map supposedly created by a European Jesuit priest, the map suggests an incomplete knowledge of Europe, omitting altogether the Papal States, Tuscany and Florence.

To add to the intrigue, the 1602 map contains an annotation in Chinese, located above the depiction of Spain, that suggests it was drawn 'some 70 years after' the first diplomatic relationship between China and Europe. This refers to the exchange of diplomatic credentials between China and the West that occurred when an embassy from the last Mongol emperor of the Yuan dynasty, Temür, visited Pope Benedict XII at Avignon in 1338 and the Pope reciprocated with an embassy to the Mongol court four years later. On this basis, the origin of the map lies during the period of the seven great voyages of Zheng He's treasure ships between 1405 and 1433, when Chinese maritime exploration was pre-eminent until it was abruptly shut down.

All of this and more suggests that Ricci's 1602 map may owe more to his Chinese collaborators than to any European knowledge and that it may possibly reflect Chinese cartography developed during Zheng He's treasure fleet voyages. One scholar of the subject – distancing himself from the methodology and reasoning in Gavin Menzies' controversial book *1421: The Year China Discovered the World* – contends that during the early Ming dynasty the Chinese reached America at least 60 years before Christopher Columbus.

The puzzling *mappamondo* aside, the Jesuits undoubtedly introduced European culture on a broad scale to China, including Euclidean geometry, Copernican astronomy, Renaissance perspective drawing and Western musical theory. But the reverse also applied. Their copious writings, careful observations and numerous reports conveyed Chinese culture to Europe. Between 1735 and 1795, Jesuits in Beijing translated for European consumption 'more than four hundred works from Chinese'. For Edmund de Waal, the most important feature of the encounter between the Jesuits and China was 'the walls of material, the scale of the writings of the Jesuits in China themselves' that were transmitted back to Europe.

This material formed the basis of the many accounts about China that multiplied in Europe in the seventeenth and eighteenth centuries in books, pamphlets and newspapers. This wave of information – factual descriptions, extracts of letters, enthusiastic embellishments and sometimes unsound assumptions – fired the popular European imagination and helped fuel a mania for chinoiserie.

CHAPTER 9

AN IDEALISED ORIENT

1600s–1700s

I did not write half the things I saw.

EVER SINCE MARCO POLO'S account of his travels in the late thirteenth century, Europeans had been fascinated by China. Yet most Western understanding of China existed in the realm of imagination and depended on second-hand information or enthusiastic speculation. The revelations in Polo's book were so foreign to the medieval European world of warring states, coarse chivalry and crude manners that early readers regarded Marco Polo as an inveterate romancer. His credibility was not helped by the fact that his narrative fluctuates between grandiosity and child-like wonder. Polo's famous account of his travels was even nicknamed *Il Milione* for the million marvels or lies that it supposedly contained. And it was well known that Polo's scribe, Rustichello, was a practised writer of romances and had once written a version of the Arthurian legend. At his deathbed, Polo's God-fearing family reputedly asked him to save his soul by confessing how many times he had departed from the truth, to which his legendary response was 'I did not write half the things I saw'. To add to the intrigue, half a century after the book was published, the Ming dynasty embraced a rigidly isolationist policy and closed the door to visitors from the West that the Mongols had flung wide open.

Several other medieval books followed Polo's *Travels* and helped spread and embellish its facts, myths and legends. Some even contained startling new information not mentioned by Marco Polo – that women's feet were bound; that mandarins grew their fingernails to extravagant lengths; that cormorants were tamed and trained and used for fishing; and that there existed a Great Wall. The last-mentioned was a surprising and difficult to reconcile omission. The first of the subsequent books was a travel journal written by a Franciscan missionary who visited China a few decades after Marco Polo. He spent three years in Beijing from 1324 to 1327 at a time when Kublai Khan's great grandson was the Great Khan. His journal *The Travels of Friar Odoric* (c. 1350) contains many eyewitness observations but its most important contribution was the foundation that it provided for its infamous successor, *The Travels of Sir John Mandeville* (1356).

Mandeville's *Travels* was a true medieval best-seller – and one of the greatest frauds in literary history. There was no John Mandeville, the author never travelled to China, and his 'personal experiences' were either inventions or plagiarisms mined from the accounts of Marco Polo and Friar Odoric. But readers were none the wiser and the book became highly influential. More copies of Mandeville's *Travels* survive than any other book of the period, except for prayer books. For the next two centuries, Mandeville's *Travels* was believed and accepted in Europe as a prime authority on the fabulous land of Cathay and its phantasmagorical world. Yet in significant respects, it was a 'farrago of highly coloured nonsense'.

As the China trade got underway in the sixteenth century and more reliable information gradually seeped through, European knowledge of China acquired a frisson of truth but one that was still wrapped in naïve idealisation. The Portuguese generated a small explosion of reports and chronicles that depicted China as a 'special geographic location which had brought together all the characteristics of an ideal society with regard to politics, economics, technology, administration and the legal system'. They praised

> the high quality of the roads and bridges, the perfect design of the cities, the rational organisation of production ... the efficiency of local government and the impartiality of the legal system.

By the late sixteenth century, a Spanish reference book called *The History of the Great and Mighty Kingdom of China* (1585) added to the general European enthusiasm. Men like Francis Bacon and Sir Walter Raleigh 'derived their notions of China and the Chinese primarily, if not exclusively from this work'. It was written from afar in Mexico City by a Spanish friar named Juan Mendoza who recorded stories from travellers passing through on their way home across the Pacific from China and the East. The book's influence was enormous and by the beginning of the seventeenth century, it is 'probably no exaggeration to say that Mendoza's book had been read by the majority of well-educated Europeans'.

As European exports from Canton grew during the seventeenth century, the exoticism of China loomed ever larger in Europe. What began as a fascination transformed into a collective mania for all things Chinese. The mania was strangely reminiscent of the Dutch tulip craze of the 1630s but much longer lasting. Both were to some extent irrational. China's isolation whetted the European appetite and served to increase its reputation as a fabulously exotic and prodigiously rich country. There was little hard information and even accounts by the Jesuit missionaries were sometimes tinged with a euphoric rhapsody. The image of China remained suffused in a romantic European haze.

The best hard information came from the 1615 compilation of the journals of Matteo Ricci, who died in China in 1610 after living there continuously for 27 years. The journals broke new ground because they were the first personal account by a European resident of China who was fluent in Mandarin. Ricci's journals were taken so seriously, read so avidly and discussed so earnestly, that they had 'more effect on the literary and scientific, the philosophical and the religious, phases of life in Europe than any other historical volume in the seventeenth century'. His detailed descriptions of the geography, culture, agriculture and philosophy of late Ming China captivated readers. Ricci's journals were followed later in the century by other important publications: a translation of the works of Confucius and a biography that expounded the core values and belief systems of Confucianism. The thinkers of Europe began to take note. Some even embraced Confucianism as an alternative to Christianity. The German polymath Gottfried Leibniz, the father of calculus, eulogised Chinese philosophy and laws and 'advocated a universal religion derived from the natural theology of Confucianism'.

In 1655, a Dutch embassy to Beijing in the early years of the Qing dynasty contributed for the first time amazing real-life illustrations of daily life in China. The embassy sought trade with China but the youthful Shunzhi emperor rebuffed the Dutch, haughtily suggesting they return in eight years. Fortunately, the VOC commissioned Johan Nieuhof to document the journey and make realistic drawings. His report was turned into a lavishly illustrated book with 149 prints from copper engravings. It was a lasting legacy. Nothing like Nieuhof's illustrations of life in China had been seen before in Europe. They were 'real pictures rather than conjectural whimsy' and readers pored over the vivid images of Chinese people and fashions, architecture and porcelain. One of the most startling images was that of the magnificent, but scarcely believable, white porcelain pagoda at Nanjing rising high above knots of tiny people carrying parasols and bowing formally to each other far below.

The pagoda was octagonal, nine storeys high and 79 metres tall, faced with white porcelain bricks with colourful glazed tiles at each roofline. It threw off 'a glittering light like the reflected rays from gems'. Each doorway and window was framed with deeply moulded ceramic tiles; each storey had its own shrine; hundreds of bells were suspended from its eaves; and 140 lamps glowed from its windows at night. Almost two centuries later, an admiring British naval officer and his companions ascended the pagoda's 184 steps to the summit where in the best British tradition, 'we drank the health of our Queen in champagne ... on top of the highest pagoda in China'.

Nieuhof's book with its revelatory pictures served as a major influence on the rise of chinoiserie. It was constantly reprinted and translated into German, French, English and Latin. Apart from his descriptions of daily life, Nieuhof's commentary on the Chinese system of government proved to be particularly powerful. Several features amazed him, including that 'the whole kingdom is swayed by Philosophers, to whom [all] yield an awful Reverence'. The other was the apparent high level of Chinese civility, manners and order, noting 'with what good order their People are Governed' and that the officials 'manage their Affairs with so much quietness and expedition that all things were dispatched, and with like dexterity as in a private family'.

As the seventeenth century turned into the eighteenth, European admiration for China only grew and the chinoiserie movement accelerated. Many Western admirers saw China as 'an unequalled vision of power, order and prosperity'. Few actually visited and most relied on what was written by the missionaries or depicted by Nieuhof. Some felt so impressed with the Qing administration that they regarded China as a model of state bureaucratisation and perfection. China's 'wealth beyond measure, its intricate bureaucracy regulating an expansive territory, its documented history coeval with biblical records, its enviable cultural achievements' made it an object of Western esteem and respect, even awe.

Europeans who were accustomed to the absolutism and corruption of their own feudal aristocracies and ancient monarchies, admired China's centralised government and bureaucratic rule by scholar officials appointed on merit after passing rigorous examinations. The Chinese system of a professional civil service with its integrated country-wide hierarchy of officials was an unfamiliar concept. Some Europeans were especially impressed by China's secularity – a 'model of a moral and well-governed state that needed no church ... founded on rational texts and ruled by scholars'. The absence of a powerful church in the affairs of state was striking for those all too familiar with Christianity's inquisitions, cruelty and dogmatism. Equally appealing was the apparently enlightened Confucian philosophy that 'embraced all the moral and none of the supernatural elements of Christianity'.

Leibniz, Voltaire, French economist Francois Quesnay and later the American Ralph Waldo Emerson, were just a few of the influential admirers of China. Voltaire never went to China but kept a picture of Confucius on his desk and wrote with dreamy effusion from his home in Geneva that 'One need not be obsessed with the merits of the Chinese to recognise ... that their empire is in truth the best that the world has seen'. Leibniz was busy around the courts of Europe extolling China and comparing the Chinese emperor, the Son of Heaven, to Louis XIV, the Sun King. He devoted the rest of his life to promoting closer cooperation between Europe and China and joked that he had so much news and information about China that his door should carry a sign stating 'bureau of address for China'. Quesnay, who was known as the 'Confucius of Europe', vigorously advocated the adoption of Chinese institutions. And Ralph Waldo Emerson, like many others, espoused Confucian values in his writings and shared his belief in the goodness of man.

In England as late as 1847, Thomas Meadows urged that Chinese-style public service competitive examinations be instituted, arguing that 'the long duration of the Chinese empire is solely and altogether owing to the good government which consists in the advancement of men of talent and merit only'.

However everything was not always what it seemed. The Qing civil service examinations were ruthless. Every two or three years, young men massed in large numbers outside vast halls and examination compounds across China. Once inside, they were assigned to cells where they were confined for up to three days with only ink and brushes, a water jug, a chamber pot, bedding and any food they brought with them. The Nanjing compound had 16,000 cells furnished with nothing other than wooden seats and writing boards. Interruptions and outside communications were forbidden. If a candidate died during the process – as sometimes happened – his body was wrapped in a straw mat and thrown over the high walls of the compound. And most scholars failed anyway, leaving behind great numbers of talented candidates and a glut of highly educated men with few career prospects. The result was fertile ground for bribery and admissions scandals.

Some Western thinkers never shared the enthusiasm for China. The incorrigible English contrarian Samuel Johnson sounded a characteristic note of condescension when he wrote in 1757 in the introduction to a book on Chinese buildings, furniture and design that he had

> no intention to place [the Chinese] in competition either with the ancients, or with the moderns of this part of the world: yet they must be allowed to claim our notice as a distinct and very singular race of men.

Twenty years later he wrote dismissively to his friend, Mrs Thrale, that he 'was not yet so infected with the contagion of China-fancy as to like anything ... which can be so easily broken', namely porcelain. The debate fluctuated between the classicists who favoured Greece and Rome and the Orientalists who favoured China, much as it does in the modern debate about Western civilisation. In 1759 the Poet Laureate William Whitehead placed himself firmly in the camp of the Orientalists and rejected the superiority of Western civilisation. He urged:

Enough of Greece and Rome.
The exhausted store
Of either nation now can charm no more …
To China's eastern realms: and boldly bears
Confucius' morals to Britannia's ears.

CHAPTER 10

CHINOISERIE MANIA

1600s–1700s

Peaches, peonies, chrysanthemums, camellias, gardenias, azaleas, forsythias, wisteria and crabapples.

BY THE MIDDLE OF the seventeenth century, an exotic picture of an imaginary China had been firmly stamped on the European mind, and architecture, landscape design, interior decoration and fashion were following suit. Europe was displaying unmistakable symptoms of a serious bout of China-mania. In garden landscape, Louis XIV's *Trianon de Porcelaine* fathered 'a numerous progeny of Chinese pagodas, latticed teahouses, kiosks and Confucian temples in every corner of Europe' from Sweden to Italy and from Portugal to St. Petersburg. More than a hundred years later in England, near the end of the eighteenth century, George, Prince of Wales, who was brought up in the shadow of his father's much-loved Chinese Pagoda in Kew Gardens, commenced construction of his own fanciful testament to China and the East.

The Royal Pavilion at Brighton was George's seaside retreat. With its fabulous chinoiserie interiors and Hindu exterior, it was and still is a spectacle of bizarre oriental brilliance. And like Louis XIV's *Trianon de Porcelaine*, it functioned as a discreet location where George could enjoy private liaisons with his long-time companion, the older, twice-widowed Maria

Fitzherbert, a Catholic whom he married illegally without the knowledge or approval of his father, King George III. If consent had been given and the marriage been valid, George would have ceased to be the heir-apparent and been removed from the line of succession. As George's disastrous debts – partly resulting from the construction of the Royal Pavilion – climbed to over £600,000, the royal family conceived a House of Windsor–like solution. George's father induced him to enter a legal marriage with a suitable young woman, his rather plain first cousin, the Duchess Caroline of Brunswick. It was, according to his father, the only way out of the hole. The considerable incentive was that the prince's enormous debts would be cleared by parliament if he wed his cousin, and the Catholic Maria would cease to be an embarrassment to the royal family.

George was a wastrel and he accepted the proposal, which left him in the fortunate position of having ample funds to be an enthusiastic exponent of chinoiserie. The marriage to cousin Caroline was a short-lived disaster; George was drunk at the wedding ceremony and the couple was estranged by the time of the birth of their only child. George ploughed ahead with his dream at Brighton and the Royal Pavilion represents the last of the era when chinoiserie was all the rage in English architecture and design. The interior was congested with elements of chinoiserie excess. Hundreds of dragons adorned the walls, textiles and fixtures. The Banqueting Room's crystal chandelier was suspended from a carved and silvered dragon. The Music Room was graced by four spectacular model porcelain pagodas – now in Buckingham Palace – two of which are over 5 metres high. The room's landscape murals featured at least 180 gigantic serpents and winged dragons. In the corridor, life-sized statues of Chinese men clad in oriental silk robes greeted the visitor. Painted Chinese wallpapers depicted exotic flowers with unfolding petals and hummingbirds disporting themselves against clear turquoise or coral pink skies. Chinese silk banners hung from the cornices and glittering hoards of porcelain, lacquer and cloisonné enamel were stacked around the rooms. The Princess of Lieven, the exhibitionist wife of the Russian ambassador in London and a leader of London society, said of the Pavilion that 'since the days of the Roman Emperor Elagabalus, there had not been such magnificence and such luxury'.

Prince George's extravagance at Brighton was not the first example of English chinoiserie style. It was preceded not only by his father's Chinese Pagoda but also by another structure known as the 'House of Confucius' in Kew Gardens. The 1740s House of Confucius is the earliest recorded English chinoiserie garden building. It was a beautifully coloured two-storey octagonal pavilion located beside a lake in the gardens. The building had elaborately enriched lattice work and a Chinese roof topped by a flying dragon. From that time, the English fashion for chinoiserie in the garden soared. Chinese bridges began to materialise in stately homes all over the countryside, as did little temples and pagodas. The fad and frivolity of chinoiserie, which combined brilliance of colouring with exquisite prettiness of ornament, was in sharp contrast to the melancholy Gothic ruins and classical symbolism that had long been popular in stately country house gardens.

The doyen of English chinoiserie at the time was Sir William Chambers, who had made two trading voyages to Canton as a young man with the Swedish East India Company and was the most internationally minded of British architects and designers. He became a friend of King George III, and was architect to the Crown. Chambers wrote an indispensable handbook for English designers titled *Designs of Chinese Buildings, Furniture, Dresses, Machines and Utensils* (1757), which covered almost everything imaginable. His fondness for China bordered on the obsessional and he wrote rhapsodically about Chinese gardens. His *Dissertations* (1772) includes the observation that Chinese gardeners 'take nature for their pattern ... [they] are not only Botanists, but also Painters and Philosophers' – a statement perhaps equally applicable to all true gardeners.

Chambers's books were dedicated to George III and had a revolutionary impact on English gardens, introducing

'Chinese pavilions, zigzag bridges and serpentine paths' and even inspiring George Washington to lay down serpentine paths at his country estate at Mount Vernon. Some gardening nationalists were horrified by the suggestion of any 'foreign' influence on English gardens and criticised Chambers, but the truth in the 1700s was that:

> For at least sixty years, the idea of the Chinese garden managed to be an inspiration, a justifying precedent, an ideal model and a constantly adaptive canvas on which every changing fashion in England could be painted and reflected back into the English garden.

Accompanying and enriching the fashion for the Chinese gardening style was the contemporaneous influx of never-before-seen exotic plants and flowers from China. From the 1760s onwards, the nurseries of Canton attracted a stream of English plant hunters, many of whom were sent out by Sir Joseph Banks, the long-serving president of the Royal Society. The collectors brought back 'peaches, peonies, chrysanthemums, camellias, gardenias, azaleas, forsythias, wisteria and crabapples, to mention but a few'. One could add clematis, pink jasmine and rhododendron among numerous others. Many of these plants have become so popular that 'their Chinese origins have been entirely forgotten and we have come to look upon them as our own'.

William Chambers's supreme example of chinoiserie in English architecture is the Chinese Pagoda at Kew Gardens. George III had it built in 1762, the year that his son, George Prince of Wales was born, and admired it with inordinate affection. The pagoda was 'a very large toy indeed'. Nothing quite like it had been seen before in England. It was so tall at 50 metres high, and so strange, that a suspicious London public was unconvinced that it would remain standing. But stand it did and continues to do so. The structure rose so high that Horace Walpole, the Whig politician and man of letters, was prompted to write to a friend that 'soon you will see it from Yorkshire' – about 300 kilometres away. Painted dragons with bells in their mouths peered out from each of the pagoda's ten storeys. The wooden dragons that adorned each corner of its many separate and elaborately tiled green and white roofs were covered in gold leaf. A gilded finial sat atop the structure. For the British public, the pagoda was a window into Chinese culture dominating the skyline of West London.

In the Netherlands, the manifestation of Dutch chinoiserie was a little less flamboyant. The seventeenth-century Dutch urban middle class excelled at the prominent display of collections of porcelain on their shelves and in their 'cabinets of curiosities', where they placed their exotica from the East. It was the Dutch way of demonstrating their worldliness and sophistication. Rembrandt's house with its porcelain collection is now a museum in Amsterdam. Some collectors added Delftware to their collections – a cheaper local earthenware ceramic manufactured in imitation of the Chinese style. The imagery of Chinese men and women with parasols, wearing flowing silk robes, elegantly sipping tea, gracefully reclining by the shade of a willow tree or crossing an ornamental bridge, was much copied by European artists on vases, cups, plates, screens, wallpapers and clothing. Delftware and later British Willow pattern were synonymous with such imagery.

Chinoiserie in France was of a different order altogether. The courts of Louis XIV – and those of his successors Louis XV and Louis XVI – were notorious for their masquerades and balls that exemplified oriental magnificence and exoticism. Such affairs were a feature of French courtly life throughout the eighteenth century until the revolution. A particularly memorable ball to welcome in the new century was staged by Louis XIV on 7 January 1700. The theme was China and the venue was the royal residence of Château de Marly, a retreat near Versailles where the king liked to escape from the court with his friends. A musical composition, *Masquerade of the King of China*, was commissioned specifically for the event and the evening opened with 30 musicians dressed in Chinese costume carrying in the 'King of China' on a palanquin. The celebrations continued with all kinds of oriental-themed dissipation and immoderation.

In the German-speaking states, the expression of Chinese culture could sometimes be quixotic. Princelings built exquisite chinoiserie pavilions in their parks and created Chinese rooms in their palaces but one of the strangest follies of all was a complete Chinese village called Mulang, a homage to China in the heart of the state of Hessen. It was an idealised concept of a Chinese rural scene. Quaint buildings were scattered around a stream over which an arched and fretted bridge in the Chinese style extended. The buildings included a small pagoda with red columns, a chinoiserie barn, a Chinese house for the tenant farmer, several Chinese 'houses' for milking cows and a long low building containing two dining rooms and a ballroom. It was dreamily imagined that 'in such delightful surroundings, Europeans could lead the lives of the porcelain figures – fishing in the lake, gardening and sipping tea by day and dancing through the night'.

There was, of course, more to European chinoiserie than pagodas and bridges, porcelain, tea and oriental masquerades. Fashion and furniture involved a more intimate connection to the culture of China. Chinese motifs and styles began to appear in furniture, especially in chairs, tables, commodes and cabinets, often using unconventional materials such as lacquered wood and faux bamboo. In England, Thomas Chippendale was the Shakespeare of English furniture makers. He adopted the Chinese style in his workshop in St Martin's Lane, in London's West End. Chippendale's lattice-backed chairs drew upon Chinese fretwork for inspiration and are still fashionable, as are his cabinets, bureaus and bookcases, which flourished in Europe. He achieved notoriety in 1754 when he published a book of his designs – *The Gentleman and Cabinet Maker's Director* – to wide acclaim. The name 'Chippendale' became synonymous with Chinese-inspired design.

In fashion, exotic Chinese silks and brilliantly coloured Indian cottons arrived on a wave of trade from the East. Exquisite fabrics decorated with oriental motifs, flowers and figures flooded into Europe. Italian silk weavers in Lucca and English silk weavers in Spitalfields soon produced indistinguishable copies that were widely distributed. Vibrant colours, elegant embroidery and Chinese cultural symbols such as 'lotus flowers, pomegranates, peonies, florets linked with whirls and sprays, the phoenix and dragons' reshaped fashion in men's and women's clothing, and especially in Paris and London. A wardrobe revolution took place, incorporating the colours, imagery and fabrics of the Orient. Paris, where chinoiserie was a raging obsession, became the undisputed capital of Western fashion.

The fashion for women became more colourful, brilliant and brightly coloured while that for men became at least as splendid. Never-before-seen exotic textiles and fabrics from the East turned heads, upended dress codes and transformed attitudes and tastes in men's clothing. In England, the eighteenth century became a colourful interlude between the dark severity of the Puritans and the black piety of the Victorians. Women's dresses and gentlemen's coats, jackets and waistcoats featured gorgeous palettes, opulent designs and rich embroidery. The most elaborate had weave patterns interlaced with gold, silver or multicoloured threads. Detailed finishing touches were indispensable, including intricate embroidered buttons, silk cravats, deep sleeve cuffs and lace jabots – the last-mentioned still being popular today with judges, advocates and choir boys.

As the eighteenth century drew to a close, the fashion for chinoiserie in men's clothing began to fade, although examples of richly decorated waistcoats can still be seen in portraits of the era. At least in England, it is said that Beau Brummell, the progenitor of modern male fashion, helped turn men's apparel to the pared-back monochromatic style of black, brown or navy that is more familiar today. This was the beginning of

Savile Row tailoring. Brummell asked his tailor to cut his coat and trousers with clean lines, which ran 'counter to the fripperies of King George III's court, setting a new fashion for sleek tailoring'. By about 1830, chinoiserie brilliance had been replaced by what one fashion commentator has called 'conservative dreariness'.

PART 4

Tea & Silver

CHAPTER 11

QIANLONG ERA
1700s

Much the most populous and sophisticated society in the world.

FOR MOST OF THE eighteenth century, as Europeans were gripped by a mania for chinoiserie and ships returned from Canton and Macau with wave after wave of Chinese goods, China's ruler was the Qianlong emperor. He was the last of the Qing dynasty's famous 'Three Emperors'. The other two were his father, Yongzheng, and his grandfather, Kangxi. Theirs was the period known as the 'High Qing' from 1661 to 1799. The Three Emperors ruled virtually unchallenged over what was said to be the wealthiest and 'much the most populous and sophisticated society in the world' at the time. The Three Emperors – father, son and grandson – gave China unprecedented continuity, prosperity and relative stability until the dawn of the nineteenth century. As one historian drily observed, the 'quality of life in eastern China in the 1700s appears to have left Europe behind'.

The Qing dynasty represented the Manchu people, whose ancestors were the Jurchen tribes of the north-east. The foreign Manchus were vastly outnumbered by the Han Chinese and, just as the Mongols had done centuries before, they rapidly assimilated Han ways. By the time of Qianlong, almost a century after the transfer of dynastic power, the Manchus revered Han culture and Qianlong's reign became another golden age of Chinese history. Kangxi is said to have secretly marked Qianlong out as a future emperor after witnessing his grandson's bravery and coolness under pressure when charged by a wounded bear during a hunting expedition. After ruling for six decades, Qianlong showed deference to the memory of his grandfather by formally stepping down, not wishing to surpass the length of his reign. But he remained in practical control for three more years so that his effective rule was longer than any other Chinese emperor before or since.

Under Qianlong, the empire reached its fullest flower. It was China's last period of national economic, military and cultural splendour before the twenty-first century. Qianlong's long reign gave him a nearly mythical status. He sponsored artistic projects on a scale unimaginable to Europeans and was himself a passionate poet, essayist and calligrapher. The official record of his collected writings is said, on one account, to amount to over 40,000 poems and 1300 pieces of prose. On this basis – if it is correct – he may have written more poetry in his lifetime than all the poets of the Tang dynasty, a period renowned for its poetry. And at a time when there were more book titles in China than in the rest of the world combined, Qianlong oversaw the ten-year compilation of a literary compendium containing all the most important Chinese texts. The compendium comprised more than 36,000 volumes and was called the 'Complete Library in the Four Treasuries' – the classics, the histories, the philosophers and the literary collections.

On the battlefield, Qianlong was more war-like than his Ming predecessors. By the mid-eighteenth century, his armies had brought the steppes of Outer Mongolia, the mountains of Tibet and the deserts of Xinjiang into the empire, largely settling China's modern geographic boundaries. Xinjiang, meaning 'the new frontier', had been forfeited during the late Tang dynasty. It was brought back under Chinese military control in 1759 after the conquest and genocide of the Dzungar people. The Dzungars were the last nomadic empire to threaten China and Qianlong insisted that their extermination should be 'the final solution'. The Uyghurs supported the Qing armies in the genocide. The Tibetans, whom the Qing army supported to wage a successful war against a Gurkha invasion force from Nepal, were also allies at the time.

The Qianlong era was not all triumph and victory all of the time. There were setbacks in the steamy jungles of Burma in 1769 and in Vietnam in 1789. The Burmese defeat of a Chinese incursion laid the foundation for the modern boundary between China and Myanmar, while the Vietnamese defeat of an over-confident and under-prepared Qing army during the Vietnamese New Year (Tet) was the original 'Tet Offensive' before that of the twentieth century's doomed Vietnam War. The occasional defeats aside, Qianlong referred to himself in old age as the 'Old Man of the Ten Completed Great Campaigns' and even wrote an essay in 1792 enumerating his victories.

In trade, China under Qianlong 'held all the cards', much as it did in the Song and Ming periods and much as it does today. The empire's strength in manufacturing and export caused Chinese prosperity to rise and rise. Adam Smith was in no doubt that China was 'much richer than any part of Europe'. The early English trade with China can be traced to the arrival of the ship *Macclesfield* at Canton in 1699. The ship belonged to the Honourable East India Company, the English trading company colloquially known as the 'Company' or the 'John Company', which was founded in 1600. The Company's coat of arms carried the motto *Neo Ducente Nil Nocet* – When God Leads, Nothing Can Harm.

In the early 1700s, when the Company established the first permanent European 'factory' in Canton, few Chinese anticipated the extent of future European encroachment. The general attitude was one of watchfulness but confidence in their ability to keep control of foreigners. A frustrated British diplomat later complained that China was 'the only civilised nation in the world whose jealous laws forbid the intrusion of any other people'. The issue would boil over in the nineteenth century but while Kangxi ruled, he was less worried by the Europeans and more concerned about the prospect of rebellion by supporters of the former Ming dynasty in the violent and unstable frontier society of Taiwan. In one of the great misjudgements of history, he famously speculated that 'in a hundred or a thousand years, the Europeans might cause trouble for the empire'.

Not everyone shared the emperor's confidence. Those with maritime experience who had seen European bullying in the ports of Southeast Asia urged vigilance. But the Chinese merchant lobby in Canton was too powerful and the lure of profitable commerce with the Europeans too great. For the time being, the European trade proceeded 'tranquilly and equitably, and all foreigners were sent away again when the winds were right'. But as the trade expanded and the numbers of incoming European ships multiplied, the Qianlong court became increasingly concerned by British vessels nudging progressively north in search of markets in cooler climates for English woollens.

In 1757 Qianlong decided to impose formal restrictions to confine the Europeans to Canton, in the same way that the Portuguese were confined to Macau. The essence of the restrictions was that the Europeans could only trade at the port of Canton and nowhere else; they could only reside and carry out business at the foreign 'factories' on the waterfront at Canton; they were subject to Chinese law; and their vessels could only anchor at the Whampoa roads. Firearms were also prohibited and foreign warships were definitely excluded. To the Chinese, the restrictions were known as 'The Five Counter Measures Against Barbarians'. To the Europeans, they were known as the 'Canton System'.

There was an additional overriding practical restraint on the European trade at Canton resulting from the prevailing meteorological conditions in the South China Sea. Trade was limited to the four-month period between monsoons – between the south-west monsoon ending in September, on which European vessels arrived, and the onset of the north-east monsoon in January, on which homeward-bound vessels set sail for Malacca, India and the Cape of Good Hope. A serious commercial setback would occur if a ship missed its monsoon and was delayed by a year or more in returning home.

One of the bizarre actions that reinforced Qianlong's justification for the Canton System was the conduct of an Englishman named James Flint who was a Company 'supercargo', a position responsible for overseeing the safekeeping and sale of ships' cargoes. He dressed like the English when their ships were in port but wore clothes like the Chinese when they were not. He spoke a Cantonese dialect and some Mandarin and could read and write in Chinese. Flint flouted the Chinese restrictions and championed the expansion of trading privileges beyond Canton. The last straw was in 1759 when he set off on a madcap expedition to meet the emperor. Flint carried a petition complaining about corruption in Canton and requesting permission for the British to trade at Ningbo, a port further north than Canton, closer to the centres of production of tea and silk and nearer to the colder northern climates.

When Flint reached Ningbo, he was told to go back to Canton but he ignored the command. When he continued to Tianjin, 1000 kilometres still further north where the road leads overland to Beijing, he caused a civil commotion. An official transmitted Flint's petition to the emperor and moved him into a Buddhist temple surrounded by guards to protect him from the angry mobs who regarded him as a 'foreign devil'. The emperor was genuinely concerned by Flint's report of corruption in Canton but was more deeply disturbed by his audacity in leaving Canton and circumventing the established channels of communication. Flint had sailed an English ship into ports where foreign vessels were forbidden and submitted a petition in Chinese directly to the sovereign despite having no rank or status within the empire.

Qianlong ordered Flint to return overland to Canton and to leave his ship and its crew behind. Neither the ship nor the crew were ever seen again. He was incarcerated in Macau for the next three years, then banished from the empire. The Qing governor in Canton wrote to the king in London extolling the

Chinese government's generosity in merely sentencing Flint to imprisonment. The letter described Flint's punishment as 'such amazingly gracious treatment that he should think of it with tears'. Flint's Chinese language teacher, who had facilitated his impertinence and translated his petition, was not treated so kindly. He was arrested and beheaded. Flint's failed escapade ensured that for the next 80 years, the Canton System was entrenched and Canton was the lone point of sanctioned commercial contact between China and the West.

The heart of the Canton System was the factories. By the 1750s, thirteen factories built in the European style of two or three storeys with columns, capitals, pilasters and colonnaded verandahs had established themselves along the Pearl River waterfront in Canton. They were so named because they were manned by 'factors' – locally based agents who represented the various European East India companies belonging to the growing number of nations who came to China for the trade in tea, silk, porcelain and other manufactured goods. The factories were in reality warehouses, trading posts, offices and places of residence. The old city was about 200 metres further back, surrounded by an eleventh-century wall that stretched as far as the eye could see in both directions. The wall was 'thirty feet high and crenelated, built from large blocks of sandstone at its base and smaller bricks above'. It was interspersed with towers armed with ancient cannon and sixteen massive wooden gates. The gates were winched open at dawn and shut firmly in the evening. Inside was a warren of narrow granite-paved streets where only a sedan chair could travel. Outside was a sprawling mass of habitations, shops, stalls, godowns, lanes and alleys leading to the European factory district beside the river.

The British factory was the grandest and most imposing of the European factories. It contained counting rooms, tea-tasting rooms, parlours, well-appointed living apartments, a chandeliered dining hall for 100 guests that served roast beef, potatoes and gravy, a billiard room and a substantial library. The factory buildings were arranged in a row, close together, set back from the riverbank, with gardens and a broad concourse in front leading down to the water's edge. Colossal flagpoles proudly displayed national flags at their entrances and narrow alleys with bars and liquor shacks squeezed between some of the buildings. No European women were allowed in Canton but the men made up for lost time in Macau during the non-trading season 'by seeking mistresses, or more rarely wives'. Floating brothels known as 'flower boats' cruised the waterways while 'sampan ladies' crowded around the anchorage at Whampoa, jostling for attention, offering to do laundry and odd jobs for the sailors.

During the trading season, the young men stayed alone at the factories, often reverting to childhood, 'playing leapfrog at all hours of the day and night' and behaving as if they were in a 'luxurious and very expensive' fraternity house. In time, they established a 'Canton Regatta Club' and celebrated ebulliently at sumptuous banquets. Downriver at the Whampoa anchorage, the merchant seamen remained with their ships and were only allowed the occasional brief foray for shore leave. The pipe and the bottle formed their main solace.

Despite appearances, the foreigners were not in charge at the Canton factories. They were entirely dependent on Chinese goodwill, much like the Portuguese community walled off on the Macau peninsula. About a dozen Chinese families known as 'Hong merchants' owned the factories and rented them to the Europeans. It paid to be on good terms with the Hong merchants who were given a monopoly over the commerce with foreigners. They formed a guild known as the 'Cohong' whose members were men of immense wealth. The richest of all was Howqua, who was revered by the foreign community for his integrity and honesty. Howqua became a household name in England and America and was probably the richest man in the world. In the 1830s, his estimated worth was 26 million Spanish silver dollars, a figure that exceeded the reputed fortune of Jacob Astor, the wealthiest man in the United States. Howqua's place of business in the factory compound was spartan and unadorned but he otherwise behaved like a modern Chinese plutocrat. His palatial home 'with its five hundred domestics [and] its pleasure gardens of the ten thousand pines' was famous throughout China.

The entire formal trade of China with the West was conducted from the factories where the foreigners were effectively quarantined to 'a space of just twelve acres – less than the footprint of one of the pyramids in Egypt'. In return for their lucrative monopoly rights, the Hong merchants subscribed to a code of articles that required them to guarantee the good behaviour and tax obligations of the Western traders. They determined prices and exchange rates; made loans; leased the factories; organised all aspects of the supply of the tea, silks and porcelain; managed a banking business; and arranged the overland transportation of export goods to Canton including the packing, quality control and shipboard delivery of the goods.

At the apex of the official hierarchy was the 'Hoppo', as he was known in pidgin. He was the imperial customs official in Canton responsible for maximising the flow of tariff revenue to Beijing. The Hoppo collected the duties on foreign trade, remitted them (or some of them) to Beijing, supervised the activities of the Hong merchants and controlled the customs inspectors. The nature of the work exposed the Hoppo and the inspectors to many opportunities for corruption and countless temptations for personal enrichment. They extracted *cumshaw* (bribes) from the European merchants at Canton and made many extortionate financial claims which required 'considerable and ongoing attention'. James Flint's complaints in his misconceived petition to the emperor related to a Hoppo who regularly demanded bribes and charged higher duties than he was supposed to.

The restriction of the European traders to a few acres beside the river at Canton reflected age-old Chinese prejudices and stereotypes about foreigners. They were *fanqui* or 'foreign devils' and the small part of Canton to which they were confined was known colloquially as '*fanqui*-town'. In Chinese eyes, they were 'merely a new form of inner Asian barbarian' with whom they were prepared to trade but nothing more. Long into the nineteenth century, the British minister was still referred to in official Chinese documents as the 'English barbarian chieftain'. Chinese elites had respected the earlier Jesuit missionaries who brought new knowledge and a softer approach, but China's time of engagement with the missionaries and curiosity about Western science and civilisation had passed following the prohibition of Christianity in 1724 and the gradual disappearance of the Jesuit influence.

None of this hampered the growth of foreign trade from China during the eighteenth century. As uncouth and morally inferior as the European traders were considered to be, they were permitted under strict controls to undertake commerce with Chinese merchants – just like other foreign barbarians in earlier eras. They may have been unworthy of intellectual intercourse but they were tolerated as a valuable source of silver. Chinese knowledge of Europe and Europeans remained bizarrely scant and superficial, however. In mid-century, as Canton was coming into its own as a European trading hub, official Chinese reports were sometimes humorous in their depiction of the Europeans. Some remarks seem apposite to the modern era:

> The males mostly wear wool and love to drink wine. The females when they have not yet married, bind their waists, desiring that they be slender. They wear dishevelled hair which hangs over their eyebrows, short clothing and layers of skirts ... [Their] flesh is dazzling white ... Marriages are left to mutual arrangement. The men are violent and tyrannical and skilled in the use of weapons ...

The Englishman Thomas Meadows explained that the Chinese

> are always surprised, not to say astonished, to learn that we have surnames, and understand the family distinctions of father, brother, wife, sister etc.; in short that we live otherwise than as a herd of cattle.

And when the occasional solitary Chinese managed to visit Europe in the eighteenth century, his observations tended to reflect a similar cultural bafflement. One noted that 'England has a great many prostitutes' – which was undoubtedly true of London at the time – and that 'illegitimate children have to be reared and they do not dare to destroy them'. Chinese and Western values were different then and now.

There was little European political or diplomatic engagement with China throughout the eighteenth century. Contact was largely confined to commercial exchange between merchants and traders in Canton. High-level political or cultural intercourse was insignificant or non-existent. The established Chinese order was not challenged; the diplomatic missions were few; and reciprocal incomprehension prevailed. After the failed mission of the Portuguese envoy Tomé Pires in 1520–1521, there were some delegations by representatives of the Pope, Imperial Russia, the Dutch Republic and Portugal – but only four occurred after 1727, of which just one was from Great Britain. It was led by Lord Macartney in 1793 and was funded by the East India Company. All missions except that of Macartney conformed to the historical tribute pattern and all ambassadors performed the prescribed ritual of the kowtow acknowledging the superiority of the emperor as the Son of Heaven.

The intransigent Macartney refused to prostrate himself and only kneeled ambiguously on one knee, managing to turn an exercise in mutual bewilderment into a simmering conflict that embittered both sides. His punctilious insistence on maintaining British dignity – while dressed in his finest spotted mulberry velvet, diamond star, ribbon and plume of feathers – was the sort of behaviour that troubled the British merchant class at Canton. These pragmatic men of commerce were terrified of losing their trade and were inclined to urge that conflict be avoided at all costs. On one occasion some of them wrote to the directors of the Company in London, warning them that 'the only and invariable rule of Conduct to be observed [in China] ... was on no occasion to give offence to the Chinese government'.

This timorous attitude would change before too many more decades. But at the time of the Macartney embassy, China was at the height of its prosperity and Qianlong was at the height of his reign. The population of China had doubled and now exceeded 300 million, representing one-third of the entire world. Britain's population was still less than 10 million. And Canton was the third largest city in the world after Beijing and London. But Qianlong was also insecure. His control over the vast empire was built on total and unquestioning obedience from the population and 'any foreign contact that might disturb this blind obedience was dangerous to the throne'. To maintain control, it was thought that foreign influence needed to be strictly limited, as it was at Canton and Macau.

Qianlong entertained the British embassy at the royal hunting lodge at Chengde, where he had a summer retreat in a cool mountain valley north of the Great Wall. The retreat was a complex of palaces, gardens, pagodas, hunting grounds and temples that made a great impression on Macartney, as his journal indicates. But Macartney's mission was doomed; he just did not know it. Qianlong outwardly blamed Macartney's 'presumption and self-importance' and wrote that 'if they come in arrogance, they get nothing'. Inwardly, the elderly emperor was worried about the effect of foreign influence. He rejected all the British requests, especially those for new ports to be opened to British trade and ordered Macartney and his companions to leave within three days. The mission was a failure, its dismissal a humiliation. Perversely, Macartney's decision not to perform the kowtow was regarded by some in London as the one triumph of the mission.

The brooding ambassador departed, forced to repeat the same months-long inland journey from Beijing to Canton along canals and rivers and over mountain passes on which James Flint was despatched in ignominy almost half a century earlier. Qianlong's formal responses written on imperial yellow silk were suitably imperious and famously hubristic. He declared that

> As the Greatness and Splendour of the Chinese Empire have spread its Fame far and wide, and as foreign Nations from a thousand parts of the World crowd hither over mountains and Seas to pay us their homage, what is it that we can want here?

adding in a separate edict that 'The products of our empire are abundant and there is nothing we do not have. So we have never needed products from foreign countries to give us anything we lacked'. Qianlong's conclusion was that further contact 'is not in harmony with the regulations of the Celestial Empire [and] ... is of no advantage to your country'.

Qianlong's faith in isolation would prove to be China's undoing in the nineteenth century when the West entered the Industrial Age. But at least in food and clothing, China was self-sufficient. Sir Robert Hart, a British diplomat from Northern Ireland who served as an official in the Qing government from 1861 to 1907, remarked that:

> The Chinese have the best food in the world: rice; the best drink: tea; and the best clothing: cotton, silk and fur. Possessing these staples and the innumerable native adjuncts, they do not need to buy a penny's worth elsewhere.

Unlike China, Great Britain was not self-sufficient. It needed the China trade, especially the tea trade, whose import duties and taxes had become 'the lifeblood of the British Empire'. As Macartney pondered his embarrassing dismissal by the emperor, he knew that if Britain reacted by showing aggression to China or by seeking to conquer any part of its territory, Qianlong could simply shut down the British China trade. If that were to happen, he wrote, 'the blow would be immediate and heavy'. By 1800, almost nothing was more important to Great Britain than the tea trade from China.

CHAPTER 12

TRADING TEA

1600s–1800s

Strange predilection for drinking hot water.

TEA WAS UNKNOWN IN England when the East India Company was founded in London on the last day of December 1600. William Shakespeare knew only beer and mead, claret and madeira, but not tea. Marco Polo made no reference to tea in his *Travels*. Knowledge of the decoction only began to seep through in whispers and rumours from travellers and missionaries who had observed in China and Japan a 'strange predilection for drinking hot water'. But by the late eighteenth century, tea had become Britain's single greatest import from China, far exceeding silk and porcelain.

In the early decades of the seventeenth century, not long before the Dutch-led tulip mania of the 1630s, the Portuguese and the Dutch brought the first shipments of tea to the European continent. By mid-century, small amounts began to make their way across the Channel to enterprising shopkeepers in London. The wealthy elite embraced the beguiling hot beverage whose expense and fashionability helped fuel its own mythology. It was a mildly addictive stimulant, slightly bitter and free of nutritional value, but it was new, exotic and expensive.

The person who almost single-handedly boosted tea's acceptance in England, and made it chic, was Catherine of Braganza, the Portuguese princess who disembarked at Portsmouth in 1662 to marry Charles II, the merry monarch of the Restoration. The princess arrived with chests of tea, a store of the finest porcelain and all the impedimenta of tea etiquette, as well as a fabulous dowry that included the strategic ports of Bombay in India and Tangier in Morocco, not to mention a cash contribution to the marriage of £500,000. Catherine's royal patronage elevated the ritual of tea drinking to a matter of court culture and voguish elegance, ensuring that the consumption of tea became an established aspect of elite and aristocratic social life, revolving around conspicuous display and spectacle, fine porcelain and genteel behaviour.

Catherine was so well known for her association with tea that Edmund Waller – a courtier and poet in an era that included Dryden, Wycherley and Congreve – wrote a sycophantic birthday ode to her entitled 'Of Tea, Commended by Her Majesty', which went in part:

> Tea both excels, which she vouchsafes to praise.
> The best of Queens, and best of herbs …
> The Muse's friend, tea does our fancy aid,
> Repress those vapours which the head invade,
> And keep the palace of the soul serene …

Fashionable allure was not the only reason for the success of tea among the well-to-do. It was also eulogised as a universal medicine and a panacea for all sorts of ailments. The Chinese had long popularised the beneficial effects of tea in stimulating wakefulness and ensuring sobriety, qualities that found congruence with Buddhist spirituality. Europeans also embraced tea's restorative and curative qualities and learned men of science and medicine composed treatises and published pamphlets about the benefits of tea. A notable Dutch physician wrote with unconstrained enthusiasm that:

> Not only does tea enliven the body, but it also wards off painful stones ... it counters headache, cold, inflammation of the eyes, drooping or disturbing of the spirits, weakness of the stomach, intestinal dysentery, lassitude and sleep ... Sipping this decoction, one may sometimes spend entire nights working ... without being otherwise overcome by the need for sleep.

Tea's power to subdue sleepiness was a professional benefit for another advocate, a French missionary in Macau who explained that he had 'experimented [with tea] quite often when I was obliged to listen all night to the Confessions of my good Christians'.

The early prices for tea were astronomical, as was the profiteering. Mark-ups were perhaps as high as 6000 per cent. In Amsterdam in 1657, tea was for sale but the expense 'was astonishing: £6 for a pound of tea', which one recent writer calculated to be equivalent in purchasing power to £847 today. The first enterprising English tea merchant appears to have been Thomas Garway, who marketed his tea to the upper echelon of society and trumpeted its health-giving properties, describing tea as 'the Excellent, and by all Physitians approved, China Drink'. Garway sought to attract 'all Persons of Eminency and Quality, Gentlemen, and others residing in or neer the Court, Westminster, and Parts adjacent' – presumably on the basis that they were the only ones who could afford it. Samuel Pepys, a humble naval administrator, knew of tea and recorded his first encounter with it in his famous journal in 1660, but was not an enthusiast. He preferred coffee.

For hundreds of millions of Chinese, tea was a millennia-old, everyday hot infusion created from the oxidised and dried leaves of a native shrub whose cultivation, consumption and connoisseurship were deep-rooted in Chinese culture. The shrub, which the Swedish botanist Carl Linnaeus later named *Camellia sinensis,* is found in profusion in eastern and southern Asia, from the Himalayas to Japan and Indonesia, and is part of the same family and genus as the common flowering garden shrubs *Camellia japonica* and *Camellia sasanqua.* It is bountiful among the dramatic landscape of the World Heritage subtropical Wuyi Mountains in China's northern Fujian province. The region's thin air, chilly nights and high rainfall contribute to the production of the richest black teas – Oolong and Lapsang souchong.

The cultivation of tea took place on thousands of smallholder farms that proliferated in the moist and mountainous tea-growing regions of the south-east, as well as Yunnan in the south-west. For a month during the spring picking season, the tender young fresh tips were 'plucked' by pickers, invariably women, who carried grass baskets on their backs and sometimes an infant at their front. They stayed in the fields from early morning until dusk and carried their harvest in bags slung from a bamboo shoulder pole, 'the weight of each bag being half a picul'. A *picul* was a heavy load, about 60 kilograms, as much as one person could carry on a pole. A woman travelling in China during the Victorian era remarked how 'thus heavily burdened, a party of these bright, pleasant-looking women march a dozen miles or more, chatting and singing as they go'.

A nimble tea picker could 'pluck up to thirty thousand tea shoots per day, which includes the time it takes to examine each shoot and make sure no stalk enters the mix'. The haul might result in 'as much as ten pounds of green leaf a day', which, after processing, might produce two pounds of fresh tea for sale.

Processing involved the oxidisation and fermenting of the leaves over a charcoal fire to ensure the distinctive dark appearance of black tea. The leaves for green tea were not oxidised. Workers often 'spent the night roasting, rolling and sifting the leaves under close watch'. The longer the curing process, the stronger the tannins, the darker the colour and the more bitter the flavour. The blackened roasted dried tea leaves were taken to local markets where they were assessed for quality and sold to merchants who operated tea warehouses and distribution points. From these places, thousands of baskets of black tea were transported to Canton and ultimately exported to Europe.

In Canton, the tea was weighed in *piculs* and payment was made in silver, which was counted in *taels*. The *picul* was a unit of measurement as culturally symbolic as the English bushel, the rood or the furlong. A *tael* was a unit of weight applied to silver and was also used as a unit of currency. It commonly represented about 40 grams of silver in imperial China but was later standardised to be 50 grams. The Europeans quickly became accustomed to the terminology. Ships moored at the Whampoa anchorage carried silver, which was valued in *taels*, and sailed with tea, which was weighed in *piculs*. The silver shipped to China was packed in heavy locked treasure chests made of hard wood secured by metal bands. Each chest contained about 4000 coins. The larger tea chests were made of a lighter wood with an internal lining of thin foil to ensure freshness and to protect against damp and salt. An incoming European ship might carry as many as 30 chests of silver and depart with thousands of tea chests. When the Dutch ship *Bredenhof* foundered in 1753, she was carrying 30 chests mostly of silver and some gold. All the chests were lost overboard but were recovered from the ocean floor more than 200 years later.

The Company's tea trade with China was slow to start and lagged well behind that of the Portuguese and Dutch. For a considerable time, tea was enjoyed and celebrated more in Amsterdam and Lisbon than in London. Portuguese merchants had long been purchasing tea at Macau, while the Dutch purchased tea in Japan – where Buddhist monks had long ago introduced tea from China - and from Chinese merchants who sailed their junks to Batavia. When the philosopher John Locke returned to England from Holland in the retinue of Queen Mary after the Revolution of 1688, he found English tea culture not nearly as sophisticated as that of the Dutch. In 1637, the directors of the VOC, who were known as the 'Gentlemen Seventeen', instructed Anthony van Diemen, the governor-general at Batavia – better known for his quest to discover the 'Great South Land' – that 'we expect some jars of Chinese as well as Japanese tea with all ships'.

It was not until about 1700 that the Company really began to appreciate tea's commercial potential. When the English tea trade eventually commenced, it became a phenomenon. A century later, British culture was addicted to tea and its fiscal security was dependent on it. No one could have foreseen the power and influence that tea would exert. Tea profits sustained the East India Company and tea taxes sustained the British Exchequer. And the British habit of adding sugar – which mystified the Chinese – brought tea into an unholy triangle with the Caribbean sugar plantations and the West African slave trade. Each underpinned the other. As the eighteenth century progressed, a dependable supply of tea from Canton was of 'increasing importance for the prosperity of the city of London, the financial security of its largest trading company and the livelihood of its working population'.

The *Macclesfield*'s supercargoes carried specific instructions from the directors of the Company to make 'Roome betwixt Decks for their Tea'. At that early stage, only a fraction of the Company's trade was with China, and such trade as there was consisted mostly of silks, porcelain and other wares, but not tea. As the new century opened, the trading momentum began to shift in favour of tea. In 1700, the supercargoes of another British vessel, the *Northumberland,* were informed that tea 'does very much obtaine in reputation among persons of all qualities'. The Company directors then resolved to 'drive the Trade to the utmost'. By 1717, the British tea trade at Canton was underway in earnest. Ships' masters were instructed to bring back 'Tea as much as the Ship can conveniently stow'. But they were also warned:

> The Chinese are a subtill Cunning People and are very dexterous in putting Cheats upon all that Deal with them and must be managed accordingly, However they love to be respected and you

> must therefore carry yourselves in such manner as not to affront them and yet to avoid being Cheated.

Cultural prejudice prevailed, as it still often does. The Chinese translators were supposedly 'all sharpers' and the local compradors who provisioned the ships were 'knaves'. There was certainly no shortage of fraud and theft at Canton, and innumerable tricks occurred between wharf and ship. But much the same applied when the tea chests were unloaded in London from the East Indiamen. The tea chests had to be transferred to shallow-keeled lighters at Blackwall Reach on the Thames, funnelled through the congested quays between Billingsgate and the Tower of London, then transported by cart to the Company warehouses in the old City around Leadenhall and Fenchurch Streets. Cheating and pilfering were rife in London as much as they were at Canton. It was said when the East India Docks were being constructed that:

> The Quantity of Tea Stolen in the delivery of the Ships has been on average for the last three years 210 Chests. Valuing them at ten pounds per chest, the amount of Plunder is in this Article alone 2,100 pounds per annum.

Neither cheating at Canton, nor ongoing theft in the Port of London, nor losses at sea, nor competition from the Continental smuggling trade, dented the Company's enthusiasm for the tea trade. Before long, tea became 'the god to which everything else was sacrificed' ... displacing silk and porcelain as the primary object of the Company's China trade. In 1730, The Company's directors instructed their Canton supercargoes to act aggressively towards their competitors, to 'make their European rivals sick of their voyages for tea at any cost'. As imports multiplied, the price of tea became affordable to a wider market and tea drinking became democratised. In 1756, one superior Englishman despaired that tea 'prevailed so universally' and remarked that it had done so 'for about twenty years'. By the 1770s tea had 'found an entrance in every cottage' in England. A decade later, the poet William Cowper wrote picturesquely of 'the cups that cheer but not inebriate' to describe the national drink that had replaced ale and gin as the people's favourite beverage.

Tea became a boom industry. In the eighteenth century, the flow of tea into Great Britain through official, non-smuggling channels 'more than doubled in each twenty-year period'. The import figures kept climbing, 'growing nearly 10,000 per cent by 1805'. Between 1720 and 1740, tea imports doubled from about 30,000 *piculs* each year to about 60,000; by 1765 they doubled again to about 120,000 *piculs*; and by 1795, they doubled again to 240,000 *piculs*. The demand was insatiable, the profits seductive and the import duties a boon for the government. As the century progressed, the East India Company focussed on tea and allowed the trade in porcelain, silks, lacquer wares and other Chinese goods to be undertaken increasingly by its private-trading captains, officers and supercargoes, some of whom made themselves considerably rich. Even passengers who went out on the Company ships engaged in private trade. There was profit for everyone.

The rewards from the Canton tea trade were stupefying. By the early 1800s, the Company was making an average annual profit of over £1,000,000, of which 90 per cent came from tea. The Company had so much wealth that in 1793, it could outlay £78,000 to fund the doomed Macartney mission to China in the hope that it would bring increased trading opportunities. By the late 1700s, Great Britain completely dominated the tea trade at Canton through its East India Company. The other European companies 'withdrew from the China trade one after another from the second half of the 1780s', while around the same time, at the conclusion of the American Revolutionary War, the Americans gradually ventured into the trade.

In the last years before the end of the Company's trading monopoly in China in 1834, when tea was its only export product from China, 'one tenth of England's total annual revenue brought into the British Exchequer came from the [Company's] tea trade', which was enough to fund the Royal Navy. The lion's share of China tea went to Great Britain and its colonies, which 'consumed 70 per cent or more of the tea exported from China'. Even convict transport ships from Botany Bay sought to profit from the tea trade – refitting their vessels and sailing to Canton to purchase tea after they had deposited their loads of convicts. At that time, virtually the only place in the world where the British and the Americans could obtain their tea was China and the only place in China where they could buy it was Canton.

From the trade's inception, the Europeans had paid for the purchase of tea with silver, none more so than the British. They had little else to offer. The Americans offered furs for a while until stocks were depleted, but among the Europeans, only the Dutch did not depend entirely on payment in silver. Their triangular trade through Java allowed them to sell pepper, tin and spices in Canton in exchange for tea. By the second half of the eighteenth century, the lopsided British balance of trade troubled those of a mercantilist outlook 'who feared that precious metals were being exchanged for luxury goods of dubious worth'. They believed that the measure of a nation's wealth was the amount of gold and silver held in its treasury. The English commentator Richard Campbell wrote that:

> It is much disputed how far this [East India] Company is beneficial to the Nation, since they carry out mostly Bullion, and bring us in return, for the most part, only Superfluities.

Another English commentator grumbled disparagingly about paying 'good silver and gold for Chinese shards, rags and herbs' – namely porcelain, silk and tea. Even the Swedish Carl Linnaeus complained of shipping away silver for no more than 'dry leaves of bushes and thin threads spun by caterpillars'. It was a similar argument to that once used by the elder statesmen of Rome who worried about the depletion of Rome's silver and gold resources for silk and other luxuries from the East.

It was certainly one-way traffic. As the tea trade grew, the average annual export of silver by the East India Company to the East climbed inexorably. By the 1750s, it was common for 70 to 85 per cent and sometimes 90 per cent of the value of the Company's outbound cargoes to be made up of silver, which the Company purchased mostly from the Bank of England or from the venerable London trading house of Moses Mocatta, the world's leading bullion broker. With so much silver at their disposal, the buying power of the Company's representatives in Canton during the eighteenth century made them the favourite customers of the Hong merchants.

CHAPTER 13

RIVERS OF SILVER

1500s–1800s

China carries away the silver from all Europe.

FOR MOST OF THE period from the mid-1500s to the early 1800s, China was the global centre of manufacturing production and the universal destination for much of the world's silver. Since ancient times, silver, not the more valuable gold, was the money of regular commerce that was 'most often used'. The world market economy, including on the European continent, was dominated by a de facto silver standard. Gold coins were used as a store of value and as money but silver prevailed because it was 'more numerous and appropriate for ordinary daily transactions'. The three-centuries-long, large-scale movement of silver to China was an economic phenomenon that dominated global trade. China became a 'seemingly bottomless silver sink', a 'suction pump *(bomba aspirante)*', a 'vacuum cleaner' for the world's silver. A Portuguese merchant observed in 1621 that 'silver wanders throughout all the world in its peregrinations before flocking to China, where it remains, as if at its natural centre'. China's thirst for silver overwhelmed Europe until eventually opium overwhelmed China.

The export of silver from Europe and the shipment of manufactured goods from China and gave rise to the birth of modern world trade. When Spain opened the Pacific and established a trading base at Manila in 1571, shipping trade joined all known continents, traversed all major oceans and transformed the world. Montesquieu, the eighteenth-century French philosopher, thought that the China trade, based on silver, was 'the greatest commerce of the universe'. And a modern historian explained that silver 'went round the world and made the world go round'. In the mid-eighteenth century, Scottish economist Adam Smith wrote in *The Wealth of Nations* that silver was the means by which the 'distant parts of the world are connected with one another'.

Silver made China rich. It remodelled Ming society, gilded the Chinese world and became the economic lifeblood of the nation. It altered daily life and became the overwhelming passion of late Ming China. The tax regime changed completely. No longer could taxes be paid in kind with whatever goods each household produced – predominately rice, silk, tea or wheat. The people were forced to pay their provincial taxes, their salt tax – a major historical revenue earner - and the price of their exemption from conscripted labour, in silver. China's tributary system also switched to silver, as did a myriad national levies – from land and poll taxes to the tributes of prefectural and county officials. Many were consolidated into a single silver tax known as the 'Single Whip reform', a phrase intended to connote the combining of many items into one.

The catalyst for China's silver transformation during the Ming dynasty was the fifteenth-century decision to abandon the various forms of paper money with which China had experimented for the preceding 400 years. The experiment had started with a form of promissory note dubbed 'flying cash' in the late Tang period and continued with bank notes in different forms in the Song and Mongol periods. When the Ming dynasty came to power, it issued its own paper currency sometimes known as the 'Great Ming Precious Notes' but they were not backed by gold or silver reserves. By the 1450s, inflation, counterfeiting and overissue had reduced the precious notes to a thousandth of their original value. During the short reign of the Jingtai emperor (r. 1449–1457), the government suspended further issues of notes and ended the centuries-long experiment with paper money.

Copper or bronze coins in the form of 'strings' of cash had long been in use in China and were the medium of menial wages and the rural marketplace but they suffered from variability in quality, unreliability in weight and disparities in metallic content, and had become unsuitable for large transactions. There was such a miscellany in the market that the calculation of payment sometimes depended on the particular coins proffered by the buyer. And they were heavy and cumbersome, especially in the form of multiple strings of a thousand coins joined together through square holes punched in each piece and hung around the necks of merchants. Small strings were also worn on wrists and arms as bangles. A string of cash of a thousand copper coins weighed about three kilograms.

Since ancient times, unminted, uncoined small silver ingots were a well-recognised feature of Chinese society. During the Ming and Qing dynasties, these ingots evolved to become the primary medium of exchange for domestic transactions other than the humblest. The ingots, known as *sycee* silver, were measured by their weight in *taels* and assessed for quality by money changers whom the Europeans called *shroffs*. They were made privately by individual silversmiths subject to the rules of local mercantile guilds that dictated their fineness, weight, size and shape – all of which varied from one locality to another. A small silver ingot representing a *tael* of *sycee* silver was generally equivalent to a string of thousand copper coins. Silver ingots in a bewildering variety of forms and degrees of fineness circulated in different regions, creating a Chinese currency of unparalleled complexity. Square and oval-shaped ingots were common but there were also boat-, flower- and tortoise-shaped ingots. If an amount of lesser value were needed, it was created by shaving off part of an ingot. From the seventeenth century onwards, the inflow of Spanish silver *pesos* added to the complicated currency mix.

Silver became the 'store of value, the money of account' and the medium for state payments and large transactions. China remonetized its economy, yet a singular feature of the monetary metamorphosis was that Chinese silver 'money' was not strictly money at all. Silver's value was determined not by any ruler's writ, but by the laws of supply and demand. It was more a commodity than a currency, 'worth sometimes more or sometimes less, depending on whether it was available in great abundance, just as in the case of silk and other commodities'. It had no face value guaranteed by government and was vulnerable to market fluctuations, as happened at the end of the Ming period when the fall of the dynasty was hastened by silver's oversupply and drop in value.

Merchants around the world acquired silver like any other commodity with the intention of reaping arbitrage profits upon its delivery to China where its value was greatest. For most of the time, 'supply and demand forces' meant that 'silver's [market] value in China was double its value in the rest of the world'. Some condemned silver's baneful influence. Sir Isaac Newton, who among his other roles was Warden of the Royal Mint, reported in 1717 that the value of silver in China was so high that it 'carries away the silver from all Europe'. Carl Linnaeus, like a modern Trumpian, insisted that there was 'nothing more important than to close that gate [to China], through which all the silver of Europe disappears'.

Awash with silver, Ming commerce was vibrant and money-making was a constant preoccupation. Perhaps more than ever before in China, silver ruled, conspicuous consumption reigned and merchants thrived. Manufacturing and industry reached new levels of proliferation; agriculture became more commercialised; and the pursuit of wealth and prosperity was energised. And with so much money, there was more than the usual amount of greed, corruption, indulgence and excess, including – perhaps especially – among officials. Silver consumed the people's hearts, and sometimes their minds. The material extravagance, ostentatious spending and social competition of the late Ming era exceeded even that of the Song dynastic period. There was a near-fetishism for luxurious material things. And those who could afford it enthusiastically lavished silver on the same things that the very rich have always spent their money on – art, property and food.

Epicureanism and gastronomy were aspects of this culture of excess. The writings of the Ming scholars are flooded with records of parties, menus and cuisines. Epicureanism became so fashionable that one's knowledge of cuisine was a sign of erudition and nobility. The contemporaneous erotic novel *The Golden Lotus* (1610), an allegory of late Ming society, features more than three hundred characters representing nearly every kind of person and business in society, merchants as well as officials. It is a mirror on society. The author describes the characters – in much-repeated and vividly described detail – pursuing profit, indulging in sex and enjoying food in equal and plentiful measure.

Then as now, conservative critics warned about the decay of the age and the decline of standards. The magistrate Zhang Tao fulminated in 1609 about the 'Lord of Silver' and complained about easy money, flamboyant display and moral decadence; how avarice was without limit; and how everything was for personal pleasure. But silver was so thoroughly a fact of daily life that nothing could be done about it. An increasingly wealthy Chinese middle class developed a taste for the luxuries previously enjoyed only at court: beautiful cloisonné vases, intricate filigree art, decorative lacquerware, elegant furniture and fine porcelain. Acquisitiveness became part of a growing culture. Nor was it enough for the elite to own paintings, calligraphy, bronzes, ceramics and carved jade, they also had to know how to talk about them as a means of establishing their superior knowledge to others within their rank. And it was considered important to 'restrict the downward extension of knowledge to the hoi-polloi'. Late Ming society was a new world with a familiar modern materialist ring – a far cry from the ideal that the moralising first Ming emperor, Hongwu, sought to establish.

CHAPTER 14

MANILA GALLEONS

1565–1815

I am rich Potosí, the treasure of the world.

CHINA'S GEOGRAPHY AND GEOLOGY meant that it had insufficient silver of its own; and any significant local extraction was hindered by a native prejudice against mining coupled with a traditional Confucian fear that 'mining would upset the balance of the earth' – a vital conception for geomancers and practitioners of *fengshui*. In the 1520s, huge silver deposits were discovered on the south-west coast of the Japanese island of Honshu. Official Chinese trade was not possible because Japan at the time was in a state of feudal anarchy, bedevilled by samurai warlords and competing warring states. And officially at least, the original isolationist Ming sea ban on foreign maritime trade was still in place and would continue until 1567.

The vacuum was filled by pirates and smugglers along the China coast who, in collaboration with the Portuguese, conducted a thriving illicit trade in Japanese silver and enslaved people. Piracy on the China coast was a longstanding phenomenon dating back thousands of years, but ever since Kublai Khan's failed invasion of Japan in the late thirteenth century, Japanese pirates who used the Ryukyu Island chain as their base had become a dominant and feared presence along the China coast. Their depredations and atrocities often extended a considerable way inland. The Chinese referred pejoratively to the shorter-statured Japanese as *wokou* or 'dwarf bandits' but these *ninja* pirates were renowned for their prowess as swordsmen. An apocryphal local story told of a 'dozen sword-wielding *wokou* who managed to kill 300 Chinese militiamen sent against them'.

The pirates and the Portuguese traders established extensive clandestine networks and local market emporiums where Japanese silver was exchanged for Chinese silk and other products. When legitimate trade flourished again and piracy diminished with the lifting of the Ming sea ban in 1567, the Portuguese dominated the trade from their base at Macau. The Portuguese may have been explorers in the Atlantic and conquerors in the Indian Ocean but 'in the Far East, they were businessmen'. Their slow-moving but capacious carracks, painted black with pitch for watertightness, came to Japan seeking silver and people to enslave. They were known to the Portuguese as the 'silver carracks' but to the Japanese they were the 'black ships'.

Japanese silver continued to flow through Portuguese hands to China until 1639 when the Shogun expelled all Portuguese missionaries and merchants and banned their ships. But by the late 1500s, Spain had become the major source of silver for China's booming economy. Silver from Spain's stupendously wealthy silver mines in the viceroyalties of Mexico and Peru flooded into China and the long-serving Ming emperors of the period, Jiajing and Wanli, who reigned collectively for over 90 years until 1620, could afford to rest on their laurels and ignore their ministers. The wealth of the economy took care of itself.

The greatest of all the newly discovered Spanish silver mines in the Americas was the mine at Potosí, a desolate mountain above the tree line in a remote part of the central Andes range. For the people of the Andes, the area was *puna* or uninhabitable but the harsh environment did not deter the Spaniards who discovered thick veins of high-grade silver running through the mountain when they were led there by indigenous peoples in

1545. The Spaniards called the mountain *Cerro Rico*, meaning 'rich mountain' and placed a Christian cross on the summit, as was their habit. Its riches were beyond the wildest dreams of the early conquistadores who arrived in the previous decade. The rudimentary town at Potosí's base became so valuable that it earned a Spanish royal charter and an official name: *Villa Imperial de Potosí.* The inscription on its coat of arms proudly announced 'I am rich Potosí, the treasure of the world; the king of mountains, the envy of kings'. The coat of arms was later updated to proclaim even more triumphantly: 'For the powerful Emperor, for the wise King, this lofty mountain of silver *will conquer the world*' (emphasis added). In a sense, it did.

Potosí was the world's largest single silver deposit, perhaps the richest mountain the world has ever known. Cervantes referred to Potosí in his novel *Don Quixote* (1605) and Matteo Ricci placed it on his *mappamondo* that he presented at the imperial court in Beijing in 1602. The phrase 'as rich as Potosí' came into common use. For Spain, and indirectly for China, it was a fountain of fortune. Over the next two centuries, the Potosí mine produced more than 40,000 tons of silver, much of which eventually made its way to China. The town's population swelled from zero in 1545 to an estimated 165,000 by 1605, nearly the size of Paris or London. This was equivalent, thought one scholar, to '20 million people moving to a spot on Alaska's North Slope'. The number of Potosí's casinos, dance halls and bordellos was scarcely believable but they existed side by side with approximately 80 churches. By the early 1600s, the isolated mining town in an oxygen-starved wasteland had become, on one account, 'the fourth largest city in the Christian world'. It was the 'first city of capitalism' supplying 'the primary ingredient of capitalism – money'.

Until the Pacific route to Manila was opened, the silver from Potosí followed a torturous journey to Seville and Lisbon before moving to the clearing houses of London and Amsterdam and onwards to China, which was known as 'the tomb of European moneys'. Mules and lamas carried heavy wooden chests of silver from the mine over the mountains to the coastal port of Callao near Lima. The arduous trek took two and a half months. From Callao the silver was shipped north to Panama where it was again laden on pack animals and transported across the isthmus to the Panamanian port of Portobelo, one of the three great 'treasure ports' on the Spanish Main – the others being Veracruz in Mexico and Cartagena in Columbia.

At Portobelo, the chests were loaded into Spanish 'treasure ships', which sailed in convoy across the Atlantic with other merchant vessels, all guarded by heavily armed naval ships. The fleet would sail first to the safe harbour of Havana, Cuba and then to Cadiz in southern Spain, the ocean port down-river from Seville. Seville was then the economic heart of the Spanish empire, the doorway to the new world and the centre of the world silver trade. It was where Columbus presented his credentials at the royal palace before his historic journey across the Atlantic for what he thought was China. Silver also went along an alternative, but technically illegal, route from Potosí south down the Rio de la Plata into Argentina, and from there across the Atlantic. It is no coincidence that Rio de la Plata means 'River of Silver' in Spanish and that 'Argentina', which is derived from the Latin word *argentum* for silver, means 'land of silver'.

By the eighteenth century, the Spanish silver *peso*, also later known as the Spanish silver dollar, was the dominant form of silver used for foreign exchange in China. One *peso* contained about 25 grams of silver and was worth eight Spanish *reals*. As the English translated *pesos* as 'pieces', they became known in the Anglophone world as 'pieces of eight'. The Spanish silver dollar progressively competed with and replaced everything else and was arguably the most successful money in history. Its ubiquity made it the first global currency, widely used in Europe, the North and South Americas and East Asia. The British government made it the first official currency of the colony of New South Wales where it was known as the 'Holey Dollar' because the centre was punched out to make a second coin. Shiploads of Spanish silver dollars arrived in Canton and circulated amongst the merchants and traders who dealt in export goods to Europe and Mexico. And as if to exemplify Spain's global currency dominance, the design on the face of the coin triumphantly boasted until 1772 two hemispheres representing the Old World and the New World under the Spanish crown between the Pillars of Hercules.

Spain's opening of the Pacific to trade from China to the Americas and Europe was the dream of Philip II, King of Spain who was married for four brief years to the Catholic Queen Mary of England. Philip presided over the Spanish Golden Age – or rather 'Silver Age' – when Spain was the richest country in Europe. Not content with the riches of the Americas, Philip also aspired to the 'riches of the Indies'. In 1564, he commissioned an expedition into the Pacific led by the mariner Miguel López de Legazpi. When Legazpi founded Spanish Manila in 1571, he expressed the hope that Philip could 'gain the commerce with China'.

Equally importantly, Legazpi was responsible for discovering the *tornaviaje*, the return route across the Pacific, linking China to the Americas. Since Magellan's 1519 expedition, all attempts to sail back across the Pacific had failed. Legazpi's navigator, an explorer and Augustinian friar named Andrés de Urdaneta, charted a return voyage that went north-east from Manila in a high arc towards Japan and over the 40th parallel. In those latitudes, ships encountered the favourable westerly winds and currents of the North Pacific Gyre as it rotated in a clockwise direction towards the west coast of North America. When Urdaneta's ship eventually entered Mexico's Acapulco Bay, the vessel and its scurvy-stricken crew had covered more than 13,000 kilometres.

For the first time, European ships could reliably sail the Pacific in both directions. And both China and Spain were enriched. The Spanish objective in establishing a base at Manila in 1571 was no different to the objective of the United States in colonising the Philippines three centuries later in 1898. The key was China's markets. The sixteenth century Spanish announcement that from Manila 'We are at the gate and in the vicinity of the most fortunate countries in the world' was barely distinguishable from the later American pronouncement that 'The Philippines gives us a base at the door of all the East ... And just beyond the Philippines are China's illimitable markets'.

Philip earned the distinction of being the monarch who 'joined the European world with the world of China'. Once the *tornaviaje* was established, the annual round trip of Manila galleons between Manila and Acapulco commenced its 250-year-long continuous history. The galleons, which were colloquially known as *nao de China* or 'China ships', were state-owned, armed vessels of the Spanish Crown built in the Philippines from local tropical hardwoods that were almost impervious to cannon fire and ship rot. The first galleon left Manila in 1573 filled with an extraordinary assortment of every type of silk from China. There was 'raw silk ... fine untwisted silk ... velvets ... damasks ... satins' together with a gallimaufry of other goods that were brought across in the armada of Chinese junks that descended each year on Manila.

The westward journey was relatively straightforward and usually took 45 days to two months. But the perilous return voyage eastward, even with the winds and currents of the North Pacific Gyre, was 'the longest, and most dreadful of any in the world' in those days, lasting on average seven months. The voyage was invariably accompanied by 'hunger, thirst, cold, continual watching [for storms] and other sufferings' including a universal raging itch from blood-sucking vermin swarming throughout the ship that 'run over Cabbins, Beds and the very Dishes the Men eat on'. Toward the end, 'the rats from the hold were a prized delicacy and[were] bought at high prices by famished passengers and crew'. Not for nothing did the galleons have painted on their sails in bold letters 'AMGP' meaning *Ave Maria, gratia plena*: Hail Mary, full of grace.

Cargo capacity was the primary consideration for the Manila galleons, which is why they were the largest vessels afloat in the late sixteenth and seventeenth centuries. They were broad-beamed lumbering arks with three or four full decks, deep stowage and towering superstructures. These top-heavy, oversized 'castles in the sea' were as large as 1500 to 2000 tons 'when most large ships were only a quarter of that size'. They were the super-container ships of the age. On the voyage to Acapulco, the cargo holds of the Manila galleons were fully laden – sometimes over-laden – with astonishing quantities of Chinese manufactures and Asian spices, including copious amounts of silk fabrics, textiles, porcelain and finished goods. So much merchandise came across the Pacific from China that the annual trade fair in Acapulco, which took place when the Manila galleon arrived and discharged its cargo, became 'the most renowned trade fair in the world'. Chinese goods that were once discretionary luxuries soon became must-have necessities and local industry became dependent on the China trade. Among the necessities was the Chinese raw silk on which approximately 14,000 Mexican weavers relied for local garment manufacturing.

Mexico City, the capital of the viceroyalty of New Spain, became 'the place where Asia, Europe and the Americas all met'. It was for a time the 'the first world city', arguably the 'centre of the world'. Merchandise from China was brought to the capital along a route from Acapulco that became known as the *Camino del China*. When the Prussian naturalist and explorer Alexander von Humboldt travelled the road in 1803–1804, it was sometimes called 'the road to Asia'. This humble road became fundamental to international trade. It rose from sea level at the port of Acapulco then ascended over 2000 metres to Mexico's Central Plateau, climbing through rugged country over mountains and numerous river crossings for almost 400 kilometres. The road brought silks, porcelain and other merchandise from China to Mexico City, from where it could be transported overland to the coastal port of Veracruz and then across the Atlantic to Cadiz.

For China, the crucial feature of this trade was the form of payment: silver and only silver. So important was the westward transfer of silver to China that the trans-Pacific trade route was better known to Spanish officials and merchants as *la ruta de la plata* – not the 'silk road' but the 'silver road'. Outgoing Manila galleons leaving Acapulco were like floating bank vaults – magnets for enterprising English ship's captains such as the Elizabethan favourite Francis Drake, the Georgian era's Commodore George Anson and a motley collection of freebooting buccaneers, pirates and privateers. Spanish merchants in the sixteenth and seventeenth centuries, like their English counterparts in the eighteenth century, had little else but silver to sell or exchange with the Chinese merchants. Their manufactured products could not compete with those from China in quality or cost. Nor did the Chinese desire them. Silver from Europe and the Spanish Americas brought twice as much in China as it did in the rest of the world. And the lower production and manufacturing costs in China made the price of Chinese goods lower still. The unquenchable Chinese thirst for silver meant that enormous profits were there for the taking and the Chinese were happy to oblige.

The advantage of silver's higher purchasing power in China was irrefutable and the commercial logic of transporting as much of it as possible to China was compelling. Rivers of silver linked China with the economies of Europe and the Spanish Americas. Manila became the nexus where the two hemispheres of the globe were joined in trade across the Pacific. And Mexico City became an international commercial, intellectual and cultural centre which thrived on the China trade and the Spanish colonial silver mines that financed it. In 1610, the Spanish poet Balbuena extolled the city's virtues: 'In you, Spain joins with China, Italy with Japan, and finally the whole world in commerce and order'. Mexico City was 'the richest, most opulent city with the most trade and the most treasure' where the best of Chinese merchandise and many of its ideas were absorbed and copied. And the source of all the wealth, the mint at Potosí, was 'the beating heart of world commerce'.

CHAPTER 15

GLOBAL CURRENTS

1600s–1800s

Through silver, China's upheavals became secretly bound to world trends.

WHAT HAPPENED IN CHINA no longer stayed in China. China, already the world's largest economic entity with a third of the world's population, became a central component in the first 'emerging world economy'. The conversion of its monetary and fiscal system to silver 'was bound to have a global impact of historic proportions'. Chinese demand for silver moved international markets, as does its modern demand for commodities like oil, coal, iron ore and more recently lithium, copper and gold. Financial systems around the world became more and more tightly connected through international trade in which silver was the common ingredient. It was the beginning of globalisation, when truly global trade networks became inter-dependent rather than regional in scope.

Mountains of Chinese manufactured goods were shipped to Europe and torrents of silver flowed to China. For the first time, there was 'a regular and lasting maritime connection established between the four great continents' then known to Europeans and the 'world's financial markets...became linked through the medium of silver'. Spanish silver production between 1500 and 1800 was approximately 150,000 tons, 'perhaps exceeding 80 percent of the entire world production over that time span'. Spanish supply stimulated, and Chinese demand drove, the global silver market.

Spain's silver mines generated such massive profits, underpinned by China's purchasing power, that Spanish kings were able to finance simultaneously a century of war and empire – against the English and Dutch in northern Europe and against the Ottomans in the Mediterranean. Spaniards basked in the glow of wealth and dominance that South American silver gave to their country. One observed with evident satisfaction that 'Because of the said mines, Castile is Castile, Rome is Rome, the pope is pope, and the king [of Spain] is monarch of the world'. A drawing in the same author's 1615 manuscript depicts the Spanish crown and the Church – figuratively the entire Spanish empire – being held up and supported by the Inca leader (the son of the Sun) and his four kings representing the four regions of the Inca empire.

China became 'irredeemably integrated into the rapidly expanding global economy' but its fortunes contributed to Spain's decline, as well as its rise. Interdependence worked both ways, as it still does with China. The surge of silver from the Spanish mines in Peru, stimulated by demand from China where much of the silver ended up, ultimately fuelled inflation and economic hardship in Spain. And Habsburg Spain was poorly managed as well as being uniquely vulnerable. Despite its wealth, the country had long over-extended itself. King Philip II was regarded as the 'borrower from hell', so much did he borrow from his Genoese bankers and so often did Spain default on sovereign debt. By at least 1623, Spain's interest payments on national debt exceeded total crown receipts. The predicament calls to mind historian Niall Ferguson's iron law that any great power that spends more on debt service than on defence will not stay great for very long. It was, he observed,

> true of Habsburg Spain, true of *ancien regime* France, true of the Ottoman Empire, true of the British Empire ... and [is] about to be put to the test by the United States.

As enormous quantities of silver flooded into China, the market gradually became glutted and silver's value fell everywhere – in Europe and in China. It was a contagion, not unlike a modern global financial crisis. Everything had been valued in silver and as its buying power diminished, everyone suffered. Inflation in Spain, the 'Price Revolution' as historians call it, was in reality a global phenomenon with its origins in China's demand-side dominance of the silver market. The oversupply of silver in China, its loss of value and a decline in production at Potosí during the early 1600s eventually profoundly affected both Spanish Crown revenues and the Chinese economy.

The collapse in silver's value during the late Ming dynasty caused enormous hardship to the people, who received copper in their daily transactions but had to pay their taxes in devalued silver. To add to the suffering, the catastrophic El Nino events of 1638 and 1639 led to poor harvests in 1640 accompanied by 'locust swarms, food shortages, sky-high prices and outbreaks of disease'. The El Nino–induced unseasonable weather and cold summers continued in 1641 and 1642 and brought 'the worst drought in 500 years' over the next three years. Famine, rebellion, Manchu invasions and catastrophic climate change did their worst. Armies of rebels, goaded by hunger and bitterness, roamed the countryside, hastening the collapse of Ming rule. An eyewitness wrote:

> All along our route home, we saw corpses scattered about in the fields, and innumerable children abandoned by the side of the road ... Approaching the village, we saw six or seven people stripping bark off elm trees [for food].

China had merged into the world economy through silver and its upheaval now had global consequences. As a modern commentator explained 'Through silver, China's upheavals became secretly bound to world trends'. The interconnectedness of world markets guaranteed that the effects of silver's loss of value were felt not just in China but in Spain and elsewhere. Practically speaking, the entire world economy was entangled in a global silver web. It took half a century – until about 1700 – for China's economy to recover and stabilise under the long-serving Qing emperor, Kangxi, whose name meant 'Abundant Prosperity'. In the next century China experienced a great leap forward – economically and politically – coinciding with a major revival of silver production in the high-altitude Zacatecas region of the Sierra Madre in Mexico. Once again, the fortunes of Spain and China were related.

The Zacatecas mines surpassed even those of Potosí. More Spanish silver was produced in the eighteenth century than in the sixteenth and seventeenth centuries combined. The China trade again invigorated demand to a level that 'caused the value of silver within China to spike some 50 percent above silver's price in the rest of the world'. There was another worldwide scramble to transfer massive quantities of silver to China, where the value was the highest and the profits greater. And as they had done in earlier centuries, 'merchant bankers in Europe began accumulating large stocks of Spanish silver pesos with an eye to trade with China and India, where they could potentially obtain double profits ... '. Silver flooded into China from east and west. From across the Pacific, Manila galleons 'brought approximately two million silver pesos per year from Mexico to the Philippines (and hence to Canton) ... '.

Adam Smith lived through the relentless flow of Spanish American silver to China in the 1700s and doubted neither the importance of silver in stimulating world trade, nor the central role of China. As silver production increased to meet the China demand, Spain went from an ailing empire in 1700 under the last Habsburg monarch to renewed prosperity under the Bourbons, who reigned throughout most of the eighteenth century and continue to do so. By about the middle of the century, the saturation levels of silver in China once more caused the precious metal's local value to gravitate towards its European value. Extreme profits declined but China's export trade escalated, fuelled by Europe's voracious appetite for Chinese and Asian goods.

As the century progressed, the sheer size and heft of China's manufacturing and export output created a consumer revolution in taste and usage in Europe. The Scottish philosopher David Hume wrote in 1750 that if China were 'as near us as France and Spain, everything we use would be Chinese'. A wide variety of Chinese goods, paid for in silver, became central to European material culture. Since Roman times when silk first caught the attention of the rich and prosperous, it had been common to speak of Asia as the 'graveyard of silver from the West'. So it was again, until in the early1800s the British found a way of substituting opium for silver and turned the trade on its head.

PART 5

Opium Trade

CHAPTER 16

THE HUMBLE PLANT

1800s

The technique of growing opium in India and disowning it in China.

THE HUMBLE PLANT KNOWN to botanists as *Papaver somniferum* – the opium poppy – is a native of Asia Minor and Türkiye. It flowers gloriously en masse in early spring, self-seeds in summer, then dies and disappears into barren ground in winter. It is an annual herb whose life cycle begins and ends in a single growing season. The flowers are mostly blue-purple or white, the foliage is silver-green and the plant's overall average height is about 1 metre. The centre of the flower contains a large seed pod full of a sticky, milky white sap that exudes when the pod is cut. The sap – the milk of paradise – contains the natural opiates morphine and codeine, which are the source of the opium poppy's deadly renown.

For millennia people have known and grown the opium poppy and understood its properties. The Sumerians called it the 'joy plant'. Phoenicians and Minoans traded it from Egypt around the Mediterranean. Homer's *Odyssey* refers to a gift of a drug bringing oblivion – believed to contain opium – given to Helen by the Egyptian queen. The ancients combined it with hemlock to achieve painless suicide and no doubt murder. Arab traders exported it to India and China. And in Georgian and Victorian England, laudanum, a tincture of opium dissolved in alcohol, was widely used for pain relief, sleeplessness and diarrhoea.

During the nineteenth century, opium became one of the first mass-produced, mass-marketed, global commodities, allowing the British to create 'the world's first drug cartel'. The opium trade was 'probably the largest commerce of the time in any commodity' in the world as well as being 'one of the most pernicious, yet well-organised and profitable drug trades that has ever existed'. While tea taxes underpinned the British economy, opium sales funded British rule in India and provided 'the financial wherewithal to make colonial empire-building feasible'. Without British opium, 'Chinese history in the nineteenth and twentieth centuries would have been far different', as would the history of India.

The Mughals had previously cultivated opium, which the Portuguese and Dutch sold in the East Indies. But the British East India Company expanded, corporatised, industrialised and internationalised the commercial production of opium on a never-before-seen scale. The Company developed an 800-kilometre stretch of alluvial plain in the lower Ganges River area into the world's leading opium-producing territory, surpassing Türkiye, the land of the poppy. By the second half of the nineteenth century, 'roughly half a million acres came to be sown with poppies' – enlisting 'more than a million peasant households, probably some 5–7 million people altogether' in return for pitiful cash advances.

All the administrative genius of Britain's imperial bureaucracy was applied to maximising the efficiency and profitability of its opium industry. At Patna in Bihar and at Ghazipur, near Benares (now Varanasi), the Company established mass production facilities on the Ganges River centred around immense purpose-built opium factories that sprawled over many hectares. They were 'quasi-military, fortress-like establishments surrounded by high, red-brick walls'. The factories serviced the raw product of its licensed poppy growers – the poverty-stricken peasants who farmed on thousands of small holdings and were bound by the Company's monopoly to supply the crop only to the British.

The unofficial capital of the British opium empire was Patna. The names 'Patna' and 'Benares' were so well known that they were literally global brand names, synonymous with the best of British opium, just like certain tobacco brands in the next century. Wherever one went east of Suez, you could pick up 'the local English language newspaper to discover the daily quotations for the prices of Patna or Benares opium' at the Calcutta auctions. At the Patna factory, Company officers watched, measured and scrutinised each step of a production process to which several thousand Indian workers applied themselves. The overall Company official responsible for the day-to-day management of the factory was the superintendent who lived on the factory grounds in a pleasant bungalow surrounded by a garden near to the Company's English church. The church's ringing bells marked the passage of the day ... for, incongruously, the opium factory was 'an institution steeped in Anglican piety'.

What made the opium trade so attractive to the East India Company was the high profit and the low risk. The commercial formula was simple: monopoly control, low production cost and a demand which increased in proportion to the Company's almost endless supply. Equally advantageous was that the business was so structured that the illegal smuggling of opium into China from British India was conveniently carried out not by the Company, but by independent traders. In Calcutta, the most successful independent traders were British, particularly Scots. In Bombay, Indian Parsis and Baghdadi Jews controlled the wealthiest and most prominent trading firms. In time, the latter, like the Sassoon family, used their profits to become philanthropists and loyal supporters of the British empire.

Everything and everyone touched by opium was altered in its wake. Merchants reaped extravagant profits and bought country estates in England, Scotland and Connecticut; the smugglers became rich beyond their dreams; and the British government's revenues multiplied to such an extent that it could not afford to extricate itself from the trade. Conversely, in China and India, the opium trade left a trail of human destruction: addicts suffered miserably, poppy growers were kept impoverished and workers in the opium factories were cruelly oppressed.

The Company's opium 'agency' – the Opium Department – orchestrated every aspect of the opium chain in India with minute attention to detail – from cultivation in the fields, to production in the factories, to sale at the auctions. In its efficiency and profitability, but not its morality, it was one of the jewels of the British empire, employing tens of thousands of patriotic Englishmen over the whole of the Victorian era. One such Englishman was George Orwell's father – a onetime Opium Agent, Fourth Class, whose famous son was born in Bihar and sent back to England for his schooling at Eton College.

The annual ritual of opium production began at harvest time when the farmers went into the fields to incise and bleed the sap of hundreds of thousands of green poppy pods. The sap was left to coagulate on the pod, then scraped off into earthen jars and delivered to the opium factory. If the farmer's raw resinous opium were sufficient to fulfil his contract and the quality was acceptable, he was paid the final instalment of his meagre cash advance. If not, he faced penury or greater indebtedness.

At the Patna factory, the newly arrived opium was taken to a cavernous and high-ceilinged examining hall where enormous scales were arrayed. Beside each set of scales, an English overseer sat with teams of weighmen, accountants and Indian workers. As the farmer watched, the overseer 'sahib' poked, prodded and sniffed his product, allowing some through for processing and condemning others of inferior quality. The room was full of the clamour of altercation and disappointment from the farmers. For although the Company 'regularly netted ten times more than it paid out for opium', it was miserly in its payments and brutally unsympathetic to the complaints of the farmers.

From the examining hall, the opium was transferred to a smaller area called the mixing room, where the air was hot and fetid, reeking of liquid opium and the dull stench of sweat. The centrepiece consisted of several large tanks where the raw opium was stirred into an homogenous paste by bare-bodied men, sometimes standing waist-deep in the viscous poison. The men used rakes or tramped in circles, churning and treading the opium, softening the sludge, breathing in its overpowering vapours, their already-short lives reduced by each turn of the circle. The scene was ghoulish: the men's bodies were listless, their eyes often vacant, glazed and glowing red in the dark from constant exposure to raw liquid opium. As the wretched men trudged and stirred, cane-wielding English overseers patrolled the walkways around the tanks, keeping their distance from the poison as much as they could.

When the opium was sufficiently churned, it was transferred to the assembly room, a long chamber where many hundreds of dhoti-clad men assembled opium balls, assisted by numerous runners and helpers. The average output at the Patna factory was 'between 16,000 and 20,000 cakes [or balls] daily'. The men sat before small low tables, their hands moving with practised dexterity to ladle and shape the liquid opium paste into moulds according to precise dimensions specified in London. Once formed, each opium ball was tapped out of its mould and placed inside two halves of round casing to form a rock-hard earthenware sphere – a 'neat little cannonshot to hold safe this most lucrative of the British empire's products'. Such was the men's concentration that there was little noise in the assembly room except for the pattering back and forth of hundreds of running boys carrying away the completed balls and delivering specified measures of ingredients to each assembler.

In the final stages, the earthenware spheres containing balls of opium were taken to vast rooms with lofty ceilings for drying and stacking, where the spheres were placed in row after ascending row on towering shelves lining the walls. The shelves extended well over 10 metres in height. Troops of young boys were constantly engaged in clambering nimbly from shelf to shelf, clinging to scaffolding and holding on to long ladders while they silently stacked, turned, aired and examined the balls. For every 10,000 balls, about 65 boys were employed to stack, turn and air them. Every now and then, the overseer would call out an order and the boys would toss earthenware spheres of opium to each other with one hand, while holding on precariously with the other, until the opium came to rest safely on the floor far below, ready for delivery.

When the opium balls were dried, they were packed into mango wood chests – 40 balls to each chest, in two layers, stuffed with petals and poppy leaves and trash. A small flotilla of Company boats transported the opium chests down the Ganges to Calcutta. The passage of the boats was like a triumphal march, marked by a beating drum warning other craft to make way for the precious cargo. At Calcutta, the new season's crop was offered for sale by auction in the exchange rooms in Tank Square. Calcutta was then the capital of British India, the second city of the empire, and Tank Square was its most imposing precinct. The headquarters of the East India Company, a 150-metre-long stone edifice known as the Writer's Building, lined the north side of the square and contained the exchange rooms. The building was a monument to private prosperity and imperial grandeur.

Once the opium was sold at auction in Calcutta it was out of the Company's hands. This was thought to be the masterstroke, the beauty of the process. No chests of opium passed through the Company factory at Canton. Some Company officials in Canton boasted that they had never laid eyes on an opium chest. It was a contrivance, best described as 'the technique of growing opium in India and disowning it in China'. The

Company's attempt to distance itself from the smuggling of opium into China was transparent. Its directors and officers remained heavily invested in the drug and retained a deep and abiding interest in the illegal market in Canton. The amounts paid for the smuggled opium by drug dealers in Canton directly affected the price that the Company could achieve for the commodity at the auctions in Calcutta. And the more of the Company's opium that was shipped to Canton, the more silver that came back to the Company.

In the best tradition of an international drug cartel, the East India Company acted both as wholesaler and banker to the opium traders, ensuring that silver proceeds from illegal opium sales were funnelled back to it in ever-increasing amounts. At the Calcutta auctions, some opium traders paid cash but most bought opium on credit 'upon giving security to pay the amount at the current exchange, into the [Company's] treasury at Canton'. In China, the traders were paid in silver, most of which they deposited into the Company's treasury at Canton, either in satisfaction of the credit given to them by the Company or in return for bills of exchange which they could redeem in Calcutta, Bombay and London. The more opium sold by the Company in Calcutta and smuggled by traders to Canton, the more the Company profited and the more silver it received.

This remarkable turnaround soon reversed the flow of silver that had favoured China for centuries and dramatically altered the balance of trade. The net flow of silver out of China to the British upended the direction of previous centuries. It depleted the Chinese treasury of silver while the cash 'went into the hands of British and American merchants who used to the money to bankroll their own transition to modern industrial and corporate capitalism'. The flow of British opium to Canton soon exceeded in value all the tea shipped back to England. Opium became an agent of global economic change.

Opium sales were normally completed at Lintin Island in the Pearl River estuary where Chinese smugglers rowed out in the dark of night to collect their opium from the foreign traders.

Their fast purpose-built vessels, known as 'scrambling crabs', carried as many as 60 oarsmen. They were long, sleek, heavily armed craft designed to outpace – and outgun – any pursuing Chinese officials. Once the opium was handed over, the Chinese buyers assumed all the risk of selling and distributing it within China, moving the drug along inland waterways, over mountains and along backwoods land routes and bribing officials. The traders who bought the opium in Calcutta for export faced their own separate risks, including the perils of the sea during the voyage, the fluctuations of the market and occasionally the Chinese authorities, but they could normally expect to recoup much more for their smuggled opium than they had paid.

There were no illusions about the illegality of the opium trade. The British, American and Parsi traders knew that opium had long been outlawed by the Chinese emperor. It was forbidden in China from 1729 to 1860 but until the Daoguang emperor took active steps to quash the trade in the 1830s, enforcement was minimal. The directors of the Company in London knew that opium was contraband and the British parliament knew it as well. But the growth of the opium trade was phenomenal and so many people were becoming inordinately rich from the trade that there were few brave voices of misgiving, at least initially. Even Edmund Burke's House of Commons review of the Company's opium trade raised no ethical questions but was more a eulogy to free trade – the rallying cry that the British later used to justify war and invasion of China. It was a mantra, the nineteenth century equivalent of the modern cry for freedom and democracy, also sometimes used to justify war and invasion.

The year 1820 was a watershed. The East India Company dramatically increased opium production partly in response to competition from growers in the princely states of the Malwa region of western India, which the Company did not control. The number of chests shipped annually to China quadrupled over a decade and kept on rising. The thundering rise of the opium trade seemed unstoppable – from about 5000 chests in 1820 to 60,000 chests in 1847. Not only were the quantities stupendous but the demand was endless and the prices were irresistible. Between 1810 and 1823, a 'Bengal opium chest (of 149 lbs) was seldom sold to the Chinese dealer at less than 1,000 Spanish [silver] dollars'. The trade figures were so favourable for the Company that the balance of trade effectively 'made the import of tea free'.

The independent traders who did the real work of smuggling the opium from India to China formed a community of their own in Canton, working in the shadow of the East India Company. Their leader was William Jardine, a Scot who had joined the Company as an eighteen-year-old surgeon's mate in 1802 before quitting and becoming a free merchant. In 1830, he perversely described the opium trade in Canton as 'the safest and most Gentlemanlike speculation that I am aware of'. In 1832, Jardine and another Scot, James Matheson, established the firm of Jardine Matheson & Co. They became the most successful traders in Canton's illegal opium trade. Their firm acted as agent for dozens of British and Parsi opium merchants in India and negotiated the sale of their cargoes of contraband to Chinese opium smugglers and drug peddlers. Both men became extraordinarily wealthy.

Matheson justified his initial presence in Canton by securing an appointment as the Danish consul, while Jardine became the Prussian consul and their firm 'operated under the protection of the Prussian flag'. They conducted their business two doors from the Company factory. In his retirement, Matheson purchased the Hebridean island of Lewis and built Stornoway Castle, becoming at his death the second-largest landowner in the United Kingdom. Jardine took a seat in the House of Commons in 1841 where the future prime minister, Benjamin Disraeli, could not conceal his dislike. His description of Jardine in his novel *Sybil* (1845) is only thinly disguised:

> Oh, a dreadful man! A Scotchman, richer than Croesus, one Mr Druggy, fresh from Canton, with a million in opium in each pocket, denouncing corruption and bellowing free trade.

The opium traders were close-mouthed about their activities. They knew the drug was forbidden but it had long been moderately prevalent among the wealthiest elite in China. In 1820, the number of users in China amounted only to 'a few hundredths of a percent of the population'. After that date, the massive influx of opium from India created an ever-expanding, seemingly limitless class of users that extended across all levels of Chinese society. This was the opium traders' paradox. To shun the trade on moral grounds meant giving up 'the easiest and most effective way to succeed at trade in China'. For most of them, the temptation was too attractive to resist.

These men were in the East to make money as fast as they could. Later in the century, one who was 'honest and outspoken enough to tell the whole truth' about the Far East trade in general, explained to a British diplomat:

> ... it is my business to make a fortune with the least possible loss of time ... In two or three years at farthest, I hope to realise a fortune and get away ... You must not expect men in my situation to condemn themselves to years of prolonged exile in an unhealthy climate for the benefit of posterity. We are money-making practical men. Our business is to make money, as much and as fast as we can ...

For their part, the directors of the East India Company put revenues before morals and were unashamedly disingenuous. In response to criticism, they pronounced that:

> Were it possible to prevent the use of the drug altogether except strictly for the purpose of medicine, we would gladly do it *in compassion to Mankind*, but this being absolutely impractical, we can only endeavour to regulate and palliate an evil which cannot be eradicated (emphasis added).

In truth, the Company did not attempt to regulate and palliate the evil but knowingly accelerated it.

Some opium made its way to England, mostly from Türkiye, and was freely available from tobacconists, barbers, stationers and wine merchants. Poets and writers such as Elizabeth Barrett-Browning, Byron, Shelley, Keats and Coleridge were all occasional users. The Chinese fashion for the ritual of smoking opium differed markedly from the way in which the drug was taken in Britain. The most tangible difference was that a smoker could easily consume an amount of opium in one day that would kill someone who ingested it directly. Central to the smoking ritual were the long opium pipes known as 'yellow dragons'. The wealthy favoured gorgeously wrought pipes and fine accessories but however beautiful the pipe, the process of smoking was the same.

A tiny pellet of opium was roasted on the end of a needle over the flame of a lamp until it sizzled and bubbled. A globule of opium paste was then placed in the bowl of a long-stemmed pipe and held above an oil-burning lamp until it smoked and vaporised. This was the moment for the user, reclining on his side, to empty the air from his chest, inhale deeply from the pipe and fill his lungs with the morphine and codeine-infused smoke, which swamped the head and poured into the body like a flood coursing through the veins. The consistency of the smoke was 'almost that of a dense, oily and intensely perfumed' liquid. When the tide ebbed, the recumbent man or woman was left with a startling stillness, a 'serenely peaceful nullity, a pain-free void', leading, if too often repeated, to a physically debilitating and soul-destroying addiction.

Most Westerners all but blamed China itself for the nation's drug use. Ordinary citizens of London and Boston began to imagine China as a world of addiction, horror and drug-induced torments. As ever, very few visited China but the state of admiration for Chinese society that had prevailed in earlier centuries slipped further and further away, fuelled in part by the dramatic imagery evoked by Thomas De Quincey's *Confessions of an English Opium-Eater* (1821), which painted a horrifying picture of an Oriental nightmare. Coleridge's revelation that his famous poem, whose full title was 'Kubla Khan, Or A Vision in a Dream: A Fragment' (1816), was 'composed in a sort of Reverie brought on by two grains of Opium' fed the same imagery.

As the British and Americans were increasingly presented with a disturbing, opium-addled image of China, a parallel phenomenon developed, which in due course would contribute further to the destabilisation of Chinese society. A powerful Protestant missionary movement evolved, especially among Americans, fostering a fantasy that 'Christian and American values would change China' and bring salvation to its people. By the 1830s, the amount of opium being poured into China was 'more than two and a half million pounds by weight each year'. And it kept growing late into the nineteenth century, carried forward by a rapacious Anglo-American trade that generated an equally expanding demand.

CHAPTER 17

A STORM BREWING

1800–1820

The most advantageous monopoly it possesses in the Universe.

FOLLOWING BRITAIN'S SUCCESS IN the Seven Years War (1756–1763) and France's descent into revolution in the late eighteenth century, the world order started to change, as it is shifting in the twenty-first century. Just as the Portuguese, Spanish and Dutch empires dominated trade for most of the sixteenth, seventeenth and eighteenth centuries, the nineteenth century would belong to Great Britain. And as British imperiousness came of age, a more sceptical, and probably more realistic, approach to China developed. China's grand mystery and hypnotic appeal began to fade and enthusiasm for its institutions and model of society diminished. The failure of the Macartney mission in 1793 was a tipping point. Critics at home decried its 'strange want of decent and manly spirit' and Macartney became a standing joke. As the nineteenth century drew near, the words of Baron Grimm, a German man of letters, rang true:

> The Chinese Empire has become in our time the object of special attention and of special study. The missionaries first fascinated public opinion by rose coloured reports from that distant land, too distant to be able to contradict their falsehoods. Then the philosophers took it up. Then [China] became in

> a short time the *home of wisdom, virtue and good faith, its government the best possible and the longest established, its morality the loftiest and most beautiful in the known world; its laws, its policy, its art, its industry were likewise such as to serve as a model for all nations of the earth.* (emphasis added)

There had long been English mutterings about the pride of the Chinese. And the religiously minded were always troubled by the idea that Chinese history extended beyond the biblical record, while others resorted to racist stereotyping, regularly sprinkling their criticisms with adjectives like 'wily', 'crafty', 'deceitful' and 'pretentious'. During and after the Napoleonic wars, deeply held anti-French and anti-Catholic sentiment led to a growing British distaste for the too-generous accolades heaped on China by French philosophers, French writers and French Jesuits. Voltaire, whose writings not only extolled Chinese society but influenced the French Revolution, was the object of a uniquely British disdain. As one British writer put it 'Nothing can exceed the *gullibility* of the French *philosophistes* except that of those who were misled by them'. Few now embraced Macartney's glowing remark – written in his journal en route to Beijing before Qianlong humiliated him and sent him away – that China was 'not only a very powerful empire, but a very wise and virtuous nation'. Attitudes changed then as they have changed in recent times in some quarters of the West.

On his return to England, Macartney expressed his resentment, his bruised dignity, his wounded pride, in a series of essays whose theme was that China was less prosperous or stable than Europeans had previously imagined. He wrote that China's grandeur and power were illusory and that 'She may perhaps not sink outright ... she may drift some time as a wreck, and will then be dashed in pieces on the shore'. The longer Macartney continued, the more his judgement darkened, leading him to fulminate about revolution and regime change. He believed that China's day of reckoning was imminent and would result in the destruction of the Qing dynasty empire. He was prescient, but about a century ahead of his time.

In a mirror of current times, the South China Sea became militarised. The Royal Navy increased its presence and changed the name of its command at Madras from the 'East Indies Station' to the 'East Indies and China Station' to reflect the new geopolitical priorities – just as in modern times the United States Pacific Command has renamed itself the 'Indo-Pacific Command'. In Canton, the changes were unsettling and destabilising. The tide seemed to be turning. The Hong merchants and Company supercargoes had built a century of commercial predictability based on their mutual trust and reciprocal pursuit of profitable trade. Neither the Royal Navy nor the American traders had the same understanding or, in the case of the Americans, the same loyalties.

The first serious threats to the stability of the Canton trade emerged early in the 1800s. Both resulted from moves by Britain to annex Macau before the French could do so. The British had already taken Penang in 1786, Cape Town in 1795 and Ceylon in 1796 and they would soon annex Java, Singapore and Malacca. All were strategic bastions along the sea route to China and the East. But Macau's unique status as a Portuguese outpost under Chinese sovereignty made its considerations different. Any interference with Macau would not just involve Britain and Portugal but could easily draw the Chinese into the conflict and affect the all-important trade. In Canton, the Company warned that whatever concerns the Admiralty may have about France in the region, conflict with China must be avoided.

The arrival of a Royal Navy fleet at Macau in 1802 caused great consternation in Beijing. The Jiaqing emperor (r. 1796–1820), the fifteenth son of Qianlong, was convinced that the British intended to take the town and called the commander's assurances of peaceful intent 'lying words' and 'dissembling'. He wanted the fleet gone and cut off its access to fresh water and food. Fortuitously, hostilities were avoided by the news of the mid-war Treaty of Amiens (1802), which established a twelve-month long period of peace in Europe – removing the immediate threat of a French assault on Macau and allowing the British naval fleet to return to India.

Six years later in 1808, the Company's China trade had become more important and profitable than ever – 'the most advantageous monopoly it possesses in the Universe'. Seen from its headquarters in the City of London, the bounty of the East seemed to be limitless. Even the design of East India House in Leadenhall Street – rebuilt in the 1790s in the neoclassical style – was intended to portray the Company's unprecedented wealth and territorial power. Six towering Ionic columns complemented the august edifice and the tympanum showed King George III defending the commerce of the East. A massive allegorical painting of *The East Offering its Riches to Britannia* dominated the interior. The painting, now hanging incongruously in the Foreign Office, depicts a lion sitting at Britannia's feet while two complaisant female figures representing the wealth of China and India make offerings to her. In the background, a fully laden East Indiaman is shown heading home under full sail with its cargo of exotic riches.

The rivers of profit and taxes from the China trade made it a national as well as a Company priority, but the geopolitical circumstances made it more vulnerable than ever. Napoleon was then supreme in continental Europe and there was no light of British victory on the horizon. France and Russia briefly became allies in 1807 and 'French cruisers were everywhere ... in Southeast Asia in particular'. Unfounded rumours of a joint Russian-French invasion of British India and unaccredited whispers of French troops being sent to Macau were troubling but the Company's directors in London were commercial men, not military strategists. They did not want to risk a rupture with the Chinese government and a catastrophic loss of the China trade. They believed – as they had at the time of the first alarm over Macau in 1802 – that they should do everything possible to avoid provoking Beijing.

In Canton, the newly appointed 'taipan' – the senior Company official in China – was John Roberts. He was the president of the Company's governing body in Canton known as the 'Select Committee of Supercargoes'. Roberts had boundless confidence in British imperial might and was imbued with a bolder, almost religious, approach toward China. He was the type of Englishman who would become more familiar in the Victorian era – a 'superior-minded Christian' whose bigoted views of the Chinese were mostly contemptuous. Roberts's attitude was a far cry from the open-mindedness that had generally prevailed among Company officials in both India and China during the more liberal eighteenth century. But the times had changed and his appointment coincided with the decision of the London Missionary Society to despatch the first Protestant missionary to China: Robert Morrison, a Presbyterian from Northumberland who turned out to be a kindred spirit of Roberts.

Roberts was convinced that China's Qing leadership had neither the means nor the will to counter a display of British military force if Macau were taken. He requested a naval fleet from Madras to capture Macau and pre-empt the French but the fleet commander, Admiral Drury, believed that war with China would be self-defeating. If the China trade were shut down, the Company – and therefore the United Kingdom (as Great Britain had become in 1801) – would lose the most valuable trade it possessed. Like a modern China hawk, Roberts insisted that Britain should not give way to the Chinese 'so long as they persevere in their haughty conduct'. Drury ignored Roberts and withdrew his fleet, acknowledging the moral justification of China's protests at the incursion. He declared that the Chinese position was 'dictated by Wisdom, justice and dignified manhood, in support of those Moral Rights of Man, of Nations, and of Nature, outraged and insulted'. It was a reaction unlike that of most other Englishmen during the nineteenth century.

In London, the Company's directors were astounded by the behaviour of Roberts who, they said, had endangered 'the property ... of the Company, their footing in China and the most valuable trade they possess'. They voted unanimously to remove him and recalled him home, out of harm's way. They also made a clean sweep of all other members of the committee. For the time being, the foreign trade at Canton flourished once more but constant rumblings and anti-Chinese sentiment continued. Admiral Drury's restraint and his respect for the Chinese would soon be a thing of the past.

In the next decade, after Napoleon was defeated at Waterloo in 1815 and the long war with France came to an end, Britain was invigorated. The Royal Navy had doubled in size and was the most powerful maritime force in the world while China was becoming increasingly destabilised by internal rebellion and corruption. The new emperor Jiaqing lacked his father's authority and leadership while the Chinese military had less resources and funding and was significantly weaker than it had been in the eighteenth century.

The situation was a reverse mirror of twenty-first century geopolitics in the region. Britain was a rising power and China was a diminishing one. By 1840, the British empire exercised dominion over a quarter of the world's population and nearly rivalled the size of China. Its strategic maritime outposts stretched in an octopus-like web of colonies, protectorates, residencies and possessions along the sea lanes to China and the East. Britain was following to the letter the advice of Sir Walter Raleigh in 1616: 'Whosoever commands the sea commands the trade; whosoever commands the trade of the world commands the riches of the world, and consequently the world itself'. The Royal Navy controlled the choke points of Gibraltar at the entrance to the Mediterranean, Aden at the entrance to the Red Sea and the Strait of Hormuz at the entrance to the Persian Gulf. In the South Atlantic Ocean, it controlled the Cape colony including Cape Town and the islands of Ascension, St Helena and Tristan de Cunha. In the Indian Ocean, it controlled Mauritius, Diego

Garcia, Ceylon and the Indian ports of Bombay, Madras and Calcutta. By 1826, it also dominated the twin choke points of the Malacca Strait and the entrance to the South China Sea through its 'Straits Settlements' at Penang, Malacca and Singapore.

The China that was once eulogised was now more often demonised. Rudyard Kipling's famously insular line 'East is East, and West is West, and never the twain shall meet' would not appear in print for another 70 years but British public opinion was already moving in the direction of that sentiment. In 1816 at the end of the Napoleonic Wars, a second British embassy to China was proposed. The Company and the British government were planning for the world after peace and wanted to convey British power and might to Beijing. Both wanted to ensure that the Chinese understood that Great Britain had pacified Europe and 'was now unrivalled as the dominant military power in Europe'. Britain was in the equivalent position after 1815 that the United States found itself in after 1945.

The second British embassy was led by Lord Amherst. Its members had a deep sense of entitlement that was a product of 'the confidence of being the pre-eminent military and commercial power on earth'. They were bolder, less respectful and less diplomatic than Macartney's first embassy had been. Along the China coast, Amherst's ships began aggressively charting the coastline, taking notes of populations, climate, geology, military installations and anchorages, and bestowing ill-suited English names on Chinese landmarks. At ports along the way, they handed out Christian Bible tracts prepared by the Protestant missionary Robert Morrison, who accompanied them.

The Chinese were bewildered by the British but what ultimately killed off the mission was the ceremonial issue, once again. Amherst initially believed that he should do no more than Macartney had done which, as he understood it, was not the formal kowtow. A great debate ensued between officials on both sides as to what Macartney had done. Jiaqing, who was present when Macartney attended on his father Qianlong in 1793, said that Macartney performed the kowtow at the

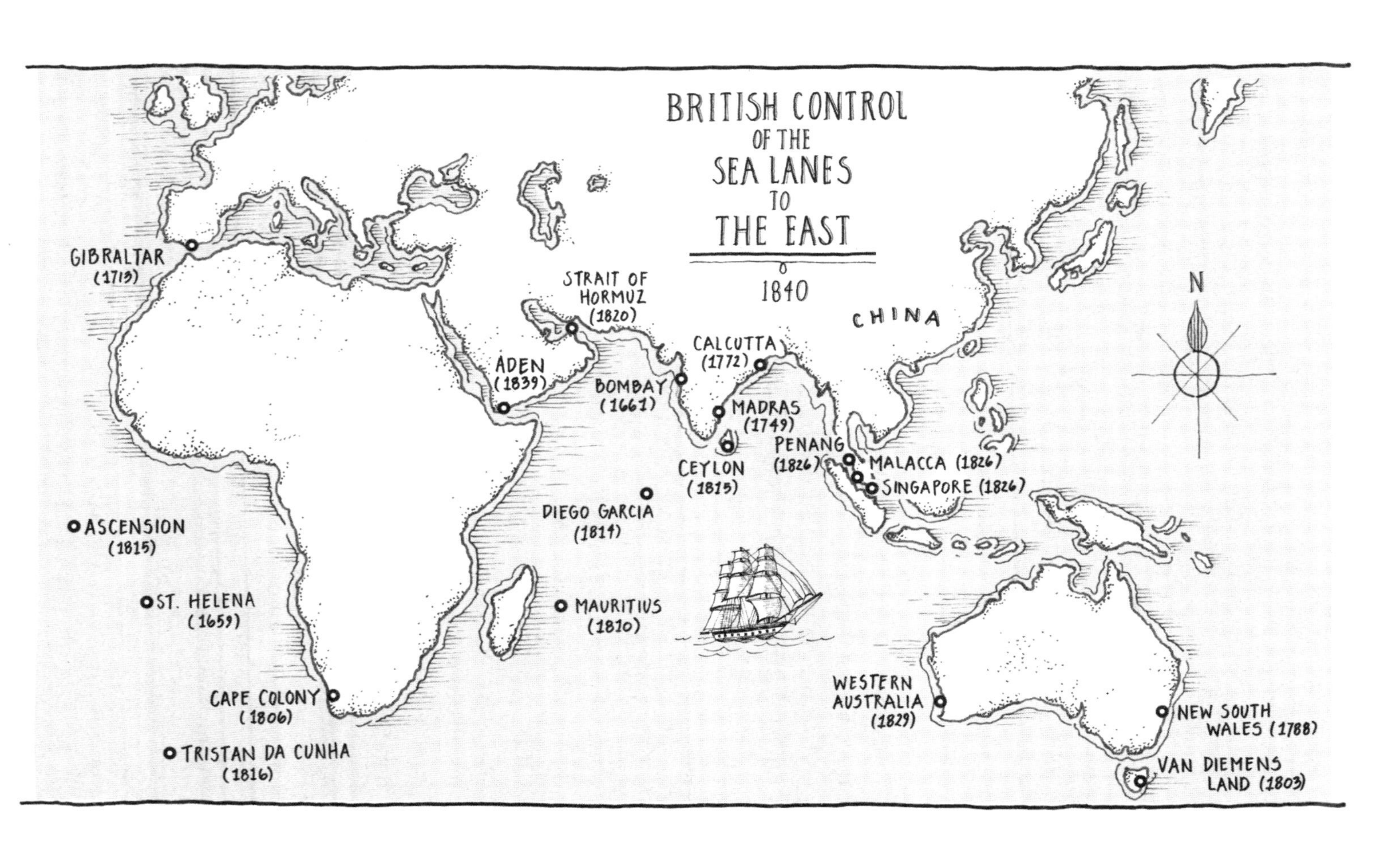

BRITISH CONTROL
OF THE
SEA LANES
TO
THE EAST
1840
GIBRALTAR (1713)
STRAIT OF HORMUZ (1820)
CHINA
CALCUTTA (1772)
ADEN (1839)
BOMBAY (1661)
MADRAS (1749)
PENANG (1826)
MALACCA (1826)
SINGAPORE (1826)
CEYLON (1815)
DIEGO GARCIA (1814)
ASCENSION (1815)
ST. HELENA (1659)
MAURITIUS (1810)
CAPE COLONY (1806)
TRISTAN DA CUNHA (1816)
WESTERN AUSTRALIA (1829)
NEW SOUTH WALES (1788)
VAN DIEMENS LAND (1803)
N

emperor's banquet at the imperial summer retreat at Chengde. There was some confirmation of this in the hand-written diary of the then twelve-year-old George Staunton, who accompanied Macartney. The diary noted that 'at a signall being made, we bent on one knee and bowed down to the ground. *We repeated this ceremony nine times with the other mandarins*'. (emphasis added) Amherst was astute enough to realise that given the loose, voluminous robes that hid most of Macartney's body from view, his nine repeated deep, kneeling bows on one knee may have been almost indistinguishable from the kowtow when seen from the distance of the throne.

To the horror of some of his officials, Amherst decided that he would just go ahead and perform the kowtow as requested. He did not think that hair-splitting distinctions between bowing and prostration, between kneeling on one knee or two, should be allowed to jeopardise the mission. Amherst's officials were horrified by his threatened behaviour and begged him to wait, suggesting that the matter be submitted to a vote. Against his better judgment, Amherst allowed the vote, which fatefully resulted in a majority deciding that the British emissary should refuse to perform the kowtow. Amherst obliged and instructed his secretary to despatch a letter to the emperor's representative. The letter contained some flattering blandishments but stated emphatically that His Majesty's ambassador 'found it utterly impossible' to perform the kowtow.

From that moment, the embassy was doomed. In fact, it went to hell. The emperor summoned Amherst to an audience at an impossibly inconvenient hour in the imperial retreat at Chengde, requiring his party to travel through the night. They arrived exhausted, dishevelled and beleaguered. Amherst was bleary and unkempt. He protested that his treasured coronation robes that he had brought for the occasion had not arrived. An argument ensued with the emperor's representative. The emperor was waiting but Amherst refused to budge. Qing officials gathered closely around him. One took hold of Amherst's arm as if to drag him into the audience chamber.

Amherst responded violently and pushed the official away. There was a melee. Attendants leapt forward, reaching for their swords in order, in Amherst's words, 'to resist force by force'.

The fracas torpedoed the planned imperial audience. The British blamed Jiaqing, whom they labelled a 'capricious despot', but it is not entirely clear that it was his fault. Behind the scenes, Jiaqing had, initially at least, been willing to accommodate the British more than they knew. Only a few days before the proposed audience, he had instructed his officials:

> Do not be so severe and exacting about ceremonials that you lose track of the etiquette for managing foreigners … it was just like this in 1793, and we made the best of the situation then. Generally speaking, it is better to meet with them than send them away …

That is, better to have dialogue than put up barriers. In the aftermath, on the day after the audience that never happened, Jiaqing wrote to George III – unaware that he had become permanently deranged in 1810 – to express his regret, making clear that it was not the fault of the king himself. Jiaqing added earnestly:

> In the future, there is no reason you should have to send another ambassador from so great a distance and give him the trouble of crossing over the mountains and seas.

His final remark was 'If the king would just tend to the boundaries of his own empire … there would be no need for a British mission ever to come to China again'.

On Amherst's eventual return to England, the public response was predictably indignant, not unlike the reaction when Macartney returned home two decades earlier. One writer was nonplussed by China; another praised those who were attempting to debunk the myth of Chinese civilisation; and another insisted that the British should stand firm against the

Chinese for 'the less that is conceded to this pusillanimous and insolent people, the more will their fears for the consequences begin to operate'. In contrast, the reaction of Napoleon Bonaparte, with whom Amherst had an audience at his island prison of St Helena on the voyage home in 1817, was more discerning.

Napoleon said it was absurd that Amherst should have refused to kowtow. 'Different nations have different customs' he said, and an ambassador to the Chinese court, British or not, should have followed Chinese customs. 'You have no right to send a man to China to tell them that they must perform certain ceremonies because such are practised in England.' What would have happened, he mused,

> if the British custom were to kiss the king on his arse instead of his hand? When they got to China, would they have ordered the emperor to remove his trousers?

All that the Amherst mission achieved, said Napoleon, was to lose the friendship of China and imperil British trade over a ridiculous matter of protocol. When it was put to Napoleon that the British had the Royal Navy and therefore did not need the friendship of the Chinese, Napoleon's tone changed and he pronounced darkly:

> It would be the worst thing you have done for many years, to go to war with an immense empire like China ... You would doubtless at first succeed ... but you would teach them their own strength. They would be compelled to adopt measures to defend themselves against you ... build ships ... put guns into them ... build a fleet and, in the course of time, defeat you.

At that time, no Englishman was thinking ahead to what might happen in 'the course of time', let alone to the twenty-first century. A dangerous momentum for the fantasy of teaching China a lesson was building. The *casus belli* would be opium.

CHAPTER 18

FIRE & SMOKE

1820–1839

Each day is worse than the last.

AS THE VICTORIAN ERA approached and the smuggling of British opium to China increased, the traders became more audacious. The new emperor, Daoguang (r. 1820–1850), who was a grandson of Qianlong and is sometimes said to have lost one of his own sons to opium, became so concerned that he lamented in an imperial edict:

> The multitude of users expands day by day, and there are more and more people who sell it; they are like fire and smoke, destroying our resources and harming our people. Each day is worse than the last.

Of all the opium traders, William Jardine and James Matheson were the loudest, the most belligerent. They were always at the vanguard, always ready to find a pretext to advocate a more aggressive stance against China to further their immense financial interests. They disliked the East India Company for its monopoly but they loathed the Chinese government even more for its restriction of foreign trade to Canton. In the years 1830–1831 Jardine and Matheson began a public campaign against the Chinese authorities. It was sparked by an incident involving the new Company taipan, a man named Baynes who was a protégé of John Roberts, the one who had attempted to incite a British invasion of Macau several decades earlier.

Contrary to the rules, Baynes had allowed his wife to sneak into Canton in February 1830 and reside with him at the British factory for the remainder of the winter trading season. Mrs Baynes – the prettiest woman in Macau – initially dressed in disguise but soon felt confident enough to promenade in 'full unadulterated London fashion, puffy-sleeved dresses and all'. Her walkabouts led to a minor mob scene as local Chinese crowded around to glimpse the Englishwoman. Several entrepreneurial Chinese with river boats charged admission to see her. Two more British wives came across to join Mrs Baynes and later a fetching young American lady named Miss Harriet Low. The Chinese prohibition against foreign women in Canton had never been tested but when Baynes decided to repeat the experiment in October at the start of the next trading season, it was too much for the governor to endure. He ordered Mrs Baynes to leave immediately and requested the British to stop defying the rules of the compound. Officials posted notices around the factory district explaining in blunt and undiplomatic terms how immoral the British had become and calling upon them to act like civilised people.

The opium traders led by Jardine and Matheson – who liked to call themselves 'free traders' – seized on the opportunity to demand that the Company do something about this allegedly terrible offence to their country. They complained that the posters were 'grossly insulting' and held up 'foreigners to the eyes of the Chinese as an inferior and abject class'. It was an entirely overblown reaction and a mere pretext for a demonstration of hostility. Baynes protested the notion that the British were in any way uncivilised or unruly but the governor held firm. Through the respected senior Hong merchant, Howqua, he requested Baynes to nominate a date by which his wife would return to Macau and warned that soldiers might be sent to remove his wife.

The simultaneous reference to 'soldiers and wife' sent Baynes over the edge. Jardine and Matheson watched gleefully as the situation turned into an international incident. Baynes called for an armed force to protect his wife and a hundred British sailors landed at Canton with naval carronades to strike fear into the hearts of the Chinese. The Select Committee of Supercargoes, chaired by Baynes, declared that anything less than a forceful response to the governor's threat 'would be highly injurious to the Interests and Honour of the British Nation'. The mystified governor quickly clarified that he did not really intend to send soldiers into the factory merely because a foreign woman was living there but he did remind Baynes that the regulations against women had been in place since 1760.

To the directors in London, Baynes's destabilising behaviour was preposterous. The next Company ship to arrive in Canton carried orders for his removal, away from trouble. He 'was relieved of his duties ... and ordered home along with his pretty wife'. But in the echo chamber world of the foreign enclave in Canton, the opium traders refused to let go of the supposed insults. In December 1830, they sent a petition to the British parliament complaining that they had 'long submitted in silence to the absolute and corrupt rule of the Chinese government' and requested that their government take a strong hand in putting the Canton trade on a more favourable basis. They emphasised their call for military force by repeating the supposedly distressing fact that the British were being depicted 'as a barbarous, ignorant and depraved race, every way inferior'.

Some months later, the opium traders manufactured another insult. In the off-season the Canton governor had visited the British factory to investigate reports of illegal construction and sat down in the dining hall with his back to a portrait of George IV. His response to this ostensibly grave offence was that he had no idea who the man in the portrait was. This inflamed the situation further. Nothing would placate the British opium traders. On 30 May 1831, they sent another petition to parliament declaring that the Canton governor's 'gratuitous insult offered to the picture of the King of England' and 'his violent entry' into the Company factory, demonstrated 'a deliberate plan to oppress and degrade British subjects'. They demanded a Royal Navy fleet to uphold their nation's honour in China – 'to preserve our national character and interests unimpaired'.

On the sidelines, the American Robert Forbes was tickled by the absurdity of the British grievances. He wrote to his cousin John Perkins Cushing, an opium smuggler who became a philanthropist, that the Qing governor 'had the temerity to enter their Hall and turn his back on the King's portrait ... [a] matter of sufficient import to despatch a ship to Calcutta' to request a naval fleet. To his uncle Thomas Handasyd Perkins, another philanthropist who became rich from opium smuggling, he wrote that the British were crying out for redress of imaginary wrongs. Later he added 'Who would barter the present free trade ... for a regular commercial System of duties, entry permits and a myriad of forms like those in London'?

The British opium traders were building a pathway to war. Their rhetoric and provocation, antagonism and demonisation of the government in Beijing were following an all-too familiar modern playbook for the lead-up to conflict. But for the time being, they did not have the support of parliament, which slapped down their petition. Lord Graham, First Lord of the Admiralty, decried the British traders' 'notions of self-importance and ... haughty defiance mixed with contempt for the laws and customs of an independent people'. He added 'Trade with China is our only object ... and commerce never prospers where force is used to sustain it'.

The wisdom of Lord Graham was soon overtaken by political changes that worked to the advantage of the opium traders. A liberal wave was sweeping Britain and the Reform acts of 1832 gave the industrial north and the manufacturers of Liverpool, Manchester and Glasgow exceptional power and voting rights. They had agitated long and hard to sell their goods and textiles to a third of the world's population in China. Like the opium traders, they railed against the Company's monopoly over the China trade. For the most zealous free trade advocates, the dismantling of the Company's monopoly in China was almost a religion. Free trade lobbying societies swamped the House of Commons with hundreds of petitions. In May 1834, parliament voted to end the East India Company's monopoly over trade with China, opening the trade to all comers – and causing the opium smuggling business to expand ever more.

Meanwhile, foreign commerce was still limited to the port of Canton, a restriction that rankled with British traders who cast their ambitious eyes to ports further north. William Jardine organised a secret exploratory expedition to the north that 'required much management and great attention' on his part. He found enterprising adventurers in Karl Gutzlaff, a German Lutheran missionary, and Hugh Hamilton Lindsay, the son of one of the directors of the East India Company. In 1832, the two would-be explorers found a private vessel at Lintin whose captain was eager to make charts of the coast. By a strange coincidence, the ship's name was the *Lord Amherst*.

The voyage of Gutzlaff and Lindsay explored Chinese ports never before visited by the British. Gutzlaff spread the gospel of the Bible and Lindsay spread the gospel of free trade. Lindsay reported that 'just about everyone, everywhere he went, wanted opium'. The two men wishfully reported, and *The Times* enthused, that 'as a nation, China is politically weak' and that its naval defences were 'contemptible'. On his return, the missionary Gutzlaff joined Jardine's firm, riding its opium smuggling ships with his boxes of Christian tracts – 'cheerfully distributing them from one side of the vessel while opium went over the other'.

In the new post–Company monopoly era, a British 'chief superintendent of trade' was appointed to represent British interests in Canton. The first appointment was Lord Napier who quickly aligned himself with the opium traders and became a firm friend of Jardine. His successor, John Davis, thought Napier was 'one of the weakest minds I ever met with'. Like some modern American politicians, Napier believed that 'what China really needed was a war' and fantasised about being the man to break China open and 'how easily a gun brig would raise a revolution and cause them to open their ports to the trading world'. But Napier's belligerence was so badly received by the Cantonese and British merchants (except Jardine and Matheson) that he was very soon forced to retreat to Macau where he died in illness and humiliation only two months after his arrival.

Jardine and Matheson soon sought to capitalise on Napier's death, which they blamed on the Chinese authorities. In December 1834, they formulated another petition, this time addressed to the king in council. It demanded satisfaction for 'China's heinous insults to Lord Napier and the British nation' as well as insults 'offered to your Majesty's flag' for having fired back at Napier's gunships when they blasted Chinese forts. The grounds of complaint were risible and the foreign secretary, Lord Palmerston, wisely ignored them, but Jardine and Matheson would not give up. They shamelessly used Lady Napier to drum up support for a war against China. Lady Napier said that 'Mr Jardine will do anything to meet my wishes'. And Matheson adopted a pastoral role towards her and her daughters, obsequiously taking the opportunity to accompany Lord Napier's exhumed remains to Scotland for reburial and promising to ensure a proper commemoration for his 'sacrifice'. In July 1835, Lady Napier, who had a level of influence with the British government in London that Matheson did not, wrote effusively to Palmerston introducing 'my friend Mr. Matheson'.

As Matheson was cultivating Lady Napier's influence, Lindsay was also in London writing long letters to Palmerston with the same object. Lady Napier fully supported their call for war, declaring that:

> If some show of apology is made, if we succeed in obtaining a commercial treaty, increasing trade, intercourse, civilisation

> and in God's good name *Christianity* will follow, and it will not be altogether in vain that Lord Napier sacrificed his health and life in the path he considered his duty and for his Country's advantage.

Matheson enthusiastically spread his war message in pamphlets and newspapers, telling his readers that although Providence had granted to the Chinese 'the possession of a vast portion of the most desirable parts of the earth and a population estimated as amounting to nearly one-third of the human race', they were 'a people characterised by a marvellous degree of imbecility, avarice, conceit and obstinacy'. Matheson called on the British people to vindicate 'our insulted honour as a nation'. But the old China hand, George Staunton, soon to become the member for Portsmouth, tried to point out how wrong, how mischievous and dangerous, were the views of Matheson and Lindsay. In language that should have a striking modern relevance, he said that 'China was not some enemy but a friendly power, with which, for upwards of an hundred years, we have carried on a most beneficial commercial intercourse'. He emphasised that 'To go to war seems to me outrageous, and quite unparalleled'.

Through the summer of 1837 and into 1838, Chinese authorities redoubled their war on drugs. The next chief superintendent, Charles Elliot, a very different man to Napier, worried about the high-handed racism of British opium traders towards the Chinese and feared an outbreak of violence. He noted that 'It is the fashion of the young men particularly to treat the Chinese with the most wanton insult and contumely'. The opium traders began to throw themselves ever more recklessly into harm's way in China. The traditional division between the legitimate trade and the opium trade – the former in the inner waters of Canton and the latter at Lintin Island and on the coast – was disappearing. The same ships now increasingly carried both contraband and aboveboard cargoes.

In late December 1838, the emperor appointed the scholar-official Lin Zexu to destroy the opium trade at its heart in Canton. Lin was a beacon of honesty and virtue who is forever known to history as 'Commissioner Lin'. There are statues of him in Macau and New York City and his nickname was 'Lin, Clear as Heaven'. In the Chinese way, Lin's punishments were severe: opium smokers were condemned to death by strangulation and opium dealers to beheading. Lin's single-mindedness soon created a frenzy among the British opium traders. Jardine wrote forlornly in the same month as Lin's appointment: 'Not a Broker to be seen, nor an Opium pipe; they have all vanished' the authorities have been vigilant in 'seizing smokers, dealers and shopkeepers innumerable'. Ever the optimist, he added 'We must hope for better times and brisker deliveries'.

William Jardine chose this moment to leave Canton after living in China for almost 20 years. At his farewell dinner in January 1839, surrounded by a bevy of stewards and a band playing Scottish airs, while his colleagues drank themselves silly on claret and madeira, Jardine remained defiant, or perhaps obtuse. As the last notes of 'Auld Lang Syne' died away, he rose, misty-eyed, and bellowed to his fellow British and American traders,

> We are not smugglers, gentlemen! It is the Chinese government, it is the Chinese officers who smuggle and who connive at and encourage smuggling, not we; and then look at the East India Company: why, the father of all smuggling and smugglers is the East India Company!

adding that his conscience was 'quite at rest on this point'.

Meanwhile, Commissioner Lin arrested known Chinese dealers, confiscated thousands of pipes and seized large quantities of opium. On 18 March, he ordered the foreign community to surrender all of their opium stocks and gave them three days to comply. He was confident that their legitimate trade was sufficient to generate adequate riches. The opium traders were stunned. They ignored Lin's orders, doubting that he could really be serious, but their judgement was wrong. When the deadline passed without compliance, Commissioner Lin ordered the Hoppo to stop all trade and announced that no foreign merchant would be permitted to leave the Canton factory compound until all of them had surrendered their opium.

Chinese valets, porters, cooks, compradors, linguists and other attendants were allowed to leave the factory buildings but their masters were left to fend for themselves. Official supplies of fresh food were shut off, rear entrances to the factories bricked up, troops stationed at the open sides of the compound and access from the river blocked by guard boats. Approximately 350 Britons, Americans, Dutch and Parsis were confined inside, including about 30 sailors and Indian lascars on shore leave who found themselves in the wrong place at the wrong time. Lin's intention was to intimidate the foreigners to force them to surrender their illegal opium, not to provoke a conflict, but he misjudged the reaction.

In reality, there was no real hardship for the imprisoned foreigners during their six weeks of captivity in the factory compound. They had ample food; the blockade of supplies was fairly relaxed and 'no one suffered from want of provisions'. Robert Forbes joked that they 'suffered more ... from absence of exercise and from over feeding than from any actual want of the necessaries of life'. One captive is said to have asked 'Are they trying to fatten us or starve us?' The stranded sailors and lascars were shared around to help with cooking; clothes were collected for washing and mending; and special requests for oranges or cleaning were happily met. The light-hearted captivity included amusements each afternoon when the foreigners gathered in the square to 'participate in or watch games of cricket and leapfrog' and other frivolity.

At the beginning of the blockade, Elliot was not to know that the captivity would be relatively benign. He had a vision of starvation and mass execution on his watch. On Sunday 24 March at sundown, standing solemnly at the stern of a small pinnace, he was rowed ashore to the factory compound, dressed in his full post captain's uniform, wearing his cocked hat and with his ceremonial sword by his side. According to Matheson, Elliot was 'a good deal excited'. He called a meeting of all foreigners and read a public notice that referred melodramatically to the 'imminent hazard of life and property' and the 'dark and violent' nature of Lin's threats. Elliot concluded his address with the dangerously impassioned words 'I will remain with you to my last gasp'. The American Robert Forbes referred to Elliot's moments of panic, to which he was noticeably prone, as 'Elliot's mad freaks'. Sometime later, Elliot confessed to his sister that he was losing his mind; that he had 'great difficulty at times in preserving a hold, a firm hold, over my thoughts'.

Two days later, Elliot announced a plan that was so strange, so unexpected, that the merchants could hardly believe it. He ordered all foreigners in possession of British opium to surrender their opium to him, in return for which he would sign promissory notes guaranteeing that the British government would reimburse them at full market value. To the hard-headed opium traders, it was a stunning deal, too good to be true, 'the most fortunate thing that could have happened' according to Matheson. But it was wholly unauthorised. In fact, Palmerston had repeatedly told Elliot that the opium smugglers must suffer their own consequences. The opium traders knew that whether authorised or not, contracts signed in good faith with Britain's official representative in Canton would provide a powerful case for compensation from the British government. This was a far better option than losing their contraband to Commissioner Lin. All told, a staggering 20,283 opium chests 'containing more than one million kilos', worth millions of pounds sterling, were offered up.

On 4 May, when Commissioner Lin was satisfied that all the opium was going to be surrendered, he removed the blockade of the factories and all foreigners were set free except for the worst opium traders who remained for a few more weeks until the last of the opium was collected. Throughout June, the opium was publicly destroyed in large trenches which Lin's men excavated near the Tiger's Mouth. Each ball was laboriously broken down, submerged in water and fermented with lime and salt. According to Indian writer Amitav Ghosh, it was hard work: 'five hundred men, working long hours, can destroy only about three hundred chests a day'. On the eve of the destruction, Lin composed a prayer, an elegy to the God of the Sea, asking that all aquatic creatures be protected from the poison that would soon be pouring out.

When the blockade ended, the foreign commerce at Canton did not return to normal. Commissioner Lin required the merchants to sign bonds promising that they would not trade in opium in the future – on pain of death – but the British refused. Elliot fell into paroxysms of rage over this issue, tearing up the bonds 'into a thousand pieces' and throwing them into the fireplace. He ordered all British subjects to abandon the factory compound in Canton and move to Macau, out of Commissioner Lin's reach. The Americans took a different approach, signing the bonds with an eye to increasing their trade when the British left. In late August, as relations deteriorated further, Elliot ordered the British to move again, this time to the safety of Hong Kong harbour, where at Kowloon on 4 September 1839, the first minor skirmish of the so-far unofficial British–China war took place.

PART 6

Opium Wars

CHAPTER 19

FIRST OPIUM WAR

1839–1842

The noble lord would call it an explanatory declaration.

LIN WAS SINCERE BUT he did not realise the seriousness of his actions. His resolve was too fixed while Elliot's reaction was too alarmist. And the latter's decision to offer an indemnity on behalf of the British government to all opium traders was without authority and seemingly without consultation. It was according to one writer 'the bizarre actions of an unhinged chief superintendent in China'. Elliot presumably had in mind the indemnity offered to British slave owners when slavery was abolished by parliament in 1833 – but enslaved people were recognised legal property at the time while opium was mere contraband. And the slavery compensation to about 3000 British slave-owning families was so huge that it took the government nearly two centuries – until 2015 – to repay its borrowings that financed the compensation. The British government simply did not have the money to compensate the opium traders, apart altogether from the moral difficulty of reimbursing smugglers and lawbreakers. The prime minister Lord Melbourne was firmly opposed and the Chancellor of the Exchequer, Francis Baring – of the famous Baring banking family – stressed that no funds were available. *The Times* reported that the nation was 'wholly unprepared to meet it'.

The cost and consequences of Elliot's decision would eventually lead the high-handed and opportunist foreign secretary Lord Palmerston to propose a war to make China atone for what Britain was unable or unwilling to pay. He had been deluged by merchant lobbyists – opium traders, investors, weavers of cotton in Manchester, producers of woollens in Leeds and tea importers from Bristol – demanding trading privileges in China. In the face of their calls for action, Palmerston returned to something that he had consistently rejected in the past: the pleas for an armed expedition against China that had been advanced by the self-interested opium traders. The person with the greatest influence on Palmerston during his deliberations was William Jardine himself, who had only recently returned to England. Jardine wasted no time getting to Palmerston's office on Whitehall where he had a lengthy audience three days before cabinet was scheduled to meet at Windsor Castle.

Jardine put his case to Palmerston, made his recommendations, provided his charts of the China coast and volunteered ships and crews from his own smuggling fleet to assist in the campaign. He later prepared a memorandum with detailed plans for the war that he wanted the British government to wage. It contained recommendations on strategy, useful harbours and the distribution of force. Cabinet met over two days and only reached the China issue on the second day. In an echo of more recent times, conflict in Syria was the main concern. Buoyed by Jardine's suggestions, Palmerston outlined a plan to blockade the China coast with 'a small squadron of one line-of-battleship, two frigates and some small armed vessels with two or three steamers'.

When discussion turned to what to do about Elliot's offer of an indemnity to the opium traders, the president of the Board of Trade thought it appropriate that the East India Company should be made to pay the indemnity as it was responsible for creating the India–China opium trade in the first place; and the Company could afford it while the government could not. Palmerston had a different view and urged that China should be made to pay, even though his past position had been that the government 'cannot interfere for the purpose of enabling British subjects to violate the laws of the country to which they trade' and that any opium loss 'must be borne by the parties who have brought that loss on themselves by their own acts'.

The cabinet supported Palmerston's proposal 'with barely a sideways glance at the morality of the war' on which they were embarking. When the ministers left the meeting on 1 October, they were in good spirits, joking light-heartedly about how they had just made war on 'the master of one third of the whole human race'. The 20-year-old Queen Victoria was in the background and went riding with Lord Broughton in Windsor Great Park after the meeting. It was less than a year since Britain had launched its fateful invasion of Afghanistan which, in another echo of the twenty-first century, resulted in a disastrous evacuation and retreat from Kabul.

Only Palmerston knew that Jardine had 'literally masterminded the government's approach towards China and the Opium War'. In November, he issued secret instructions to the Admiralty that approximated Jardine's recommendations 'down to details such as the size of ships to be deployed and the terms of the treaty to be proposed to China.' From February 1840, soldiers began arriving at the huge Fort William complex in Calcutta. Others gathered in Madras and at Ceylon. The largest contribution was non-English, made up of Indian sepoys from the Madras Native Infantry Regiment.

In April an attempt was made in the House of Commons to stop the expedition. The young William Gladstone, who later served four terms as prime minister and became the pre-eminent British statesman of the century, castigated Palmerston. The war had no proper basis, he said, no just cause, other than to 'exact reparation for insult and compensation for confiscation' of opium. Gladstone famously added that:

> a war more unjust in its origin, a war more calculated in its progress to cover this country with permanent disgrace, I do not know, and I have not read of.

His conclusion was that 'justice, in my opinion, is with them [the Chinese]'. Gladstone's passion, but not his acuity or the truth of his claims, may have been influenced by the fact that his younger sister Helen was afflicted by an opium addiction.

The vote was taken at four o'clock in the morning after three long nights of vigorous debate. A majority of just nine votes (271–262) supported Palmerston's war. If the cabinet ministers whose decision was the subject of attack had abstained, the result would have gone the other way and the war may have been stopped. A last chance in the House of Lords failed when the aged Duke of Wellington swung the vote with an adamantly pro-Palmerston speech based on Elliot's exaggerated reports of insult and injury. Across the Atlantic, another septuagenarian of the Victorian era, the former American president John Quincy Adams, also supported the war. He somewhat curiously declared that the war was perfectly just and admirable and that 'the cause of the war is the kowtow – the arrogant and insupportable pretensions of China'. Adams's opinion did not reflect the popular American revulsion at the British opium trade and he had difficulty finding a publisher for his remarks.

The government's supporters in parliament claimed to be 'acting in defence of national honour and avoidance of shame'. Palmerston was fond of saying that the 'Flag of England *must* be respected' but pursuing or redressing notions of 'honour', 'shame' or 'respect' could not be a reasonable justification for war. Even less so were the purely mercenary motives of the British opium traders. They cared only about getting paid for their opium, opening new ports and expanding trade access. The opium traders desired 'what not one single person in Parliament had called for: the opening of China'. The tail was wagging the dog and the decade-long aspirations of Jardine, Matheson and the opium traders were coming to fruition in the dexterous hands of Lord Palmerston, whose critics variously described him as 'shifty', 'shuffling', 'slippery', 'brazen' and 'cheating'.

As is so often the case, parliament did not know what it had unleashed by choosing the path of war. No member knew that Palmerston secretly supported the traders to the hilt; that his instructions to Elliot embraced 'every claim or demand the traders had nagged the British government with over the years'; or that they 'represented far more the avaricious desires of the free traders than the rightful claims of the British nation'. Palmerston worked hard to keep the full picture out of the public domain and ensured that his despatches to and from Elliot were 'locked up in the Foreign Office for as long as he possibly could'. When responding to repeated questions about the rumoured hostilities in China, he was dissembling and insisted that 'the proposed operations' were 'communications' not hostilities. It was a denial of the truth as weird as Vladimir Putin's 'special military operation'. *The Times* scoffed, saying memorably that 'if the town of Canton were blown to atoms, the noble lord would call it an explanatory declaration'.

Parliament did not claim a unilateral right for Britain to use military force to encroach on China's sovereignty to compel trading concessions and obtain access to Chinese territory but Palmerston was following the Jardine blueprint. He intended to open China for British trade. And he wanted the Chinese government to pay more, much more, than compensation for the opium. Palmerston's objectives included the 'cession of one or more islands on the coast'; the opening of multiple ports beyond Canton for British trade; the right of British men and women to reside in those ports 'freely and without restraint'; an end to the monopoly of the Hong merchants to allow British traders to deal with whomever they liked; and payment of the entire expenses of the British naval expedition. Later, under fire, he conceded that payment for 'the expenses of war' was 'certainly unusual in European warfare' but was necessary 'in order to make the Chinese sensible of the extent of the outrage they had committed'.

In May 1840, the warships of the British invasion force began forming up in Singapore, the expedition's place of rendezvous. There was not much to the British settlement of Singapore at that time. From the distance of the outer harbour, it appeared to be little more than a clearing in the jungle. Supply vessels and merchant transports carried thousands of Irish, Scots and Indian troops under English command. Some of the masters of the transports also carried chests of opium in the expectation that they would profit from the opening of new ports and an anticipated spike in prices. The expedition was not exactly what Palmerston had suggested to cabinet. It was a virtual armada of fighting ships, transport ships, supply vessels, brigs, sloops, schooners, bomb ships and hospital ships as well as approximately 4000 troops and all the supplies, stores and impedimenta of a substantial fighting force. The expedition also included four steamships of the East India Company, which were joined in November by the shallow draught, flat-bottomed, steam-powered *Nemesis*.

The *Nemesis* would live up to her name. She was a secret British weapon – the country's first iron-clad gunship, its first warship with watertight bulkheads and the first iron ship to round the Cape of Good Hope. The ship was built entirely of iron, except for the deck, and her bottom was almost perfectly flat. She would prove to be unassailable in the shallow rivers and estuaries of China's coast, where the ships of the line could not go. The Chinese had never seen anything like the *Nemesis* and referred to her as the 'devil ship'. Her apparently supernatural powers spread fear and panic. Everything about the *Nemesis* was secret. She was commissioned by the East India Company but not listed among the Company's ships. She was not requisitioned by the Admiralty under the articles of war. Her captain and first and second officers were Royal Navy men but the rest of the officers and crew were civilian. Even the ship's mission to China was kept secret. When she set sail from Liverpool, it was publicly suggested that the *Nemesis* was bound for Odessa on the Black Sea.

The *Nemesis* embodied Britain's superior technology. In contrast, Daoguang's troops were mostly 'underfed, underpaid, undertrained, underequipped – or not at all'. They had no field artillery and their muskets were 'a wretched thing, crudely made, of small calibre'. Worse, they were matchlocks, an inferior weapon that had not been issued to British line regiments since the reign of Queen Anne. The Chinese cannon lacked sighting devices and swivelling mechanisms and their gunpowder was coarse and unreliable. And bows and arrows, rattan shields, spears and halberds were commonplace military issue. But the greatest Qing weakness was their war junks, which were only patrol vessels carrying around ten guns, which could not compete with the firepower and professionalism of Britain's copper-plated men-of-war whose potency had been honed over two centuries of naval conflict with France, Spain and the Dutch.

The campaign began without a declaration of war and the Chinese did not know what was happening at first. When a detachment of the British fleet first appeared at Macau in June 1840, Commissioner Lin reported to the emperor that they were probably just opium ships and that 'there is really nothing they can do'. The reality hit home next month when the fleet headed north and captured the large island of Zhoushan about halfway between Canton and Beijing. They were following to the letter Jardine's recommended strategy to 'occupy Zhoushan and blockade the eastern seaboard ... then press on to the capital to make Britain's demands'. When the order to fire was given at Zhoushan, a thunderous broadside belched smoke and flashing fire from the decks of the warships. In nine short minutes the guns sent a deadly message to the Chinese. An eyewitness recalled that:

> the crashing of timber, falling houses, and groans of men resounded from the shore ... When the smoke cleared away a mass of ruin presented itself ... crowds were visible in the distance flying in all directions.

When the British soldiers landed, they were unopposed, greeted only by 'a few dead bodies, bows and arrows, broken spears and guns'.

The pitiful scene at Zhoushan was replayed again and again during the war. The British suffered little resistance and few casualties except from disease. From Zhoushan, the remainder of the fleet sailed further north to the river known as the Peiho, which connects Beijing through Tianjin to the coast. It is the entry point for Beijing from the Yellow Sea. The emperor had no desire for war and the conflict might have ended there. He thought the British complaint was limited to Commissioner Lin's actions in Canton and banished him to the far western regions in the hope that it would salve British concerns. On 30 August, the local regional viceroy, Qishan, invited Elliot to discuss terms of peace in a reception tent near the mouth of the river, safely away from Beijing.

Elliot behaved strangely once again. He would not press Palmerston's formal demands because his firm personal view was that Britain should not use the war as an excuse to further the ends of the opium traders who had caused all the trouble in the first place. Elliot considered that the British merchants had a right to compensation for their confiscated opium and were entitled to a guarantee of safety in their future trade but to go further would be inconsistent with the 'character and dignity of England'. And he worried that a protracted war would cause many civilian casualties and provoke the 'deep hatred' of the Chinese people.

After several months, the parties adjourned to faraway Canton. The negotiations stalled and Elliot suspected obfuscation. On Boxing Day 1840, after the British military had feasted on roast beef and plum pudding, he reluctantly ordered the commencement of a blockade of the Pearl River and the bombardment of the Chinese forts. It was a brutal reminder of British strength, 'costing the Chinese two forts, most of their fleet and five hundred men'. The bombardment had its intended effect and in late January Qishan staged a huge placatory feast on the banks of the Pearl River where, in an inner chamber draped in yellow silk, he and Elliot reached an accord. The atmosphere was 'more village fete than parley: the riverways were crammed with brightly coloured official boats, the path up to the conference marquee strewn with bunting'. Elliot contributed to the festive occasion, bringing with him 'sixteen drumming and piccolo-tooting musicians' of his own.

Their tentative agreement would get them both into trouble. Elliot agreed to accept payment of 6 million Spanish silver dollars to cover the opium that Lin had destroyed – to be paid in instalments by the Hong merchants in Canton without the emperor even being notified of it. The British would withdraw from Zhoushan but would be allowed residence on the much smaller island of Hong Kong, where China would establish a customs house and the British merchants would pay the same fees and taxes as applied at Canton. And the trade at Canton would resume. There was no 'opening' of China as Palmerston intended, no payment of the expenses of the war and no expansion of trade to northern ports. When Palmerston and Daoguang heard about the terms of the agreement, both were enraged – the former with Elliot for settling for too little and the latter with Qishan for giving away too much. Neither government would ratify the agreement.

Everyone was unhappy. Qishan received the same fate as Commissioner Lin and was banished to the western regions. Elliot was peremptorily dismissed and ordered home on the next ship, accused by Palmerston of treating his instructions as 'wastepaper', which is exactly what he did. Queen Victoria, now 21 years old, 'stamped her little foot' and wrote to her uncle Leopold that '*All* we wanted could have been got, if it had not been for the unaccountably strange conduct of Charles Elliot who ... *tried* to get the *lowest* terms he could'. Palmerston grumbled that Hong Kong was 'a barren island with hardly a house on it' and would never be a centre of trade. And the Queen quipped that Albert was 'much amused at my having got the island of Hong Kong ... we think [daughter] Victoria ought to be called Princess of Hong Kong in addition to Princess Royal'. Lord Minto thought his cousin Elliot had gone native and 'become more of a Chinese than an Englishman'. Elliot himself later said that 'Much travel ... has pretty nearly un-Englished me'.

The hostilities resumed and the Chinese were soon on their knees again. In late May 1841 a British bombardment of Canton inflicted terrible damage – 'all you could hear was the noise of burning and death'. After a week, Elliot called a truce and announced that he was sparing the city out of concern for 'the protection of the people of Canton and the encouragement of their goodwill towards us'. Canton was once more left to itself. Commerce picked up and continued through the worst of the following year's hostilities. The opium trade kept going – 'soldiers, officials and militiamen were shuttling back and forth' often selling the foreign smoke 'while the sky was dark with smoke and flames and the guns blazing'.

Elliot's replacement, the veteran Henry Pottinger, arrived in August. Pottinger was a hard-headed Anglo-Irish career soldier who had served in India for almost 40 years. He shared none of Elliot's respect or affection for the Chinese people and was determined to drive the war in China to its fullest and most profitable extent. It was a dark turn of events. Toughness was in the family. Pottinger's nephew Eldred achieved cult status in Victorian England when he travelled alone, disguised as a horse dealer, to Herat in Afghanistan where he survived a year-long siege of the city by Russian and Persian forces. Later, as British envoy to the Afghan court, he was held as a hostage by Akbar Khan, which fortuitously enabled him to avoid the massacre of the British army retreating from Kabul.

The battles in China under Henry Pottinger's command were generally swift and bloody. The coastal cities north of Canton fell with ease, blasted away with relentless British cannon. Amoy (Xiamen), a prosperous port in Fujian province on the Taiwan Strait, was the first to succumb to Pottinger's lethal guns; then Zhoushan again, a thousand kilometres further north, which the British took for the second time after pounding the coastal forts at dawn; then Zhenhai, on the coast opposite Zhoushan, where forts guarded the river approach to Ningbo; then Ningbo itself, a further 30 kilometres upstream on a branch of the Grand Canal and close to China's centres of production of tea and silk. The Ningbo–Zhenhai–Zhoushan axis was, and still is, a hugely important industrial and transport hub. There was some resistance at Zhenhai under the brave leadership of Yuqian, a Confucian warrior super-hero who killed himself rather than submit to his enemies but the outcome, as usual, was pitiable. On one account 'one and a half thousand Qing soldiers perished [and] at most sixteen British were killed and a few wounded'. When four British steamers and four warships sailed upriver to Ningbo, they found it ungarrisoned, its defenders in flight.

The Qing armies had no answer to British naval cannon and field artillery but the victories were 'increasingly self-defeating for British morale as their troops racked up atrocities against helpless Chinese civilians and soldiers' without finding a way to compel the Qing government to surrender. The letters and journals of some British officers reveal discomfit, unease and embarrassment at the wanton bloodshed and destruction. One confessed that 'many most barbarous things occurred disgraceful to our men'. Another described the horror of a sea 'quite blackened with floating corpses' and the inside of a bombarded fort 'bespattered with brains'. Towards the end of the war, the admiral of the fleet requested that his forces be spared from having to invade any more Chinese cities because 'our visitations are so calamitous to the wretched inhabitants'.

When Elliot arrived back in England in late 1841, he pointed out to the government that the only path to the kind of victory Palmerston desired was through 'the slaughter of an almost defenceless and helpless people, and a people which, in a large portion of the theatre of the war, was friendly to the British nation'. But the Conservative administration wanted only to conclude the drawn-out war and would not listen. It resorted to the now familiar modern tactic of a 'surge' in men and materiel. More artillery, supplies, soldiers and ships were added. The number of troops almost tripled to about 10,000 men and ship numbers increased to over 70, including 48 transports.

The end drew near in July 1842 when the reinforced British fleet moved further north to the mouth of the Yangtze River. From there, the fleet turned west and began its stately progress towards Nanjing, the ancient capital 300 kilometres upriver from Shanghai. The sails of the ships were a fearsome sight along the river – like 'a white cloud three miles in extent'. The Chinese never expected the British to attack so deep up the Yangtze. At Zhenjiang, the final Qing stronghold about 60 kilometres from Nanjing, near the confluence of the Yangtze and the Grand Canal, the resistance of the soldiers was desperate, but futile. The British force captured the city in a single day under a summer sun so hot that seventeen British sailors and marines died of sunstroke. It was the last battle of the First Opium War, enabling the British to block the transport network of grain throughout the empire.

The catastrophic loss of Zhenjiang, the crossroads of China's inland commerce, led to despair and suicide among the Qing military, including by the supreme commander Hai Ling and his entire family. Among the British, the horrors of the war caused some to be sick at heart, if they were not already so afflicted. In the wreckage of the fallen city, one officer wrote of 'groups of old men, women and children cutting each other's throats, and drowning themselves by the dozen'. Others described unutterable scenes of woe and despair – children thrown into wells and collections of 'fourteen, even twenty bodies found hanging from rafters in single houses'.

As the walls of Nanjing came into view, Lieutenant Bingham, who came to China like many others of his countrymen with the ambition of knocking off a few mandarins' heads, rejoiced that 'the energy of British character under the blessing of the Almighty, had placed, without an accident, a fleet of seventy sail ... in the heart of the Celestial Empire!'. Within days, the 'dishonourable war', as *The Times* called it, came to an end. Lady Napier had her revenge. At the outbreak of war, she had written to Palmerston to convey the joy she felt at the news and remarked 'I knew the day of Retribution must come, and I ... shall rejoice most sincerely when the Chinese are thoroughly humbled, a lesson they have long required'. The Chinese were indeed humbled, defeated and humiliated. Not a shot was fired in anger at Nanjing; not a shot was needed. The First Opium War ended with the Treaty of Nanjing on 29 August 1842.

CHAPTER 20

SECOND OPIUM WAR

1856–1860

We are so strong and so right.

THE TREATY OF NANJING marked a watershed in the Western realisation that 'one could get what one wanted from China through violence'. As well as an exorbitant indemnity of 21 million Spanish silver dollars that covered the confiscated opium, war reparations and the cost of the British invasion, the treaty granted Hong Kong Island to Britain in perpetuity, ended the Canton system, finished the monopoly of the Hong merchants and opened five ports for foreign trade and foreign residence – Canton and Xiamen, Fuzhou, Ningbo and Shanghai. The emperor Daoguang felt such intense feelings of regret and despair that he later wrote:

> Hounded by such unspeakable bullying, so much anger and hate bottle up inside me ... I can only blame myself and feel utterly ashamed ... I just want to strike and strike my chest with clenched fists.

The crushing victory convinced most Britons that it had been right to initiate the war. Their attitude was a manifestation of that phenomenon of self-justification with which victors often convince themselves of the validity of their actions. The war's opium origins were ignored. Supporters revelled in rousing cries for free trade, open markets and Christian civilisation. Many letters to *The Times* reflected what a 'great and glorious thing' the war had been. A widespread mindset developed that it was good for both Britain and China to open forcibly 'a new continent to the increasing activity of all Europeans'; that the war was a service to world civilisation; and that 'vast hordes of populations ... will now enjoy the freedom of a more expanded civilisation'. A minority considered the conflict to be

> the most disgraceful war in our history ... we lost about 69 men and killed between 20,000 and 25,000 Chinese. There is no honour to be gained in a war like that.

One critic wrote that 'No man with a spark of morality in his composition ... has dared to justify that war'. In fact, most merchants and traders, diplomats and missionaries, journalists and scholars, and naturally politicians, did justify the war. Not only did they justify the war, they also wanted more. They wanted to open China to an even greater extent and to subdue what some called 'the insufferable sins of the Chinese that had necessitated the first war'. They could not stomach the Chinese 'pride, their xenophobia, their resistance to change, their heathen cruelty and immorality'. Opinion had emphatically tilted against China. A Sinophobia, not unlike that which emerged during the Covid-19 pandemic, generally prevailed. Even the literary Charles Dickens, an opium user himself, took the opportunity to 'sneer at the comic fragility of China' whose millennia of civilisation he labelled a 'waste and desert of time'.

Contrary to the emperor's hopes, the treaty did not cut off forever all causes of war. Instead, it stored up trouble for the future. And its implementation proved to be disappointingly difficult. Daoguang wanted the British tenure at the new ports to be limited, confined to a certain area during the trading season, as it had been at Canton for more than a century. Before the signing ceremony, he issued an impractical edict stating that in trading at the new ports, the British 'must not take possession and dwell for a long time' and that Fuzhou, the capital of the great tea province of Fujian, 'absolutely may not be conferred' as a place for trade, although another port might be substituted for it. Qiying, the emperor's representative, ignored the edict and signed the treaty in the form prepared by the British. It allowed the opening of Fuzhou and, according to the British interpretation, granted permanent residence at the port cities. The Chinese version referred to the residence of British subjects only 'at the harbours or anchorages of the five port cities' – not permanently but only temporarily for the duration of the trading season.

The difference of interpretation laid the seeds for another war, starting once again at Canton. Treaty or no treaty, the Cantonese did not want the British to live among them: 'It was enough to have a few hundred of them squeezed into the factory space' beside the river. The aversion of the Cantonese to letting the British into the city was understandable. During the war, Canton had been bombarded by the British, who on at least one occasion had gone on a spree of rape, treasure-hunting and grave-robbery. Cantonese mothers often quietened their children by 'threatening to throw them to the *fanqui*, the bogeyman foreigner' down by the river.

In 1847, the British decided to force the issue of entry to Canton by bringing a fleet of steamers up the river, taking Chinese forts and spiking their cannon along the way. In response to this show of force, Qiying, who was now the imperial commissioner in Canton, half-relented and agreed to allow entry to the British 'not immediately ... but in two years' time'. It was an odd reprieve and it made things doubly hard for Qiying's successor, Xu. In 1849, as the two-year period was coming to an end, Xu wrote to the emperor informing him that:

> The moment the entry question is raised, popular anger soars to the point of wanting to eat [the Britons'] flesh and sleep on their skin. Persuasion is useless. Nearly a hundred thousand militiamen have already gathered in Canton for its protection.

The government in Beijing knew that, despite Qiying's promise, if they buckled to British demands, there would be a popular uprising.

The intractable problem of foreign access to Canton was not repeated to quite the same extent in Shanghai. The Shanghai authorities, like their counterparts in Canton, did not want foreigners to reside inside the city itself and confined them to a rectangular parcel of marsh land crossed by numerous canals that stretched for about a kilometre along the riverfront to the north of the walled city. The foreigners accepted the restriction and the site became known as the British Settlement and later as the International Settlement. The area adjacent to the waterfront would become more famously known as the Bund. The real issue in Shanghai was that foreign ships were not permitted to go further along the Yangtze to tap into the trunk lines of inland trade traffic where most of China's markets lay. The British had long singled out Shanghai as the most promising of the treaty ports but its foreign trade growth was initially disappointing. The desire to have inland treaty ports along the Yangtze became a source of agitation.

In 1849, as the deadline for access to Canton drew nearer, the emperor issued another edict stating that 'A date should be set for a temporary entrance to the city'. Whether temporary or not, Xu knew how strongly the people of Canton felt about foreigners and believed that their loyalty had to be retained, even if it meant risking war ... or even if it meant issuing a false edict in the name of the emperor. He wrote to the emperor seeking authority to resist the British and warned that if they were allowed to enter, it would mean rebellion. Then and now, and in centuries past, Beijing worried about domestic unrest: 'Foreign threat is worrying ... but domestic rebellion is even more unnerving'. In the words of Henry Kissinger, China's 'greatest fear remains domestic upheaval at home'.

The looming British entrance to the city created an atmosphere of crisis in Canton. The militia was called up in readiness and inflammatory notices were posted around the city 'urging the people to pour boiling congee from their rooftops onto the heads of the British troops'. Xu could not continue to hold off the British. Nor could he wait for a response from the emperor to his despatch. On 1 April, he risked his neck by forging an imperial edict stating that 'The Central Empire cannot oppose the People in order to yield to the men from a distance'. When the false edict was handed to the new British representative, George Bonham, a successor to Pottinger, Bonham did not suspect duplicity. He also knew that the people of Canton stood ready to oppose any British intrusion. With nothing more than a mild warning to Xu that he would report this 'unsatisfactory evasion of the treaty' to his government, he withdrew his forces.

The Cantonese were euphoric and Beijing was jubilant. Xu had achieved what has been called – with considerable overstatement – 'the first great Chinese diplomatic coup of the nineteenth century'. At the end of the month, a genuine imperial edict arrived in Canton endorsing Xu's stance and reversing the emperor's earlier position. Daoguang stated unequivocally 'Do not let [the barbarians] enter the city ... If they enter the city, there will be harm but no profit'. To the enduring frustration of the British merchants and traders, the standoff continued for the next seven years until 1856.

Palmerston brooded resentfully over the rebuff, which caused him to utter a memorable piece of imperial condescension: 'These half-civilised Governments ... all require a Dressing [down] every eight or ten years to keep them in order'. For the British merchants, the continuing exasperation over access to Canton added to their disenchantment with the Treaty of Nanjing. While British imports of tea and silk continued to grow, exports to China did not. In British eyes, China continued to be inexplicably resistant to the attraction of its goods. One eminent Sheffield firm sent out a large consignment of knives and forks and 'declared themselves prepared to supply all China with cutlery', presumably hoping to replace chopsticks. Others sent pianos and worsteds that generated little interest.

The opium traders were dissatisfied as well, as the continuing illegality of opium left their property and person at risk. A popular groundswell developed that the hoped-for expansion in trade – for legitimate goods as well as opium – would only occur when British products could penetrate the vast inland regions 'particularly in the rich Yangtze valley and along the Grand Canal' and not be limited to the five treaty ports nominated in the Treaty of Nanjing.

The idea of inland trade expansion enthused Palmerston. In 1850 he instructed Bonham to approach Beijing officials to obtain treaty revisions that would give British subjects free access to the interior for trade – as if it were that simple. When Bonham had no success, Palmerston thundered menacingly 'I clearly see that the Time is fast coming when we shall be obliged to strike another Blow in China'. The treaty did not allow for the revision of any of its terms but Palmerston soldiered on as if it did not matter. In 1854 he tried again, issuing instructions to Bonham's successor, Sir John Bowring, to seek a formal revision of the treaty's terms.

Bowring concluded that he could not claim a legal right to revise the Nanjing treaty but went ahead anyway and met officials from Beijing because, in his words, 'I *have* an end and an object, *to open China*' – by force if necessary. The new emperor Xianfeng (r. 1850–1861), Daoguang's 23-year-old son, bluntly rejected Bowring's request for revision. He would make no concessions. Xianfeng 'had grown up fervently loathing Westerners' and had been selected by his father in the hope that he would be more able to resist the West. One of his first acts as emperor was to condemn Qiying for being too conciliatory and 'always caving in to foreigners at the cost of the country'. Xianfeng would prove to be a thorn in the Western side.

In early 1855, after many years as foreign secretary, Palmerston became prime minister and a new phase in international relations began. The interests of Britain, France and the United States coalesced on an issue that would occupy the West's attention for the next half century and beyond: the expansion of trading opportunities in China. Palmerston was 'tired, septuagenarian and gout-ridden' but more belligerent than ever. President Pierce of the United States shared Palmerston's ambitions and instructed his newly appointed commissioner to China – a physician and missionary named Peter Parker – to obtain 'unlimited extension of our trade, wherever within the dominions of China commerce may be found'.

Palmerston continued to fulminate about the Chinese. He called them 'most strikingly arrogant' for their refusal to 'recognise any obligation to concur in a revision of the [British] treaty'. In September 1856, Palmerston authorised his ambassador in Paris to propose to the French a joint naval expedition to announce to the Chinese emperor that Britain and France wanted their treaties revised – so that 'the vast resources of that Empire [be] opened up to the industrial enterprise of foreign nations'. The despatch to the ambassador added menacingly that the emperor should be advised that he 'better consult the interests of his Empire by deferring to the wishes of the Treaty-Powers'.

At that stage, there was no plausible pretext for war, as much as Palmerston wanted one. A few weeks later, a pretext conveniently came along, or so the British contended. It began with a precocious junior British consul named Harry Parkes who had come to China as a thirteen-year-old boy to serve the interests of the empire and 'swaggered about ... defending British dignity ... all the while denouncing the natives ... as a most obstreperous race'. By 1856, his experience had given him an excellent knowledge of the Chinese language but minimal sympathy for the Chinese themselves. In London, on a trip home earlier that year, Palmerston flattered him with a private interview in which, it seems, he 'encouraged [Parkes] to find a pretext on which to force the question' of entry to Canton and to be 'on the lookout for a *casus belli*'. Parkes was more than ready for some excitement, even if he had to manufacture it.

The opportunity arrived on 8 October when the Chinese governor in Canton, Ye, ordered the arrest of a group of smugglers and the seizure of the cargo on a ship called the *Arrow*. The ship was Chinese-built, Chinese-owned and Chinese-crewed but she was nominally captained by a 21-year-old British ne'er-do-well from Belfast named Kennedy. The only function of a British 'captain of convenience' was that of a scarecrow – to help stave off Chinese maritime police. Such men were usually 'some loose fish, some stray person, or runaway apprentice, or idle young seaman [who] was not expected to take part in the working of the ship' and whose sole value was in being British. Such ships were registered – 'by means of some mystification' – with the British authorities in Hong Kong entitling them to fly a British ensign.

At the time of the arrest, the captain was not on board, the ship's registration had expired and she was almost certainly not flying a British ensign. The *Arrow* was not entitled to British protection but when Parkes arrived at the dock in Canton, he affected outrage and came to blows with the Chinese officers who were trying to do their duty. During the fray, Parkes was struck and made loud protests about the 'insult' – either to him or the British flag or both. His cheek and pride still stinging, the young consul then wrote to Ye, warning him that 'An insult so publicly committed must be equally publicly atoned'.

Bowring fully supported Parkes and through October the two men 'deliberately, cynically and illegally war-mongered to vent their dissatisfactions with China and the post-1842 status quo'. Bowring wrote privately to Parkes enquiring 'Cannot we use the opportunity and carry the City [of Canton] question?' He was so consumed with the issue that an uncomprehending House of Lords later dismissed him as a 'monomaniac'. The most senior judge, Lord Lyndhurst, the Lord Chancellor, doubted Bowring's sanity and Lord Derby said, 'I believe he dreams of the entrance into Canton ... [and] thinks of it the first thing in the morning [and] the last thing at night'.

What followed was a tragicomedy. Unknown to London, about a week after the *Arrow* incident, Parkes and Bowring unleashed another undeclared war on China and persuaded the British naval commander, Admiral Seymour, to open hostilities. Bowring rejoiced: 'We are *so* strong and *so* right'. For his part, Seymour, who had lost an eye to the Russians in Crimea, knew only one way to conduct himself. In late October 1856, he began a months-long bombardment, setting fire to Canton, destroying thousands of houses and killing many of its people. The bombardment and the extensive fires turned stretches of the city into 'one mass of smoke'. Parkes and Bowring kept from the admiral their knowledge that the *Arrow*'s registration had expired and that she had almost certainly not been entitled to British protection.

When news of the bombardment of Canton reached London in December, there was outrage and vigorous condemnation in some quarters. But before any debate in parliament, Palmerston's cabinet, fresh from its war to contain Russia on the Crimean Peninsula, decided that it would also wage war on China. There was as much British popular and political antagonism towards Russia and China then as there is now. The commander's formal instructions were to coerce China into revising the Nanjing treaty – to destroy all Chinese forts up to Canton and blockade the Yangtze and Peiho rivers, 'thus cutting off all access by water to the capital and, thereby, supplies from the southern provinces'. Later in the House of Lords, Lord Grey mourned:

> Almost for the first time in our history, we were engaged in a war which had not been formally made known to their Lordships by a Message from the Crown, and which Parliament had not been called upon to consider ...

Actually, the last time had probably been the First Opium War. The secret exercise of the war power by government without public, parliamentary or congressional scrutiny was an issue then, as much as it is in some countries today. A censure motion was passed, parliament was dissolved in March and a general election known as 'the Chinese election' was scheduled for April. During the election, Palmerston was bolstered by a frenzy of anti-Chinese jingoism, especially from the mercantile communities of Manchester, Liverpool, Bristol and the City of London, as well as the popular press. The 'uproar of the merchant princes' resulted in boardroom meetings, public gatherings, mass petitions and deputations to Palmerston. British xenophobia was in full cry. Opponents of Palmerston's war against China were labelled 'un-English' and the opposition was called the 'Chinese coalition'. Gladstone was decried as 'seraphic'. Disraeli was condemned. The Canton governor Ye was accused of being an insolent barbarian. Some enthusiasts felt that 'the whole civilised world ought to combine ... to teach these wretches the common principles of humanity'.

On the hustings, Palmerston slandered the Chinese wherever he could. His rhetorical strategy was simple: 'to repeat loudly that violence against China was honourable and inevitable until, in the popular imagination, it became so'. When the election was held, the result overwhelmingly endorsed Palmerston and 'returned the warmongers on a platform of jingoistic Sinophobia'. Palmerston was given a free hand to fight a second China war as he wished. It was already underway anyway. Before the election, he had appointed Lord Elgin to be the leader of the British expedition to China. Elgin's name was well known. His father was notorious for having removed the priceless Parthenon Marbles from Athens and shipped them to Britain.

The French joined the war as a British ally, seeking unlimited access to the interior for their missionaries. In December 1857, an Anglo-French force under Elgin's command bombarded Canton into submission once again, with almost no reply from the town. Elgin wrote privately that the date of the bombardment was the Massacre of the Innocents in the Christian calendar. He confided that 'I never felt so ashamed of myself in my life ... I feel that I am earning for myself a place in the Litany, after plague, pestilence and famine'. The bombardment cowed the Cantonese people – 'shells and rockets from thirty-two warships battered the city walls without a break for twenty-seven hours'. On the next day, British redcoats and French bluejackets stormed into the city and occupied all the government buildings.

The irrepressible Parkes was at the forefront, taking personal pleasure in hunting down his old enemy Ye through the narrow streets of the walled city. It was not altogether unlike the hunts for Saddam Hussein in Baghdad and Osama bin Laden in Abbottabad. 'Ye was my game', Parkes exulted. He eventually 'sniffed out' the governor who was arrested as he tried to get over the rear wall of his residence. In breach of diplomatic protocol, Ye was treated as a prisoner of war and callously shipped off to exile in India, to a place outside Calcutta where he died of 'sickness and ennui a year later'. Parkes was left 'warlord governor' of Canton, which subsided into anarchy.

The next target was Beijing. In May 1858, the Anglo-French fleet sailed north to the entrance to Beijing at the Peiho River. The fleet had little trouble taking the forts known as the Taku Forts that guarded the mouth of the river – and protected the approach to Beijing - before proceeding 60 kilometres upriver to occupy Tianjin. At this point, the emperor Xianfeng reluctantly accepted the inevitability of another humiliating defeat and finally came to terms. The one-sided negotiations 'were little more than an exercise in armed extortion'. Elgin described his diplomatic method as 'fighting and bullying and getting the poor commissioners to concede one point after another'. To his wife he confessed

> I have seen more to disgust me with my fellow countrymen than I saw during the whole course of my previous life ... in our relations with the Chinese we have acted scandalously ... anyone could have obtained the Treaty of Tianjin.

The French and the British were the sole warring parties against China but the Russians and Americans came along to Tianjin to share the spoils of war. In June 1858 four separate Treaties of Tianjin were signed with the British, Russians, French and Americans. They were in similar terms, focussed as much on the spread of Christianity as on the expansion of trade. Christianity in the form of the Russian Orthodox, Protestant and Catholic religions was now allowed to be practised and missionaries were permitted to travel throughout China. Ten new ports, including four along the Yangtze upriver from Shanghai, were opened and limits were placed on Chinese customs duties. Permanent Western diplomatic establishments were allowed in Beijing for the first time. To satisfy Western pride, the term 'barbarian' was forbidden when referring to the treaty powers or their officials. And more onerous financial penalties were imposed on the Qing empire: two million *taels* of silver to France and four million for Britain, comprising two million for military expenses and two million as compensation to British merchants. A *tael* was then worth more than a Spanish silver dollar.

CHAPTER 21

PLUNDER & PILLAGE

1860

This is what civilisation has done to barbarism.

WORSE WAS TO COME in 1860. Emperor Xianfeng hated the Tianjin treaties that had been forced on him. The French envoy, Baron Gros, depicted the young emperor, still only 26 years old, as having had no effective choice with a 'pistol at the throat'. For months Xianfeng ruminated and agonised over Western bullying. In desperation, he proposed that the treaties be annulled in return for waiving all import duties, but there was no agreement. Formal ratification of the Tianjin treaties was due to take place in Beijing in June 1859, a year after they were signed, and Xianfeng was determined to do what he could to frustrate Western implementation. He devoted much of his energies during the intervening twelve months to improving Beijing's defences and strengthening the Taku forts at the entrance to the Peiho River.

While Xianfeng plotted and schemed, Elgin returned to England and looked forward to a more tranquil existence. He accepted the gratifyingly less arduous posts of Postmaster-General and Rector of Glasgow University and was given the Freedom of the City of London. In China, where his brother, Frederick Bruce, was left behind to be the British 'minister' (or ambassador), things began to unravel. Bruce, who looked uncannily like the elderly, bearded Charles Darwin, insisted on travelling up the Peiho River to Beijing for the ratification of the British treaty accompanied by a large military force. Xianfeng would not countenance such hubris and required that the British representative travel with an entourage of 'no more than 10 men, no arms ... no sedan chairs or processions ... and that he leave Beijing the moment the ratification is done'.

The American minister John Ward showed more concern for the emperor's sensitivities and made the journey with an escort of only 20 men. He was received, it is said, with 'high consideration and respect, with unceasing attention and courtesy'. Bruce not only refused to compromise but decided in the inimitable British way of the times to blast his way through, opening fire on the Taku forts. The resulting engagement was a disastrous surprise and the attempt to obtain ratification failed. The British mission never got past the recently strengthened forts. The Chinese fired back with focussed accuracy, leaving 519 British soldiers and sailors dead, another 456 wounded and six British gunboats sunk or disabled. The infantry landing parties suffered enormous carnage. The shock of the repulse caused some of the British combatants to doubt whether the enemy was truly Chinese. A young Jacky Fisher, a future first Lord of the Admiralty, wrote home in disbelief 'they must have been Russians; no Chinaman ever fought like those fellows did'.

The emperor was so elated by the reversal of fortune that he unwisely decided to repudiate the treaties. In London, *The Times* screamed 'Our loss is awful' and 'We must strike a signal blow and amply revenge our slaughtered countrymen'. Palmerston needed no persuading. He turned once again to Lord Elgin, who despite his misgivings, agreed to return to China in April 1860 with a combined Anglo-French force. His mission was to complete the job and obtain ratification of the Tianjin treaties. Elgin had a Victorian sense of duty but he was also a reluctant imperialist. He was a deeply sensitive, contradictory man who had not relished his first China posting and regarded the *Arrow* incident as a shameful pretext for starting the Second

Opium War. In his words, it was 'wretched ... embarrassing ... a scandal ...[and was] so considered by all except the few who are personally compromised'.

En route to China, Elgin read Darwin's recently published masterpiece, *On the Origin of Species*, and pondered:

> Can I do anything to prevent England from calling down on herself God's curse for brutalities committed on another feeble Oriental race? Or are all my exertions to result only in the extension of the area over which Englishmen are to exhibit how hollow and superficial are both their civilisation and their Christianity.

The Anglo-French force was considerably stronger than that of two years earlier. It now consisted of 13,000 British and 7000 French troops, and this time they knew what to expect. The opening engagement in August 1860 resulted in heavy casualties on both sides. The alpha male Parkes wrote home 'I am very cheerful ... We lost 201 men in killed or wounded ... The enemy must have lost 1,200 or probably 1,500'. The British artillery bombardment was merciless but the Chinese defended so stoutly that one participant recommended recruiting them for 'an experimental Anglo-Chinese corps' in India. The Taku forts were eventually stormed and British honour was restored. The expedition's chaplain, horrified by the maimed and dead Chinese bodies, expressed gratitude that the new, lethal Armstrong artillery guns 'were in our hands – ours, who would use them more to preserve the peace of the world than ever to make an aggressive or unjust war'. It was a display of moral certainty reminiscent of that which prevailed after the testing of the atomic bomb in the New Mexico desert in 1945 or the more recent suggestion of an American Air Force general that, of all nations, the United States can be trusted with AI because it is 'a Judaeo-Christian society'.

The reluctant aggressor Elgin now held back. Rather than advance on Beijing, he sought to negotiate with the Qing leadership. Elgin's hesitancy failed to impress Parkes, whose youthful judgement was that he was not a great man. Elgin for his part, would soon become so seriously desensitised, enraged and possibly destabilised that he would completely change course and commit what some in modern China consider to be the flagship act of Western aggression. The trigger was the capture, interrogation and torture of the British negotiating party, including Harry Parkes and *The Times* journalist Thomas Bowlby. The Chinese decision to capture the negotiating party was influenced by the war faction among the emperor's inner circle who were opposed to the peace process. It has been said – although possibly with questionable authority – that in Chinese warfare, to harm the enemy's messenger was 'the ultimate way of sending the message: we will fight you to the death'. Most of the men were thrown into the Ministry of Punishments prison in Beijing where their captors 'tied their feet and hands together behind their backs as tightly as possible, afterwards pouring water on the chords to increase the tension'.

The capture of the negotiating party made Elgin decide to push on. As the Anglo-French force approached Beijing in late September, the soldiers freely engaged in 'the killing of prisoners, reprisals against the civilian population and widespread looting'. On one occasion, a funeral procession was attacked, the coffin thrown into a ditch and the mules confiscated. The degeneration of discipline within the British ranks was so severe that Elgin and his senior general, Hope Grant, had 'their own personal wine stock (a mere fifteen hundred bottles) stolen by soldiers of the 60th Regiment'. The circumstances recalled the Duke of Wellington's harsh rebuke, when angered by the looting of his soldiers at Vitoria in Spain during the Peninsular War, that they were 'the scum of the earth' who enlist for drink.

By 21 September, the Anglo-French armies were close to Beijing but Xianfeng was in residence at the Old Summer Palace about 20 kilometres north-west of the Forbidden City. When news arrived of the approaching French and British troops, the court packed up in panic and Xianfeng fled north across the Great Wall to the imperial country retreat at Chengde – where Qianlong had once entertained Lord Macartney. The Empress Consort Zhen and Xianfeng's concubine Cixi – the mother of his son – accompanied him. Xianfeng never returned from Chengde. He was determined to avoid contact with the invading powers and chose to spend the grim winter in the northern wilderness, despite his delicate constitution. He fell ill, coughed blood and was confined to bed. In his final days, Xianfeng indulged his passions for opera and music, which were performed for him almost every day including for several hours on the last days of his life. Eleven months after arriving at the retreat, Xianfeng died, but not before announcing that he had chosen Cixi's five-year-old son to be the next emperor.

The Old Summer Palace was known in Chinese as *Yuanmingyuan*: the garden of Perfect Brightness. It was a testament to China's glorious eighteenth century under the Three Emperors. Its construction began under the emperor Kangxi in 1709 and was greatly enlarged by his son Yongzhen and his grandson Qianlong, whose name meant 'Heavenly Greatness'. The palace and gardens were a perfect paradise, built at colossal expense with exquisite care, using the finest materials and artisans. Inside the palace buildings was an unimaginable collection of masterpieces of art. In Victor Hugo's words 'All the treasures of our cathedrals could not equal this formidable museum of the Orient'. Hugo never visited China nor saw the Old Summer Palace, but he did have a Chinese lounge in his Paris apartment. His description was nonetheless poetic:

> There was, in a corner of the world, a wonder of the world, this wonder was called the Summer Palace … People spoke of the Parthenon in Greece, the Pyramids in Egypt, the Coliseum in Rome, Notre Dame in Paris, the Summer Palace in the Orient. If people did not see it they imagined it. It was a kind of tremendous unknown masterpiece, glimpsed from the distance

in a kind of twilight, like a silhouette of the civilisation of Asia on the horizon of the civilisation of Europe.

The palace's 860 acres 'extended for six or seven miles in every direction' – an area five times the size of the Forbidden City that included hundreds of buildings, public audience halls, private apartments, studios, libraries, temples, theatres and pavilions. It was the most luxurious and important imperial establishment in China. There was even a series of European-style palaces, known as the 'Western mansions', planned and designed by French Jesuits at the court of Qianlong. These buildings were built largely of stone and set in their own carefully crafted landscape settings. In one of the palaces, built in the style of Louis XV, there were rooms lined with Gobelins tapestries, the arms of France and 'portraits of the beauties of the court of France'.

On 6 October, a few weeks after Xianfeng and his court fled the Old Summer Palace, the first European forces arrived at the gates. They expected to find the emperor or his senior government officials there but instead they encountered only a small sentry detachment and a few eunuchs who offered little resistance. Over the next two days, the French and British engaged in an orgy of desecration. The men ran around in a temporary delirium of looting and destruction. They seemed to be gripped by a frenzied madness. The second day of looting, 8 October, when the British threw themselves into the task, was according to one British general, 'a memorable day in the history of plunder and destruction'. 'Imagine' said another British officer, 'Christie's, Hunt and Roskell's, Howell and James's, half a dozen watch and clockmakers, two or three upholsterers, and that fine fan-shop in Regent Street, all being under the same roof'. The British chaplain, M'Ghee, who strolled around gazing in contemplation, wrote 'If you can imagine fairies to be the size of ordinary mortals, this then was fairyland. Never have I beheld a scene which realised one's ideas of an enchanted land before'. A man must be, he thought, 'a poet, a painter, an historian, a virtuoso ... to give you even an idea of it'.

An eyewitness recorded that 'Officers and men ... seized with a temporary insanity ... were absorbed in one pursuit, which was plunder, plunder'. In some rooms, silks had been pulled out of boxes and thrown on the floor so that 'you would sink above your knee [in silk] as you entered the room'. The rolls of silk – 'satin or silk, plain or figured, white, blue, yellow (the imperial colour), purple, stone or fawn' – attracted much attention from the sepoys who 'carried them off in cartloads'. The French also coveted the silks. Their camp outside the palace gate was 'blazing with silk of every hue, and the richest embroidery'. The English were equally captivated. The bizarre scenes included 'army cross-dressers dancing around in the gorgeous embroidered gowns of the emperor's concubines'.

Destruction was as common as plunder. 'Everything that could not be moved was being smashed, and property that the Chinese would have ransomed for a million was being carried away or destroyed'. Elgin went to see for himself and described a scene of desolation among rooms once filled with exquisite curios, handsome clocks, bronzes, porcelain, gold and silver, pearls and other precious stones, jade ornaments, furs, carpets, enamels, lacquered screens, books and engravings:

> There was not a room I saw in which half the things had not been taken away or broken in pieces ... Plundering and devastating a place like this is bad enough, but what is much worse is the waste and breakage.

Demonstrating that private capacity for liberal regret that would belie his public actions ten days later, Elgin noted 'War is a hateful business. The more one sees of it, the more one detests it'.

As the plunder and pillage continued into its second day, the emperor's brother, Prince Gong, who had been left in charge in Beijing, released Harry Parkes and six other members of the captured negotiating party. The released men were in fair condition but over the next week, the remaining living captives were returned – only barely alive – and were followed by the dead. The British chaplain wrote that

> I never saw a more pitiable sight than the return of the *sowars* [Indian cavalry soldiers] ... Hardly able to walk, they dragged their legs along and held their hands before their breasts in a posture denoting great suffering ... with running sores at the wrists ... some were shrivelled like a bird's claw and appeared [to] be dead and withered.

After days of lacerating agony, 21 men, including Bowlby from *The Times*, had died. It was an atrocious wrong, which galvanised the enigmatic Elgin. The reluctant warrior became God's avenging angel. He decided on an exemplary punishment

> as expiation of the foul crime of which the Chinese government have been guilty ... to mark by a solemn act of retribution the horror and indignation with which we were inspired.

The funeral service for the dead men was held on 17 October. It was a day when 'the heavens were black, and bitter was the cold north wind, which cut into the very marrow of our bones'. On the day after the funeral, Elgin issued instructions to destroy the Old Summer Palace ... forever. It became a benchmark of European atrocity. Elgin's chosen method of annihilation was fire. The French condemned the destruction of the palace and refused to cooperate. They considered Elgin's decision to be 'a Goth-like act of barbarism'. On 18 October, troops of the British First Division began to systematically torch and incinerate every building. It was hard work stretching over two days. When the order was given, a wreath of smoke began curling upwards and

> in a few minutes other wreaths of smoke arose from half-a-hundred different places ... Soon the wreath becomes a volume, a great black mass, outburst a hundred flames, the

> smoke obscures the sun, and temple, palace, buildings and all, hallowed by age … with all their contents, monuments of imperial taste and luxury.

When the destruction was over, the chaplain M'Ghee reflected in sadness that

> No one will ever again gaze upon those buildings which have been doubtless the administration of the ages, records of bygone skill and taste, of which the world contains not the like. You have seen them once and forever, they are dead and gone, man cannot reproduce them.

In moral equivalence, the destruction rivalled the Taliban's detonation of the giant Buddha statues in the Bamiyan Valley in Afghanistan in 2001. But with that indomitable moral certainty that characterised Englishmen of the period, M'Ghee justified the destruction with the rider that 'It was a sacrifice of all that was most ancient and most beautiful … offered to *the manes of the true, the honest, and the valiant*' (emphasis added).

Victor Hugo wrote afterwards in deep sorrow from Paris that:

> One day two bandits entered the Summer Palace. One plundered, the other burned … The devastation of the Summer Palace was accomplished by the two actors acting jointly. Mixed up in all this is the name Elgin, which inevitably calls to mind the Parthenon. What was done to the Parthenon, was done to the Summer Palace, more thoroughly and better, so that nothing of it should be left … One of the two victors filled his pockets; when the other saw this he filled his coffers. And back they came to Europe, arm in arm, laughing away. Such is the story of two bandits.

The imperial treasures of China passed to unappreciative amateurs, 'dispersed and undocumented', slipping with humiliating carelessness through the hands of the soldiers and officers into private and public collections across Europe, never to be returned. The soldiers converted emblems of imperial culture into military souvenirs and commodities. Some items appeared in London exhibitions and some briefly resurfaced in auction catalogues that sought extra lustre by promoting their provenance as being 'loot' from the Old Summer Palace. Paintings and calligraphy, not perceived as valuable by the soldiers, were neglected and later consumed by the destructive British firestorm. Of the treasures that were removed, on some estimates, 'well over a million objects emanating from the Summer Palace adorn some 2,000 museums and numerous private collections throughout the world'. Notable exceptions include Yves St Laurent's bronze fountainheads in the shape of Chinese zodiac animals, the rat and the rabbit, which were pillaged from the water clock fountain designed for the emperor by the Jesuit Michel Benoist. After much controversy, the bronze fountainheads were returned to the National Museum of China in 2013.

As the soldiers pilfered, Lord Elgin and French General Montauban tried to identify the greatest objects for their respective sovereigns. Those earmarked for Queen Victoria were absorbed into royal collections where they remained sequestered. Those for Napoleon III were put on temporary public display in the Tuileries Palace and later dispersed to the Artillery Museum or mixed with other Asian items at Empress Eugenie's Chinese Museum at Fontainebleau, to which access was limited. Victoria received trifles as well as treasures, including a female Pekingese dog that lived with her until its death more than a decade later. She blithely named it 'Looty'. Montauban had three jade necklaces made into a rosary, which he presented to Eugenie after having it blessed by the newly restored Bishop of Beijing.

There was no more fight left in the Qing. A few days after the Hadean fire, Elgin was carried in a sedan chair borne 'by sixteen Chinamen dressed in royal crimson liveries and accompanied by an army band playing God Save the Queen'. The escort 'consisted of six hundred men, besides one hundred officers'. The emperor's younger half-brother, Prince Gong, pale as death and frozen with fear, capitulated to all demands and agreed to the 500,000 *tael* ransom demanded by the British and French. On 24 October 1860 the Treaties of Tianjin were finally ratified. To rub salt into the wound, three additional treaties with Britain, France and Russia were imposed on Beijing. They were known collectively as the Convention of Beijing. The Convention quadrupled the indemnities payable to the British and French governments – from two million to eight million *taels* each – and granted everything else for which European merchants, politicians and missionaries had been agitating since the end of the First Opium War. Kowloon, a peninsula opposite Hong Kong Island, was ceded to Britain in perpetuity. Russia acquired over one and a half million square kilometres of territory in Manchuria, including a long strip of Pacific coastline that included the Vladivostok region. And Christian missionaries were given free rein to evangelise throughout the land.

As Elgin's private secretary, Henry Loch, travelled back to England with the ratified British treaty and a clutch of Pekingese dogs, he was preceded and overtaken by dispatches from flag-waving journalists that worked the country into a 'frenzy of anti-Chinese patriotism'. Most thought that the year 1860 marked the commencement of a glorious new era – 'not only in the history of the Empire of China, but of the world, by the introduction of four hundred millions of the human race into the family of civilised nations'. It was easy to forget the pretext on which the war had been provoked.

Watching the destruction of the Old Summer Palace was Garnet Wolseley, a young officer who later became a field marshal and commander-chief of the British Army. In his memoir 43 years after the China campaign, he reflected with what may or may not be prescience that:

There is no nation, numerically as great as China … To me they are the most remarkable race on earth and I have always thought and still believe them to be the great coming rulers of the world. They only want a Chinese Peter the Great or Napoleon to make them so … and in my idle speculation upon this world's future, I have long selected them as the combatants on one side at the great battle of Armageddon, the people of the United States of America being their opponents.

PART 7

Neo-Colonialism

CHAPTER 22

AMERICA & JESUS

1784–1860

A backward people who could use a stiff dose of American Puritanism.

IN SOME WAYS, THE Americans were 'the war's greatest beneficiaries' for they were able to share most of the advantages of Britain's forced opening of China's ports 'without any of the violence or the lasting stain on their national character'. The American presence in China had always been focussed on commerce more than conflict. Merchants from the nascent United States of America began arriving in Canton almost as soon as the ink had dried on the Treaty of Paris (1783) that formally ended the revolutionary war. The first American ship to enter the China trade was the *Empress of China*, whose historic voyage in 1784–1785 was enthusiastically supported by future presidents James Madison and Thomas Jefferson and backed by Robert Morris, the financier of the American Revolution. The ship sailed symbolically from New York Harbour on the birthday of George Washington and the senior agent on board was Samuel Shaw, a close friend of Washington. Supporters loftily declared that the voyage was guided by 'the hands of Providence, who have undertaken to extend the commerce of the United States to that distant, and to us unexplored, country'.

The sailing route of the *Empress of China* went by the Cape of Good Hope and halfway across the Indian Ocean to Amsterdam Island, then north by Java Head and the Sunda Strait to the South China Sea. The ship carried Spanish silver and a type of ginseng that grew wild on the banks of the Hudson River and returned with as much as 800 chests of tea and 64 tons of porcelain. Washington acquired an elaborate porcelain dinner service from the ship's cargo for his country estate at Mount Vernon. When the ship returned to New York, she was greeted by cheering crowds who lined the quayside, excited by the prospect of an immense new market for American trade. At the time, China's population was about 60 times that of the United States.

Over the next decades, as the French revolutionary wars took hold in Europe, French merchants abandoned Canton and Americans enthusiastically filled the gap, eventually taking over the French factory on the waterfront and raising the Stars and Stripes where the Tricolour once flew. In the words of one merchant, 'We raise the fortunes of the United States on the wreckage of France'. American commerce at Canton grew so rapidly that British merchants began to resent their competition, although it never amounted to anywhere near as much as the British trade. One British free trade advocate pointed to how well the Americans were faring without the obstacle of the East India Company's monopoly and complained that the American intercourse was 'yearly increasing at our expense'.

The intercourse naturally included opium. By 1830, American opium traders led by the firm of Russell & Co had secured a substantial foothold in the China opium trade. Russell & Co's business, like that of Jardine & Matheson and many others in Canton, had two sides: 'the above ground trade in tea, silk, cotton ... that took place openly in Canton, and the underground trade in opium that took place at Lintin Island'. The firm operated from the American factory, five doors along from Jardine & Matheson, and eventually handled 'more than a fifth of the Indian opium arriving at Canton'. It represented the greatest challenge to the dominance of British traders like Jardine and Matheson.

Russell & Co was a unique institution. Most of its partners were part of a 'gifted, prolific and powerful kinship group in eastern Massachusetts' that represented a roll-call of what were some of the most illustrious and wealthy East coast families – the Perkins, Forbes, Cushing, Russell, Low, Cabot and the Delano families. Warren Delano was the grandfather of Franklin Delano Roosevelt. A young Robert Forbes, a contemporary of Warren Delano, defended his participation in the opium trade with Russell & Co by noting that:

> some of America's best families were involved, those to whom I have always been accustomed to look up as exponents of all that was honorable in trade – the Perkins, the Peabodys, the Russells and the Lows.

These men accumulated truly fabulous fortunes from the China trade, well before the Carnegies, Vanderbilts and Rockefellers of the gilded age. Their opium profits shaped the city of Boston and helped finance the boom in railways. The Perkins family 'built Boston's Athenaeum, the Massachusetts General Hospital and the Perkins Institution for the Blind'. Opium profits helped finance railways such as

> the Boston and Lowell (Perkins), the Michigan Central (Forbes), the Chicago, Burlington and Quincy (Forbes), and the Chesapeake and Ohio (Low).

The founder of Russell & Co, Samuel Russell, who began acquiring opium in Türkiye and smuggling it to China and ran America's biggest smuggling operation, built one of the finest Greek Revival mansions in the north-eastern United States at his home in Connecticut. Warren Delano purchased a sumptuous townhouse in Lafayette Square in New York City near John Jacob Astor. And Robert Forbes built a Greek Revival mansion for his mother at Milton, Massachusetts. Russell encouraged ambitious young men to join the firm to seek their fortune and score what the China traders called a 'competence' – 'a profit of $100,000 before they were thirty years old'. It was enough at that time to ensure a life of financial independence, social leadership and philanthropic beneficence.

Following closely behind the American traders in Canton were the Protestant missionaries. They came to China as part of a sweeping revitalisation of religious piety known as the Second Great Awakening, which was especially virulent in the United States. For these believers, the Bible was the indispensable passport to Jesus. They were convinced that if the Christian Gospel could be translated and rendered into Chinese, then China would eventually become a Christian country. They believed that books could travel where preachers could not and that 'all a person needed was a book of scripture, in a language he or she could read, and that would be enough to become a practising Christian'. It was a formula that met with limited success but was something of a Protestant obsession. The Englishman John Roberts, the East India Company's taipan earlier in the century, hoped that one day he could give a copy of the Bible in Chinese to his Confucian counterparts and gloat, as he put it, that 'This volume *we* deem the best of books'.

Elijah Bridgman, the first American Protestant missionary in China, was deeply troubled by the opium trade on which his countrymen had been making themselves rich for years and worked tirelessly to expose the harm to the Chinese. He publicly attacked the opium problem and published article after article on the subject. Bridgman hoped to turn Western or at least American opinion against the opium trade. He believed that a well-informed public would readily recognise the evils of the opium trade and would wish to see it halted. He even attended Commissioner Lin's historic destruction of the confiscated opium at the mouth of the Pearl River. Partly because of Bridgman's efforts in publicising the harm caused by opium, the American public regarded the British opium trade as reprehensible, while being generally unaware of their own opium barons. And even if they were sometimes aware, American popular opposition to the opium trade often 'conveniently left out of the picture the unsavoury and indefensible role of their fellow citizens'.

The opium traders and the missionaries held contrasting moral values but they were united by a common goal. Both had a grand vision of opening China. The missionaries even adopted the language of a military campaign in the pursuit of God's will – conquest, attack, victory. When a new American missionary was sent out in 1834, the *Boston Recorder* wrote that his objective was to 'penetrate' the Chinese empire; that he would work in eastern China while another missionary 'attacks the centre'; and that they would meet in the middle 'as conquerors of this vast kingdom'. Part of the military campaign involved the dissemination of cultural propaganda through a Society for the Diffusion of Useful Knowledge whose mission statement proclaimed that its object was 'to engage in warfare'. Elijah Bridgman was one of the society's secretaries and the British drug traders James Matheson and William Jardine were its first and second presidents. In their enthusiasm and hubris, the founders pronounced that 'we are sure that the victors and the vanquished will meet only to exult and rejoice together'.

In the United States, preachers regaled their followers from church pulpits with shocking tales of pagan and idolatrous practices; of a 'backward people who could use a stiff dose of American Puritanism'. The hyperbole reflected familiar American moral extremism, old and modern. Missionaries to China were instructed that 'The manifold needs of China ... will be met permanently, completely, only by Christian civilisation'. Admiral Alfred Mahan, America's greatest naval strategist of the nineteenth century, warned that China's future power might equal her geographic size, 'so Americans should expose the Middle Kingdom to Christian values ... to absorb the ideals which in ourselves are the results of centuries of Christian increment'.

It seems counter-intuitive but many missionaries supported the Opium Wars. Henrietta Shuck, the first American female missionary to China, was positively delighted when the first war was imminent:

> how these difficulties do rejoice my heart; because I think the English government may be enraged, and God in his power break down the barriers which prevent the gospel of Christ from entering China.

The English Methodist Reverend Piercy, shedding crocodile tears, wrote that:

> We, as missionaries, weep over the miseries let loose on these [Chinese] people; but we cannot shut our eyes to the fact that nothing but the strong arm of foreign power can soon open the field for the entrance of the Gospel.

A belief took hold that only Christ could save China from opium but only war could open China to Christ. To the missionaries 'it appeared more and more obvious that four hundred million Chinese would never attain the Christian life save by the road that led through opium and war'.

The missionaries believed that the opening of China for free trade was the will of God – the same right by which the 'aborigines of North America and New Holland [Australia] were driven from their indisputable homes by the governments of the United States and Great Britain' – namely the right that 'barbarism must vanish before civilisation, ignorance succumb to knowledge'. It was a far cry from the approach of the Jesuit missionaries in earlier centuries, but their presence and influence in China had dwindled to nothing and the Protestant missionaries now represented the dominant Christian presence in China. They considered themselves to be 'representatives of Christendom, in the providence of God brought face to face with China, the representative of paganism'. It was good versus evil again.

The mantra was not entirely universal. A French missionary who travelled extensively through China between the First and Second Opium wars wrote of the Chinese that:

> They are not Christians but have hospitals for orphans ... for the old and the sick ... welfare offices where food is provided for the destitute and medicines for the sick ... along the roads they provide shelters for the free use of travellers. *How dare one say that a nation that displays such enlightenment, generosity and wisdom is inferior in any way to we Europeans?*' (emphasis added)

Similar criticisms have long been made. One former China resident and correspondent for the *New York Tribune* in the early twentieth century found the Christian missionary approach in China so deeply unsettling that he wrote:

> There was fundamentally something unhealthy and incongruous in the whole missionary idea ... to go out to a race of high culture and long tradition, with philosophical, ethical and religious systems antedating Christianity, and to go avowedly to save its people from damnation as dwellers in heathen darkness – in that there was something not only spiritually limited but also grotesque.

The religious zeal of the American missionaries tended to exceed that of the British. And as for the opium traders, the British exhibited almost no virtue while the Americans were inclined towards a false virtue. As the First Opium War loomed in 1839, some American opium traders professed to distance themselves from the British-dominated trade. In January of that year, at the farewell dinner for William Jardine in the chandeliered dining hall of the British factory, when Jardine railed against everyone else and refused to accept responsibility for the opium trade, Robert Forbes and Warren Delano were enthusiastic table-thumping, spoon-banging participants. But soon afterwards Forbes told his wife that the opium trade had devolved into a renegade commerce 'carried on in spite of law and reason by a parcel of reckless individuals' and 'that we cannot compromise ourselves by dealing in it'.

In a sudden but ultimately short-lived about-face, Forbes, Delano and their partners decided to do what their British counterparts would never do. In February of that year, Russell & Co, the American firm with the largest share of the drug trade, issued a public circular announcing that it would no longer do business in opium. In May when Commissioner Lin's blockade of the factories was lifted, they signed the bonds that the British had refused to accept. And when the British left Canton, the Americans stayed in their factory to continue to trade without competition. But circumstances changed and the temptation to profit was too great. The American renunciation of the opium trade, which had always been tinged by opportunism, did not last. When the war was over, the 'Americans of Russell & Co – proving themselves to be more pragmatic than angelic – jumped right back in again'. And other firms followed.

In Washington, the United States government was opposed to the opium trade and sought to distance itself from the British. The government was influenced by public opinion at home, not to mention a still-lingering animosity towards Britain. The public face of the American approach was exemplified by Caleb Cushing, a distinguished Harvard man whose family had once profited handsomely from the opium trade. Immediately after the First Opium War, President Tyler selected him to lead the first-ever American mission to China. Before his departure, Cushing made abundantly clear his strong anti-British, anti-opium convictions, saying, not entirely accurately, that the Americans in Canton:

> have manifested a proper respect for the laws and rights of the Chinese empire, in honourable contrast with the outrageous

> misconduct of the English there ... God forbid that I should entertain the idea of cooperating with the British government in the purpose – if purpose it have – of upholding the base cupidity and violence, and highhanded infraction of all law, human and divine, which have characterised their despicable actions with respect to opium in China.

President Tyler saw Cushing's mission to China as an opportunity to secure a treaty for the United States and to present America as a friendly Western power that would be 'a hedge against the aggressions of the British'. His diplomatic strategy was accompanied by a much-used American tool: the provision of weaponry and technology to improve a foreign country's military. Instead of the British clocks and telescopes brought by Macartney and Amherst, the American mission brought 'Kentucky rifles ... six-shooter pistols of varying sizes ... a working model of a war steamer ... a full model of its engine ... books on gunnery, fortifications, shipbuilding and naval strategy'.

The American approach conveniently resonated with an ongoing debate in China that the country should 'now be arming itself with Western ships and cannons, and stock itself with foreign rockets and gunpowder'. It was said that by this means, 'the special skills of the Westerners would become the special skills of the Chinese'. It was an echo of Napoleon's warning to Lord Amherst when they met on St Helena. An influential Chinese thinker at the time, Wei Yuan, predicted that once the naval fleets and coastal defences at Canton and the other treaty ports were fully modernised, 'It would open a new era of Chinese naval power ... such as had not been seen in a thousand years'. That did eventually happen, but not until the twenty-first century.

The outcome of Cushing's American mission was the Treaty of Wangxia (1844), which was signed in a Buddhist temple in a village outside Macau. It was the first treaty between a Western country and China signed in peace. And it provided 'most of the same privileges that the British had fought their atrocious and demoralising war to secure' without the extortionate war reparations or compensation for seized opium. Some provisions reflected overriding American ambitions for the spread of Christianity, including a concession to China that excluded any American citizens dealing in opium from the extraterritorial protection of American law; a provision allowing Americans, especially missionaries, to study the Chinese language with local teachers; and another that provided general protection for American missionaries in China.

The treaty brought hope and excitement to missionaries and merchants alike. The former were elated at the prospect of establishing Protestant missions in the five treaty ports while the latter believed that the new order established by the treaty was 'one of the greatest commercial revolutions that ever took place' – to be compared with the 'discovery of a new continent'. Americans had long dreamed of the day when the hundreds of millions of Chinese would 'generate a tidal wave of profitable consumerism', while evangelists dreamed of China's hundreds of millions of immortal souls waiting to be saved. They both aspired to the 'opening' of China and both believed that each helped the other. The missionaries saw almost no distinction between spreading the doctrine of free trade and spreading the doctrine of Christianity. For them, free trade was God's ambassador. Both traders and missionaries were to be disappointed.

Caleb Cushing was sincere in his desire to stem the American opium traffic but the opening of additional treaty ports had the effect of multiplying the illegal opium trade, which flourished more than ever along the China coast. And American consular officials in China, conflicted by their own vested opium interests, made little effort to stop the trade. In fact, Russell & Co controlled the consulates in Shanghai and Canton and had no genuine interest in curtailing the opium trade. One of its principals, Paul S. Forbes, was later forced to resign his position as consul following public condemnation of his involvement in the opium trade.

As opium fumes wafted on the breeze and the trade proliferated along the coast, even the respected British Peninsular and Oriental Steam Navigation Company, established by royal charter in 1840, began carrying opium on a regular schedule. The expansion of the trade made the preaching of the gospel increasingly frustrating, even fruitless, as the Chinese accused the missionaries of hypocrisy. British and American missionaries preached virtue to the Chinese while their merchants kept them addicted to opium. The illegal activities of the opium traders discredited the missionaries and undermined the idea that Christianity represented a superior foundation for moral behaviour. Some Chinese called the drug 'Jesus opium' and queried: 'Is it not brought from your country? Are not your Jesus Christ's men engaged in selling it to us?' Others complained that opium traders could not be Christians 'for they killed the Chinese with opium merely for gain' in breach of the Sixth Commandment.

Missionaries had such little success in winning converts to Christianity that they started to believe that their failure could only be explained by the 'frown of God' on the Chinese. Elijah Bridgman began to rationalise that nothing could, or need, be done to stop the opium trade because the ravages to China and its people were part of God's will:

> Amid the distresses and perplexities which have overtaken the inhabitants of this land – by the introduction of opium, by the continuance of war ... God is evidently carrying on his own great designs; and in wrath he will ... bring order out of confusion, good out of evil ... His promises are sure; none can stay his hand; the heathen shall be given to his Son; and all the ends of the earth praise him as Lord of all.

By the mid-1850s, a transformation had taken place. Leading members of the American missionary community in China, like the opium traders themselves, began to advocate for the legalisation of the drug – to bring an end, they said, to the deceit, violence and corruption; to somehow make it less morally degrading; and to legitimise what had become an integral part of Western trade in China. A fundamental reversal of position emerged. Missionary concern for the impact of opium on the health and welfare of the Chinese people was superseded by a 'greater concern over the impact of its illegality on the reputation of Westerners in general – and thus on the winning' of converts to Christianity. The missionaries believed that legalisation of the opium trade would remove it as an obstacle to their sacred ambitions.

When Britain initiated the Second Opium War in 1856, the United States remained neutral, as it had done in the First Opium War – 'carefully watching developments from abroad and wishing to partake of the benefits likely to accrue from the gunboat diplomacy of the British and French'. The president sent William Reed as his representative to explore whether the United States could obtain treaty revisions including the access to inland ports that the British and French were seeking. When Lord Elgin's fleet sailed upriver to Tianjin in 1858, Reed's American contingent trailed inconspicuously behind, knowing they could rely on British force. They were, said one commentator, like the opportunist who stands 'under the tree with his basket, waiting for his associates to shake down the fruit'.

The prohibition of opium was not addressed by the Tianjin treaties but Reed had been convinced by American traders in Shanghai that the overwhelming majority of foreign residents in China, including missionaries, now thought that 'legalisation was preferable' to the continuance of the smuggling trade. Legalisation, it was contended, would remove the stigma of lawlessness that obstructed the spread of Christianity. Reed convinced Elgin that opium could be legalised – not through the treaties, but indirectly by the stratagem of including it among the list of goods subject to Chinese tariff in a supplementary commercial agreement contemplated by the treaty. By this means, without having to negotiate a formal treaty or involve the emperor, 'the British and Americans won by stealth that which they would have been embarrassed to secure under military coercion at the Treaty negotiations'. And the missionaries, for the sake of easing their consciences and hoping to facilitate the spread of the gospel more effectively, helped open China to the importation of infinitely more opium.

CHAPTER 23

UPHEAVAL & TURMOIL

1850s–1860s

The smell of burning was in the air.

THE GRADUAL DECLINE OF China in the first six decades of the nineteenth century during the reigns of Qianlong's son (Jiaqing), grandson (Daoguang) and great grandson (Xianfeng) turned into a spiral after the Second Opium War. The now-legalised opium trade expanded exponentially; the influx of evangelising Christian missionaries soared; foreign vultures and predators began to circle; and China's slow degeneration reached the point of no return. Aggressive Western colonisation began to tear China apart, exacerbated by China's resistance to modernisation, the weakness of its leadership and traumatic internal fissures. Before too long, 'the smell of burning was in the air'.

The death of the emperor Xianfeng in 1861 marked the beginning of the last half-century of the two-millennia-old empire. Xianfeng died leaving a power vacuum and an only son by Cixi, his 25-year-old concubine. Cixi became empress dowager along with the emperor's official wife, Zhen. Their relations were cordial, even friendly. Cixi's son became the emperor Tongzhi (r. 1861–1875) and China was briefly governed by a board of regents. The board was led by the firmly anti-Western Prince Sushun, who had been responsible for the disastrous hard-line foreign policy failures of Xianfeng's reign. But in a series of events worthy of Machiavelli, the two young widows, the empress dowagers, staged a coup and established themselves as regents of the boy-emperor. They were supported by Prince Gong, who was flexible towards the West and had concluded the treaty negotiations at Tianjin with Britain, France, Russia and the United States.

The coup brought Cixi personal acclaim and popular approval. She was the moving force, aided and abetted by Prince Gong, while Empress Dowager Zhen tended to take a back seat. Prince Gong served as Prince-Regent and as head of the Grand Council. The famed military commander and later reformer Zeng Guofan was so impressed with Cixi that he wrote in his diary:

> I am bowled over by the Empress Dowager's wise, decisive action, which even great monarchs in the past were not able to achieve. I am much stirred by admiration and awe.

The British consul reported to London that Cixi was 'a woman of mind and strong will'. She demonstrated her strength and ruthlessness when she magnanimously granted a reprieve to the emperor's three main regents who had been sentenced to death by slow slicing. Instead she ordered that Sushun be publicly beheaded and that the other two be sent white silk scarves with which to hang themselves.

The all-women regime – aided by Prince Gong – came to power at a perilous time. The Qing dynasty had survived the British and French Opium Wars but it was facing a more deadly enemy from within. The Taiping Rebellion convulsed China from 1850 to 1864 and caused more social dislocation than both Opium Wars. It was only the latest in a series of civil disturbances that had beset the empire since the end of the Qianlong era – as Macartney had predicted. At the end of the eighteenth century, uprisings by brotherhoods and secret societies began to eat away at Chinese society. The rebels were invariably against Confucianism, against the Manchu Qing emperor, against feudal landlords and in favour of the peasants and the poor. Frequently, they brandished watchwords such as 'Restore the Ming'. As the old ethos broke down, communities were increasingly prey to disorder and social dissension.

The Taiping movement was the latest disturbance and the most damaging of all. It had its origin after the First Opium War in a chance meeting in Canton between a disappointed twice-failed imperial examination scholar, Hong Xiuquan, and an American Protestant missionary, Edwin Stevens. Stevens had attended Yale College and Yale Divinity School but wore Chinese clothes and kept his hair in a Qing-style queue as he illegally distributed Christian tracts on the streets of Canton. He gave Hong a pamphlet containing several homilies and an attack on Chinese religions as well as a form of the Bible in vernacular Chinese. In the aftermath of the humiliating First Opium War, the tracts began to work on Hong's mind, especially` it has been suggested, the words of Isaiah: 'Your country lies desolate; your cities are burned with fire; in your very presence foreigners devour your land. Why be downtrodden anymore? Rise up and revolt'.

Hong headed to the hills where he found mass poverty, unemployment and corruption. It was fertile ground for revolution and he began to preach a new age of justice. He identified the Christian god with the high god of ancient China – as Matteo Ricci had long ago tried to do – and announced that he wanted to create God's kingdom on earth by overthrowing the corrupt Qing empire. He envisioned a golden age of equality for the poor and the rich where society lived in harmony and justice. His new world would be called the Taiping Heavenly Kingdom. By some process of delusion, Hong also came to believe that his celestial older brother was Jesus Christ and that he himself was 'God's Chinese son'. By 1852, he had gathered an army of approximately 100,000 men, to which flocked disaffected bandits, the unemployed, seasonal labourers and enemies of local elites wherever he went. They captured ammunition, stole cash from government offices and purchased armaments from always-willing foreign merchants in treaty ports.

Hong declared himself the 'Heavenly King' and imposed strict discipline on his followers. Opium, tobacco, alcohol, foot binding, prostitution and gambling were banned; sex was prohibited; the death penalty was imposed on homosexuals; and private ownership of land was abolished. The Qing imperial forces were sent to restore order in southern China but the Taiping army defeated them and the rebels soon marched on Nanjing, gathering supporters and engaging in fanatical onslaughts against Manchus along the way. In March 1853,

> the Heavenly King entered the southern capital of Nanjing in style, borne aloft in a golden palanquin and wearing the dragon robe of a Chinese emperor plus the tinsel crown of a Christian king.

The march of the Taipings to Nanjing, where the founder of the Ming dynasty had centuries before proclaimed his rule, had taken them from obscurity to centre stage. Some Westerners were initially impressed by the discipline and dedication of the Taipings, as well as by their idealism, puritanical abstinence and quasi-Christian beliefs. And some missionaries – just as they had supported the First Opium War as a way of opening China to Christianity – urged support for the rebels, 'sensing a triumph beyond their wildest dreams.' One of the missionaries, the American Presbyterian William Martin, enthused that the Taipings would 'revolutionise the empire, rendering all its vast provinces open to the preachers of the Gospel'. Another American, the Southern Baptist Issachar Roberts, was so thoroughly convinced of the utility of the Taiping movement in spreading Christianity that he briefly became its director of foreign affairs.

But Western disillusionment grew in the face of the unrelenting devastation that the Taiping unleashed, not to mention concerns about Hong's hypocrisy. As the Heavenly King preached sexual abstinence, he surrounded himself with dozens of concubines while his peasant rebel followers indulged in the wanton slaughter of the innocent and the blameless. As they burned villages and towns wherever they went, they shattered a huge area across the Yangtze heartland. The fertile and prosperous area between Nanjing and Shanghai became a bloody wasteland. The conflict eventually resulted in approximately 20–30 million deaths. It traumatised the whole body politic of China and was one of the worst wars in global history.

The British, French and Americans were anxious to see the rebellion ended so that their newly expanded rights to trade and proselytise would not be disrupted, especially at Shanghai, which had become the major commercial port. They were prepared to offer assistance to the emperor but Xianfeng so detested the Western powers that he would not entertain any offer of foreign help. After his death, the matter was raised again and Cixi and Prince Gong concluded that to defeat the Taiping, they needed amicable relations with the treaty powers who had kept their word after the Treaties of Tianjin and withdrawn their troops.

Gunboats, transport, munitions and loans were made available to the Qing but it was a step too far for any foreign army to be allowed to return to Chinese soil. A small number of courageous French, British and American officers were permitted to lead Chinese volunteer units composed mainly of irregulars. The French-officered unit was sometimes referred to as the 'Unvanquished Army' and its Anglo-American equivalent rejoiced in the name of the 'Ever-Victorious Army'. Their dashing exploits – with modern rifles, howitzers, field guns and inspirational, often crazed, commanders – eventually helped reclaim Nanjing in 1864 and drove the remnant rebels into the highlands, effectively ending the civil war.

Once the Taiping Rebellion was suppressed, the devastated Chinese communities faced years of rebuilding and restoration but there was no holding back the now legitimised opium trade.

British and American opium ships proliferated up and down the coast, free to ply their trade and distribute the drug as far as they wished. And while politicians and merchants in London and Washington brayed about 'the civilizing mission of Free Trade', the opium-selling business in China, and the opium-financing business in London, leapt ahead. At the height of the trade in the 1870s and 1880s, 90,000 chests of British opium were leaving Indian ports every year, compared to 25,000 chests at the onset of the First Opium War. The mid-nineteenth-century opium trade to China was so huge, so profitable, that it became structural to the global economy, centred less on the trading houses of Canton and Shanghai and more on the financial institutions of the City of London – an 'entire interlocking system of London brokers, banks, discounting and accepting houses and, of course the Bank of England'.

Bills of exchange issued to opium traders, purchased through the London bill market and accepted by British merchant banks underpinned the opium trade and 'kept the world economy moving'. They were used by British traders to buy American cotton; by American traders to buy Chinese tea; and by Cantonese merchants to buy British opium. London bills became such a crucial mechanism for financing opium transactions that the opium trade 'could not be extirpated without seriously damaging world commerce'. And like some complex modern debt instruments, they developed a life of their own, creating a system of fictitious credit where 'bills were no longer drawn because commodities had been sold, but rather commodities sold in order to draw bills which could be discounted and converted into money'.

As City gentlemen in London grew rich trading in bills, an increasingly substantial part of China's population became mired in an epidemic of opium addiction – to which, after legalisation, the Chinese contributed by growing their own opium in Sichuan and Yunnan. By the 1880s, Chinese domestic production of opium 'had begun to equal imports'. Estimates of the number of addicts vary but the Anglo-American historian

Jonathan Spence concluded that 'Undeniably, opium was being smoked in China on a gigantic scale'. Some estimates are 'nearly 30 or 40 percent of the population'. Opium also brought other evils. Bubonic plague was endemic among rodents in western Yunnan and is believed to have travelled with the opium trade from western Yunnan to Canton in the late nineteenth century. In 1894, the disease killed 80,000 Cantonese and spread to Hong Kong.

Opium was a personal as well as social tragedy. Its presence in the bloodstream made digestion more difficult and diminished the bodily functions. The first symptom of chronic addiction was the inability of the metabolism to absorb food. The nervous system was impaired and vital internal organs ceased to secrete their fluids. As the addiction increased, malnourishment often followed. Addicts became thin and cadaverous, pale and listless, glassy-eyed and sweating. Many simply starved to death. The physical effects were plain for all to see as emaciated and sickly men and women filled opium dens in the streets and laneways of Canton, Shanghai and all the treaty ports.

The flood of opium had the result that by the last quarter of the nineteenth century, in yet another reversal, Protestant missionaries who had earlier supported legalisation of the drug, once again became fervent crusaders against opium. Most concluded that 'the trade in the past was a monstrous wrong, and thus it is still a gigantic evil'. The founder of the China Inland Mission was convinced that the opium traffic was 'doing more evil in China in a week than Missions are doing good in a year'. Some however remained recalcitrant. The Englishman Arthur Moule, Archdeacon of the Church Missionary Society, told the Society for the Suppression of the Opium Trade that frequently when preaching to the Chinese, 'Someone shouts out "Who sells Opium?". My answer has been, I fear, not a very Christian answer "Who smokes Opium?" I have thus silenced them hundreds of times.' This was the standard British response. And the American Presbyterian Henry Candliss was not alone in adhering to the old canard that 'I think [opium] is the judgment of God on a dishonest race'.

The affliction of opium in China was not the judgement of God but a consequence of supply creating its own demand. Just as tea became a national pastime in Britain, so opium became a national pastime in China. Both tea and opium were unstoppable foreign exports – like tobacco in the twentieth century – relentlessly promoted by powerful Western trading and financial interests. It took a half-century after 1860 before the tide began to turn in China and in Britain. As it had once done with the slave trade, public opinion on both sides of the globe moved overwhelmingly in favour of prohibiting the opium trade. Eventually in 1906, the British parliament resolved that the opium trade to China was 'morally indefensible'. The mood of the country so excited the Chinese ambassador in London that Cixi, still in a position of power, announced her intention to eradicate opium production and consumption in China within ten years. A Chinese opium prohibition movement developed with a focus on 'renovating the people' into a modern nation. The effect on the nation was dramatic – 'farmers stopped cultivation; smokers abandoned the habit by millions; it became unfashionable to smoke in public'. And finally the British government 'agreed to restrict opium from India', but incrementally: 'by one-tenth each year'.

Opium addiction was not the only pervasive social ill in China in this time of unrest and upheaval. Foreign gunrunners, adventurers, deserters and mercenaries joined the civil war on the Taiping side; piracy flourished along the China coast; and foreign hustlers and carpetbaggers grew in numbers. The casualties of conflict, the homeless and impoverished, fled to the major coastal ports in their hundreds of thousands where a worse fate awaited them. The Chinese coolie trade evolved to replace the trade in enslaved Africans and served the same function: as a source of labour to work colonial plantations. The British government sanctioned the trade for fear that if labour could not be obtained, plantation land would fall out of cultivation and 'whites will disappear, and with them civilisation, morality and religion'. On paper, coolies were indentured labourers who voluntarily agreed to work for a period, usually eight years, at a specified rate of pay before being released from their contract as free men. In reality, for all intents and purposes, the coolie trade was slave labour.

Chinese coolies sent to work on the sugar, tobacco and cotton plantations of Cuba and Peru were usually never released, rarely remunerated, seldom ever got home and more often died of overwork in the fields. In most cases, coolies were 'taken away, never to be seen again: they vanished, as if into the netherworld'. They were rounded up by 'crimps' in south China ports who were paid a capitation fee (a fee-per-coolie) by emigration agents and ship's captains eager to fill their holds. Sometimes they were simply kidnapped or shanghaied. There was no limit to the mix of dishonesty and trickery to which the crimps resorted to lure the coolies into holding pens, where they were confined in captivity before their Pacific crossing to the far side of the world. An eyewitness explained that once secured inside, when all exit was prevented, 'we perceived how we had been betrayed, but there was no remedy'. The crowded pens were known as 'barracoons', the same word used for the enclosures in which European slave traders once held enslaved Africans pending their Atlantic crossing. The conditions inside were inhuman and death from disease or suicide while waiting for a ship was a common occurrence.

The voyage across the Pacific was an even worse ordeal than imprisonment in the barracoons. The major promoters of the Chinese coolie trade usually had form in the slave trade and drew on their experience. At least one of them had been previously tried in London for violating the slave trade abolition laws. And the crews on coolie ships were the international

ABOVE: Relief of Bactrian camel among ruins of Persepolis in ancient Persia. The shaggy, heavy-bodied and sure-footed two-humped Bactrian camel excelled in the high mountains and exposed deserts to China's west (page 7).

RIGHT: One of two twin stone pagodas built by Buddhist monks at the maritime port of Quanzhou on the Fujian coast. The pagoda symbolises the multiculturalism of Quanzhou, which was a centre of shipping and trade and the starting point for the maritime silk road. Marco Polo marvelled at the amount of shipping in the harbour (pages 12, 19).

ABOVE: A full-sized model of what is said to be a 'middle-sized treasure ship' (63.25 metres long) of the Zheng He treasure fleet at the Treasure Boat Shipyard in Nanjing. The commissioning of these huge junks by the Yongle Emperor (1402-1424) was one of his greatest achievements. The object of the treasure fleets was to project China's wealth and cultural superiority to foreign civilisations. In a sense, it was an earlier version of the Belt and Road Initiative (page 27).

LEFT: A replica of Columbus's flagship, the Santa Maria, which left Spain on 3 August 1492 and ran aground on Christmas Day near Haiti. The tiny Portuguese and Spanish ships of Dias, Columbus and Vasco da Gama were Lilliputian compared to the largest Chinese junks of the Song, Mongol and early Ming periods (page 37).

5

Afonso de Albuquerque, an early viceroy of Portuguese India (1509-1515). He was a 'warrior of the cross' who saw his mission as threefold – combat Islam, spread Christianity and secure trade (page 37).

RIGHT: The Ming dynasty was famous for its blue and white porcelain that had long been produced in unfamiliar shapes with geometric designs and Arab script for export to the Persian Gulf (page 71).

LEFT: Qing porcelain, produced in a variety of bright colours, was in high demand in Europe and was known for its high quality glaze, decoration and inscriptions. A stream of commissions came from Europe for multi-coloured scenes that were entirely unfamiliar to local artists in Jingdezhen and Canton (page 71).

Left: The Chinese Pagoda at Kew Gardens was built by George III in 1762, the year of birth of his son, George, Prince of Wales. It was so tall and so unusual that Horace Walpole wrote to a friend to say that 'soon you will see it from Yorkshire'. It was a window into Chinese culture that dominated the skyline of West London in the eighteenth century. (page 95).

Below: The Royal Pavilion at Brighton was the dream of George, Prince of Wales who became king in 1820. With its fabulous chinoiserie interiors and Hindu exterior, it was and still is a spectacle of bizarre oriental brilliance (page 92).

10

An eighteenth century, double-sided, embroidered Chinese, silk crêpe shawl that belonged to Queen Mary with typically romantic scenes evoking the colours and imagery of the Orient (page 98).

ABOVE: Strings of cash of a thousand copper coins were hung around the necks of merchants with square holes punched in each piece. They continued in use in China until the early twentieth century. Each string weighed about three kilograms (page 127).

BELOW: The Spanish silver mine at Potosi in the central Andes range was the largest silver deposit the world had ever known in the seventeenth century. For Spain, and indirectly for China, it was a fountain of fortune (pages 131–32).

The Spanish silver peso contained about 25 grams of silver and was worth eight reals. In the Anglophone world, it was known as a 'piece of eight'. The ubiquity of the Spanish silver peso (or dollar) made it the first global currency (page 133).

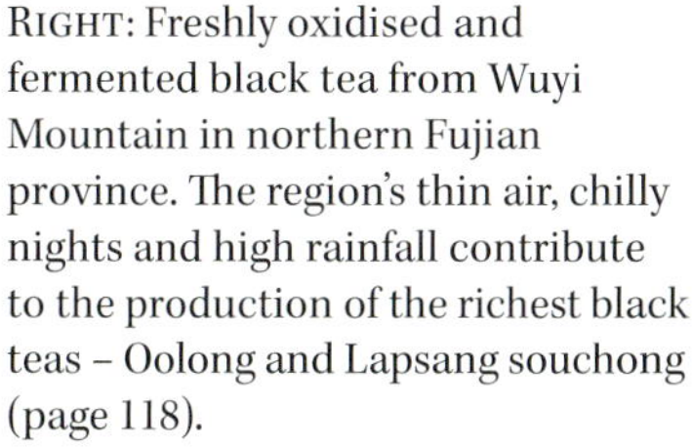

RIGHT: Freshly oxidised and fermented black tea from Wuyi Mountain in northern Fujian province. The region's thin air, chilly nights and high rainfall contribute to the production of the richest black teas – Oolong and Lapsang souchong (page 118).

LEFT: A typical narrow valley in the Wuyi Mountain tea growing district. Robert Fortune was sent into the forbidden hinterland by the East India Company after the First Opium War to steal tea plants and seeds and learn the secrets of tea production, so as to break the Chinese monopoly on tea and establish a tea industry in British India (page 249).

15

ABOVE: This massive allegorical painting *The East Offering its Riches to Britannia*, by Spiridione Roma, depicts a lion sitting at Britannia's feet while two complaisant female figures representing the wealth of India and China make offerings to her. The painting dominated the interior of East India House in London, which was rebuilt in the 1790s to portray the Company's unprecedented wealth and power (page 162).

BELOW: By the 1750s, thirteen factories built in the European style of two or three stories with columns, capitals, pilasters and colonnaded verandahs had established themselves along the waterfront at Canton. The British factory was the grandest and most imposing of all and included a chandeliered dining hall for 100 guests that served roast beef, potatoes and gravy (page 108).

18

The Hong merchant Howqua was revered by the foreign community for his integrity and honesty and was probably the richest man in the world. In the 1830s, his estimated worth was 26 million Spanish silver dollars, a figure that exceeded the reputed fortune of Jacob Astor (pages 109–110).

19

20

21

TOP: A busy stacking room in the opium factory at Patna, India. The East India Company expanded, corporatised, industrialised and internationalised the commercial production of opium on a never-before-seen scale along an 800-kilometre stretch of alluvial plain in the lower Ganges River area. Mass production facilities that were purpose-built, quasi-military, fortress-like establishments were created at Patna and Benares. The names Patna and Benares became global brand names, synonymous with the best of British opium (pages 151–52).

MIDDLE: A busy mixing room in the opium factory at Patna, India (page 151).

LEFT: Opium poppies. The milky white sap exuding from the pod contains the natural opiates morphine and codeine (page 147).

Right: Lord Elgin was the son of the 7th Lord Elgin who removed the Parthenon Marbles from Athens and shipped them to Britain. The younger Lord Elgin was a sensitive but contradictory man who was responsible for what the Chinese regard as the benchmark of European atrocity – the destruction of the Old Summer Palace in 1860. The French refused to participate and considered Elgin's decision to be a Goth-like act of barbarism (page 217).

Below: The ruins of the Old Summer Palace, or Yuanmingyuan, have been left undisturbed. They are now an historic site visited by many Chinese and foreign tourists (page 214).

23

24

LEFT: Cixi was a concubine of the Xianfeng Emperor. He died in 1861 leaving a power vacuum and an only son by Cixi who became Empress Dowager along with his official wife Zhen. Until her death in 1908, the ruthless Cixi clung to power by one ruse or another – exercising actual or de facto authority, first behind the throne of her son, Tongzhi and then behind that of her adopted son, the emperor Guangxu (pages 238, 278).

BELOW: Elgin's Anglo-French fleet gathered in the bay of Hong Kong in 1860 prior to the assault on Beijing and the destruction of the Old Summer Palace (pages 211–12).

25

RIGHT: The famous French cartoon from *Le Petit Journal*, 16 January, 1898 depicting Queen Victoria, Kaiser Wilhelm II, Czar Nicholas, the Marianne symbol of France and a Japanese samurai, with knives poised, carving up the 'cake' of China as a Qing official holds up his hands, powerless to stop them (page 282).

BELOW: Four Chinese prisoners, possibly Boxers, beheaded in front of a group of Chinese officials. Tens of thousands of Chinese were massacred in public executions on behalf of the foreign forces by General Yuan's pro-foreign 'Right Division' (page 293).

27

Xuantong (r. 1908-1912), the last emperor of China. Known as Puyi, he was born in 1906 and was a nephew of Cixi, who revealed her choice of new emperor on 13 November 1908. The emperor Guangxu died the next day and was probably poisoned. Cixi died on the following day. The letter of abdication, bringing an end to two millennia of imperial rule, was signed by Empress Dowager Longyu, the long-suffering widow of Guangxu (page 297).

detritus of the sea – 'misfits and castaways of society, many of them fleeing from justice', united by 'their dislike of the Chinese, whom they regarded as less than human'. They used the cat-o'-nine-tails freely and stowed the coolies like chattels in the between-deck where they slept on narrow wooden shelves along the ship's sides, head to toe. Each shelf rarely exceeded a width of about 50 centimetres.

Many hundreds of coolies and 'sometimes more than a thousand' shared 'the same hot, cramped, dimly lit, poorly ventilated, foul space'. The food, often putrid, was provided in quantities that barely sustained life; the hatches were covered with iron grates to keep the coolies below deck; and the quarterdeck was protected 'by a massive barricade, from behind which the heavily armed crew kept a wary eye on the passengers'. Sixteen-pound canons were kept in place, aimed at the coolies, but even they were not enough to prevent the desperate attempting grisly mutinies – 'about one voyage in every eleven experienced a mutiny' and 'over 4,000 emigrants, 12 captains and a minimum of 200 sailors lost their lives in these revolts on the high seas'. For some ship's captains, the coolie trade was just too dangerous.

In the middle years of the century, almost 150,000 Chinese were shipped to Havana, of whom 17,000 died en route. The survivors were 'offered for sale in the men-market' where they were stripped and examined by buyers, as if they were horses. As ownership of enslaved Africans in Cuba persisted until 1886, Chinese coolies were put to work in the fields alongside the Africans and were treated the same. The British consul general at Havana reported that

> The Chinese coolie is treated precisely as a slave. He is beaten, ironed and often cruelly punished, frequently driven to suicide or crime; he can be sold or transferred like any other chattel ...

During the 1860s, the rate of Chinese coolie suicide in Cuba was 'one hundred times more than whites and fourteen times more than slaves', giving Cuba the highest suicide rate in the world at the time.

Another 100,000 Chinese coolies were shipped to Peru where many were consigned to the guano mounds of the desolate Chincha Islands. Mining guano, compared with work on the sugar, tobacco and cotton plantations, was especially hellish. More Chinese coolies were worked to death mining guano in Peru than those who died working in Cuban fields. The small granite islands were thickly covered in centuries of the accumulated faeces and urine of cormorants, boobies, gannets, gulls and other sea birds. The resulting concoction was called 'guano' and was rich in nitrogen and phosphorous. In some places, the mounds 'were more than 150 feet thick'. The American correspondent for *The New York Times* visited in 1853 and described the labour of the coolies as more severe than that of the Negroes on our Southern plantations, noting that 'Each coolie, strong and weak alike, had to dig five tons of guano per day, and transport it by wheelbarrow up to a quarter mile away and dump it in chutes leading into the holds of the ships'.

China's mid-century civil and foreign wars, the civic disruption of widespread opium addiction and the social dislocation of the coolie trade were devastating, especially in the huge and populous Yangtze Delta. The ever-thoughtful Garnet Wolseley observed at the time that the 'distress and misery of the inhabitants were beyond description'. Into the bargain, the growing presence of lawless foreign adventurers intent on profit and rapine disturbed the old order of things. European and American gunrunners sailed up the Yangtze River to Nanjing, vying with each other to sell weapons and gunpowder to the Taiping rebels. Western deserters and mercenaries joined the war on both sides – some with the rebels and others against them.

Some of them followed the American freebooter Frederick Ward, who had spent his life as a sailor and mercenary in Central America and Crimea, and established his own 'Shanghai Foreign Arms Corps', a private army funded by two Shanghai merchant-officials, answerable to neither side. Along the coast, swarms of vicious pirates including 'British, American, French and other foreign renegades, who often worked in league with Chinese merchants', were a constant threat to opium clippers. The most famous pirate renegade was an American sailor called Eli Boggs, who ran a pirate 'fleet of between thirty and forty junks' and many hundreds, if not thousands, of men. His nemesis was an even more famous American sailor, Captain Bully Hayes, who claimed the bounty on Boggs's head – demonstrating the truth of the adage that there is no honour among thieves. He then decamped to the relative safety of blackbirding in Australasian and Pacific waters.

Chinese sovereignty no longer seemed to matter. Foreigners were all over China in search of opportunity. European and American ships sailed or steamed anywhere they wanted. The British in particular thought they could do whatever they liked. After the First Opium War when foreigners were confined to the five coastal treaty ports, the East India Company brazenly sent a Scotsman named Robert Fortune into China's forbidden hinterland to steal tea plants and seeds and learn the secrets of tea production. Not a moment's consideration seems to have been given to the legality or morality of the task. It was, said one American writer, 'the greatest theft of trade secrets in the history of mankind ... as if he had stolen the formula for Coca-Cola'. The object of the expedition was to break the Chinese monopoly on tea – the 'symbol of the one major country on earth that still resisted Britain's empire' – and create a tea industry in British India.

Fortune disguised himself by adopting the manner of the Chinese – learning the rise and fall of their voices, how to stand, when to bow, whether to look in someone's eyes, when to avert his gaze, what the shake of the head means, how to eat and how to dress. He shaved the front of his head in the Qing style and added a braided ponytail, a queue, at the back. And he fitted himself out in the clothes that any dignified travelling Chinese merchant might wear:

> a grey silk garment that buttoned down the front, with a high stand-up collar; flowing trousers with legs so wide that two men might have walked in them; sleeves that hid his large gardener's hands; and thin slippers ... Over this he wore a padded coat that was sashed and had deep pockets.

His height and facial features were a distinct problem but it was well known that Chinese subjects from the far west or outside the Great Wall could be 'very tall and extremely brutish' in appearance. Fortune's tonsure and queue marked him as a subject of the emperor, erasing initial doubts about his appearance.

He was in constant danger but survived largely unmolested by those from whom he stole. In the Wuyi Mountains of northern Fujian, where the aromatic tea fragrance of the hillsides could be detected from far away, Fortune took thousands of cuttings from the choicest black tea plants and hired small children to collect many more thousands of seeds. He also persuaded young rural men from the tea districts of China to leave their tearful families and travel to India to employ their tea-making skills working for the British at Darjeeling in the foothills of the Himalayas. The mission was an exceptional success. 'Within twenty years of Fortune's theft, the tea trade shifted away from China to British dominions.'

Just as the pottery workshops of Stoke on Trent learned to make Chinese porcelain, so British tea planters at Darjeeling learned to grow Chinese tea. By 1860, not only had Britain and France defeated China in war, but the secrets of China's ancient silk, porcelain and tea production had all now passed to the West. China's centuries-long economic dominance was crumbling. After the continuity, wealth and power of Qianlong's long eighteenth-century reign, China's downward spiral during the nineteenth century was a profound reversal of fortune.

CHAPTER 24

MAKE CHINA STRONG

1860s–1870s

Exceedingly special and strange in the utmost.

CIXI'S COUP IN 1861 heralded a change of direction in China but the change was hardly comparable with what had happened in the West – and what was about to happen in neighbouring Japan under the Meiji regime. At the end of the First Opium War, China had no steam engines or industrial machinery. Little had changed. The country's progress to modernisation over the next 50 years would be uneven, stuttering and stubbornly resistant. Cixi accepted in principle Prince Gong's advice that good relations with foreign powers were necessary and that China should be modernised, strengthened and opened to the West, but her embrace of modernisation was quixotic and often reluctant.

The symbolic first step in the reform of China's relations with the West was the establishment by Prince Gong of a foreign policy office. Its name, *Zongli Yamen,* meant 'Office in Charge of Affairs Concerning all Nations' and signified a departure from thousands of years of Confucian traditionalism. China had never had a dedicated foreign affairs office or any permanent foreign ambassador. Foreign nations traditionally came to it, not the reverse. Prince Gong was well-liked by all the foreign representatives in Beijing and the establishment of the foreign office was well received. Algernon Mitford, the British diplomat and grandfather of the more famous Mitford sisters, wrote fondly of Prince Gong as being 'quite charming'. And Lord Elgin's brother, Frederick Bruce, the first British ambassador to Imperial China, was so encouraged that he reported to London that these were 'statesmen who understand our character and motives sufficiently to place confidence in us'. Palmerston himself noted that 'China is now prepared to enter into relations with foreigners instead of … endeavouring to prevent all intercourse whatever with them'.

The ambition of Cixi and Prince Gong was to pull China 'out of the dead end into which it had been rammed by Emperor Xianfeng's all-consuming hatred' of the West. The ensuing decade – known as the Tongzhi Restoration after the imperial name of Cixi's son – saw the first green shoots of China's voluntary opening to the West. It was helped along by an idea called the 'Self-Strengthening Movement', another grand slogan like many others in China's history. But the self-strengthening movement had more to do with strengthening the military than strengthening the nation and less to do with Western-style industrialisation. Some of its supporters naively believed that 'China just needed to build a few steamships and buy some foreign guns' to be strong again. It was far from enough and China's problems went much deeper.

The millennia-old forces of Confucian traditionalism remained formidable and the exercise of power continued to be rooted in ancient ritual. In the countryside, local loyal magistrates and civic-minded gentry continued to support the ideals of Confucian society while at imperial audiences, the boy-emperor still sat on a throne, small feet overhanging, in front of a yellow silk screen facing the members of the Grand Council who prostrated themselves before him. Behind the screen, only vaguely visible, were the two empress dowagers who discussed business with the officials and issued edicts in the name of the emperor. The struggle between traditionalism and modernisation in China, between reformists and conservatives, between following the West or pursuing a separate path, would continue for the next half-century. In a sense, it is still going.

In 1861, the immediate task was to restore peace and security by defeating the Taiping rebels who were wreaking havoc. When the buccaneering American mercenary Frederick Ward, who had become the leader of the Ever-Victorious Army, died in battle in 1862, the Chinese asked the British to appoint one of their own as leader. They requested 'a man of good temper, of clean hands and a steady economist' – a man unlike Ward's associates who were disliked for their greed and alcoholism. The British selected Major Charles Gordon, who proved to be an inspired choice. Gordon was a man of high principle, strict discipline, great courage and apparent celibacy who helped turn the tide against the Taiping. He made himself famous in China under the nickname 'Chinese Gordon' and even more famous later as a martyr at the Siege of Khartoum. Cixi and her court officials trusted and respected Gordon, whose achievements and behaviour helped to soften their traditional apprehension that Westerners were all barbarians.

Other Europeans also earned the trust and respect of Cixi's court and contributed to the improvement of China's relationship with the West. The most outstanding and influential was the British diplomat Robert Hart, who became the inspector-general of China's Imperial Maritime Customs Service and remained in the role until the early twentieth century. He and Prince Gong worked closely together under the government's motto 'Make China Strong'. As foreign trade increased at the treaty ports and Shanghai became China's pre-eminent commercial centre, import duties rose and rose. Hart's Customs Service transformed itself from an antiquated government office prone to corruption to an efficient modern organisation that generated enough money in import duties for China to pay off its indemnities from the Second Opium War 'with minimal pain to the country at large'.

Hart, who had three children by a Chinese woman named Ayaou, never ceased trying to modernise China, despite opposition, cultural prejudice and conservative Confucian traditionalism. He proposed various industrial projects: 'railroad, telegraph ... all the old stories that have been trotted out a hundred times' by Western industrialists and diplomats. But China was not yet ready for them and most projects were rejected. Even the most reform-minded senior official, Li Hongzhang, who became a valiant pioneer of China's modernisation, initially opposed mining, telegraph and railway projects because they would 'deface our landscape, invade our fields and villages, spoil our *feng-shui* and ruin the livelihood of our people'. It was believed that such projects would disturb the spirits of the dead that dwelled in the ancestral tombs dotted all over the countryside and that if a man's ancestral burial site were destroyed, he would not join his ancestors and 'all his family would become homeless ghosts after death, condemned to eternal loneliness and misery'.

Court officials also worried that railway lines 'would give a foreign power a strategic advantage in traversing Chinese terrain'. Their preoccupation was with the defence of China. Militarisation was preferred to industrialisation. For Cixi, the motto 'Make China Strong' meant military strength – 'the only way to ensure that foreign countries will not start a conflict against us ... or look down on us'. It is a continuing modern Chinese priority. Cixi's court pressed ahead with militarisation while lagging on industrialisation. It established three major arsenals, one of which, in a quirk of history, was entrusted to the supervision of Halliday Macartney, a British diplomat and descendant of the original Macartney in China who became a life-long civil servant of the Qing government. Another European who helped improve China's military strength in the early years after the Second Opium War was the French naval officer Prosper Giquel, who arrived in China with the Anglo-French invasion force and later led the French-officered Unvanquished Army against the Taiping rebels. In 1866 Giquel was made director of China's flagship defence infrastructure project – the Fuzhou Naval Shipyard in the coastal province of Fujian on the Taiwan Strait.

The ambitious Fuzhou project involved the construction of a modern shipyard, a metal-working forge, a fleet of naval steamships and a naval college for navigation and marine engineering. Approximately 40 European engineers and mechanics and about 2000 Chinese labourers worked on the project. The fleet-building exercise was akin to creating a modern nuclear-powered submarine fleet from scratch for a foreign nation with no nuclear submarines or expertise of its own. Within a short time, the shipyard produced China's first steamship, the patriotically named *Qing Forever*. By completion, the project had produced a fleet of eleven steamships of modest horsepower that were 'mostly wooden ... and thus vulnerable to European ironclads. Nor were they equipped with latest compound engines'.

Almost at the same time, China took its first tentative steps in the field of international diplomacy. In 1866, Prince Gong assigned a 63-year-old Manchu named Binchun to travel with Robert Hart to Europe as the leader of a small group of Chinese students. Binchun was a strangely inappropriate choice as he was merely a clerk in the Customs Service, and far too old, but everyone else who was approached for the mission declined to accept the job. Binchun became, as he proudly wrote in his travel diary, 'the first person to be sent to the West from China'. The mission was successful in introducing a select group of young Chinese men to the West. They travelled to eleven countries, had an unlikely audience with Queen Victoria and visited cities, palaces, museums, factories, shipyards, hospitals, even zoos. At a ball given by the Prince of Wales, Binchun was dazzled by the dancing and entranced by the beauty of European women. Travelling on to the United State, one of the students again mentioned the beauty of the women and that 'the fragrant aroma of their whole bodies was so enticing'. Binchun rode trains on numerous occasions and described the sensation as 'like flying through the air'. His travel diaries, which were delivered to Prince Gong on his return, were full of rhapsodic superlatives.

The exploratory expedition by Binchun was only a prelude to the appointment of China's first envoy to the West. No Chinese official yet spoke a foreign language or had any familiarity with foreign countries. In 1867 Prince Gong therefore made the astonishing suggestion to Cixi that an American – Anson Burlingame, who had completed his term as President Lincoln's representative in Beijing – be appointed as China's own 'Ambassador Extraordinary' to lead a diplomatic mission to visit the treaty powers of Britain, France, Russia and the United States. Gong told Cixi that Burlingame was a 'fair and conciliatory' man who had 'the interests of China at heart' and was 'always willing to help China solve its problems'. Naturally, Confucian conservatives were contemptuous of the appointment but the foreign community was impressed by its inspired initiative. The English-language *North China Herald* heralded it as 'singular and unexpected'.

The imperial court could not have had a more suitable spokesman than Anson Burlingame. Burlingame believed in the equality of nations, was respectful to China and was not adversarial. Compared to modern times, he represented a more enlightened approach. He was the first 'American Architect of the Cooperative Policy in China'. In a speech to a New York audience in 1868, Burlingame condemned those who 'tell you that the present dynasty must fall, and that the whole structure of Chinese civilisation must be overthrown'. And he pointed out that the idea being advocated by eager American business barons that China should be coerced into quick industrialisation was 'born of their own interests and their own caprice'.

Burlingame did more than present China's case. He also signed China's first 'equal treaty'. The Burlingame Treaty in 1868 was an attempt to protect Chinese immigrants to America and finally stop the coolie trade to Cuba and Peru, in which American involvement had been substantial. Over the ten years from 1852, 'sixty-two ships flying the American flag engaged in the coolie trade' and one estimate was that in the first six of those years, 'American ships carried forty thousand Chinese, earning the shipowners millions of dollars'. The treaty resolutely declared:

> The United States and the Emperor of China ... join in reprobating any other than an entirely voluntary emigration ... and agree to pass laws making it a penal offence ... to take Chinese subjects ... to the United States or any other foreign country without their free and voluntary consent.

Ultimately however, racial prejudice in the United States won out. In the 1880s, American anti-Chinese public sentiment was so heated that the Burlingame treaty was watered down and the first Chinese exclusion law was introduced – the first in American history to place broad restrictions on immigration.

Burlingame died in office in St Petersburg during a Russian winter while representing China and was replaced by his deputy, Zhigang, who continued the diplomatic tour. On his return, Zhigang's analysis of the West was more objective than the effusive enthusiasm of his less-qualified predecessor Binchun. He believed that some things would not work in China and that the West had serious flaws. The Chinese valued sense, he claimed, the Europeans sensuality; Christianity was hypocritical as Westerners preach the love of God and the love of man, yet they wage war with gunboats and cannon to conquer people by force; the love of God, he wrote, is less real than the love of profit; and democratic elections, he ruminated, gave opportunities to immoral self-promoters – as is all too often evident.

Zhigang returned to Beijing at the end of 1870 and advocated for China's industrialisation. At a minimum, he favoured the telegraph which would not intrude on the land or ancient customs as much as railways or mining. He reported that 'If we are able to do what they are doing, there is no question we, too, can be rich and strong'. Li Hongzhang, who was now a major force behind modernisation, was anxious to move forward with a comprehensive agenda. Yet nothing happened. For the next five years until 1875, the imperial court was paralysed by one of those internecine power struggles that were a feature of the last decades of the Qing dynasty. Zhigang lamented that 'Unexpectedly, the situation changed. Alas! There is nothing I can do but wring my hands'. The primary culprit was Prince Chun, whose pedigree was exceptional: brother of the late emperor Xianfeng, husband of Cixi's sister and half-brother to Prince Gong. The two princes were the sixth and seventh sons of the Daoguang emperor and, like Cain and Abel, they differed.

Prince Chun was not a modernist. He favoured China becoming stronger to avenge itself on the Western powers but did not want China to discard its Confucian traditionalism. He had originally supported Cixi in the coup because he wanted to remove those in power whom he blamed for China's defeat in the Opium Wars and he had wrongly assumed that Cixi held the same views. But as the 1860s progressed, Prince Chun began to see that retribution was not on Cixi's agenda; that she was, in his view, soft towards the West. In 1869, he presented Cixi with a list of demands that began with a reminder of the burning of the Old Summer Palace and the death of her husband in exile. He then outlined what she should do: expel all Westerners; close China's door; boycott foreign goods; destroy all Western products in the palaces; and compile a list of all foreigners in Beijing. Most alarmingly of all, he urged Cixi to

> issue a decree to all provincial chiefs telling them they are to encourage the gentry and the people ... to burn foreign churches, loot foreign goods, kill foreign merchants and sink foreign ships.

The inflammatory memorandum was the beginning of Prince Chun's vendetta against Cixi and the West. Soon afterwards, the prince was instrumental in the execution of Cixi's favourite eunuch, known as 'Little An', with whom she was reputed to be in love. Cixi suffered a nervous breakdown and retreated into herself. China's modernisation stalled while Prince Chun led cries for revenge against the West and Christian missions. Within a short time, a deadly riot erupted at a French mission in Tianjin, encouraged and inflamed by Prince Chun. He wanted the whole country to do as had been done at Tianjin. Instead, Cixi's government condemned the riot, sent an apology mission to France and agreed to pay compensation for the actions of the rioters – narrowly avoiding war.

Prince Chun was unrepentant and wrote long letters to Cixi, criticising her for not encouraging the Tianjin rioters, for allowing foreigners to run even more rampant and for not expelling them. His old-school views continued to act as a brake on improved relations with the West. Cixi, Prince Gong and Li Hongzhang preferred peaceful coexistence. Things took a turn for the worse in 1873 when the sixteen-year-old Tongzhi became old enough to assume the office of emperor in his own right. The two empress dowagers were no longer required as regents and Cixi was forced to take a back seat. The yellow silk screen was removed and the two women retired into the women's quarters in the inner palace. Tongzhi was youthful and guileless and his short reign, with one exception, achieved little. The exception related to the kowtow, which had bedevilled European and American relations with China. In a historic moment on 29 June 1873, after many representations from the British ambassador and with Cixi's approval, Tongzhi dispensed with the kowtow and received the foreign legation ministers without requiring them to kneel, let alone touch their heads to the ground. The conservatives at court were appalled.

After less than two years officiating as emperor, Tongzhi died of smallpox leaving no heir. Cixi and Zhen then announced – in a second naked power grab – that they would adopt an infant son and continue to rule as regents, as they had done before. This was unorthodox but the coup de grace was the selection of Prince Chun's three-year-old boy as their adopted son. The boy became, at the stroke of an ink brush, the new emperor Guangxu (r. 1875–1908). Prince Chun was so shocked that he fell to the ground, stupefied and unconscious. Not only was he losing his only son but protocol dictated that the father of the emperor, if alive, must resign all official posts to avoid any possibility of conflict. Prince Chun's forced resignation deprived him of all pretensions to power. Cixi graciously – or perhaps mischievously – gave him responsibility for the mausoleums of the Qing emperors.

China's small steps towards modernisation had faltered under the weight of internal court politics and the inconvenient fact of Tongzhi's short reign, but, following the premature death of Tongzhi, Guangxu's reign from 1875 under the regency of Cixi and Zhen revived hope for the future. Cixi and Zhen regained effective power and the arch-conservative Prince Chun was consigned to powerless obscurity. Cixi's supporter Prince Gong was still head of the Grand Council and the modernist Li Hongzhang was now one of the government's most prestigious Grand Secretaries. Li wrote optimistically to Cixi that 'From now on all sorts of things will be introduced into China, and people's minds will gradually open up'. He was too optimistic.

Later that year, Robert Hart wrote a memorandum aimed at the expansion of foreign trade, with an eye to increasing the all-important customs duties. Under pressure from the European and American powers, the government opened many more ports to foreign trade, mainly along the Yangtze, into the country's heartland. Eventually there were 'over eighty of them'. The motto 'Make China Strong' began to share equal billing with another aspirational motto: 'Make China Rich'. But industrialisation remained backward. Cixi relented on a few projects but not others. Military strengthening remained her focus. The telegraph was installed in Fujian but only effectively for military purposes to facilitate communication with Taiwan in case of Japanese aggression. Two trial areas for modern coal mining were designated against fierce opposition and in 1878 Hart's Customs Service expanded to incorporate the independent 'Great Qing Post'.

Most significantly for relations with the West, Cixi agreed to the groundbreaking appointment of Guo Songtao as China's first permanent ambassador to the United Kingdom and later to France. When Guo arrived in England on a steam-powered P&O liner in 1877, it was the real beginning of China's modern international diplomacy. Guo was a brilliant, forward-looking man and an advocate for the radical transformation of China through technological innovation and educational reform. He had topped the imperial examinations and been admitted to the Hanlin Academy, the learned institution for the most elite classical scholars. Its Chinese name was sometimes translated in English as the 'Academy of the Forest of Pencils'.

Nothing impressed Guo more than British railways. He was convinced that they would transform the life of China and wrote that 'The railways will pass through the country rather as blood circulates in the human body'. It is happening in modern China with high-speed rail but Guo was ahead of his time. He travelled by rail from London to Ipswich and met the famous railway engineer Rowland Stephenson, the architect of the railway system in British India, who gave him a map of a projected Chinese rail system. It was, thought one writer, 'the founding moment of what is today the world's most extensive and up-to-date rail network'. Guo and his reform-minded colleagues dreamed of building a line from Canton to Wuhan, all along the Yangtze River, east to Nanjing and north to Tianjin and Beijing, and 'when this line is up and running, we can go on to open branch routes to reach every town and city, and so change the face of China.' But a Chinese rail system was not to be, not yet. On this issue Cixi herself, let alone her conservative Confucian officials, were full of anxiety and doubt. It touched on something akin to religion.

Guo was criticised, marginalised and made the target of a vicious campaign by purist scholar-officials, whom he likened, pointedly, to a 'Chinese Oxford Movement: a Confucian High

Church Tory Revival' that aimed to purify national life by opposing the introduction of Western thought. He returned to China in 1878, intimidated by his opponents and fearful for his life. And like many an out-of-favour Chinese official before and since, he was forced to retire from public life and died disappointed and in seclusion. Even Guo's journals were regarded as wrong thinking and were barred from publication, just as, centuries earlier, the official records of Zheng He's groundbreaking treasure fleet voyages were considered to be inappropriate for public consumption and were officially 'lost'.

FRIPP.
PEKING

PART 8

Decline & Fall

CHAPTER 25

ROAD TO RUIN

1870s–1890s

My country is hampered by traditions and customs.

CHINA'S RESISTANCE TO MODERNISATION placed it on a road to ruin. And after Japan savagely defeated and humiliated her in 1895, China was on a road to revolution. The country was semi-colonised by Western powers, ending thousands of years during which China had developed in isolation from the West. Its trade policy was turned on its head; its legal framework was undermined; and the authority and sovereignty of the imperial court in Beijing were weakened. And infighting in the imperial court prevented any substantial progress to industrial modernisation. China's Imperial Customs Service was an indispensable source of revenue for Beijing but, paradoxically, it was also a pillar of the foreign presence in China, employing over 700 Western officials under Sir Robert Hart.

The most significant feature of the semi-colonisation of China was the granting of extraterritorial rights to foreign nations. The privilege of being exempt from Chinese law and justice was first introduced in the Treaty of Nanjing in 1842 and was replicated and expanded in every subsequent treaty with a foreign power. As treaty ports encroached deeper and deeper into China's interior, each new place of business carried extraterritorial privileges for foreigners. And each new treaty port placed larger and larger numbers of foreign merchants, missionaries and consuls in the midst of local populations. Conflict was impossible to avoid: Westerners clamoured for their treaty privileges and spread their influence while local Chinese found their age-old Confucian networks of social, religious and legal relations threatened and often upturned. Anti-Western sentiment, especially against missionaries, festered dangerously.

Within a few years after the Treaty of Nanjing, nineteen foreign powers – representing the first surge of foreign countries to seek trading advantages in China – were granted extraterritoriality. Great Britain, the chief imperialist, led the way followed closely by Russia, the United States and a near–football team of European powers of the day: France, Germany, Austria-Hungary, Spain, the Netherlands, Belgium, Italy, Portugal and Switzerland, not to mention the Scandinavian nations, Sweden, Norway and Denmark, and the relatively new countries of Peru, Brazil and Mexico. The up-and-coming Japan – like it does today – joined forces with the Western powers.

Extraterritoriality insulated foreigners from the real China. It introduced foreign values, foreign banks and foreign legal systems that ran counter to the laws, principles and institutions of Chinese law. Europeans and Americans could shelter behind the jurisdiction of their home countries, while a Chinese businessman dealing with them had to accommodate himself to foreign law and foreign courts, rather than the reverse. Not only were disputes between Chinese and Westerners determined according to the law of the treaty power but the 'judge' was typically the foreign consul. By the end of the nineteenth century, at least 273 foreign consulates had mushroomed in China. They were islands of foreign culture and influence – and in any given dispute, the likelihood of partiality and prejudice was heavily weighted in favour of the foreigner.

Britain went further than any other foreign nation and operated its own 'Supreme Court for China' from a grand purpose-built colonial building in Shanghai where its judges sat behind a façade of stately Corinthian columns. The United States kept matters away from scrutiny within its consulate. The Netherlands sent serious cases to Java. Portugal conducted a consular court in China but discouraged appeals by requiring unsuccessful litigants to go to the high judicial court in Goa and afterwards to Lisbon. When it came to prisons, Britain, France, Japan and the United States bypassed China's system and ensured that any of their citizens sentenced to imprisonment were placed in custody in their own foreign-operated prisons, not those of China.

In banking, extraterritoriality provided something of a Western financial free-for-all. It allowed British and European banks to enter the market unregulated by the Chinese government, to make and receive loans and even issue their own banknotes for circulation. The historically confused Chinese money system became more chaotic and complicated than ever. British banks, led by the Hong Kong and Shanghai Banking Corporation (HSBC) in 1865, had an effective monopoly on foreign banking and enjoyed complete control over China's international remittance and foreign trade financing until late in the century, when the Russo-Asiatic Bank and German, Japanese and French financial institutions provided competition. By that stage, there were 171 branches of foreign note-issuing banks in the treaty ports of China.

Within their own areas of operation, and at their own cost, foreign businessmen made modernising advances. In Shanghai, they established a Western-style stock exchange called the Shanghai Share Broker's Association, the first in China. And they introduced electric lighting in the International Settlement in 1882 for their own use – in the same year that it was introduced in New York and only a few years after London. But China's government continued to be slow to industrialise. Nothing better reflected China's failure to modernise than the ideological resistance by Cixi and her court to the introduction of railways. While China dithered, extensive railway networks crisscrossed Europe, North America, India and Japan. By the early 1890s, on the eve of the calamitous war with Japan, China stood in stark contrast to the rest of the civilised world: the Orient Express ran from Paris to Constantinople; an Austro-Hungarian line ran from Vienna to the seaport of Trieste; the Liverpool and Manchester Railway had been running for 60 years; a transcontinental railroad connected the Atlantic and Pacific coasts of the United States; the Moscow–St Petersburg Railway had been running for 40 years; a railway line connected the new Japanese capital of Tokyo with the port of Yokohama; and in British India, railway networks crisscrossed the country linking Peshawar, Calcutta, Bombay and Madras.

It was not for want of trying by Western businessmen but the opposition to railways from officials in the imperial court was unyielding. One demonstration model – a 600-metre stretch of narrow-gauge rail line built in Beijing in 1865 – met a brick wall of incomprehension and distrust from nonplussed court officials who promptly had it dismantled. An almost equally bizarre episode occurred in Shanghai in 1876 when the firm of Jardine Matheson took matters into its own hands, hoping to create an entry wedge for the general introduction of railways to China. Their undertaking – surreptitiously conceived and illicitly constructed – was pushed by the American vice-consul and deliberately concealed behind a veil of corporate complexity. The Jardine Matheson front company, misleadingly called the 'Wusong Road Company' to hide its true purpose, acquired land and constructed a 15-kilometre stretch of narrow-gauge rail line from the outskirts of the American concession in Shanghai to the port town of Wusong. The train line caused considerable hostility among the local people and great concern and resentment among officials. Within a year, the Chinese authorities took possession of the rail line, disassembled it and left it to rust.

The first standard gauge railway in China, and the first railway to survive, was a short 10-kilometre line at a coal mine at Kaiping south of Canton. When the line was laid, the train was pulled by horses and mules until in 1881 the local viceroy permitted a rudimentary steam locomotive engine, christened the 'Rocket of China', to be used. Despite this modest advance, Cixi remained wary of embracing railways, although her trusted advisor, Li Hongzhang, was one of their strongest proponents. In 1888, in order to secure her support, Li went to the trouble of commissioning from a European manufacturer a small train with luxurious carriages for her use within the Sea Palace, where she preferred to live adjacent to the Forbidden City. A trial run in 1889 does not seem to have been a success. After witnessing the black smoke and hearing the engine chuffing and clanking, Cixi ordered that the train be stored away – only ever to be brought out afterwards for visitors. On those occasions, 'eunuchs pulled the carriages, using long yellow silks twisted into ropes' to avoid disturbing the *fengshui* of the imperial city.

As Beijing was prevaricating over the introduction of railways during the 1870s and 1880s, Russia, France and Japan were each threatening the country's territorial integrity. The areas of dispute were, and remain, perennial hotspots for China – Xinjiang, Taiwan, the Ryukyu Islands and northern Vietnam. Xinjiang was strategically important then, just as it is a hub of China's Belt and Road Initiative today. In 1871, Russia occupied the Ili Valley territory in northern Xinjiang, asserting that it was doing so to protect Russian citizens. Three years later, in 1874, Japan invaded Taiwan. It withdrew five years later but then annexed all of the adjoining Ryukyu Islands and transformed them into the Japanese prefecture of Okinawa. And in 1884, France launched the Tonkin War against China in northern and central Vietnam. The French navy attacked along the Fujian coast, briefly invaded Taiwan and destroyed China's southern fleet. Ironically, it blew up the Fuzhou Naval Shipyard that had been built under the supervision of its own Prosper Giquel. France and Russia agreed to resolve their claims by treaty but Japan stood apart and remained an outlier.

During this rolling foreign aggression, while Beijing's attention and resources were directed to building its defences and confronting its aggressors, the most lethal drought and famine in imperial China's long history descended on the northern provinces. The calamity was caused by a series of El Nino events at the beginning of the reign of the infant emperor Guangxu followed by an extensive three-year drought from 1876–1878. The usual climatic consequences of an El Nino event in China are flooding in the south, drought in the north and a cold summer in the north-east. All five northern provinces withered and baked, drastically diminishing crop production. The drought led to a destructive three-year-long famine centred on the Yellow River basin. It came to be called the 'Incredible Famine' and by the time conditions began to stabilise in 1879, as many as 13 million people had died.

Cixi professed to be a devout Buddhist and occasionally dressed as the compassionate Bodhisattva Avalokiteshvara. The rhetoric of her court was that the first essential task of officials was to ensure that 'not a single person was left to starve'. But it was a hollow promise. The state was beleaguered – not just by foreign aggression but also by fiscal woes and paralysing internal division. While some officials insisted that the first priority of a benevolent Confucian state was to nourish the people, supporters of the self-strengthening movement insisted that China's limited resources should be spent on defence projects, notably coastal defence. As a result, little was done to alleviate the suffering of the people.

In the West, the China Famine Relief Fund, a London-based philanthropic committee of missionaries, diplomats, scholars and merchants, distributed harrowing woodblock prints to illustrate the extent of China's humanitarian tragedy. They were described as 'Pictures that Might Draw Tears from Iron'. The pictures showed parents selling their children; farmers taking their houses to pieces to sell the materials; people stripping bark from trees and digging up roots for food; the old and the weak, the starving and helpless, hanging themselves from beams or throwing themselves into the rivers; a mother in labour dying in the open air; unburied corpses being devoured by birds and beasts; and people with the appearance of living skeletons engaging in cannibalism.

The government's sluggish progress towards modernisation and its inability to deal effectively with the famine reflected the waverings of a weak Qing court. It would continue that way and progressively worsen until revolution would finally bring the dynasty to an end in 1912. The self-strengthening movement, whose rationale was to make China strong, had tried to copy and adopt Western ideas in military technology and shipbuilding. But when put to the test, it was singularly unsuccessful, as France revealed in its war with China in 1884 and Japan would demonstrate most emphatically in its war with China in 1894–1895. It took the French Navy only a few hours at most, possibly 'only fifteen minutes', to annihilate the Chinese Southern Fleet in the harbour at Fuzhou in August 1884.

At the time, Taiwan's strategic location generated almost as much boosterism from Western armchair experts as it does today. An early Taiwan enthusiast was Sir Edmund Hornby, the founder of the British Supreme Court for China, who vigorously encouraged France to take Taiwan from China. He wrote in the *Pall Mall Gazette* from his retirement in Devon that:

> For the French to take the Island of Formosa would be a stroke of statesmanship ... I do not think that there would be any Power in Europe that would not secretly rejoice ... [for Taiwan] lies, as it were, *on the high road of foreign commerce, in the midst of rough and dangerous seas.* (emphasis added)

France did not accept this advice but Japan coveted the strategically situated island. Japanese dominance of East Asia was an eventuality for which China was ill prepared. The ten-year period that preceded the outbreak of war with Japan in 1894 was marked by constant, simmering dysfunction in the imperial court and wilful blindness to Japan's aggressive intent. At the beginning of that period, Prince Gong, the most powerful person in the empire after Cixi herself, who had been head of the Grand Council for a quarter century and had stood by Cixi's side for two decades, fell out of favour. In a move with many parallels in old and modern China, he was peremptorily stripped of position and power and slipped out of sight. Cixi did not see Prince Gong again for nearly a decade – until she recalled him during the dark early days of the war with Japan.

At the same time in the mid-1880s, Cixi prepared to 'retire' and unwittingly invited a scandal that distracted officials and damaged China's war effort. The issue involved the construction of her dream retirement home adjacent to the gardens of the Old Summer Palace. Cixi knew that the cost would be difficult to justify and would result in a chorus of disapproval. She was defensive from the outset, issuing an imperial decree in 1886 that misleadingly described the project as 'very limited repair work' and offering an assurance that the construction would 'not touch any funds from the Ministry of Revenue, so would not affect the livelihood of the people'. Cixi's edict concluded by imploring 'all in the empire to show understanding'.

In practice, Cixi financed the project with brazen unscrupulousness, unable to resist using state funds that were earmarked for naval modernisation. She reckoned that 'the country need not know of her scheme'. It is not clear how much Cixi took but 'she may have siphoned off some three million *taels*' of silver. Her stratagem was bound to be detrimental to the navy, some suggest irretrievably. At one stage, Cixi appeared to worry about the wrath of Heaven and issued a decree halting the work. But then construction resumed and she followed its progress with eager expectation. The finished project, including Kunming Lake, became a brilliant example of traditional Chinese landscape gardening and remains a jewel of Beijing. It is known today as the Summer Palace *(Yiheyuan)*, as distinct from the Old Summer Palace, which was left in ruins after its destruction by the British in 1860.

Another major distraction occurred in 1889 when the boy emperor Guangxu came of age, married and assumed power. Guangxu's mentor and father figure was Grand Tutor Weng whose influence put him 'in a position to shape the policies of Emperor Guangxu's reign'. Encouraged by Weng to rule as a Confucian purist, the emperor returned to the old ways of running the empire. He was indifferent to industry, modernisation, trade or diplomacy; detached from foreign policy; and content to labour over the classics in isolation inside the Forbidden City. He did not follow up Cixi's reforms – such as they were – or continue her naval and military development and did not grant an audience to the foreign diplomatic corps for two years after he assumed power. When Cixi moved into her completed Summer Palace in 1891, Guangxu promptly issued a decree in her absence – on the advice of Grand Tutor Weng – formally discontinuing all naval and army purchases as 'there is no war on the coast'.

The deeply fractious relationship between Guangxu and Cixi exacerbated imperial dysfunction and intensified China's unpreparedness for the coming war with Japan. A major source of discord was Cixi's choice of her loyal niece as Guangxu's imperial wife. Guangxu detested his chosen wife, Empress Longyu. He was physically weak, timid and nervous, inclined to speak in whispers, vulnerable to cold from the slightest draught and disinterested in physical activity. And he had no sexual interest in his wife, preferring the company of a lively concubine named Pearl, who dressed like a man and made no unwelcome demands on him.

Japan meanwhile continued its march to martial supremacy and China seemed powerless to recognise or prepare for it. Japan's navy was modelled on Britain's Royal Navy: its officers were trained in gunnery and seamanship by British advisors, and its best war ships were British- or French-built. When it became apparent that war was imminent, Guangxu appointed Grand

Tutor Weng as his war advisor. Robert Hart wrote at the time that China would find that 'her army and navy are not what she expected them to be … [and] with her old tactics, will have many a defeat to put up with'. Guangxu's incompetence and unsuitability for the impending conflict were quickly apparent and when Cixi realised the gravity of Japan's aggressive intent, she came out of retirement and returned to Beijing. She had no formal power but managed to have Prince Gong reinstated as head of the Grand Council. It made no difference.

As the war progressed from bad to worse, an immense power struggle ensued between Cixi and the young emperor that continued until Guangxu's death in suspicious circumstances in 1908. Near the end of 1894, Cixi coerced Guangxu into allowing her to have full access to all information in the imperial decision-making process, but by then it was too late. China was already doomed to defeat. Guangxu, Prince Gong and the rest of the Grand Council did not want to fight and were willing to accept any Japanese compromise. They were mortified by the prospect of the Japanese marching on Beijing only 30 years after Lord Elgin's Anglo-French force had done so. Robert Hart wrote in a letter at the time that 'Things look bad here. The officials have no fight in them and despair is gradually settling down on all'.

The outcome of the war was predictable. China suffered one catastrophic defeat after another, first on land on the Korean Peninsula and then at sea. In September 1894 in the Yellow Sea, the Imperial Japanese Navy destroyed almost the entire Chinese Northern Fleet. The defeat shattered Chinese naval morale and was a major propaganda victory for Japan. *The New York Times* likened the battle to Waterloo although Trafalgar may have been a more accurate comparison. The remainder of the Chinese Northern Fleet was subsequently destroyed or surrendered in the Chinese harbour at Weihai, a major port on the Yellow Sea.

Western powers were scandalised and contemptuous that China seemed incapable of a decent fight. Cixi was enraged but her involvement would not have changed the outcome. In April 1895, when Li Hongzhang was forced to travel to Shimonoseki in Japan to accept the terms of China's humiliating surrender – where he suffered a pistol wound during an assassination attempt – he acknowledged China's unique difficulty in achieving social change let alone political change. Japan's prime minister, the urbane and sophisticated Ito Hirobumi, asked him in fluent English 'Why is it that up to now not a single thing [in China] has been changed or reformed?' Li reflected on three decades of attempted modernisation and responded through an interpreter:

> My country is hampered by traditions and customs: one can hardly do what one wants. China has people who understand modern affairs; but there are too many provinces, with strong sectionalism, just like your country in the feudal period.

Unlike the position today, China lacked strong central control. Its modernisation movement had failed dismally. Nor had the self-strengthening movement achieved anything like adequate military power. According to one writer, in three decades China 'had yet to find a firearm for every conscript, a field gun for every detachment, or sufficient ships – bought, built, reconditioned – for a couple of fleets'.

CHAPTER 26

ROAD TO REVOLUTION

1895–1900

The beginning of the end for imperial China.

THROUGHOUT THE WHOLE OF the period from her coup in 1861 until her death in 1908, the Empress Dowager Cixi clung to power by one ruse or another – exercising actual or de facto authority, first behind the throne of her son the emperor Tongzhi and then from 1875 behind that of her adopted son, the emperor Guangxu. In the later stages of the Cixi period, imperial authority suffered and collapsed under the weight of a decade of agitation, revolts and uprisings culminating in the revolution of 1911. It was an end-of-empire time in Chinese history. After the Japanese war, China's implosion, already hastened by the Opium Wars, the Taiping Rebellion and the Western pursuit of trading advantages, disintegrated into a spiral. The Treaty of Shimonoseki, the peace treaty that ended the Japanese war, was a tipping point. Charles Denby, an American diplomat who helped negotiate its terms, wrote afterwards that 'The Japanese war was the beginning of the end for imperial China'.

The treaty ruined China. Its terms were merciless. Apart from an astronomical indemnity, China was required to open yet more treaty ports and cede to Japan some of its most valuable real estate in perpetuity, including Taiwan and the strategically important Liaodong Peninsula in southern Manchuria. Losing Taiwan was a heavy blow. It was a jewel that filled Beijing's coffers with taxes that were sorely missed. And the Liaodong Peninsula was in such a geographically sensitive location in north-east China that Russia, Germany and France all objected. They feared that its occupation by Japan might 'put the Chinese capital in a permanently threatened position' that could lead to an expanded Asian threat. Kaiser Wilhelm II was so agitated by the prospect of the Asian threat that he coined the expression 'Yellow Peril'.

The size of the indemnity – 200 million *taels* – was crippling. It was many times the amounts demanded by the British and French following the Opium Wars. In 1842 at the end of the First Opium War, China was required to pay to Britain 21 million Spanish silver dollars (equivalent to about 15 million *taels*); in 1860, at the end of the Second Opium War, the total amount paid to Britain and France was 16 million *taels*. The 200 million *taels* demanded by Japan in 1895 bore no relation to any previous indemnity and no connection to the actual costs of war. It was simply a form of collective punishment. The position became worse when Japan, under pressure from Russia, Germany and France, agreed a few months later to give up the Liaodong Peninsula if China paid a further 30 million *taels*. The final indemnity of 230 million *taels* was equivalent in weight to 8 million kilograms of silver and was 'more than four times Japan's total revenue'.

To make matters worse, China had no option other than to borrow from the West to meet its obligation to pay Japan. The Russo-Chinese Bank facilitated the loans and Russia's lending relationship with China became a lever for its foreign influence – a strategy which the British and Americans also made an art form. In 1896, China's sovereignty was further eroded by a secret unequal treaty with Russia. The treaty terms were tantamount to the annexation of north-east China by

Russia in all but name. Beijing granted a concession to allow the Russian Trans-Siberian Railway to run across Manchuria to Vladivostok; it allowed Russian warships to use Chinese ports; it permitted Russian troops to be stationed in Manchuria; and it agreed not to interfere with the movement of Russian troops or munitions. Coming on top of the onerous Japanese peace treaty, the unequal treaty with Russia over Manchuria further inflamed anti-foreign sentiment in China.

The Japanese victory and the Russian intrusion in Manchuria were the beginnings of an unseemly foreign scramble for China. HB Morse, historian and former China customs official, wrote that no country

> had ever been subjected to such a series of humiliations, or to so many proofs of the low esteem in which it was held, as China had been subjected to in the six months from November 1897 to May 1898.

The leading foreign bully was Queen Victoria's grandson, Kaiser Wilhelm. He wanted the port of Qingdao in Shandong province, a few hundred kilometres south of the Peiho River where the British had sailed up to Beijing during the Second Opium War. Looking for a 'desired opportunity and pretext', German warships cruised threateningly along the China coast, like modern American warships in the Taiwan Strait. The opportunity presented itself when two German missionaries were murdered in a village in Shandong. The fleet anchored at Qingdao, guns bristling, and gave the Chinese garrison 48 hours to vacate the port. The timid Guangxu, fearing an invasion, absolutely forbade any fighting, then handed over on a platter the strategic port to Germany under a 99-year lease. It was March 1898.

Almost immediately after Germany took Qingdao, Russian warships arrived at Port Arthur on the tip of the Liaodong Peninsula about 400 kilometres to the north and demanded the port for themselves, using the same bullying tactics and threats

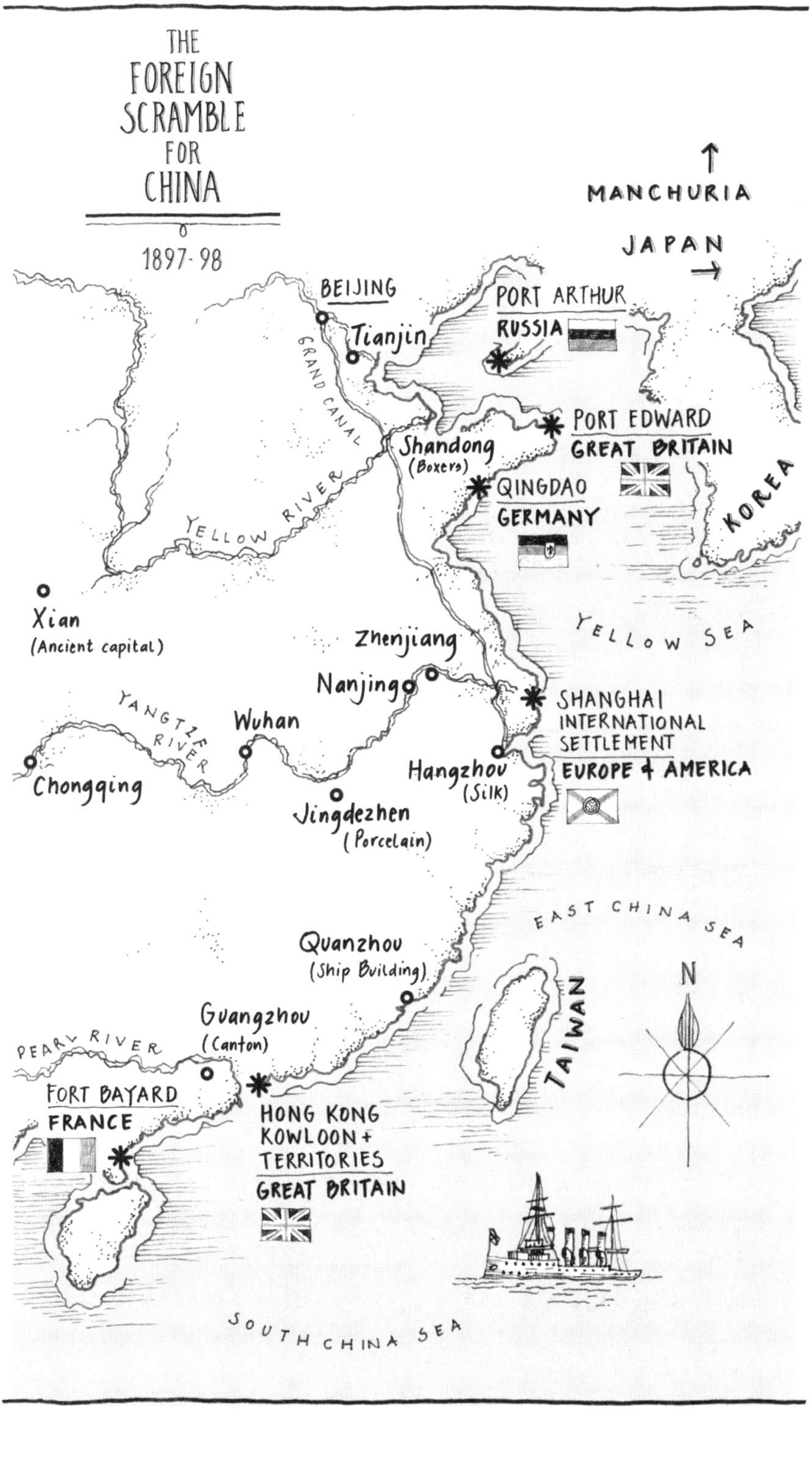

THE FOREIGN SCRAMBLE FOR CHINA

1897–98

MANCHURIA
JAPAN
BEIJING
Tianjin
GRAND CANAL
PORT ARTHUR
RUSSIA
PORT EDWARD
GREAT BRITAIN
Shandong
(Boxers)
QINGDAO
GERMANY
KOREA
YELLOW RIVER
Xian
(Ancient capital)
YELLOW SEA
Zhenjiang
Nanjing
SHANGHAI
INTERNATIONAL
SETTLEMENT
EUROPE & AMERICA
YANGTZE RIVER
Wuhan
Chongqing
Hangzhou
(Silk)
Jingdezhen
(Porcelain)
EAST CHINA SEA
Quanzhou
(Ship Building)
TAIWAN
N
Guangzhou
(Canton)
PEARL RIVER
FORT BAYARD
FRANCE
HONG KONG
KOWLOON +
TERRITORIES
GREAT BRITAIN
SOUTH CHINA SEA

of violence that had worked for Germany. Russia reasoned – notwithstanding its recent treaty with China – that if Germany had Qingdao, Russia must have nearby Port Arthur (now Lushun). When the emperor meekly signed away Port Arthur, Britain responded with its own demand that if Germany had Qingdao and Russia had Port Arthur, Britain must have the strategic Port Edward (now Weihai) on the Shandong Peninsula. Port Edward and Port Arthur lay opposite each other and together controlled the seaward approach to Beijing. Once again, the emperor capitulated and Port Edward and its surrounds became a British foreign territory – a summer anchorage for the Royal Navy's China Station with its own British territorial flag on which the Union Jack was juxtaposed against a pair of Mandarin ducks.

The new German, Russian and British territories and naval bases in north-east China were all within easy striking distance of Beijing. To the south, Britain also greatly expanded its Hong Kong base – demanding and receiving the New Territories, a thousand-square-kilometre section of the mainland many times the size of the adjacent Hong Kong Island and Kowloon Peninsula. The 99-year British lease of the New Territories expired in 1997, the year when the sun finally set on the British empire in the East.

Further south, France was not to be left out. It reasoned that if Britain had a 99-year lease in southern China, it must have one as well. France duly demanded and acquired a deep-water port south of Canton pursuant to a lease also expiring in 1997. It was called Fort Bayard (now Zhanjiang), which Charles de Gaulle graciously returned to China in 1945. By mid-1898, the major foreign powers could take what they wanted in China – a point well made in the famous French cartoon from the daily newspaper *Le Petit Journal* depicting Queen Victoria, Kaiser Wilhelm II, Nicholas II of Russia, the Marianne symbol of France and a Japanese samurai, with knives poised, carving up the 'cake' of China as a Qing official holds up his hands, powerless to stop them.

As if the European encroachments were not enough, something else was happening in mid-1898, something that would destroy the Qing dynasty from within. The young emperor Guangxu fell in thrall to the brilliant, scheming political reformer Kang Youwei, whom some liked to call 'Wild Fox Kang'. The emperor's mentor, father figure and long-time teacher, the conservative Confucian Grand Tutor Weng, tumbled out of favour. Guangxu even refused to see him to say goodbye. Kang was a strange and delusional creature, not unlike Hong Xiuquan, the founder of the Taiping movement. The supremely self-confident Kang believed he was the reincarnation of Confucius and wrote an autobiographical manuscript titled *The History of Me*. He was intent on being by the emperor's side, making decisions for him, perhaps even supplanting him. In a whirl of undue influence from Kang, Guangxu suddenly displayed an urgent and uncharacteristic desire to improve Chinese society. Guided by Kang, he issued a cascade of reformist decrees that became known to history as the Reforms of 1898 or the Hundred Days Reforms.

The events that followed were so bizarre, so outlandish, so sadly comical, that they are almost impossible to fathom. They ended, once again, with another coup by Cixi and the house arrest of the emperor. In the beginning, many fresh ideas tumbled out of Kang and were embraced by Guangxu. Some received Cixi's initial approval. As to others, she was more guarded. Most of them were strongly opposed by the conservative elites. One of Kang's ideas was for the establishment of an advisory board to the emperor with its own executive powers. Kang would, of course, sit on the board. The board was a deeply unsettling concept for traditionalists in China, where the emperor was a metaphorical Atlas who alone carried the load of empire and made all decisions.

Cixi was cautiously supportive of some sort of advisory board concept, but her officials were not. Later in her life, according to her lady in waiting, 'Princess' Der Ling – whose husband was Thaddeus C. White, an American – Cixi expressed sympathy for reform of the Chinese governance system. She compared her role unfavourably with that of Queen Victoria: 'I have 400 million people, all dependent on my judgment ... I have the Grand Council but anything of an important nature I must decide myself'. On the other hand, 'Queen Victoria had the able men of parliament' who 'discussed everything until the best result was obtained, then she would sign the necessary documents'. Kang was clearly obsessed by the idea of an advisory board, presumably as a vehicle for his own advancement, but officials were wary that the board could be stacked, fall into the wrong hands and imperil the empire. And a democratic election of board members was so foreign as to be unthinkable. The advisory board was not to be.

Kang blamed the court elite for blocking it and heaped absurd flatteries on the insecure young emperor, describing him as 'the wisest ever in history', with abilities 'sublime and unparalleled even compared with the greatest emperors of all time'. The guileless Guangxu was so affected that he had all of Kang's petitions and proposals collected and lovingly bound in a volume named *The Petitions of the Hero*. Urged on by Kang, he dismissed with a single sweep of his ink brush a host of officials and closed down a number of offices. When Cixi expressed her alarm and disapproval, the emperor issued even more edicts without first showing them to her, in defiance of their working protocol. In 'one wrathful, crimson-inked edict' in early September 1898 Guangxu dismissed the head of the all-important Ministry of Rites and five other top ministry officials and appointed accomplices of Kang to replace them. Matters were getting out of hand.

At the same time, Kang reignited a concerted campaign to establish an imperial advisory board, pushing the emperor inexorably towards it. The board was Kang's road to the throne. Guangxu made up his mind to go ahead with the idea but Cixi blocked Kang's leap to the top, making it utterly clear to the emperor at an audience in the Summer Palace on 14 September 1898 that her position was non-negotiable. Kang's ambitions were thwarted but his malevolence was not. He conceived a plan to kill Cixi and sent an emissary to General Yuan, the emperor's personal commander, to outline a proposal that his troops surround the Summer Palace and capture the empress dowager so that she could be slain. But Kang chose the wrong man. General Yuan, who would become the first president of the republic, was no saint but he was stupefied by the proposal and subsequently denounced the plot to Cixi.

Over the same few days, a series of surreal parallel events were taking place in Beijing. Of all people, Ito Hirobumi, the former prime minister of Japan and mastermind of the catastrophic defeat of China in 1895, was in town and was scheduled to have an audience with the emperor. Under Kang's influence, Guangxu had developed an unlikely pro-Japanese attitude. Some officials believed that China and Japan should unite to resist the Europeans while other wiser heads did not trust Japan, which had recently refused China's request to extend the payment deadline for its crippling indemnity. A chorus led by Wild Fox Kang submitted petitions calling for the emperor to make Hirobumi his adviser. A Japanese-owned newspaper in Tianjin backed the idea 'not only for the good fortune of China and Japan but also for the survival of Asia and the Yellow race'.

A deeply concerned Cixi, alarmed by the turn of events, travelled from the Summer Palace to the Forbidden City on 19 September, having made up her mind what to do. The outward serenity of her autumn boat journey across Kunming Lake and along the Imperial Canal belied the tumult she was about to unleash. At the palace, the empress dowager was not expected but nonetheless attended the imperial audiences as if business were as usual. During the emperor's audiences with Yuan and Hirobumi, Cixi appeared unperturbed. But on the next day, she moved to implement her plan – her third and last coup. Troops loyal to Cixi and Yuan placed the emperor Guangxu under arrest and confined him to a villa on a small islet in the middle of the lake in the Sea Palace. It was reachable only by a long bridge that could be closed. To prevent rescuers or kidnappers, large iron locks and bars from the royal ironsmith were added to the villa; brick walls were erected; and steps were taken to prevent underwater intrusion in summer and over-ice intrusion in winter. Cixi made the emperor her prisoner.

Eight days later, the executions started. Six of Kang's leading accomplices, including three who were now secretaries of the Grand Council, were summarily beheaded without trial. The peremptory executions shocked the public and upset officials. Cixi's actions seemed unreasonable and questionable. The six men went down in history as heroes who fought for the reforms, becoming known as the 'Six Gentlemen of the Hundred Days Reform'. Their executions were followed by those of the four eunuch chiefs who facilitated communication between Guangxu and Kang. In her bitterness, Cixi specified 'no coffins or funerals for them, just throw them into the mass burial pit'. Ten other eunuchs were beaten and severely punished. Kang fled Beijing and was taken in by the British and then by the Japanese, who invited him to stay in Japan. The Hundred Days Reform collapsed.

Cixi was cast in the international press as a reactionary and vicious villain – which was probably somewhat true – while Guangxu was widely regarded, probably somewhat incorrectly, as a tragic, reformist hero. British ambassador Sir Claude MacDonald reported to London that 'the rumoured plot is only an excuse to stop Emperor Guangxu's radical reforms'. From Japan, Kang vilified Cixi and tried to persuade foreign governments to overthrow her. In the Forbidden City, Cixi and Guangxu kept up appearances and attended the morning audiences together, with Cixi occupying the main throne and Guangxu now pointedly sitting on a stool at her side. The foreign legations all supported the embattled emperor and criticised Cixi. Some in Beijing speculated that Guangxu might not remain on the throne for much longer and that Cixi would surely murder him and seize the throne.

In the next year, Cixi came up with a new scheme to supplant the emperor. It involved another adoption, another young boy and a resolution to adopt an heir-apparent to the imperial throne. She presented the proposal to Guangxu on the ground that he was clearly never going to have children. The subsequent imperial edict, written by Guangxu in his own hand in January 1900 at Cixi's insistence, stated implausibly that he had repeatedly asked the empress dowager, and she had graciously agreed, to designate an heir-apparent for the sake of the dynasty. The chosen heir apparent was Pujun, the fourteen-year-old son of the arch-conservative, anti-foreign Prince Duan.

CHAPTER 27

END OF THE ROAD

1900–1912

I fear nothing but bad will result.

AS CONFLICT IN THE imperial court in Beijing seethed, the people of the neighbouring province of Shandong were suffering the effects of flood and famine. In the late summer of 1898, the Yellow River burst its banks producing an 11-kilometre-long breach near the provincial capital of Jinan. A vast area of the rich North China Plain was submerged; crops were destroyed; cattle were drowned; homes washed away. Several thousand people immediately lost their lives and at least two million people were reduced to hunger and famine. The ruin and wretchedness of villagers and farmers exacerbated their longstanding resentment towards foreigners and missionaries. Suspicion and distrust turned to violence, initially against the heavy-handed Germans in Shandong. Younger men formed a secret martial arts society called the Society of Righteous and Harmonious Fists and began murdering missionaries and Christians and destroying foreign-owned railroads, trains and telegraphs. They were known as the Boxers.

The Boxer uprising spread from coastal Shandong to inland Shanxi and throughout north-east China. The enemy was foreign influence. Many atrocities – explicable but no less horrendous – were inflicted on foreigners and missionaries.

Posters appeared in Beijing calling for the 'killing of all foreigners in three months' and 'Support the Qing! Destroy the Foreigner!'. In June 1900, frenzied Boxers laid siege to the Legation Quarter in the heart of Beijing where approximately 500 foreign civilians from eleven countries, and thousands of Chinese Christians, lived. The foreign press at first reported inaccurately that everyone in the Legation Quarter was massacred, creating a titanic alarm in Whitehall and other Western corridors of power. A joint military force from Britain, Russia, Japan, France, Germany, the United States, Italy and Austria-Hungary was assembled and soon began the march to Beijing to relieve the foreign legations. A small Australian contingent later joined in. Cixi, encouraged by the hard-line anti-Western Prince Duan, fatefully chose to support the Boxers and issued an imperial edict that was effectively a declaration of war against the West. Her 'Kansu Braves', a unit of loyal Muslim troops armed with modern rifles but dressed in traditional uniforms, joined forces with the Boxers.

After fierce fighting in late June and July, the foreign forces finally reached Beijing and brought a bloody end to the siege on 14 August. The British arrived first; the Americans an hour or so later; the Japanese and Russians were delayed by Chinese resistance; and the French got lost. When the foreign troops commenced to occupy Beijing, the Empress Dowager Cixi had already fled the Forbidden City accompanied by the emperor Guangxu, his wife the empress, the heir apparent, the concubine Jade (but not the emperor's favourite concubine, Pearl), and a dozen or so princes and princesses. Pearl, who had been under house arrest with Guangxu, was ordered to commit suicide but she refused and was thrown to the bottom of a well. The small imperial troupe, escorted by Kansu Braves, travelled to Xian, the once-great former capital away to the south-west. Their undignified departure began in disguise, rumbling through the streets of Beijing in mule carts and ragged clothes. Once settled in Xian, Cixi continued to exercise de facto imperial authority as best she could while

Prince Qing and Li Hongzhang were left behind in occupied Beijing to negotiate the terms of a peace.

For the next twelve months after the lifting of the siege of the Legation Quarter, foreign forces carried out punitive reprisals to teach China a 'lesson'. The armies of the eight-nation alliance sought out Boxers and sympathisers for arrest and execution and undertook a collective program of humiliation against 'the symbols of Chinese sovereignty and civilisation'. The exorbitant reprisals reflected an eternal phenomenon, one that at the time of writing is being played out in modern Gaza. The miseries and hatred of the Boxers towards Christians and foreigners spawned atrocities that begat more violence and culminated in overwhelming retaliation that inflicted greater violence.

Military sappers and engineers had a field day. A key aspect of the reprisals was the bombing, blasting, exploding and destruction of the physical features of Chinese imperial civilisation. It was part of 'Euro-American lore that walls and gates were the proudest symbols of a Chinese city' and that their destruction would strike hard at its people. In Tianjin and other places where missionaries were killed, city walls and gates were blown up and temples destroyed. In Beijing, the British blew a hole in the massive city walls for the purpose of running a railway into the Temple of Heaven and trampling a Chinese cemetery. It was dubbed the 'Great British Gate'. The Americans blew open the gates leading to the Hall of Supreme Harmony. Other Western cannon blasted open the centre door of the Qian Gate, the door that was reserved exclusively for the emperor.

When the guns fell silent and the Boxers scattered, foreign soldiers celebrated with boisterous parades, the blare of military bands and the hoisting of flags. Terrified shopkeepers posted signs pleading not to be shot. Two weeks after ending the siege, the eight-nation military force staged a combined triumphal march to portray Western power and humiliate the Chinese. Contingents from the eight armies marched up the central avenue leading through the imperial city, making a point of passing through doorways reserved exclusively for the emperor. They were followed with a 21-gun salute by British artillery. Since 1861 when foreign legations were first allowed in Beijing following the Second Opium War, no European or American had been allowed to enter the central audience halls or the private apartments in the Forbidden City. The innermost shrine of Chinese exclusiveness was now open to penetration, its secrets soon to be exposed to the world and made available to Edwardian-era tourists from the West.

There were other actions designed to crush the spirit of the Chinese and to cause China's rulers to lose face: British troops bivouacked in the Temple of Heaven – an imperial sacrificial altar set in gardens that is now a World Heritage site - and played hockey in the temple grounds; American troops pitched their tents in the Temple of Agriculture; all the foreign troops roamed through the courtyards and halls of the Forbidden City, sitting on thrones, entering the private apartments of the emperor and the empress dowager, removing and appropriating valuable items. Precious Buddhist books were burned and Qing palaces and homes of nobles were looted, ransacked and sometimes commandeered as residences for occupying forces.

Looting was rife. Almost immediately after the relief of Beijing, members of the eight armies, as well as civilians, diplomats and missionaries, started to fill their pockets. As had occurred at the Old Summer Palace 40 years before, a loot fever gripped the foreigners. Some British accounts accused the Russians, their arch-rivals in the Great Game, of being the worst looters. But the Englishman Bertram Simpson suggested that everyone had been made 'savage' by loot fever and that there were no restraints on anyone. One of the most eager looters was the wife of the British ambassador, Lady Claude MacDonald, who filled 87 cases with valuable treasure. Herbert Squiers, the Secretary of the American Legation, filled several railway carriages with his loot and artefacts. Japanese officers were particularly interested in Chinese art and antiquities, and located the Qing treasury with unerring accuracy, making off with its store of bullion.

There were differences between the looting after the Second Opium War and the looting after the Boxer Uprising. In 1860, the looting was confined to the palace and its gardens and was carried out by Anglo-French troops. In 1900, the looting was carried out not merely by soldiers but also by civilians from multiple nations. And it was not confined but took place across the whole of Beijing and surrounding districts. Places of plunder outside the city included Cixi's re-built Summer Palace and virtually every city and town in the neighbouring province of Zhili. The British represented the height of organisation, systematising their looting and conducting daily public auctions in the grounds of the British Legation. Newspapers at home expressed shame. The London *Daily Express* said that 'The great Christian nations of the world are being represented in China by robbing, rapine [and] looting soldiery'. *The Sydney Morning Herald* called it the 'carnival of loot' and the Irish war correspondent George Lynch called it 'the biggest looting excursion since the days of Pizarro'.

Worse than the looting and symbolic destruction were the executions and punitive reprisals. The senior British officer, General Stewart, said that after the siege was lifted, summary 'justice' was meted out through September and into the middle of October. It continued well into 1901. Patrols were sent out ostensibly to hunt for Boxers but more often innocent Chinese were killed. All Chinese people 'appeared to be fair game'. The head of the United States China Relief Expedition, General Chaffee, reported that:

> It is safe to say that where one real Boxer has been killed since the capture of Peking, fifty harmless coolies or laborers on the farms, including not a few women and children, have been slain.

George Lynch reported that officers in the German sector used torture during interrogations and immediate execution by firing squad afterward. German troops were encouraged by Wilhelm II's chilling imprimatur when farewelling them from Bremerhaven. The Kaiser exhibited no recognition of the rules of war or the Hague Conventions of 1899 but in a bloodcurdling address known as the 'Hun speech', exhorted his soldiers:

> No quarter will be given! Prisoners will not be taken! Whoever falls into your hands is forfeited! Just as a thousand years ago the Huns ... made a name for themselves, one that even today makes them seem mighty in history and legend, so may the name Germany be affirmed by you in such a way in China that no Chinese will ever again dare to look cross-eyed at a German!

The Japanese army frequently adopted beheading. Russian Cossacks were indiscriminate and the French, Italian and Austro-Hungarian forces were not without blame. Suspected Boxers were beaten and bayoneted and entire village populations were sometimes burned and killed. Mass public executions were thronged by victorious crowds of leering soldiers and civilians from all nations as well as photographers and even missionaries. The British and Americans singled out German, Russian and Japanese troops for their ruthlessness and willingness to execute Chinese of all ages and backgrounds – but they were not innocent themselves. They enlisted the support of General Yuan Shikai, a member of the pro-foreign faction in the imperial court, to hunt, kill and suppress Boxers on their behalf. Yuan's 'Right Division' massacred tens of thousands of Chinese in public executions after the siege – by beheading, strangulation and other gruesome methods.

It was the worst of times. The convulsive Boxer Uprising and its aftermath shook China and the world. The terminal dysfunction and chaotic dissension of imperial China were painfully evident. A significant group of Han provincial governors and viceroys in the south-east and in Sichuan and Shaanxi provinces were unwilling to participate or support the Qing court. They ignored Cixi's imperial edict supporting the Boxers and declared their neutrality, ensuring that the doomed conflict was localised in north-eastern China. Of the Chinese armies that participated, some supported the Boxers against the foreigners while others like Yuan's Right Division fought on the side of the eight-nation alliance against the Boxers. Deep political ruptures – together with Cixi's savage reaction to any dissent – further eroded support for the Qing court. When six senior officials including the Roman Catholic Xu Jincheng, China's respected envoy to France and other European nations, protested to Cixi and urged a diplomatic settlement, she was so outraged that she sentenced all of them to death for wilfully and absurdly petitioning the imperial court and building subversive thought. The executions were carried out in late July and their heads placed on public display as the foreign forces approached.

Eventually in September 1901, after all the reprisals, the desecration and the executions, eleven foreign nations agreed on the terms of the Boxer Protocol with the representatives of the emperor, while Cixi remained in Xian. Three additional European nations – Belgium, Spain and the Netherlands – added themselves to the eight nations who had formed the original foreign military alliance. The treaty was more a diplomatic protocol than a peace treaty and acted as a means for perpetrating control and foreign influence in China. Its primary objects were punishment and penalty but the unprecedented scale of the indemnity – far outstripping the already crippling Japanese indemnity – would be a dominant feature of China's financial affairs for years to come. Qing authority was destroyed and Chinese relations with the West were fundamentally re-ordered. China was too weak to regenerate, fatally weighed down by political and trade restrictions and saddled with unmanageable debt. The terms of the protocol were even more remorseless than those of the Japanese peace treaty. The dynasty was on its knees and nothing could stop the coming revolution that would bring down the empire.

The first order of business under the Boxer Protocol was the Western requirement for punishment of high officials. At the head of a long list were three imperial princes who were blood descendants of the Daoguang and Kangxi emperors, including Prince Duan, father of Pujun, the heir apparent. The protocol recited, in many cases retrospectively, the punishments demanded – either execution, exile, life imprisonment, suicide or deprivation of office. The conduct of the Boxers and Cixi's senior officials who supported them was characterised as 'crimes unprecedented in human history ... against the laws of humanity and against civilisation'. In fact, the legal concept of a crime against humanity was only first recognised and enforced by the international community in 1946, when the Nuremburg trials were conducted with scrupulous formality and in the public glare. In China in 1901, there were no such safeguards. The Western powers punished crimes against humanity summarily without trial.

A litany of other punishments was laid out: imperial examinations were suspended in all cities where foreigners had been massacred; express apologies were prescribed for Germany and Japan; 'expiatory monuments' were required to be erected in foreign or international cemeteries; the importation of arms and ammunition by China was prohibited; Chinese people were prohibited from residing in the Legation Quarter; the Taku forts protecting the approach to Beijing were ordered to be destroyed; and imperial edicts were to be published in all cities banning membership of anti-foreign societies. Maritime access to Beijing along the Peiho River, and to Shanghai along the Huangpu River, was also required to be improved to assist the Western shipping trade. The greatest irony was the requirement that the groundbreaking *Zongli Yamen* foreign office, established by Prince Gong after the Second Opium War, be abolished and replaced by an 'Office of Foreign Affairs' that would take precedence over all other ministries of state. After two millennia in which China had no need to concern itself with a formal foreign relations structure, it was now forced by foreign powers to make foreign affairs its top government priority.

The cruellest cut was the Boxer Indemnity. The amount was a staggering 450 million *taels* – and China bore the currency risk.

The protocol stipulated that it 'constituted a gold debt' calculated at the rate of exchange of the *tael* to 'the gold currency of each country'. Sir Robert Hart, still head of the Imperial Maritime Customs, wrote of the indemnity that 'The future looks very dark indeed and I fear nothing but bad will result'. The indemnity was 'approximately three times the annual revenue of the government' and the question was not so much whether China could pay the indemnity – it could not – but whether it could repay the loans advanced by Western powers to meet it.

The burden was heavy in the extreme. China's creditworthiness was already restricted by past indemnities, including the huge 230 million *tael* penalty imposed by Japan in 1895. All the valuable customs revenues not already pledged were secured, and revenues traditionally assigned to provincial governments were diverted to repayment of the Boxer Indemnity. As revenue streams from tariffs, duties and taxes were tied up, less money was available for the administration of government or distribution to provinces, adding to the disintegration of Beijing's authority and the loss of its central control. The parlous financial circumstances contributed to a nationwide brew of agitation and revolt that eventually led to revolution in 1911 and imperial collapse in 1912. The agitation and conflict were made worse by Cixi's belated and controversial introduction of a program of modernising and educational reforms that conservatives criticised as too radical and reformers as too slow.

In 1908, the emperor Guangxu died at the age of 37 years, still under house arrest. His death was not peaceful nor was it likely natural. It was preceded by violent stomach pains and his face turned blue: typical symptoms of arsenic poisoning. On the following day, Cixi herself died and rumours swirled of foul play masterminded by her. A century later, the *China Daily* newspaper reported that forensic tests carried out at the request of the National Committee for the Compilation of Qing History revealed that the level of arsenic in Guangxu's remains was at least 2000 times higher than normal. Experts concluded that the emperor died of acute arsenic poisoning. It seems likely that the relationship between Cixi and Guangxu had turned literally toxic.

On 13 November 1908 – the day before Guangxu met his demise and two days before Cixi's own death – the Empress Dowager revealed her choice of new emperor. The previous heir apparent, Pujun, had long ago been consigned to history. His appointment was annulled when his father, Prince Duan, was sentenced to death for his role in encouraging the Boxer movement. Duan was permitted to spend the rest of his life in exile in Xinjiang, where his family was also despatched. Pujun in any case proved to be a strange and seemingly inappropriate choice. He is said to have shown no aptitude for state affairs and more interest in 'caring for his many pets – dogs, rabbits, pigeons and crickets'.

Cixi decreed that the ever-weakening imperial line would stay in the family and the two-year-old Puyi, her great nephew and son of the second Prince Chun, would be Guangxu's successor. Guangxu and the second Prince Chun were half-brothers. The second Prince Chun would give up his son to the throne just as their father had given up Guangxu to the throne in 1875. Unlike his father, who had to give up all his positions of power, the second Prince Chun was appointed as regent. No one, probably excepting Cixi, knew quite how soon the new emperor and the regent would take up their roles. A few weeks later – after Guangxu and Cixi were entombed – the coronation ceremony took place. The tearful child was carried to the throne by his father. His regnal name was Xuantong (r. 1908–1912), the last emperor of China.

The second Prince Chun, still in his twenties, proved to be inept and stepped aside as Puyi's regent shortly after the revolution broke out in late 1911. He was replaced by Guangxu's long-suffering widow, the Empress Dowager Longyu, who left her mark on history by signing the letter of abdication on 12 February 1912, drawing the curtain on the empire and ending two millennia of imperial Chinese rule.

Conclusion

THE WEIGHT OF THE Boxer indemnity hung like a millstone around China's neck long after the collapse of the Qing dynasty. Loan piled on loan to service more loans, and arcane negotiations over the reconstruction and reorganisation of China's financial obligations to the West finally ended only with the termination of foreign extraterritoriality in 1943 and the establishment of the People's Republic in 1949. The Boxer Indemnity essentially bankrupted China, hindered foreign investment and delayed its industrial modernisation. Sir Robert Hart's fear that 'nothing but bad will result' was 'too fully realised'. The size and vindictiveness of the indemnity reflected the same 'narrow and grotesque political short-sightedness' that most of the same nations repeated two decades later when they imposed crippling reparations on Germany after World War I – making a further European conflict inevitable.

In 1820, as the British opium trade was getting into its stride, China had the largest share of the world's gross domestic product. By the end of empire in 1912, the country was a social and economic shambles and would remain so until late in the twentieth century. In 1949 after a civil war, there emerged a new government, another 'dynasty'. For three decades it endured grievous strains and difficulties, committed horrendous mistakes, made cruel missteps and caused incalculable human tragedy, before settling on a path to prosperity that accelerated in the twenty-first century under a government system that has emphasised 'political centralisation paired with economic decentralization'.

Over time, the China trade recovered, as it has generally always done. In the twenty-first century, China has ceased to be pre-eminent in porcelain but is still the world's largest producer of tea and silk. The scourge of opium has been eradicated, silver *taels* have been abolished and the *yuan* has become a stable national currency, achieving a greater share of global trade finance in 2023 than the euro. China's strength remains its manufacturing, trade and export industries, as it was in centuries past. In 2024, China was the world's 'sole manufacturing superpower' with the largest trade surplus in world history and an output greater than the nine next largest manufacturing nations. Technological innovation has also accelerated. Even before the introduction of its groundbreaking open-source AI model, DeepSeek, China was the global leader in 57 of 64 critical technologies, according to a 2024 report by the Australian Strategic Policy Institute.

Paradoxically, as China endured an existential struggle for survival in the twentieth century, a terror of retribution for past iniquities became a staple of popular Western culture and politics. As one historian noted, 'it stood to reason that they would exact vengeance for the humiliations suffered at the hands of the West'. *The Times* wrote that China was 'a nation teeming with vitality … eager for expansion, perhaps for conquest, for world power, if not for revenge for wrongs inflicted upon it by nearly every European power'. Edwardian children's serials, Christmas annuals for boys and girls, magazines, novels and newspapers popularised fantastic stories of Chinese invasion and world domination. The hugely popular American novelist Jack London wrote of the 'menace to the Western world … [from] the four hundred millions of yellow men'. Western anxieties grew that the sleeping giant – to borrow a phrase attributed to Napoleon Bonaparte – would turn on its former aggressors. The fear has never quite gone away.

Notes

Preface

xi elsewhere that I love: de Waal, 127
xi global heartland: see Mackinder, 2020 [1904]; also Noorali and Ahmadi, 2022

Introduction

xiv Newton lamented: Newton, 1717
xv What are the intentions: Juvenal, *Satires VI*, 400–3
xv He who does not forget: quoted in Ropp, 54
xv is inscribed on China's: Westad, 2
xvi no claim to academic: Norwich 1998, xli

Chapter 1: Before the Europeans

3 almost brushed against: Galli, 4
4 changed the whole course: Keay, 16
4 Qin road network: Schuman, 47, citing Michael Nylan, 'The Power of Highway Networks during China's Classical Era (323–316CE): Regulations, Metaphors, Rituals, and Deities', ch. 2 in SE Alcock, J. Bodel, and RJA Talbert (eds), *Highways, Byways and Road Systems in the Pre-Modern World*, Wiley-Blackwell, 2012
4 the name Qin: Keay, 97–8; Hansen, 18–19
5 stronger than a comparable: Tonti, 109
5 the first Romans to see: McLaughlin, 6
6 with their standards: Florus, 46.3.11
6 Many legionnaires had: Plutarch, *Crassus*, 25
6 Chinese steel making: McLaughlin, 5
6 wondrous than: Pliny the Elder, 19:6
6 white breasts resplendent: Lucan, X:136–93; also St. Clair, 86
7 a woman who wears: Seneca, 7–9
7 shimmer in public: Pliny, 6–20
7 graveyard of silver: Topik et al., 17
7 shifting sand dunes: Shifting Shapes of Sandy Scapes, Earth Observed website: https://earthobservatory.nasa.gov/blogs/eokids/shifting-shapes-of-sandy-scapes (accessed 6/4/2024)
8 tame compared to the Taklamakan: Hanbury-Tension, 109
8 Mardi Gras of snow: ibid., 10
8 singing boys: Schoff, 77
8 dramatically higher prices: Bernstein, 4
8 every farming household: Liu, 10
9 Once this economic: McLaughlin, 44
9 corrupt them with wealth: Fairbank, 28
9 in terms of both: Whitfield, 21
9 one of the most important: Nylan and Vankeerberghen, 3
9 eight broad boulevards: Xiaoneng Yang, 233–6
9 averaged about six metres: 'Appian Way', Britannica website: https://www.britannica.com/topic/Appian-Way (accessed 19/5/2024)
10 when merchants went by sea: see Schottenhammer, 117
10 a flowering of trade: Paine 2013, 297
10 a waterfront for the world: Hourani, 64
10 the 6,000 mile voyage: Severin, 18
10 hallway to China: ibid., 24
10 gateway to China: Hourani, 78
10 Gates of China: ibid., 72
10 Arab shipwreck: Paine 2013, 292–3
11 over vast distances: Heng, 24
11 Is not this revenue better: Lo 1995, 499
11 utility of money: Lien-sheng Yang, 36–52
11 first introduction of paper money: Cribb, 193
12 limited liability stock company: Carlen, 110–13

12 **the port was clogged:** Paine 2013, 309
12 **ocean liners boasting staterooms:** Lo 1995, 500
12 **more than 100 cabins:** Jordanus, 55
12 **anything but warriors:** Polo (Yule and Cordier), 3
13 **leaped into the sea:** Paine 2013, 350

Chapter 2: The Mongols

17 **came from nowhere:** Keay, 350–1
17 **God only knows:** Colin Thubron 'Pleasure Domes and Postal Routes', *The New York Review*, 22 July 2021
18 **uprooted from one part:** Shea, 388
18 **spectacle of thousands:** ibid., 402
18 **secret trade agreement:** Silk Roads Programme, UNESCO website: https://en.unesco.org/silkroad/content/venice#:~:text=Indeed%2C%20a%20trade%20treaty%20between,grain%20to%20porcelain%20and%20pearl (accessed 14/4/2024)
18 **records of silk-producing areas:** Lopez, 73
18 **unlimited amounts:** Inalcik, 218
18 **never-ending stream:** Frankopan 2015, 181; see also Kuhn, 6–7
19 **a virgin with a gold dish:** Thubron, *Shadow of the Silk Road*, 305
19 **China is the safest:** Frankopan 2015, 184
19 **I can assure you:** Paine 2013, 352–3
19 **a hundred ships:** Frankopan 2015, 185–6
19 **international major currency:** Ding, 209
19 **economically crippled:** Norwich 2006, 140
20 **hundred different destinations:** Wyman, 172
20 **Polo was in China:** see Vogel 2013
20 **I did not write half:** Polo (ed. Rugoff), xxvii
20 **homage to the Father of Christendom:** Habig, 22
21 **dressed in festive vestments:** ibid., 25
21 **mother was a Nestorian:** Jaivin, 101
22 **four great prophets:** Polo (ed Rugoff), 101
22 **oppression of the ethnic Han:** Kerr, 73–4
22 **detested the rule:** ibid.; see also Ebrey, 174
23 **wide enough for nine horseman:** Weatherford, 198
23 **bounced from brother:** ibid., 241
24 **bubonic plague:** Spryou et al. 2022
24 **consequential population decline:** Deng 2004
24 **politically and ritually sealed:** Wakeman 1974, 4

Chapter 3: Great Ming

25 **honoured and the mean:** Postrel, 187
25 **people tend to respect:** ibid., 187–8
26 **In the morning I punish:** Ebrey, 192
26 **gilded sedan chairs:** Keay, 394
26 **executed over 30,000 subjects:** Ebrey, 192
26 **return of native rule:** ibid.
26 **vanished and was probably murdered:** Dreyer 2007, 33–4; Wakeman 1993
26 **death by a thousand cuts:** see Brook et al., 117
26 **to the ninth degree:** 'Nine familial exterminations': Wikipedia: https://en.wikipedia.org/wiki/Nine_familial_exterminations (accessed 17/4/2024)
27 **leviathans of the seas:** see Paine 2013, 373–4
27 **more reasonable:** Sleeswyk, 12; Paine 2013, 374
27 **object of Yongle's treasure fleets:** Wills 2011(a), 9; Paine 2013, 368–9
28 **Yongle's chosen commander:** Wakeman 2009, 9–10
28 **spoutless teapots:** See, 222. The Chinese method of castration involved slicing off the penis as well as the testicles.
28 **sucking need for power:** ibid., 228
28 **carried 17 imperial eunuch ambassadors:** Wakeman 2009, 10; also Crawford, 124
28 **both the throne and the administration:** ibid., 127
28 **succession of powerful eunuchs:** Lo 1958, 164
29 **promotion or dismissal:** Crawford, 136
29 **Chinese army was crushed:** Keay, 391
29 **hundreds of thousands of men:** ibid., 390
29 **probably at the hands of his own officers:** ibid., 392
29 **palace floor was steeped in blood:** ibid., 392
30 **reversal of policy was attributable:** see Paine 2013, 369
30 **vanity and waste:** Wills 2011(a), 10
30 **compromised from the start:** Wakeman 2009, 12
30 **on the day of his coronation:** Dreyer 1982, 222
30 **manipulated the child emperor:** Siu, 103
30 **death, at least in theory:** Villiers, 66
31 **deceitful exaggerations:** Paine 2013, 370
31 **best bureaucratic minds:** Lo 1958, 168
31 **Why must you speak of profit:** Mencius, Readings 1, n.p.
32 **relied almost solely:** Crawford, 124
32 **global centre of porcelain:** Hunt 2021, 5
32 **left most of the wealth:** Mote 1988, 7

32 **largest and wealthiest:** ibid.
32 **cog running the wheel:** Flynn and Giraldéz 2002(b)
32 **How important to the people:** Brook 1981, 186
33 **Those who went out as merchants:** Brook 1998, 86; also Frank, 221
33 **healthier and more numerous society:** Mungello, 3
33 **beginning of major population growth:** Banister, 6
33 **may have tripled:** Frank, 109
33 **merchant clans:** see Hang 2015

Chapter 4: Age of Discovery

34 **alter the course:** Schuman, 212
34 **came crashing into each other:** ibid.
34 **Chinese cannon invented:** Gwei-Djen et al. 1988; also Andrade 2016
35 **rivals for monetary primacy:** Sevket Pamuk, 6–8; also Bacharach 1973
35 **Cairo and Mecca:** Paine 2013, 413
35 **only five thousand miles west:** ibid., 393
36 **366 marginal annotations:** Urresti, 186; see also Polo (ed. Rugoff), p. xi which refers to 'seventy marginal notes'
36 **realms of the Grand Khan:** Paine 2013, 390
36 **reached the outskirts:** ibid., 396
36 **six stars low down over the sea:** ibid., 386–7
37 **in search of Christians and spices:** Ames, 50
37 **obsession with Moors and mosques:** Subrahmanyam, 1365
37 **very great deed, Sire:** Earle and Villiers, 413
38 **patently they were not:** Paine, ibid., 397
39 **at the end of one monsoon:** Tomé Pires, *Suma Oriental*, Hakluyt Society, 2nd series, 1944, 286, cited in Earle and Villiers, 67
39 **Whoever is lord of Malacca:** Paine, ibid., 413
39 **Lord of the Conquest:** ibid., 400

Chapter 5: Trading Posts

41 **led by Captain d'Andrade:** T'ien-Tse Chang 1962, 47
41 **informed of China and the Chinese:** ibid., 50–1
41 **improper conduct of the Portuguese:** ibid., 49
42 **climbed up its wall:** ibid., 51
42 **inhuman, wanton marplot:** Jesus, 6
42 **so far as to seize the children:** T'ien-Tse Chang 1962, 52, 57; also Schuman, 215
42 **laws banning the buying:** Dias, 71
42 **preliminary imperial audience:** see Wills 2011(b), 29–30
43 **We must not receive:** T'ien-Tse Chang 1934, 51
43 **hustled out and returned:** Wills 2011(b), 30; Schuman, 215
43 **untamed and disregard:** T'ien-Tse Chang, 1962, 59
43 **forty-two of their men:** ibid., 62
43 **sentenced to death:** T'ien-Tse Chang 1934, 59
44 **absurd bellicosity:** Wills 2011(b), 36
44 **500 *taels* of silver:** ibid.; Ptak, 466
44 **ground rent:** Wills, ibid., 37
44 **Dread our greatness:** Villiers, 69–70
45 **robbers and insurrectionaries:** ibid., 75
45 **great town spread out:** Blusse 1988, 651–2
45 **executed all but three:** Wills 2011(b), 46; Paine 2013, 444
45 **in order to inflict damage:** Steensgaard, 128
46 **more than doubled the VOC's capital:** Paine 2013, 444
46 **it is lawful for any nation:** Grotius; see also Paine 2013, 444–6
46 **not lawful for the Pope:** Armitage, 108
46 **as European pirates:** Paine 2013, 448
47 **drunken negro slaves:** Boxer 1968, 83
47 **Austronesian-speaking people:** Paine 2013, 448
47 **repeated El Nino events:** Frankopan 2023, 412–3
47 **Pagoda tree:** possibly folklore but the tree, or its replacement, has become a national landmark and tourist attraction
48 **coastal overlord clans:** Keay, 433
48 **more than a thousand ships:** Platt, 106
48 **32-kilometre-wide corridor:** Mote 1999, 849
48 **wailing everywhere:** Faure, 173
48 **re-imposed the early Ming ban:** von Glahn, 1996(a), 440
49 **Hitherto this island:** Campbell, 423
49 **China's first great victory:** Andrade 2011, 298–303
49 **swiftly annexed the island:** Elman, 286

Chapter 6: Porcelain's Puzzle

53 **seemingly improbable:** Gleeson, 43
53 **transparent as glass:** Bushell, 133
54 **made from a certain juice:** Degenhardt, 153
54 **eggshells and shells:** ibid.
54 **one selflessly far-sighted generation:** ibid., 156–7
54 **artificial cement:** Bacon and Rawley, 165
54 **nothing lovelier could be imagined:** Polo (trs. Latham), 201
55 **nothing like it in European pottery:** Ricci, 14–15

55 **immunity against poison:** Degenhardt, 152
55 **first began to appear:** Finlay, 254
55 **I would counsel all princes:** ibid., 70
55 **largest collection of porcelain:** see Krahe, 221
55 **over 300 pieces of porcelain:** De Luca 2021
56 **modest gift of sixteen pieces:** de Waal, 151
56 **more than 1500 pieces:** Marchand, 14
56 **half of England's treasury:** Cartwright 2020
56 **about 3.5 million guilders:** Finlay, 253
56 **who did not marvel:** ibid., 254
57 **most dynamic economic region:** Finlay, 258; also Schama, 174–88, 304–19.
57 **common presence in Dutch households:** Weststeijn, 213
57 **daily use with the common people:** Finlay, 254
57 **exceeding 200,000 pieces:** Marchand, 14
57 **everyday life of a large part:** Finlay, 261
57 **any house of indifferent quality:** Brook 2009, 74
57 **inventory of the possible:** ibid., 74
57 **certainly the most busie:** ibid.
58 **consuming society enthralled:** Finlay, 56
58 **preceded and stimulated:** ibid., 261–2
58 **curvaceous and voluptuous:** see Fraser 2006
58 **escape to for intimate dinners:** de Waal, 123
59 **to evoke Louis XIV's Trianon:** Finlay, 275
59 **piling their china upon:** Defoe, 65
59 **same is true for oranges:** de Waal, 151
59 **Rumours first started:** Gleeson, 18–21
60 **knew 'everything about everything':** de Waal, 166
60 **I pity the poor goldmaker:** ibid., 170
60 **such an important creature:** ibid., 173
61 **I can happily recognise:** ibid., 177
61 **I need to see you:** ibid., 186
61 **vaults of the Jungfern bastion:** Menzhausen, 11
61 **burst into hysterical laughter:** ibid.
62 **no place in the world:** Gleeson, 140
62 **theorised over by mineralogists:** de Waal, 252; also Penderill-Church 1972
62 **mission of industrial espionage:** Finlay, 49
63 **Cookworthy's royal patent:** Webster, 40
63 **monopoly of stones and earth:** de Waal, 297–8
64 **firm and secure hold:** ibid., 304
64 **Wedgwood Cornish Clay Company:** Hunt 2021, 236
64 **pair of porcelain swans:** 'Sculpture Reported Given to Mao', *The New York Times*, 25 February 1972: https://www.nytimes.com/1972/02/25/archives/sculpture-reported-given-to-mao.html (accessed 5/5/2024)

Chapter 7: Kilns of Jingdezhen

65 **year-round thunder and lightning:** de Waal, 41
65 **noise of tens of thousands of pestles:** Elvin, 285
65 **ten thousand chimneys smoke:** Finlay, 20
66 **whole city is on fire:** Tichane, 60
66 **midst of a carnival:** Finlay, 18
67 **quantity of it is so great:** ibid., 21
67 **more than 600,000 ceramics:** ibid., 21
67 **took away forty tons:** ibid., 21–2
67 **precisely 499,061 porcelains:** ibid., 22
67 **Jingdezhen alone has the honour:** Jenyns1959, 25
67 **coordinated effort, specialised skills:** Finlay, 21
67 **division of labour:** Smith, Adam 22–6
67 **the hot fire men:** Finlay, 30
68 **Unless the fire is hot and strong:** ibid., 30
68 **kaolin gives porcelain:** see Gleeson, 49, 67–8
68 **a never-ending line of boats:** de Waal, 36
68 **up to three rows of boats:** ibid.
68 **skimmed off the creamy residue:** Finlay, 26
69 **one hair or one grain of sand:** ibid.
69 **wooden spatulas day and night:** ibid., 26–7
69 **six categories of decorator:** de Waal, 38
69 **one workman draws:** Jenyns 1959, 7
69 **at least seventy craftsmen:** ibid., 6
70 **but it is commonly believed:** Finlay, 18
70 **10,000 loads of rice:** ibid., 43
70 **11,000 kilograms of wood:** ibid., 43
70 **knock-kneed, flattened:** ibid., 31
70 **26,350 bowls with dragons:** Jenyns 1953, 110
71 **one tried to strangle him:** Wu Mingren, 'When Concubines Fought Back: The Plot to Eliminate a Mad and Sadistic Emperor', *Ancient Origins*, 20 January 2018: https://www.ancient-origins.net/history-famous-people/when-concubines-fought-back-plot-eliminate-mad-and-sadistic-emperor-009468 (accessed 19/5/2024)
71 **stream of commissions:** Beurdeley and Beurdeley, 264–8
71 **copying is a valued pathway:** de Waal, 68
71 **superimposing one coat of arms:** Finlay, 28

72 **I procured two separate engravings:** Detweiler, 90
72 **formative period for modern:** see Kingston 2007
72 **sold at auction in London:** Jörg, 59; Finlay, 22
72 **inland navigation much more extensive:** Smith Adam, 25
73 **intersecting network of rivers:** Ricci, 12
73 **dedicated to the true Queen of Heaven:** Finlay, 43
74 **finally encountered an adversary:** ibid., 295; de Waal, 322

Chapter 8: Infiltration in Beijing

75 **history of intercourse:** Udias, 463
75 **The encounter between:** de Waal, 101
76 **China's Catholic centuries:** Waley-Cohen 2000, 56
76 **close to being baptised:** Mungello, 32
76 **cross-legged on Schall's bed:** ibid., 32–3
76 **changed her name to 'Helena':** Waley-Cohen 2000, 67
77 **European invasion force:** Ross, 119
77 **advocates of military conquest:** ibid., 44, 119
77 **Eurocentric understanding:** ibid., 42–3
77 **five hundred per cent:** Keay, 18
78 **totally different from Greek or German:** Hong, 92
78 **something utterly incompatible:** Ross, 119–20
78 **Four Books:** ibid., 126
78 **Holy Commandments:** Hong, 91
78 **Chinese Character Table:** ibid., 92
78 **Euclid's Elements:** Zong, 953
79 **Christ and Cicero:** Wills 2011(a), 21
79 **almost two hundred courtiers:** Waley-Cohen 2000, 67
79 **queried long-cherished ideas:** ibid., 66
80 **Chinese medicine did not manage:** de Waal, 120
80 **engineers who made major contributions:** Keay, 430–1
80 **settling China-Russia border:** Szczesniak 1969
80 **permanently known to all peoples:** Li, 26
80 **Westerners are petty indeed:** ibid., 22
81 **shut down and re-used:** Rowe, 140
81 **remain in privileged positions:** Waley-Cohen 1993
81 **stagnated as a result of:** Landes, 11–12, 15
81 **modern European celestial instruments:** Udias, 469; Ma, 8–9
81 **15 of the King's Mathematicians:** Jami, 6
81 **all-important Board of Astronomy:** Udias, 468
82 **huge map of the world:** Lee 2012, 306
82 **impossible black tulip:** Lee 2018, 5
82 **considerably superior:** Lee, 2012, 310
82 **some 70 years after:** ibid., 316–7; Lee 2018, 5
82 **exchange of diplomatic credentials:** Habig, 21–2
83 **at least 60 years before:** Lee 2012, 306–10, 330–1
83 **more than four hundred works:** Finlay, 47
83 **walls of material:** de Waal, 101

Chapter 9: An Idealised Orient

84 **Polo's scribe, Rustichello:** Honour, 8
84 **I did not write half:** *Travels*, Polo (ed. Rugoff), xxvii; Honour, 9
85 **Mandeville's Travels:** ibid., 13
85 **farrago of highly-coloured nonsense:** ibid., 15
85 **special geographic location:** Zhu, 70
86 **quality of roads and bridges:** ibid., 69
86 **derived their notions of China:** Boxer 2008, xvii
86 **majority of well-educated Europeans:** ibid.
87 **more effect on the literary:** Ricci, xix
87 **advocated a universal religion:** Zhu, 242
87 **real pictures rather than:** de Waal, 123
88 **reflected rays from gems:** Loch, 180
88 **drank the health of our Queen:** ibid., 184; de Waal, 83
88 **swayed by philosophers:** Honour, 19
88 **with what good order:** ibid.
88 **unequalled vision of power:** Platt, 9
88 **wealth beyond measure:** Ellis et al., 14
89 **model of a moral:** Platt, 9
89 **embraced all the moral and none:** Honour, 22
89 **One need not be obsessed:** Brown 2021, 175
89 **bureau of address for China:** Perkins, 115
89 **Confucius of Europe:** Neill, 154
89 **long duration of Chinese:** Meadows, 124
90 **Nanjing compound:** Wood 2020, 420
90 **If a candidate died:** Miyazaki, 18–25
90 **no intention to place:** McCutcheon, 560
90 **contagion of China-fancy:** Johnson, 70–1
91 **Enough of Greece and Rome:** Murphy 1759

Chapter 10: Chinoiserie Mania

92 **numerous progeny of Chinese:** Honour, 53
93 **over £600,000:** By 1795, the actual figure was £630,000, De-la-Noy, 55
94 **since the days of the Roman Emperor:** Honour, 190
94 **not only Botanists:** Chambers, 13, 14; also Honour, 156–7

95 **Chinese pavilions, zigzag bridges:** Kilpatrick, 31
95 **For at least 60 years:** Bertram, 36
95 **peaches, peonies, chrysanthemums:** Valder, 12
95 **Chinese origins have been entirely forgotten:** Kilpatrick, 9
95 **very large toy indeed:** Honour, 155
96 **see it from Yorkshire:** Paterson, 27
97 **30 musicians dressed in Chinese:** Honour, 62–3
97 **In such delightful surroundings:** ibid., 114; see also Alexandra Loske, review of 'Siting China in Germany: Eighteenth-Century Chinoiserie and Its Modern Legacy' by Christiane Hertel, *Journal of the History of Collections*, vol. 33, issue 1, 2021, 144–5.
97 **Thomas Chippendale:** Thomas Williams, 'Collecting guide: Thomas Chippendale Snr', Christie's website, 18 October 2024: https://www.christies.com/en/stories/a-guide-to-thomas-chippendale-senior-e412b365b3a14c5fb6cf7c0d5bb20b4b (accessed 27/4/2024)
98 **lotus flowers, pomegranates:** see Richard Martin and Harold Koda, *Orientalism: Visions of the East in Western Dress*, The Metropolitan Museum of Art, 1994
99 **counter to the fripperies:** Charlie Porter, 'Savile Row is back in style – so why is the street so empty?', *Financial Times*, 18 April 2023: https://www.ft.com/content/70ac37b8-d49d-402c-8fa6-240578773e4c (accessed 27/4/2024)
99 **conservative dreariness:** Alexandra Rowland, 'Beau Brummell Wasn't a Hero of Modern Men's Fashion. He Was a Villain. A Boring, Uptight Villain', *Esquire*, 20 March 2019, https://www.esquire.com/style/mens-fashion/a26870204/beau-brummell-style-toxic-masculinity/ (accessed 27/4/24)

Chapter 11: Qianlong Era

103 **most populous and sophisticated:** Keay, 431
103 **appears to have left:** Platt, 10; also Pomeranz, 36–9, 116–22
104 **bravery and coolness under pressure:** Elliott 2009, 8
104 **fullest flower:** Platt, 46; also Elliott, 2012
104 **collected writings amounts:** 'A Golden Age of China: Qianlong Emperor (1736–1795)', exhibition, National Gallery of Victoria media release, 19 January 2015: https://www.ngv.vic.gov.au/media_release/a-golden-age-of-china-qianlong-emperor/ (accessed 23/4/24)
104 **Complete Library in the Four Branches:** Platt, 45; see *Siku Quanshu*, UC Santa Barbara Library, https://guides.library.ucsb.edu/az/databases?a=s
105 **the final solution:** Westad, 10
105 **referred to himself in old age:** Waley-Cohen 1996, 869
105 **held all the cards:** Platt, xxiv
105 **much richer than any part:** Smith Adam, 195
105 **only civilised nation in the world:** Anderson 1795
106 **in a hundred or a thousand years:** Wills, 198
106 **urged vigilance:** see Fu, 122–7
106 **tranquilly and equitably:** Cranmer-Byng and Wills, 199
107 **ever seen again:** see Platt, 7
108 **such amazingly gracious:** ibid.
108 **arrested and beheaded:** Wakeman 1974, 49
108 **thirty feet high and:** Platt, xvii
108 **warren of narrow:** Wakeman 1974, 14
109 **seeking mistresses:** Boxer 1979, 747
109 **known as flower boats:** ibid.
109 **playing leapfrog at all hours:** Ian Morris, 'The Opium War and the Humiliation of China', review of *The Opium War and the End of China's Last Golden Age* by Stephen R. Platt, *The New York Times*, 2 July 2018
109 **luxurious and very expensive:** Downs 1968, 424
109 **Canton Regatta Club:** Dolin, 185
109 **richest man in the world:** Platt, 202
110 **with its five hundred domestics:** Wakeman 1974, 44
110 **a space of just twelve:** Platt, xxi
110 **prices and exchange rates:** Fairbank 1964, 51
110 **considerable and ongoing:** Ellis et al., 70
110 **regularly demanded bribes:** Fairbank 1964, 49–50
111 **merely a new form:** ibid., 7, 9
111 **English barbarian chieftain:** ibid., 9
111 **time of engagement and curiosity:** ibid., 9, 14
111 **The males mostly wear wool:** ibid., 12
111 **are always surprised:** ibid., 19
112 **a great many prostitutes:** ibid., 17
112 **funded by the East India Company:** Waley-Cohen 2000, 103
112 **historical tribute pattern:** Fairbank 1964, 14
112 **embittered attitudes on both sides:** Cranmer-Byng and Wills, 245
112 **finest spotted mulberry velvet:** Lindorff, 442

112 only and invariable rule of conduct: Wood 1940, 142
113 one third of the entire world: Ping-ti, 23, 264, 270, 278
113 third largest city: Platt, 67
113 any foreign contact: Jung Chang, 21
113 as his journal indicates: Macartney, 124–6
113 come in arrogance, they get nothing: Edict of QL58/8/6 (10 September 1793) in Platt, 38
114 As the Greatness and Splendour: 'Letter from the Emperor of China to the King of England', British Library India Office Records in Platt, 39–40
114 Chinese have the best food: Hart, 61
114 lifeblood of the British empire: Platt, 41
114 blow would be immediate and heavy: Macartney, 212–3

Chapter 12: Trading Tea

115 strange predilection: Ellis et al., 19
116 Catherine's royal patronage: ibid., 38
117 Not only does tea enliven: Nicholas Tulp, *Medical Observations*, Amsterdam, 1641 (trans. Boris Ginsburgs, 2011) 400–3, in Ellis et al., 34
117 experimented quite often: Alexandre de Rhodes, *Divers voyages et missions du père Alexandre de Rhodes*, Paris, 1654, 62–3, in Ellis et al., 24–5
117 6,000 per cent: de Rhodes, 62–3 in Ellis et al., 24
117 astonishing ... £847: Ellis et al., 32
117 the Excellent, and by: *Mercurius Politicus*, 23 September, 1658
117 all Persons of Eminency: Ellis et al., 26–7
117 Samuel Pepys: Pepys, vol. 1, 25 September, 1660, 253, and vol. VI, 13 December 1665, 328
118 weight of each bag: Rose, 153
118 Thus heavily burdened: ibid.
118 pluck up to thirty thousand: ibid., 155
118 as much as ten pounds: ibid.
118 workers were woken: Ball 1848
118 the next day's plucking: ibid.
119 4,000 coins: Gotu, 15
119 Dutch ship Bredenhof: UNESCO: Silk Roads Programme, Bredenhof (1753), https://en.unesco.org/silkroad/silk-road-themes/underwater-heritage/bredenhof-1753
119 philosopher John Locke returned: Ellis et al., 46
120 we expect some jars: Schlegel, 469
120 increasing importance for prosperity: Ellis et al., 116
120 Roome betwixt Decks: ibid., 63
120 does very much obtaine: ibid., 58
120 drive the Trade to the utmost: Directors of the English Company to President Catchpole and Council in China, 27 June 1700, in Ellis et al., 56
120 as the Ship can conveniently stow: Hosea Ballou Morse, vol. 1, 158
120 subtill Cunning People: Despatches to the East, India Office Records in Ellis et al., 66
121 all sharpers ... knaves: Charles Lockyer, *An Account of the Trade in India*, London, 1711, 116–17, in Ellis et al., 66
121 innumerable tricks occurred: Ellis et al., 66; Rose, 90
121 Quantity of Tea Stolen: Pudney, 50
121 the god to which everything else: Gotu, 10
121 make their European rivals sick: Chung, 77
121 tea prevailed so universally: Ellis et al., 182
122 an entrance in every Cottage: ibid., 180
122 the cups that cheer: William Cowper, 'The Task: A Poem', in *The Poems of William Cowper*, John D Baird and Charles Ryskamp (eds), vol. 2, Oxford, 1995, 187–8
122 more than doubled: Ellis et al., 182
122 growing nearly 10,000 per cent: Greenberg, 3; also Platt, 12
122 tea imports doubled: Cranmer-Byng and Wills, 210
122 captains, officers and supercargoes: Gotu, 11
122 over a £1million: ibid., 12
122 £78,000: McCutcheon, 564
122 withdrew from the China trade: Gotu, 13–14
123 one tenth of England's total revenue: Greenberg, 3
123 consumed 70 per cent or more: Pritchard, 285
123 convict ships from Botany Bay: Regina Ganter, 9
123 only place in the world: Platt, 12
123 triangular trade through Java: Gotu, 17
123 feared that precious metals: Bowen, 446
123 It is much disputed: ibid.
123 Chinese shards: Lisbet Koerner, *Linnaeus; Nature and Nation,* Harvard University Press, 1999, 96, 116–7, 136, in Finlay, 54
123 dry leaves of bushes: Finlay, 54
124 trading house of Mocatta: Bowen, 453: see discussion in note 19

Chapter 13: Rivers of Silver

125 most often used ... more numerous: Ryan McMaken, 'Why Did the World Choose a Gold Standard Instead of a Silver Standard?', *Mises Wire*, 1 May 2022: https://mises.org/mises-wire/why-did-world-choose-gold-standard-instead-silver-standard

125 seemingly bottomless ... vacuum cleaner: Flynn and Giraldez 1995, 206
125 silver wanders throughout all the world: von Glahn 1996(a), 433
126 greatest commerce of the universe: Montesquieu, 392
126 went round the world: Frank, 131
126 distant parts of the world: Smith Adam, 212
126 Single Whip reform: Flynn and Giraldez 1995, 208–9
126 decision to abandon: see Cribb, 194; also von Glahn 1996(a), 430
126 a thousandth of their original value: Cribb ibid.
127 miscellany in the marketplace: Flynn and Giraldez 1995, 207–8
127 string of a thousand coins: Cribb, 185
127 like bangles on wrists and arms: Ghosh 2011, 334
127 dictated their fineness: Cribb, 196
127 shaving off part of an ingot: ibid., 190
128 store of value: Pomeranz, 159
128 sometimes more or sometimes less: von Glahn, 433
128 silver's [market] value: Flynn and Giráldez, 1995, 206, 215
128 carries away the silver: Newton, 2.
128 nothing more important than: Lisbet Koerner, *Linnaeus; Nature and Nation,* Harvard University Press, 1999, in Finlay, 5
128 conspicuous consumption: Xu, 134–5
129 exceeded even that of the Song dynastic period: Brook 2010, 187–212
129 Epicureanism and gastronomy: Xu, 133–4
129 enjoying food in equal and plentiful measure: Jaivin, 119
129 decay of the age and the decline of standards: Brook 1981, 173
129 magistrate Zhang Tao fulminated: Brook 2009, 173–4
129 extension of knowledge to the hoi polloi: Clunas, 34–6

Chapter 14: Manila Galleons

130 upset the balance of the earth: Cribb, 189–90
130 huge silver deposits: von Glahn 1996(a), 432
130 depredations and atrocities: Blue, 69–70
131 apocryphal local story: Brook 2009, 90
131 extensive clandestine networks: Antony, 44–6
131 in the Far East, they were: Villiers, 69
131 dominated the trade: ibid., 71
131 known as the 'black ships': see Cushner 1961, 533–42
131 led there by indigenous peoples: Brook 2009, 157
132 I am rich Potosí: Gordon and Morales, 52
132 For the powerful emperor: ibid.
132 perhaps the richest mountain: John Maxwell Hamilton, 'The Glory That Was Once Potosi', *The New York Times*, 29 May 1979
132 phrase 'as rich as Potosí': Brook 2009, 158
132 40,000 tons of silver: von Glahn 1996(b), 124–41
132 town's population swelled: Flynn and Giraldez 1995, 209; Brook 2009, 158
132 20 million people: Flynn and Giraldez, ibid.
132 casinos, dance halls and churches: Gordon and Morales, 53
132 fourth largest city: Patrick Greenfield, 'Story of cities #6: how silver turned Potosí into "the first city of capitalism"', *The Guardian*, 21 March 2016
132 first city of capitalism: ibid.
132 tomb of European moneys: Brook 2009, 159
133 arduous trek took: Flynn and Giraldez 2020, 14
133 centre of world silver trade: Brook 2009, 159
133 technically illegal: ibid.
133 pieces of eight: Brook 2009, 261–2
133 first global currency: Gordon and Morales, 62
134 two hemispheres representing: ibid., 61
134 aspired to 'the riches of the Indies': RJH de Jesus, review of Dámaso de Lario (ed), 'Re-shaping the World, Phillip 11 of Spain and His Time', *Philippine Studies*, vol. 58, no, 3, 2010, 429
134 mariner Miguel López de Legazpi: see Cushner 1965
134 gain the commerce with China: Letter from de Legazpi to Marques de Falces in Blair and Robertson, vol. 3, 43
134 all attempts to sail back: Gordon and Morales, 16
135 We are at the gate: ibid., 17–18, citing Blair and Robertson, ibid., vol. 2
135 Philippines gives us a base: Senator Albert Beveridge, 'In Support of an American Empire', 9 January 1900, *The Senate, Classic Speeches 1830–1993*, US Government Printing Office,1994, vol.3, 493
135 joined the European world with: de Jesus, 430
135 built in the Philippines: Lugar, 30
135 raw silk ... fine untwisted silk: Gordon and Morales, 22–3
135 longest, and most dreadful: Lugar, 38

135 **hunger, thirst, cold:** Gordon and Morales, 28
135 **rats from the hold:** Lugar, 36
136 **when most large ships:** Gordon and Morales, 25
137 **most renowned trade fair:** von Humboldt, vol. 4, 71
136 **14,000 Mexican weavers:** Gordon and Morales, 36
136 **arguably the 'centre of the world':** ibid., 40
137 **la ruta de la plata:** ibid., 4
137 **little else to sell:** Brook 2009, 160
137 **Mexico City became:** Boyer, 455
137 **In you, Spain joins:** Bernardo Balbuena, *The Grandeur of Mexico City*, 1604, cited in Gordon and Morales, 46
137 **richest, most opulent:** ibid., 41
137 **beating heart of world commerce:** Richard Mills, 'The Role of Silver in Chinese History', AheadOfTheHerd website, 29 December 2022, https://aheadoftheherd.com/the-role-of-silver-in-chinese-history/

Chapter 15: Global Currents

138 **emerging world economy:** Atwell, 236
138 **global impact of historic proportions:** Flynn and Giraldez 2020, 8
138 **regular and lasting maritime connection:** Boxer 1969, 17
138 **world's financial markets:** Gordon and Morales, 66
139 **perhaps exceeding 80 percent:** Ward Barrett, 'World Bullion Flows, 1450–1800', in James D. Tracy (ed.), *The Rise of Merchant Empires: Long-Distance Trade in the Early Modern World, 1350–1750*, Cambridge, 1990, 237, cited in Flynn and Giraldez 1995, 202
139 **century of war:** Flynn and Giraldez 1995, 216
139 **Because of the said mines:** Guaman Poma quoted in Evan M. Bourke, 'Silver and the Spanish Empire', 7 December 2021: https://storymaps.arcgis.com/stories/d1fa8efad3a24a2abe00ccc570e974e3
139 **A drawing in:** ibid., drawing no. 375
139 **irredeemably integrated into:** Waley-Cohen 2000, 52
139 **borrower from hell:** see Drelichman and Voth, 2014
139 **true of Habsburg Spain:** Gerald Seib, 'Will Debt Sink the American Empire?', *The Wall Street Journal*, 21 June 2024: https://www.wsj.com/politics/policy/will-debt-sink-the-american-empire-8459096b
140 **Price Revolution:** see Flynn and Giraldez 2020, 16–20
140 **locust swarms, food shortages:** Frankopan 2023, 412
140 **worst drought in 500 years:** ibid.
140 **All along our route:** Brook 2017, 28–9
140 **Through silver, China's upheavals:** Xu, 146
141 **It took half a century:** Cranmer-Byng and Wills, 196
141 **More Spanish American silver:** Flynn and Giraldez 2002(a), 12–13
141 **merchant bankers in Europe began:** Topik et al., 19
141 **two million silver pesos per year:** ibid., 20
142 **as near us as France or Spain:** Hume to Oswald, 1 November 1750 in Hume, 198
142 **graveyard of silver:** Topik et al., 17

Chapter 16: The Humble Herb

147 **the joy plant:** Brownstein 1993
147 **drug bringing oblivion:** Bell and Copeland, 242
148 **world's first drug cartel:** Realuyo, 133
148 **one of the most pernicious:** Trocki, 5
148 **the financial wherewithal:** Brook and Wakabayashi, 1
148 **Chinese history would:** ibid.
148 **roughly half a million acres:** Ghosh 2024, 50
148 **quasi-military, fortress-like:** ibid., 62
149 **local English language newspaper:** Trocki, 2
149 **The church's ringing bells:** Ghosh 2008, 94–5
149 **like the Sassoon family:** see Sassoon 2022
150 **kept impoverished:** Soutik Biswas, 'How Britain's Opium Trade Impoverished Indians', BBC News, 2 September 2019: https://www.bbc.com/news/world-asia-india-49404024 (accessed 14/5/2024)
150 **regularly netted ten times more:** Trocki, 66–7
151 **between 16,000 and 20,000 cakes:** ibid., 70
151 **neat little cannonshot:** Ghosh 2008, 102
152 **ten metres in height:** ibid., 100
152 **For every 10,000 balls:** Trocki, 70
152 **technique of growing:** Greenberg, 110
153 **upon giving security:** Trocki, 76
153 **in return for bills of exchange:** Platt, 185; also Downs 1968, 433–4
153 **went into the hands of British:** Trocki, 58–9
153 **exceeded in value all of the tea:** Platt, 187
154 **scrambling crabs:** Bradley, 22
154 **eulogy of free trade:** Owen, 34
154 **The thundering rise:** Chung, 81; also Rose, 176, Platt 187–8

155 **Bengal opium chest:** Chung, ibid.
155 **made the import of tea free:** Parvez Mahmood, 'Addiction of a Nation', *The Friday Times* [Pakistan], 26 May 2017: https://thefridaytimes.com/26-May-2017/addiction-of-a-nation (accessed 15/5/2024)
155 **safest and most Gentlemanlike:** Jardine to R Rolfe, 6 April 1830 in Platt, 195
155 **Matheson justified his initial presence:** Grace, 104
155 **Matheson purchased the Hebridean:** ibid., 299
155 **Oh, a dreadful man:** in Lovell, 26
156 **a few hundredths of a percent:** Platt, 213
156 **easiest and most effective:** Platt, 194
156 **It is my business to make:** Alcock, 37–8
156 **Were it possible to prevent:** Trocki, 75
157 **most tangible difference:** Platt 213.
157 **almost that of a dense, oily:** Ghosh 2015, 395
157 **a serenely peaceful nullity:** ibid., 474
158 **composed in a sort of reverie:** Platt, 197–8
158 **Christian and American values:** Bradley, 6
158 **more than two and a half million:** Platt, 199

Chapter 17: A Storm Brewing

159 **strange want of decent:** *The Chinese Repository*, Bridgman and Williams (eds), vol. 6, May 1837, 18
159 **The Chinese Empire has become:** Honour, 22
160 **long been English mutterings:** McCutcheon, 559
160 **resorted to racist stereotyping:** ibid.
160 **Nothing can exceed the gullibility:** Platt, 121
160 **not only a very powerful empire:** Macartney, 112
160 **She may perhaps not sink:** ibid., 212–13
160 **He believed that China's day:** ibid., 239
161 **lying words:** Platt, 73
162 **most advantageous monopoly:** Drury to Roberts, 8 November 1808 in Wood 1940, 150
162 **French cruisers were everywhere:** Platt, 89
162 **Rumours of a joint Russian-French invasion:** Hopkirk, 33–4
163 **superior-minded Christian:** Platt, 88
163 **Robert's attitude was a far cry:** see generally Dalrymple 2004
163 **so long as they persevere:** Peter Auber, *China: An Outline of Its Government, Laws, and Policy*, Parbury, Allen & Co, 1834, 233, cited in Platt, 92
163 **dictated by Wisdom:** Wood 1940, 153
163 **endangered 'the property.'** ibid., 156
164 **By 1840, the British empire:** Platt, 117
164 **Whosoever commands the sea:** in Tan, 132
165 **Great Britain was now unrivalled:** Platt, 151
165 **The deeper sense of entitlement:** ibid., 155
167 **at a signall being made:** George Thomas Staunton, Diary 1793–4, entry for 17 September 1793, *Staunton Papers*, Duke University, cited in Platt, 161
167 **Amherst was astute enough:** Amherst to Canning, 20 February, 1817 in ibid., 161
167 **found it utterly impossible:** English draft of Amherst's letter in ibid., 164
168 **to resist force by force:** Amherst to Canning, 8 March, 1817 in ibid., 167
168 **capricious despot:** Clark Abel, *Narrative of a Journey in the Interior of China*, Longman, 1818, 111, in ibid., 169
168 **Do not be so severe:** Jiaqing edict, 25 August, 1816 in ibid., 169
168 **If the king would just tend:** Jiaqing edict, 30 August, 1816 in ibid., 170
169 **the less that is conceded:** 'Chinese Drama – Lord Amherst's Embassy to China', *Quarterly Review*, 16, no. 32, January, 1817, 412, in ibid., 173
169: Different nations have different customs: O'Meara, vol. 1, 471
169 **It would be the worst thing:** ibid., 471–2

Chapter 18: Fire & Smoke

170 **The multitude of users expands:** Platt, 216
171 **full unadulterated London fashion:** Platt, 232; also Hillard, 73, 110, 141
171 **soldiers and wife:** Platt, 235
171 **grossly insulting:** Morse, vol. 4, 236
172 **would be highly injurious:** ibid., 237–8
172 **relieved of his duties:** Platt, 236
172 **long submitted in silence:** 'China Trade: Copy of a Petition of British Subjects in China', House of Commons, 20 March, 1833 reproduced in Le Pichon, 553–9,
172 **barbarous, ignorant and depraved:** Platt, 238
172 **had no idea:** Morse, vol. 4, 286
173 **gratuitous insult offered:** 'Resolutions of the British Merchants of Canton', 30 May 1831 in Morse, vol. 4, 311
173 **to preserve our national character:** secret letter from the Select Committee to the Court of Directors, 18 June 1831, in Platt, 239
173 **had the temerity:** Forbes to Cushing, 30 June, 1831 in ibid., 239

173 **Who would barter:** Forbes to Perkins, 21 December, 1831 in ibid., 239–40
173 **notions of self-importance:** C.S. Parker, *Life and Letters of Sir James Graham, 1792–1861* in ibid., 244
174 **required much management:** Jardine to Matheson, 28 January, 1832 in Le Pichon, 143–5, in ibid., 264
174 **just about everyone:** Platt, 264
174 **as a nation, China:** 'Mr Gutzlaff's Voyages along the Coast of China', *The Times*, 26 August, 1834
174 **cheerfully distributing:** Fay, 89
174 **one of the weakest minds:** Davis to Staunton, 20 October, 1834 in Platt, 301
175 **what China really needed:** Platt, 280
175 **how easily a gun brig:** Napier Diary, entry for 26 October, 1833 in ibid., 269
175 **China's heinous insults:** 'The Petition of the Undermentioned British Subjects at Canton', 9 December, 1834 in Platt, 298–9
175 **Mr Jardine will do anything:** Lady Napier to Alexander Hunter, 4 November, 1834 in Platt, 302
175 **my friend Mr Matheson:** Lady Napier to Palmerston, 14 July, 1835, in Platt, 303
175 **If some show of apology:** Lady Napier to Lindsay, 18 January 1836, in Platt, 305
176 **the possession of a vast portion:** Matheson 2012 [1836],
176 **China was not some enemy:** Staunton, *Remarks on the British Relations with China, and the Proposed Plans for Improving Them*, 1836 in Platt, 307
176 **It is the fashion:** Elliot to Lennox-Conygnham, 12 June 1837, in Platt, 325
177 **Not a broker:** Jardine to Jauncey, 10 December, 1838, in Platt, 342
177 **We are not smugglers:** 'Public Dinner to Mr. Jardine, on the occasion of his departure for Europe', *Canton Register*, 29 January 1839 in Platt, 347; also Ghosh 2011, 427
178 **no one suffered:** Hsin-pao Chang, 157
178 **suffered more:** Platt, 355
178 **Are they trying:** Ghosh 2011, 53
178 **participate in or watch:** Hsin-pao Chang, 154
179 **a good deal excited:** Matheson to Jardine, 1 May 1839 in Platt, 353
179 **imminent hazard:** John Slade, *Narrative of the Late Proceedings and Events in China*, Canton Register Press, 1839, 53, in ibid., 353
179 **I will remain:** Slade, 54 in ibid., 354
179 **Elliot's mad freaks:** Forbes to Rose Forbes, 31 January 1840 in ibid., 358
179 **great difficulty at times:** Elliot to Emma Hislop, 12 May 1840 in ibid., 400
179 **He ordered all foreigners:** Hsin-pao Chang, 164–5
179 **the most fortunate thing:** Matheson to Middleton, 9 April, 1839 in Platt, 357
179 **containing more than:** Jung Chang, 22; also Hsin-pao Chang, 175–6
180 **five hundred men:** Ghosh 2011, 562; cf. Hsin-pao Chang, 175
180 **into a thousand:** Hsin-pao Chang, 185

Chapter 19: First Opium War

185 **the bizarre actions:** Platt, 372
185 **wholly unprepared:** *The Times*, 23 October, 1839
186 **a small squadron of:** Melancon, 869
187 **cannot interfere:** Palmerston to Elliot, 15 June 1838 in Melancon, 859
187 **with barely a sideways:** Lovell, 101
187 **master of one third:** Platt, 372
187 **literally masterminded:** Wong, 311; also Hsin-Pao Chang, 193–4
187 **down to details:** Wong, 311
187 **a war more unjust:** 'War with China–Adjourned Debate', *House of Commons Debates*, 8 April, 1840, vol. 53, 816–8: https://api.parliament.uk/historic-hansard/commons/1840/apr/08/war-with-china-adjourned-debate
188 **younger sister Helen:** Isba, 2003
188 **pro-Palmerston speech:** Hansard, *House of Lords Debates*, 12 May, 1840, vol. 54, c. 35–6: https://hansard.parliament.uk/Lords/1840-05-12/debates/aff9f17e-4c46-47cd-98d8-d84ea36da554/HouseOfLords
188 **the cause of the war:** John Quincy Adams, 'Lecture on the War with China', Massachusetts Historical Society, December 1841 in Platt, 416
188 **acting in defence:** Melancon, 857–8
188 **Flag of England:** Palmerston to Grey, 14 September, 1832 in Melancon, 857
188 **what not one single person:** Platt, 392
188 **shifty, shuffling, slippery:** Lovell, 106
189 **every claim or demand:** Platt, 396
189 **locked up in:** Lovell, 103
189 **if the town of Canton:** 'The House of Lords Last Night', *The Times*, 11 March 1840
189 **Palmerston's objectives:** Platt, 397
189 **certainly unusual:** Jung Chang, 23, footnote 2
190 **She was a secret British weapon:** Fay, 262
190 **devil ship:** Paine 2000, 115
190 **Everything about the *Nemesis*:** Fay, 261–2
191 **underfed, underpaid:** Lovell, 150
191 **Chinese cannon:** Fay, 345
191 **bows and arrows:** Lovell, 111–12

191 there is really nothing: Waley, 103
191 occupy Zhoushan and blockade: Lovell, 110
191 in nine short minutes: Lord Jocelyn, *Six Months with the Chinese Expedition*, John Murray, 1841, pp. 55–7 in Lovell, 100–111
192 character and dignity: Platt, 397–8
192 On Boxing Day 1840: Lovell, 129
192 costing the Chinese two: Wakeman 1974, 11
193 more village fete: Lovell, 137
193 wastepaper: Platt, 399–400
193 stamped her little foot: Lovell, 169
193 ***All*** **we wanted:** Queen Victoria to Leopold, King of the Belgians, 13 April, 1841 in Benson and Esher, vol.1, 329–30
193 was a barren island: Palmerston to Elliot, 21 April 1841 in Platt, 399
193 much amused: Victoria to Leopold, 13 April 1841, in Benson and Esher, ibid.
194 become more of a Chinese: Platt, 400
194 Much travel has: Lovell, 174
194 all you could hear: ibid., 154
194 the protection of the people: Fay, 294
194 soldiers, officials and militiamen: Lovell, 143–4
195 One and a half thousand: John Elliot Bingham, *Narrative of the Expedition to China*, 2nd edn, Henry Colburn, London, 1843, 280–1 in Lovell, 189
195 increasingly self-defeating: Platt, 404
195 many most barbarous ... bespattered with brains: ibid.
195 our visitations are so: Parker to Minto, 30 July 1842 in ibid.
195 the slaughter of: Elliot to Aberdeen, 25 January, 1842 in ibid.
196 a white cloud: Sir Henry Keppel, *A Sailor's Life under Four Sovereigns*, London, 1899, vol. 1, 269 in Fay, 351
196 groups of old men, women: Granville Loch, *The Closing Events of the Campaign in China*, John Murray, 1843 in Lovell, 218–9
196 fourteen, even twenty bodies: Lovell, 218
197 the energy of British character: John Elliot Bingham, *Narrative of the Expedition to China*, Henry Colburn, 1843, vol. 2, 356 in Lovell, 222
197 the dishonourable war: *The Times*, 24 December 1842
197 I knew the day of retribution: Lady Napier to Palmerston, 12 March 1840 in Platt, 410

Chapter 20: Second Opium War

198 one could get what: Platt, 406
198 Hounded by such unspeakable: Jung Chang, 25
199 great and glorious: Lovell, 241
199 a new continent to: *The Times*, 23 November 1842
199 vast hordes: Thurin, 5
199 the most disgraceful: *The Times*, 17 March, 1857
199 no man with a spark: *The Times*, 30 October 1858
199 the insufferable sins: Lovell, 243
199 sneer at the comic: ibid., 242
200 must not take possession: Fairbank 1964, 102
200 at the harbours: Nolde 1961
200 It was enough to: Lovell, 247
200 threatening to throw: Wakeman 1974, 54, note 3
200 not immediately ... but: ibid., 134
200 The moment the entry question: ibid., 134
201 A date should be set: Wakeman, 1974, 102
201 Foreign threat is worrying: Wong, 119
201 greatest fear remains: Henry Kissinger explains how to avoid world war three', *The Economist*, 17 May 2023
202 urging people to pour: Wakeman, 1974, 94
202 The Central Empire cannot: ibid., 103
202 unsatisfactory evasion: ibid.
202 first great Chinese diplomatic: ibid., 104
202 Do not let the barbarians: ibid., 103
202 These half-civilised Governments: Costin, 152
202 declared themselves prepared: George Wingrove Cooke article in the *Economist*, 4 September 1858 in Wong, 263, note 14
203 particularly in the rich: Bonham to Palmerston, 15 April, 1850 in Wong, 263
203 I clearly see: Fairbank 1964, 380
203 I ***have*** **an end:** Bowring to Clarendon, 5 September 1854 in Wong, 265
203 had grown up fervently loathing: Jung Chang, 25
203 always caving in: ibid., 26–7
204 tired, septuagenarian: Lovell, 254–5
204 unlimited extension of our trade: Wong, 272
204 most strikingly arrogant: Clarendon to Cowley, Despatch 1099, 24 September 1856 in Wong, 266
204 the vast resources: ibid.
204 swaggered about: Lovell, 245
204 encouraged [Parkes] to find: Lovell, 251; also Wong, 269
205 some loose fish: Wong, 3–4
205 by means of some mystification: Wong, 3
205 An insult so publicly: Parkes to Yeh, 8 October 1856 in Wong, 72–3
205 deliberately, cynically and illegally: Lovell, 253

205 **Cannot we use the opportunity:** Bowring to Parkes, 16 October 1856 in Wong, 88
205 **monomaniac ... dreams of entrance to Canton:** Hansard, 3rd series, v. 144, cols. 1177, 1184, 1204: https://api.parliament.uk/historic-hansard/lords/1857/feb/24/resolutions-moved-debate-adjourned#column_1177; also Wong, 105–6
206 **We are *so* strong:** Bowring to Parkes, 21 October 1856 in Wong, 90
206 **one mass of smoke:** 'Memorandum of Operations at Canton, 5–13 January 1856' [sic] dated 14 January 1857 in Wong, 101
206 **their knowledge ... expired:** fully discussed in Wong, 70–1, 87, 91 & 103; also Lovell, 252
206 **thus cutting off:** Foreign Office to Admiralty, 9 February, 1857 in Wong, 289–90
206 **Almost for the first time:** Hansard, 9 March, 1857, 3rd series, v. 144, col. 2042: https://api.parliament.uk/historic-hansard/lords/1857/mar/09/motion-for-opinion-of-the-judges#column_2042
207 **was an issue then:** see Petition to the Queen, 2 February 1857 in Wong, 288
207 **uproar of the merchant princes:** Wong, 305
207 **un-English ... seraphic:** *Morning Post*, 17 March 1857 in Wong, 227
207 **Chinese coalition:** Wong, 225
207 **whole civilised world:** Gourley to Hammond, 24 March, 1857 in Wong, 217
207 **to repeat loudly:** Lovell, 255
207 **returned the warmongers:** ibid., 256
207 **I never felt so ashamed:** Theodore Walrond (ed.), *Letters and Journals of James, Eighth Lord Elgin*, Cornell University Library, 2009 [1872], 212 in Newsinger, 119–20
208 **shells and rockets:** George Wingrove Cooke, *China:Being The Times Special Correspondence* [sic] *from China in the Years 1857–58*, 2023 [1858], 318–19 in Newsinger, 120
208 **Ye was my game:** Stanley Lane-Poole, *Sir Harry Parkes in China*, Methuen, 1901, 272 in Lovell, 258
208 **sickness and ennui:** Lovell 258
208 **warlord governor:** Lane-Poole, 181, in Lovell, 258
208 **were little more than:** Newsinger, 131
208 **fighting and bullying:** Walrond 252–3 in ibid.
208 **To his wife he confessed:** ibid.

Chapter 21: Plunder & Pillage

210 **pistol at the throat:** Jung Chang, 27
211 **no more than 10 men:** ibid., 28
211 **high consideration and respect:** Immanuel Hsu, *The Rise of Modern China*, Oxford University Press, 1983, 214 in Newsinger, 133
211 **they must have been Russians:** Gerald Graham, *The China Station: War and Diplomacy 1830–1860*, Clarendon Press, 1978, 377 in Newsinger, 134
211 **Our loss is awful:** 'The Disaster in China', *The Times*, 16 September 1859
211 **We must strike a signal blow:** 'Allied Expedition to China', *The Times*, 12 September 1859
212 **wretched ... embarrassing:** Lovell, 260; Walrond, 209; Wong, 460
212 **Can I do anything:** Walrond, 325 in Newsinger, 134
212 **I am very cheerful:** Lane-Poole, 227 in Lovell, 258
212 **an experimental Anglo-Chinese:** David Rennie, *The British Arms in North China and Japan*, London, 1864 in Newsinger, 135
212 **were in our hands:** Rev RJL McGhee, *How We Got to Pekin*, Richard Bentley, 1862, 114–15 in Newsinger, 134–5
212 **a Judaeo-Christian society:** 'Pentagon AI more ethical because of Judeo-Christian society', *The Washington Post*, 22 July, 2023: https://www.washingtonpost.com/national-security/2023/07/22/air-force-general-ai-judeochristian/
213 **the ultimate way:** Jung Chang, 29
213 **tied their feet:** ibid., 30
213 **the killing of prisoners:** Newsinger, 136
213 **their own personal wine stock:** ibid.
213 **scum of the earth:** Wellington to Earl Bathurst, 2 July, 1813 in Brown 2015, p.1
214 **chosen Cixi's five-year:** Jung Chang, 40
214 **All the treasures of:** Victor Hugo, Letter to Captain Butler, 25 November, 1861 in 'The Chinese Expedition: Victor Hugo on the Sack of the Summer Palace', 1861, Napoleon.org website: https://www.napoleon.org/en/history-of-the-two-empires/articles/the-chinese-expedition-victor-hugo-on-the-sack-of-the-summer-palace/ (accessed 19/5/2024)
214 **in a corner of the world:** ibid.
215 **extended for six or seven:** McGhee, 211–12 in Roote, 59
215 **portraits of the beauties:** Roote, 111
215 **a memorable day:** Captain JH Dunne, diary entry 8 October, 1860 in Roote, 84

215 **Christies, Hunt and Roskell's:** ibid., 86–8
215 **If you can imagine:** McGhee, 204–5
215 **a poet, a painter:** ibid., 285–9
216 **Officers and men ... seized with:** Wolseley 2005 [1862], 227
216 **you would sink:** McGhee, 210 in Roote, 57
216 **satin or silk:** ibid.
216 **blazing with silk:** McGhee 206–7 in Roote, 64
216 **army cross-dressers:** Lovell, 263
216 **Everything that could not:** Dunne, *From Calcutta to Peking*, Samson Low 1861, 128–9 in Roote 2017, 85
216 **There was not a room:** Walrond, 361–2 in Newsinger, 137
216 **War is a hateful business:** ibid.
217 **I never saw a more pitiable:** McGhee, 252
217 **as expiation of:** Robert Swinhoe, *Narrative of the North China Campaign of 1860*, Smith, Elder, 1861, 329 in Lovell, 265
217 **the heavens were black:** McGhee, 258 in Roote, 66–7
217 **Goth-like act of barbarism:** Wolseley, 279 in Roote, 247
217 **in a few minutes other wreaths:** McGhee, 287 in Roote, 69
218 **No one will ever again:** ibid.
218 **It was a sacrifice:** McGhee, 289 in Roote, 70
218 **One day two bandits:** Victor Hugo letter to Butler, in ibid.
218 **dispersed and undocumented:** Thomas 2008.
219 **promoting the provenance:** see ibid.
219 **well over a million:** Andrew Hillier, review of *Collecting and Displaying China's "Summer Palace" in the West*, Reviews in History website, 2018: https://reviews.history.ac.uk/review/2223 (accessed 19/5/2024)
219 **by sixteen Chinamen:** *Illustrated London News*, 5 January 1861 in Hevia, 114–15
220 **consisted of six hundred:** ibid.
220 **Prince Gong, pale as death:** ibid., 115
220 **frenzy of anti-Chinese patriotism:** *The Times*, 10 & 11 December 1860
220 **not only in the history:** Lovell, 268
221 **There is no nation, numerically:** Wolseley 2022 [1903], vol. 2, 2

Chapter 22: America & Jesus

225 **without any of the violence:** Platt, 416, 420–21
225 **the hands of Providence:** Schmidt, 4
226 **800 chests of tea:** Dolin, 84
226 **Washington acquired an elaborate:** Detweiler, 86–90
226 **We raise the fortunes:** Platt, 71
226 **yearly increasing:** Platt, 172, citing 'Chinese Embassy and Trade', *Edinburgh Review* 29, no. 58, February 1818, 433–53
226 **the above ground trade:** Platt, 191
226 **the firm operated from the American factory:** Yen-p'ing, 215
227 **gifted, prolific and:** Downs 1968, 429–30
227 **some of America's best families:** Bradley, 22
227 **built Boston's Athenaeum:** ibid., 29
227 **the Boston and Lowell:** ibid., 30
228 **competence – a profit of $100,000:** ibid., 19
228 **all a person needed:** Platt, 125
228 **This volume *we* deem:** M. Broomhall, *Robert Morrison: A Master Builder*, Turnbull & Spears, Edinburgh, 1927, 57 in Platt, 88
228 **the American public regarded:** Downs 1972, 144–5
229 **often conveniently left out:** Dolin, 257
229 **penetrate ... attacks the centre:** 'Mission to China', *Boston Recorder*, 31 May 1834
229 **to engage in a warfare:** *Chinese Repository*, December 1834, 380 in Platt, 468, note 24
229 **we are sure that the victors:** ibid.
229 **backward people who:** Bradley, 37
229 **The manifold needs:** AH Smith, *Chinese Characteristics*, Fleming H Revell, NY, 1894 in Bradley, 39
229 **so Americans should expose:** Young, 221
230 **how these difficulties:** Fay, 331
231 **We, as missionaries, weep:** *The Wesleyan-Methodist Magazine*, January 1957, 181 in Wong, 320
231 **it appeared more and:** Fay, 331
231 **aborigines of North America:** 'Barbarism. Civilisation', *Canton Register*, 30 December 1834 in Platt, 267
231 **representatives of Christendom:** Bradley, 39
231 **They are not Christians but:** Wood 2020, 403–4
231 **There was fundamentally:** Nathaniel Peffer, *The Far East: A Modern History*, University of Michigan Press, Ann Arbor, 1958, 117–8 in Bradley, 40
232 **carried on in spite of:** Robert Bennet Forbes to Rose Forbes, 27 February 1839 in Platt, 346
232 **The Americans of Russell & Co:** Platt, 424
232 **have manifested a proper:** Dolin, 256–7
233 **a hedge against:** Platt, 418

233 **the American mission brought:** 'List of Articles for the Legation to China', 11 April 1843 in ibid., 419
233 **now be arming thousand years:** ibid., 423–4
233 **most of the same privileges:** ibid., 420
234 **one of the greatest commercial:** Freeman Hunt, *Hunt's Merchant's Magazine*, January 1845, 79–80 cited in Dolin, 284–5
234 **generate a tidal wave:** Dolin, 285
234 **Paul S Forbes ... resign:** He, 13
235 **Peninsular & Oriental:** Harcourt, 1–83
235 **Jesus opium:** Lazich, 215
235 **for they killed:** ibid., 220
235 **frown of God:** ibid., 215
235 **Amid the distresses:** ibid., 211
236 **greater concern over:** ibid., 217
236 **carefully watching developments:** ibid., 219
236 **under the tree with:** Dennet, 305
236 **legalisation was preferable:** Stelle, 128
236 **Reed convinced Elgin:** Wong, 414
237 **the British and Americans won:** Lazich, 222

Chapter 23: Upheaval & Turmoil

238 **opium trade expanded:** Dolin, 287
238 **smell of burning:** Wood 2020, 430
239 **I am bowled over by:** Jung Chang, 50
239 **a woman of mind:** Robertson to Foreign Office, 30 November, 1861 in Jung Chang, 50
239 **The Taiping Rebellion:** Wood 2020, 413
240 **Your country lies desolate:** Wood 2020, 406; also Keay, 469–73
240 **God's Chinese son:** Wood 2020, 408
241 **Heavenly King entered:** Keay, 473
241 **sensing a triumph:** ibid.
241 **revolutionise the empire:** Bennett, 2009
241 **Southern Baptist:** Teng 1963
242 **dozens of concubines:** Jung Chang, 58
242 **20 to 30 million:** Wood 2020, 414
242 **Unvanquished ... Ever Victorious:** Keay, 477
243 **civilizing mission:** Lovell, 251
243 **ninety thousand chests:** Richards, 163
243 **entire interlocking system:** Banaji, 4
243 **kept the world economy:** Lovell, 251
243 **could not be extirpated:** Downs 1968, 434
243 **And like some complex modern debt instrument:** Banaji, 4
243 **had begun to equal:** Lovell, 273
244 **Undeniably, opium was being:** Spence 1975, 154
244 **nearly 30 or 40 percent:** Jung Chang, 331
244 **killed 80,000:** Cohn, 336
244 **the trade in the past:** Lodwick, 30
244 **doing more evil:** ibid., 50
244 **Someone shouts out:** ibid., 33
245 **I think [opium]:** Park, 62–3
245 **morally indefensible:** UK Parliament, Hansard, vol. 158, Wednesday 30 May 1906, 'The Opium Traffic': https://hansard.parliament.uk/Commons/1906-05-30/debates/706e6e2b-465e-404f-b188-aeb4245a2369/TheOpiumTraffic
245 **renovating the people:** Lovell, 303
245 **farmers stopped cultivation:** Jung Chang, 331
245 **agreed to restrict:** *Anglo-Chinese Ten Year Opium Suppression Agreement, 1907* is comprehensively discussed in Reins, esp. at 133 ff
246 **whites will disappear:** 'Memorial on Immigration into the West Indies', 18 February, 1859 in Meagher, 37
246 **taken away, never:** Ghosh 2008, 75
246 **we perceived how:** Deposition of Ye Fujun in 'Report of the Commission Sent by China to Ascertain the Condition of Chinese Coolies in Cuba', in Wakeman 1993, note 14
247 **misfits and castaways of society:** Meagher, 180
247 **sometimes more than:** Dolin, 293; Meagher, 153
247 **by a massive barricade:** Dolin, 293
247 **about one voyage in every:** Meagher, 179
247 **men-market:** Wakeman 1993 citing Juan Pérez de la Riva, *El barracón: Esclavitud y capitalismo en Cuba* [*The Barracks: Slavery and Capitalism in Cuba*], Barcelona, 1978, 107
247 **The Chinese coolie is treated:** Crawford to Granville, Havana, 3 September, 1873 in Meagher, 214
247 **one hundred times:** Wakeman 1993, citing de la Riva, p. 67
248 **were more than 150 feet:** Dolin, 299
248 **five tons of guano:** Dolin, 300
248 **distress and misery of:** Spence 1996, 304
249 **British, American, French:** Blue, 73
249 **fleet of between thirty:** ibid., 74
249 **the greatest theft:** Rose, 34
249 **symbol of the one:** ibid., 28
250 **a grey silk garment:** ibid., 64
250 **very tall and extremely brutish:** ibid., 65
250 **Within twenty years:** ibid., 237

Chapter 24: Make China Strong

252 **quite charming:** Algernon B Freeman-Mitford, *The Attaché at Peking*, Elibron Classics, 2005, 72 in Jung Chang, 58

252 **statesmen who understand:** Bruce to Earl Russell, 12 November 1861 in Jung Chang, 55
252 **China is now prepared:** A Egmont Hake, *Events in the Taiping Rebellion*, WH Allen & Co., 1891, 87 in Jung Chang, 57
252 **out of the dead end:** Jung Chang, 55
252 **China just needed to build:** Morris, 15
253 **a man of good temper:** Faught, 29
253 **with minimal pain:** Jung Chang, 64
254 **railroad, telegraph ... :** Freeman-Mitford in Jung Chang, 240–1
254 **deface our landscape:** Jung Chang, 67
254 **all his family:** ibid., 68
254 **would give a foreign power:** Schmid and Huang, 579
254 **the only way to ensure:** Jung Chang, 66
255 **Fuzhou project:** see Pong 1987, 123–4
255 *Qing Forever*: ibid., 127
255 **mostly wooden and:** Benjamin Elman, 298
255 **first person to be sent:** *Travel Diaries and Poems of Binchun* in Jung Chang, 74
255 **fragrant aroma of:** Biggerstaff 1937
255 **like flying through:** Jung Chang, 74
256 **Ambassador Extraordinary to Europe:** Biggerstaff 1942, 277–9
256 **fair and conciliatory:** Jung Chang, 76
256 **singular and unexpected:** ibid., 77
256 **American Architect:** Anderson 1977
256 **tell you that the present dynasty:** Shore, 408–9
257 **sixty-two ships:** Dolin, 301
257 **The United States and the Emperor:** Burlingame Treaty, Article V in Jung Chang, 79
257 **first Chinese exclusion law:** Chinese Exclusion Act, 1882, National Archives, https://www.archives.gov/milestone-documents/chinese-exclusion-act#:~:text=It%20was%20the%20first%20significant,immigrating%20to%20the%20United%20States
See also: US Office of the Historian, https://history.state.gov/milestones/1866-1898/chinese-immigration
257 **Zhigang's analysis of the West:** *The Travel Diaries of Zhigang as an Envoy to the West*, 244–380, cited in Jung Chang, 80–1
257 **if we are able:** Jung Chang, ibid.
258 **Unexpectedly, the situation changed:** ibid., 82
258 **Chun memorandum:** Weng Tonghe, *The Diaries of Weng Tonghe*, Beijing, 2006, vol. 2, 671, in Jung Chang, 88
258 **issue a decree to all:** ibid., 88–9
260 **From now on all sorts:** Jung Chang, 118
260 **over eighty of them:** Wood 2020, 429
260 **Make China Rich:** Jung Chang, 123
261 **Hanlin Academy:** see Stevens 1996
261 **The railways will pass through:** Wood 2020, 427
261 **the founding moment:** ibid.
261 **when this line is up and running:** ibid.
261 **Chinese Oxford Movement:** ibid., 428

Chapter 25: Road to Ruin

268 **nineteen foreign powers:** Keller and Shiue, 61, which contains a detailed account of the introduction of extraterritoriality to China
269 **foreign note-issuing banks:** see JE Sandrock 1997
270 **Wusong rail line:** Pong 1973
271 **eunuchs pulled the carriages:** Jung Chang, 126
272 **not a single person:** *North China Herald*, 22 July 1876 in Edgerton-Tarpley, 136
272 **Pictures that Might Draw Tears:** Edgerton-Tarpley, 'Pictures to Draw Tears from Iron', The North China Famine of 1876–1879: https://visualizingcultures.mit.edu/tears_from_iron/tfi_essay_01.pdf
273 **only fifteen minutes:** Elman, 316
273 **For the French to take:** Sir Edmund Hornby in *The Pall Mall Budget,* 29 August, 1884, 10
274 **all in the empire to show understanding:** Jung Chang, 160
274 **the country need not know:** Jung Chang, 161
274 **she may have siphoned:** Association of Chinese Historians (ed.) 2000, *The Movement to Learn from the West*, vol. 3, 141, in Jung Chang 161
275 **in a position to shape:** Jung Chang, 155
275 **there is no war:** Association of Chinese Historians (ed.) 2000, *The Sino-Japanese War*, vol. 3, 177–8, in Jung Chang, 183
276 **her army and navy are not:** Fairbank and Bruner (eds), vol. 2, 974–5
276 **Things look bad here:** ibid., 991–2
276 ***The New York Times* likened:** Paine 2009, 179–85
277 **Why is it that up to now:** Schell and Delury, 71
277 **had yet to find a firearm:** Keay, 489

Chapter 26: Road to Revolution

278 **The Japanese war:** Denby, vol. 2, 147
279 **put the Chinese capital:** Fairbank and Bruner, vol. 2, 992, 1006

279 **Kaiser Wilhelm … Yellow Peril:** in an interview with Dr William Hale, 19 July 1908 in Jung Chang, 200
279 **more than four times:** Jung Chang, 202
280 **no country had ever been:** Morse, vol. 3, 127 in Jung Chang, 219
280 **a desired opportunity:** Morse, vol. 3, 106–7 in Jung Chang, 213
284 **I have 400 million:** Ling, 277
284 **the wisest ever in history:** Jung Chang, 227
284 **lovingly bound in a volume:** ibid., 228
284 **one wrathful crimson:** ibid.
285 **not only for the good fortune:** ibid., 234
286 **no coffins or funerals:** ibid., 244
286 **the rumoured plot:** ibid., 242
286 **Some in Beijing speculated:** ibid., 254
287 **The subsequent emperor's edict:** *First Historical Archives of China* (eds), 1996, vol. 25, no. 1512, in Jung Chang, 254

Chapter 27: End of the Road

289 **killing of all foreigners:** Jung Chang, 266; also see Cohen, 1998
289 **reported inaccurately:** Lovell, 278
290 **punitive reprisals:** Hevia, 196
290 **symbols of Chinese sovereignty:** Hevia, 195; also Hunt 1979
290 **Euro-American lore:** Hevia, 201
290 **Great British Gate:** ibid.
290 **Qian Gate:** A Smith, 'The Punishment of Peking', *The Outlook*, vol. 66, 1900, 498, in Hevia, 197
291 **made 'savage' by loot fever:** Bertram L Simpson, *Indiscreet Letters from Peking*, Arno Press/*NY Times*, 1907 [1970], 334, 349, 354 in Hevia, 209
291 **Lady Claude MacDonald:** FA Sharf and P Harrington, *China, 1900 The Eyewitnesses Speak*, Greenhill, London, 2000, 222–3, in Hevia, 209
291 **Herbert Squiers:** Preston, 31
291 **Japanese officers:** Sand, 654
291 **soldiers located the Qing treasury:** Hevia, 211
292 **Christian missionaries:** ibid., 217
292 **British represented the height:** ibid., 214
292 **The great Christian nations:** *Journal of Presbyterian History*, 2000, vol. 78, issues 2–4, 200; also Silbey, 2012
292 **carnival of loot:** Nicholls, 111
292 **biggest looting excursion:** Lynch, 179
292 **summary 'justice' was meted out:** Stewart, 267, 283
292 **appeared to be fair game:** Hevia, 221
292 **It is safe to say:** Lynch, 84 in ibid., 220
292 **officers in the German sector:** Lynch, 143–4 in ibid., 221
293 **Hun Speech:** Wilhelm 11, 'Hun Speech', Bremerhaven, 27 July 1900, GHDI [German History in Documents and Images] website: https://ghdi.ghi-dc.org/sub_document.cfm?document_id=755
293 **Mass public executions:** Lovell, 279
294 **Xu Jincheng:** Jung Chang, 277
295 **crimes unprecedented:** Hevia, 244
296 **constituted a gold debt:** Boxer Protocol 1901, Article VI, US-China Institute website: https://china.usc.edu/boxer-protocol-1901
296 **The future looks very dark:** Hart to James Campbell, 17 July 1902 in King, 663
296 **approximately three times:** Hevia, 248
296 **Guangxu's death:** Louisa Lim, 'Who murdered China's Emperor 100 Years Ago?', National Public Radio, Washington, USA, 14 November 2008, https://www.npr.org/2008/11/14/96993694/who-murdered-chinas-emperor-100-years-ago#:~:text=New%20tests%20show%20that%20Guangxu,the%20mastermind%20behind%20his%20murder (accessed 2023); Arsenic killed Chinese emperor, reports say, CNN, 14 November 2008, https://edition.cnn.com/2008/WORLD/asiapcf/11/04/china.emperor/index.html (accessed 27/11/2023); see also Jung Chang, 366
297 **in caring for his many:** Jung Chang, 308
297 **Puyi:** see Behr, esp. 62–3

Conclusion

298 **essentially bankrupted China:** King, 684–5
298 **nothing but bad will result:** ibid., 689
298 **narrow and grotesque:** Steil, 73
298 **world's largest gross:** Maddison, 2007
299 **sole manufacturing superpower:** Richard Baldwin, 'China is the World's Sole Manufacturing Superpower: A line sketch of the rise', VoxEU website, 17 January 2024: https://cepr.org/voxeu/columns/china-worlds-sole-manufacturing-superpower-line-sketch-rise
299 **China led the world:** 'ASPI's Two-Decade Critical Technology Tracker 'The rewards of long-term research investment', Australian Strategic Policy Institute, 28 August 2024
299 **greater share of global trade finance:** Samuel Shen and Rae Wee, 'Cheap Yuan Catapults China to Second-Biggest Trade Funding Currency', 17 November 2023, Reuters:

https://www.reuters.com/markets/currencies/cheap-yuan-catapults-china-second-biggest-trade-funding-currency-2023-11-17/

299 **it stood to reason:** Lovell, 274

299 **a nation teeming:** *The Times*, 17 January 1911

299 **Edwardian children's serials:** Lovell, 285

299 **menace to the Western world:** Jack London, 'The Yellow Peril', in *Revolution and Other Essays*, Macmillan, London, 1906, online at https://www.gutenberg.org/files/4953/4953-h/4953-h.htm

Bibliography

Alcock, Rutherford, *The Capital of the Tycoon: A Narrative of Three Years' Residence in Japan*, Longman, 1863.
Ames, Glenn, *Vasco da Gama: Renaissance Crusader*, Pearson Longman, 2005.
Anderson, Aeneas, *A Narrative of the British Embassy to China in the Years 1792, 1793, and 1794*,
J Debrett, London, 1795, Internet Archive
Anderson, David, 'Anson Burlingame: American Architect of Cooperative Policy in China, 1861–1871', *Diplomatic History*, vol.1, no. 3, 1977, 239–55.
Andrade, Tonio, *The Gunpowder Age: China, Military Innovation, and the Rise of the West in World History*, Princeton University Press, 2016.
Andrade, Tonio, *Lost Colony: The Untold Story of China's First Great Victory Over the West*, Princeton University Press, 2011.
Antony, Robert J (ed.), *Elusive Pirates, Pervasive Smugglers: Violence and Clandestine Trade in the Greater China Seas*, HKU Press, 2010.
Armitage, David, *The Ideological Origins of the British Empire*, Cambridge University Press, 2000.
Atwell, William S, 'Some Observations on the "Seventeenth-Century Crisis" in China and Japan', *The Journal of Asian Studies* 45, no. 2, 1986, 223–244.

Bacharach, Jere, 'The Dinar Versus Ducat', *International Journal of Middle East Studies*, vol. 4, no. 1, 1973, 77–96.
Bacon, Francis and Rawley, William, *Sylva Sylvarum, Or, A Natural History, in Ten Centuries*, printed by J.R. for William Lee, London, 1670.
Ball, Samuel, *Account of the Cultivation and Manufacture of Tea in China*, 1848, Longman, Brown, Green, and Longmans, https://archive.org/details/accountofcultiva00ballrich/page/n7/mode/2up
Banaji, Jairus, 'Seasons of Self-Delusion: Opium, Capitalism and the Financial Markets', *Historical Materialism*, vol. 21, no. 2, 2013, 1–17.
Banister, Judith, *China's Changing Population*, Stanford University Press, 1987.
Bell, Luke & Copeland, Ash, *Organic Chemistry*, Ed-Tech Press, 2018.
Behr, Edward, *The Last Emperor*, Bantam Books, Toronto, 1987.
Bennett, AJP, *China: Death Throes of Empire*, Perseus Books, 2009: extract available at alternate.history com website, p. 17, https://www.alternatehistory.com/forum/threads/the-smallest-possible-difference.190997/page-17
Benson, AC and Esher, Viscount (eds), *The Letters of Queen Victoria*, Longman, Green, 1907.
Bertram, Aldous Colin Ricardo, *Chinese Influence on English Garden Design and Architecture Between 1700 and 1860*, University of Cambridge, 2012.
Bernstein, William, *A Splendid Exchange: How Trade Shaped the World*, Atlantic Books, 2008.
Beurdeley, Cécile and Beurdeley, Michel, *Chinese Ceramics*, Thames & Hudson, 1974.
Biggerstaff, Knight, 'A Translation of Anson Burlingame's Instructions from the Chinese Foreign Office', *Far Eastern Quarterly*, vol. 1, no. 3, 1942, 277–9.

Biggerstaff, Knight, 'The First Chinese Mission of Investigation Sent to Europe', *Pacific Historical Review*, vol. 6, no. 4, 1937, 307–20.
Blair, Emma H and Robertson, James A (eds), *The Philippine Islands, 1493–1803*, 2020.
Blue, AD, 'Piracy on the China Coast', *Journal of the Hong Kong Branch of the Royal Asiatic Society*, vol. 5, 1965, 69–85.
Blusse, Leonard, 'Brief Encounter at Macao', *Modern Asian Studies*, vol. 22, no. 3, 1988, 647–64.
Bowen, HV, 'Bullion for Trade, War, and Debt-Relief: British Movements of Silver to, around, and from Asia, 1760–1833', *Modern Asian Studies*, vol. 44, no. 3, 2010, 445–75.
Boxer, CR, *South China in the Sixteenth Century (1550–1575)*, Kraus Reprint, 2008.
Boxer, CR, 'The Dutch East India Company and the China Trade', *History Today*, vol. 29, issue 11, 1979, 741–750.
Boxer, CR, *The Portuguese Seaborne Empire, 1415–1825*, Knopf, 1969.
Boxer, CR, *Fidalgos in the Far East 1550–1770*, Oxford University Press, 1968.
Boyer, Richard, 'Mexico in the Seventeenth Century: Transition of a Colonial Society', *The Hispanic American Historical Review*, vol. 57, no. 3, 1977, 455–478.
Bradley, James, *The China Mirage: The Hidden History of American Disaster in Asia*, Back Bay Books, 2015.
Bridgman, EC & Williams SW (eds), *The Chinese Repository*, vol. 6, May 1837–April 1838, Canton, 1838.
Brook, Timothy, 'Nine Sloughs: Profiling the Climate History of the Yuan and Ming Dynasties, 1260–1644', *Journal of Chinese History*, 1, no. 1, 2017, 27–58.
Brook, Timothy, *The Troubled Empire: China in the Yuan and Ming Dynasties*, Harvard University Press/Belknap Press, 2010.
Brook, Timothy, *Vermeer's Hat The Seventeenth Century and the Dawn of the Global World*, Profile Books, 2009.
Brook, Timothy, *The Confusions of Pleasure Commerce and Culture in Ming China*, University of California Press, 1998.
Brook, Timothy, 'The Merchant Network in 16th Century China, *Journal of the Economic and Social History of the Orient*, vol. 24, no. 2, 1981, 165–184.
Brook, Timothy, Bourgon, Jerome, and Blue, Gregory, *Death by a Thousand Cuts*, Harvard University Press, 2008.
Brook, Timothy and Wakabayashi, Bob Tadashi, *Opium Regimes China, Britain & Japan, 1838–1952*, University of California Press, 2000.
Brown, Colin, *The Scum of the Earth What Happened to the Real British Heroes of Waterloo?*, The History Press, 2015.
Brown, Kerry, '*Britain, China & the 400-Year Contest for Power*', (2024), Yale University Press.
Brown, William, *Chasing the Chinese Dream*, Springer, 2021.
Brownstein, Michael J. 'A brief history of opiates, opioid peptides, and opioid receptors', *Proc. Natl. Acad. Sci. USA*, vol. 90, 1993, 5391–3.
Bushell, Stephen W, *Chinese Art*, Parkstone International, 2012.

Campbell, William, *Formosa Under the Dutch*, SMC Publishing Inc, 1992.
Carlen, Joe, *A Brief History of Entrepreneurship: The Pioneers, Profiteers and Racketeers Who Shaped Our World*, Columbia Business School Publishing, 2013.
Cartwright, Mark, 'The Capture of the Treasure Ship Madre de Deus', *World History Encyclopedia*, 23 June 2020.
Chambers, William, *Dissertation on Oriental Gardening*, W. Griffin, printer, London, 1772: Internet Archive.
Chang, Hsin-pao, *Commissioner Lin*, WW Norton, 1964.
Chang, Jung, *Empress Dowager Cixi - The Concubine Who Launched Modern China*, Jonathon Cape, 2013.
Chang, T'ien-Tse, 'Malacca and the Failure of the First Portuguese Embassy to Peking', *Journal of Southeast Asian History*, vol. 3, issue 2, 1962, 45–64.
Chang, T'ien-Tse, *Sino-Portuguese Trade from 1514–1644: A Synthesis of Portuguese and Chinese Sources*, Late EJ Brill, 1934
Chung, Tan, 'The Britain-China-India Trade Triangle (1771–1840)', *Proceedings of the Indian History Congress*, vol. 34, 1973, 77–91.
Clunas, Craig, *Superfluous Things: Material Culture and Social Status in Early Modern China*, Polity Press, 1991.
Cohen, Paul, *History in Three Keys: The Boxers as Event, Experience, and Myth*, Columbia University Press, 1998.

Cohn, Samuel, *The Black Death Transformed*, Oxford University Press, 2002.
Costin, WC, *Great Britain and China, 1833–1860*, Oxford University Press, 1937.
Cowper, William, *The Poems of William Cowper* (ed. John D Baird and Charles Ryskamp, vol. 2, Oxford University Press, 1995.
Cranmer-Byng, John L and Wills, John E Jr., 'Trade and Diplomacy with Maritime Europe, 1644–c.1800 in John E Wills Jnr (ed.), *China and Maritime Europe 1500–1800: Trade, Settlement, Diplomacy and Missions*, Cambridge University Press, 201, 183–254.
Crawford, Robert, 'Eunuch Power in the Ming Dynasty', *T'oung Pao*, second series, vol. 49, livr. 3, 1961.
Cribb, J., 'An Historical Survey of the Precious Metals of China', *The Numismatic Chronicle*, series 7, vol. 19, 1979, 185–229.
Cushner, Nicholas, 'The Great Ship from Amacon', *Philippine Studies*, vol. 9, no. 3, 1961, 533–542.
Cushner, Nicholas P., 'Legazpi 1564–1572', *Philippine Studies*, vol. 13, No. 2, 1965, 163–206.

Dalrymple, William, *White Mughals: Love and Betrayal in Eighteenth-Century India*, Penguin, 2004.
Defoe, Daniel, *A Tour Through the Whole Island of Great Britain*, Yale University Press, 1991.
Degenhardt, Jane Hwang, 'Cracking the Mysteries of "China": China(ware) in the Early Modern Imagination', *Studies in Philology*, vol. 110, no. 1, 2013, 132–167.
De La Noy, Michael, *George IV*, Sutton Publishing, 1998.
de Luca, Lisa, 'Porcelain of the Medici Family: How Failure Led to Invention', *The Collector*, 28 February 2021, https://www.thecollector.com/porcelain-of-the-medici-family-how-failure-led-to-invention/
Denby, Charles, *China and Her People*, L.C. Page & Co., 1906.
Deng, Kent, 'Unveiling China's True Population Statistics for the Pre-Modern Era with Official Census Data', *Population Review*, vol. 43, no. 2, 2004, 332–69.
Dennet, Tyler, *Americans in Eastern Asia*, Macmillan and Co., 1922.
Detweiler, Susan Gray, *George Washington's Chinaware*, Abrams, 1982.
de Waal, Edmund, *The White Road*, Vintage, 2015.
Dias, Maria Suzette Fernandes, *Legacies of Slavery: Comparative Perspectives*, Cambridge Scholars Publishing, 2007.
Ding, Dechen, 'Internationalization Experience of Chinese Ancient Currency and Its Enlightenment', *Advances in Economics, Business and Management Research*, vol. 166, 2021, pp. 207–210.
Dolin, Eric Jay, *When America First Met China*, Liveright Publishing Corporation, 2012.
Downs, Jacques M, 'Fair Game: Exploitive Role Myths and the American Opium Trade', *Pacific Historical Review*, vol. 41, no. 2, 1972, 133–49.
Downs, Jacques M., 'American Merchants and the China Opium Trade, 1800–1840, *The Business History Review*, vol. 42, no. 4, 1968, 418–42.
Drelichman, Maurizio and Voth, Hans-Joachim, *Lending to the Borrower from Hell: Debt Taxes and Default in the Age of Phillip II*, Princeton University Press, 2014.
Dreyer, Edward, *Zheng He: China and the Oceans in the Early Ming Dynasty, 1405–1433*, Pearson Longman, 2007.
Dreyer, Edward, *Early Ming China: A Political History 1355–1435*, Stanford University Press, 1982.

Earle, TF and Villiers, John (eds/trans), *Albuquerque Caesar of the East Selected texts by Afonso de Albuquerque and his son*, Aris & Phillips, 1990.
Ebrey, Patricia, *The Cambridge Illustrated History of China*, Cambridge University Press, 2010.
Edgerton-Tarpley, Kathryn, 'Tough Choices: Grappling with Famine in Qing China, the British Empire, and Beyond', *Journal of World History*, vol. 24, no. 1, 2013, 135–176.
Elliott, Mark, 'The Historical Vision of the Prosperous Age (Shengshi)', *China Heritage Quarterly*, No. 29, March 2012.
Elliott, Mark, *Emperor Qianlong: Son of Heaven, Man of the World*, Longman, 2009.
Ellis, Markman, Coulton, Richard and Mauger Matthew, *Empire of Tea*, Reaktion Books, 2015.
Elman, Benjamin, 'Naval Warfare and the Refraction of China's Self-Strengthening Reforms into Scientific and Technological Failure, 1865–1895', *Modern Asian Studies*, vol. 38, no. 2, 2004, 283–326.

Elvin, Mark, *The Pattern of the Chinese Past: A Social and Economic Interpretation*, Eyre Methuen, 1973.

Fairbank (ed.), John King, *The Chinese World Order: Traditional China's Foreign Relations*, Harvard University Press, 2008.
Fairbank, John King, *Trade and Diplomacy on the China Coast: The Opening of the Treaty Ports 1842–1854*, Harvard University Press, 1964.
Fairbank, John King and Bruner, Katherine F., (eds), *The I.G. in Peking: Letters of Robert Hart, Chinese Maritime Customs, 1868–1907*, Harvard University Press, 1975.
Faught, C Brad, *Gordon: Victorian Hero*, Potomac Books, 2008.
Faure, David, *Emperor and Ancestor: State and Lineage in South China*, Stanford University Press, 2007.
Fay, Peter, *The Opium War 1840–1842*, University of North Carolina Press, 1977.
Finlay, Robert, *The Pilgrim Art: Cultures of Porcelain in World History*, University of California Press, 2010.
Kilpatrick, Jane, *Gifts from the Gardens of China*, Frances Lincoln, 2007.
Florus, *Epitome of Roman History*.
Flynn, Dennis O and Giraldez, Arturo, 'China and the Spanish Empire', *Journal of Iberian and Latin American Economic History*, Virtual Special Issue, 2020, 1–31.
Flynn, Dennis O and Giraldéz, Arturo, 'Cycles of Silver: Globalization as historical process', *World Economics*, vol. 3, no. 2, April-June 2002(a), 1–16.
Flynn, Dennis O and Giraldéz, Arturo, 'Cycles of Silver: Global Economic Unity through the Mid-Eighteenth Century', *Journal of World History*, vol. 13, no. 2, September 2002(b), 391–427.
Flynn, Dennis O and Giraldez, Arturo, 'Born with a "Silver Spoon": The Origin of World Trade in 1571', *Journal of World History*, vol. 6, no. 2, 1995, 201–21.
Frank, Andre Gunder, *ReORIENT: Global Economy in the Asian Age*, University of California Press, 1998.
Frankopan, Peter, *The Earth Transformed: An Untold History*, Bloomsbury Publishing, 2023.
Frankopan, Peter, *The Silk Roads – A New History of the World*, Bloomsbury, 2015.
Fraser, Antonia, *Love & Louis XIV: The Women in the Life of the Sun King*, Weidenfeld & Nicolson, 2006.
Fu, Lo-shu, *A Documentary Chronicle of Sino-Western Relations (1644–1820)*, University of Arizona Press, 1966.

Galli, Marco, 'Beyond Frontiers: Ancient Rome and the Eurasian Trade Networks', *Journal of Eurasian Studies*, vol. 8, issue 1, 2016.
Ganter, Regina, 'China and the Beginning of Australian History', *The Great Circle*, vol. 25, no. 1, 2003, 3–19.
Ghosh, Amitav, *Smoke & Ashes*, John Murray, 2024.
Ghosh, Amitav, *Flood of Fire*, John Murray, 2015.
Ghosh, Amitav, *River of Smoke*, John Murray, 2011.
Ghosh, Amitav, *Sea of Poppies*, John Murray, 2008.
Gleeson, Janet, *The Arcanum*, Warner Books, 1998.
Gordon, Peter and Morales, Juan José, *The Silver Way: China, Spanish America and the birth of globalisation 1565–1815*, Penguin Random House, 2017.
Gotu, Zhuang, 'Tea, Silver, Opium and War: From Commercial Expansion to Military Invasion', *Itinerario*, vol. 17, no. 2, 1993, 10–36.
Grace, RJ, *Opium and Empire: The Lives and Careers of William Jardine and James Matheson*, McGill-Queen's University Press, 2014.
Greenberg, Michael, *British Trade and the Opening of China, 1800–1842*, Cambridge University Press, 1951.
Grotius, Hugo, *The Free Sea, trans. Richard Hakluyt, with William Welwod's Critique and Grotius's Reply*, ed. David Armitage, Liberty Fund, Indianapolis, 2004.
Gwei-Djen, Lu, Needham, J. & Chi-Hsing, P., 'The Oldest Representation of a Bombard', *Technology and Culture*, vol. 29, no. 3, 1988, 594–605.

Habig, Marion, 'Marignolli and the Decline of Medieval Missions in China', *Franciscan Studies*, New Series, vol. 5, no. 1, 1945, 21–36.
Hakluyt, Robert, *The Principal Navigations Voyages Traffiques and Discoveries of the English Nation*, Cambridge University Press, 2014.

Hanbury-Tension, Robin (ed), *The Great Explorers: Forty of the Greatest Men and Women Who Changed Our Perception of the World*, W.W. Norton, 2018.
Hang, Xing, *Conflict & Commerce in Maritime East Asia: The Zheng Family and the Shaping of the Modern World, c. 1620–1720*, Cambridge University Press, 2015
Hansen, Valerie, *The Silk Road: A New History*, Oxford University Press, 2015.
Harcourt, Freda, 'Black Gold: P&O and the Opium Trade, 1847–1914', *International Journal of Maritime History*, vol. 6, no. 1, 1994, 1–83.
Hart, Sir Robert, *"These from the land of Sinim": Essays on the Chinese Question*, Chapman & Hall Ltd, 1901.
He, Sibing, 'Russell and Company in Shanghai, 1843–1891: U.S. Trade and Diplomacy in Treaty Port China', paper presented at Hong Kong University, 23–24 May, 2011.
Heng, Geraldine, 'An Ordinary Ship and Its Stories of Early Globalism', *Journal of Medieval Worlds*, vol. 1, no. 1, 2019, 11–14.
Hertel, Christiane, *Siting China in Germany: Eighteenth-Century Chinoiserie and Its Modern Legacy*, Penn State University Press, 2019.
Hevia, James, *English Lessons: The Pedagogy of Imperialism in Nineteenth–Century China*, Duke University Press, 2003.
Hillard, Harriet Low, *Lights & Shadows of a Macau Life*, edited by NP Hodges and AW Hummel, History Bank, 2002.
Hong, Chen, 'On Matteo Ricci's Interpretations of Chinese Culture', *Coolabah*, no. 16, 2015, 87–100.
Honour, Hugh, *Chinoiserie: The Vision of Cathay*, Harper & Row, 1961.
Hopkirk, Peter, *The Great Game: On Secret Service in High Asia*, John Murray, 1990.
Hourani, George, *Arab Seafaring*, Princeton University Press, 1995.
Hume, David, *Writings on Economics*, ed. Eugene Rotwein, University of Wisconsin Press, 1970.
Hunt, Michael, 'The Forgotten Occupation: Peking, 1900–1901', *Pacific Historical Review*, vol. 48, no. 4, 1979, 501–29.
Hunt, Tristram, *The Radical Potter: Josiah Wedgwood and the Transformation of Britain*, Allen Lane, 2021.

Inalcik, Halil, 'Bursa and the Silk Trade', Halil Inalcik and Donald Quataert (eds), *An Economic and Social History of the Ottoman Empire, 1300–1914*, Cambridge University Press, 1994.
Isba, Anne, 'Trouble with Helen: The Gladstone Family Crisis, 1846–1848', *History*, vol. 88, No. 2, 2003, 249–61.

Jaivin, Linda, *The Shortest History of China*, Black Inc, 2021.
Jami, Cathérine, *The Emperor's New Mathematics: Western Learning and Imperial Authority During the Kangxi Reign (1662–1722)*, Oxford University Press, 2012.
Jenyns, Soame, *Later Chinese Porcelain: The Ch'ing Dynasty, 1644–1912*, Faber & Faber, 1959.
Jenyns, Soame, *Ming Pottery and* Porcelain, Faber & Faber, 1953.
Jesus, Carlos Augusto Montalto, *Historic Macau: International Traits in China Old and New*, Indiana University, 1926.
Johnson, Samuel, *The Letters of Samuel Johnson: Vol III: 1777–1781* (ed. Bruce Redford), Clarendon Press, 1992.
Jordanus, Friar, *The Wonders of the East*, c.1330, translated by Henry Yule, The Hakluyt Society, London, 1763.
Jörg, CJA, The *Geldermalsen: History and Porcelain*, Kemper, 1986.
Juvenal, *Satires* VI.

Keay, John, *China: A History*, Harper Press, 2009.
Keller, Wolfgang & Shiue, Carol H., 'The Economic Consequences of the Opium War', National Bureau of Economic Research, Cambridge MA, 2023.
Kerr, Gordon, *A Short History of China: from Ancient Dynasties to Economic Powerhouse*, Pocket Essentials, 2013.
Kilpatrick, Jane, *Gifts from the Gardens of China*, Frances Lincoln, 2007.
King, Frank H, "The Boxer Indemnity –'Nothing But Bad'", *Modern Asian Studies*, vol. 40, no. 3, 2006, 663–89.
Kingston, Christopher, 'Marine Insurance in Britain and America, 1720–1844: A Comparative Institutional Analysis', *The Journal of Economic History*, vol. 67, no. 2, 2007, 379–409.

Krahe, Cinta, 'The Reception and Value of Chinese Porcelain in Habsburg Spain', in Anna Grasskamp and Monica Juneja (eds), *China, Europe, and the Transcultural Object, 1600–1800*, Springer, 2018, 221–238.

Kuhn, Wagner, 'The Christian Missions to China Under Mongol Occupation: Challenges and Opportunities', *Hermeneutica*, vol. 6, 2006, 1–17.

Landes, David S, 'Why Europe and the West? Why Not China?', *The Journal of Economic Perspectives*, vol. 20, no. 20, 2006, 3–22.

Lazich, Michael C, 'American Missionaries & the Opium Trade in Nineteenth Century China', *Journal of World History*, vol. 17, no. 2, 2006, 197–223.

Lee, Siu-Leung, 'Chinese Mapped America Before 1430', Proceedings of the International Cartographic Association, 2018.

Lee, Siu-Leung, 'Zheng He's Voyages Revealed by Matteo Ricci's World Map', in Chia Lin Sien and Sally K. Church (eds), *Zheng He and the Afro-Asian World*, Perzim, 2012.

Le Pichon, Alain (ed.), *China Trade and Empire: 1827–1843*, Oxford University Press, 2006

Li, Dun J, *China in Transition, 1517–1911*, Van Nostrand Reinhold, 1969.

Lindorff, Joyce, 'Burney, Macartney and the Qianlong Emperor, 1792–1794', *Early Music*, vol. 40, no. 3, 2012, 441–453.

Ling, The Princess Der, *Two Years in the Forbidden City*, 1st World Library, 2004.

Liu, Xinru, *The Silk Road in World History,* Oxford University Press, 2010.

Lo, Jung-Pang, 'The Emergence of China as a Sea Power During the Late Sung and Early Yuan Periods', *The Far Eastern Quarterly*, vol. 14, no. 4, August 1955, 489–503.

Lo, Jung-Pang, 'The Decline of Early Ming Navy', *Oriens Extremus*, vol. 5, no. 2, 1958.

Loch, Granville Gower, *The Closing Events of the Campaign in China: The Operations in the Yang-Tze-Kiang, and Treaty of Nanking*, Cambridge University Press, 2013 (1843).

Lodwick, Kathleen L., *Crusaders Against Opium, Protestant Missionaries in China, 1874–1917,* University Press of Kentucky, 2009.

London, Jack, 'The Yellow Peril', in *Revolution and Other Essays*, Macmillan, London, 1906, https://www.gutenberg.org/files/4953/4953-h/4953-h.htm

Lopez, Robert Sabatino, 'China Silk in Europe in the Yuan Period', *Journal of the American Oriental Society*, 1952, vol. 72, no. 2, 1952, 72–76.

Lovell, Julia, *The Opium War*, Picador, 2011.

Lucan, *Pharsalia*, Book X.

Lugar, Catherine, 'The History of the Manila Galleon Trade', *Pacific Sea Resources*, 1990.

Lynch, George, *The War of the Civilisations: Being the Record of a 'foreign Devil's' Experiences with the Allies in China,* Longmans, Green, 1901.

Ma, Chicheng, 'The Jesuits and Chinese Science', *Barcelona School of Economics*, June 2019, 56 pp.: https://events.bse.eu/live/files/2913-jesuits-and-chinese-sciencepdf

Macartney, George, *An Embassy to China: Being the Journal Kept by Lord Macartney during His Embassy to the Emperor Ch'ien-lung, 1793–1794*, edited and with an Introduction and notes by J.L. Cranmer-Byng, London, 1962.

McCutcheon, James M, 'Tremblingly Obey': British and Other Western Responses to China and the Chinese Kotow', *The Historian*, vol. 33, issue 4, 1971, 557–577.

McMaken, Ryan, 'Why Did the World Choose a Gold Standard Instead of a Silver Standard?', *Mises Wire*, 1 May 2022, Mises Institute website.

Mackinder, Halford, *The Geographical Pivot of History*, Cosimo Classics, 2020 (1904).

McLaughlin, Raoul, *The Roman Empire and the Silk Routes*, Pen & Sword Books, 2016.

Maddison, Angus, *Chinese Economic Performance in the Long Run, 960–2030*, OECD Publishing, 2nd edn., 2007.

Marchand, Suzanne L., *Porcelain: A History from the Heart of Europe*, Princeton University Press, 2020.

Matheson, James, *The Present Position & Prospects of the British Trade with China,* Cambridge University Press, 2012 (1836).

Meadows, Thomas Taylor, *Desultory Notes on the Government and People of China, and on the Chinese Language*, W.H. Allen and Co., 1847.

Meagher, Arnold J, *The Coolie Trade The Traffic in Chinese Laborers to Latin America 1847–1874*, Xlibris Corporation, 2008.

Melancon, Glenn, 'Honour in Opium? The British Declaration of War on China, 1839–1840', *The International History Review*, vol. 21, no. 4, 1999, 853–1136.

Mencius, 'On Humane Government', *Readings 1*, T. de Bary, W. Chan and B. Watson (eds), *Sources of Chinese Tradition*, 1960: https://courses.umass.edu/pols294p/documents.html/mencius.pdf

Menzhausen, Ingelore, *Early Meissen Porcelain in Dresden*, Thames & Hudson, 1990.
Miyazaki, Ichisada, *China's Examination Hell: The Civil Service Examinations of Imperial China*, Yale University Press, 1981.
Montesquieu, *Montesquieu The Spirit of the Laws*, ed. Anne Kohler, Cambridge University Press, 1989 (1748).
Morris, Ian, *Why the West Rules For Now*, Profile, 2011.
Morse, Hosea Ballou, *The Chronicles of the East India Company Trading to China, 1635–1834*, Clarendon Press, 1926.
Mote, Frederick W, *Imperial China, 900–1800*, Harvard University Press, 1999.
Mote, Frederick W, 'Introduction', in Frederick W. Mote and Denis Twitchett (eds), *The Cambridge*
History of China, vol. 7, Cambridge University Press, 1988, pp. 1–10.
Mungello, David, *The Great Encounter of China and the West 1500–1800*, Rowman & Littlefield, 2005.
Murphy, Arthur, 'The Orphan of China, a tragedy, as it is perform'd at the Theatre-Royal, in Drury-Lane', 1759: Internet Archive.

Neill, Thomas P, 'Quesnay and Physiocracy', *Journal of the History of Ideas*, vol. 9, no. 2, 1948, pp. 153–173.
Newsinger, John, 'Elgin in China', *New Left Review*, 15, 2002,119–140.
Newton, Sir Isaac, *Report to the Lords Commissioners of His Majesty's Treasury, on the state of the Gold and Silver Coin,* from Sir Isaac Newton, Master of the Mint, Mint Office, 21 September 1717, 2, UK Parliamentary Papers.
Nicholls, Bob, *Blue Jackets & Boxers Australia's Naval Expedition to the Boxer Uprising*, Allen & Unwin, 1986.
Nolde, John J, 'The "False Edict" of 1849, *The Journal of Asian Studies*, vol. 20, no. 3, 1961, 229–315.
Noorali, Hassan and Ahmadi, Seyyed Abbas, 'Iran's new geopolitics: heartland of the world's corridors', *GeoJournal*, vol. 88, 2022, 1889–1904.
Norwich, John Julius, *The Middle Sea: A History of the Mediterranean*, Chatto & Windus, 2006.
Norwich, John Julius, *A Short History of Byzantium*, Penguin Books, 1998.
Nylan, Michael and Vankeerberghen, Griet (eds), *Chang'an 26 BCE An Augustan Age in China*, University of Washington Press, 2015.

O'Meara, Barry E, *Napoleon in Exile; Or A Voice from St. Helena*, Simpkin & Marshall, 1822.
Owen, DE, *British Opium Policy in China & India*, Yale University Press, 1934.

Paine, Lincoln, *The Sea and Civilization: A Maritime History of the World*, Knopf, 2013.
Paine, Lincoln, *Warships of the World to 1900*, Mariner Books, 2000.
Paine, Sarah, *The Sino-Japanese War of 1894–1895: Perceptions, Power and Primacy*, Cambridge University Press, 2009.
Pamuk, Sevket, *A Monetary History of the Ottoman Empire*, Cambridge University Press, 2000.
Park, William H, *Opinions of Over 100 Physicians on the Use of Opium in China*, American Presbyterian Mission Press, Shanghai, 1899.
Paterson, Allen, *The Gardens at Kew*, Frances Lincoln, 2008.
Penderill-Church, John, *William Cookworthy, 1705–1780: A Study of the Pioneer of True Porcelain Manufacture in England*, Bradford Barton, 1972.
Pepys, Samuel, *The Diary of Samuel Pepys*, edited by Robert Latham and William Matthews, Bell and Hyman, 1970–83.
Perkins, Franklin, *Leibniz and China: A Commerce of Light*, Cambridge University Press, 2004.
Ping-ti, Ho, *Studies on the Population of China, 1368–1953*, Harvard East Asian Series, 1959.
Platt, Stephen, *Imperial Twilight: The Opium War and the End of China's Last Golden Age*, Alfred A. Knopf, 2018.
Pliny the Elder, *The Natural History, www.gutenberg.org*
Plutarch, *Crassus,* Internet Archive.
Polo, Marco, *The Travels of Marco Polo,* vol. 2, translated by Henry Yule and edited by Henri Cordier, Dover Publications, 1993.
Polo, Marco, *The Travels of Marco Polo*, edited and with an Introduction by Milton Rugoff, Signet Classics, 2004.

Polo, Marco, *The Travels of Marco Polo*, translated and with an Introduction by Ronald Latham, Folio Society edition, 1990.

Pomeranz, Kenneth, *The Great Divergence: China, Europe and the Marking of the Modern World Economy*, Princeton University Press, 2000.

Pong, David, 'Keeping the Foochow Navy Yard Afloat: Government Finance and China's Early Modern Defence Industry', 1866–75', *Modern Asian Studies*, vol. 21, no. 1, 1987, 121–52.

Pong, David, 'Confucian Patriotism and the Destruction of the Woosung Railway, 1877', *Modern Asian Studies*, vol. 7, no. 4, 1973, 647–76.

Postrel, Virgina, *The Fabric of Civilization*, Basic Books, 2020.

Preston, Diana, *Besieged in Beijing: The Story of the 1900 Boxer Rising*, Constable, 1999.

Pritchard, EH, 'Struggle for Control of the China Trade', *Pacific Historical Review*, vol. 3, no.3, 1934, 280–295.

Ptak, Roderich, 'Trade Between Macau and Southeast Asia in Ming Times: A Survey', *Monumenta Serica*, vol. 54, 2006, 465–489.

Pudney, John, *London's Docks*, Thames & Hudson, 1975.

Realuyo, Celina B, 'The New Opium War: A National Emergency', *PRISM*, 8, no.1, 2019, 133–142.

Reins, Thomas D, 'Reform, Nationalism and Internationalism: The Opium Suppression Movement in China and the Anglo-American Influence, 1900–1908', *Modern Asian Studies*, vol. 25, no. 1, 1991, 101–142.

Ricci, Matteo, *China in the Sixteenth Century: The Journals of Matthew Ricci, 1583–1610*, (trans. Louis J Gallagher), Random House, 1953.

Richards, John F, 'The Opium Industry in British India', *Indian Economic & Social History Review*, 39, nos. 2 & 3, 2002, 149–180.

Roote, John A., *Destruction of Paradise Triumph, Tragedy, and the Sack of the Summer Palace*, Forbidden City Books, 2017.

Ropp, Paul (ed.), *Heritage of China*, University of California Press, 1990.

Rose, Sarah, *For All the Tea in China How England Stole the World's Favourite Drink and Changed History*, Penguin Books, 2009.

Ross, Andrew C, *A Vision Betrayed: The Jesuits in Japan and China, 1542–1742*, Orbis Books, 1994.

Rowe, William T, *China's Last Empire: The Great Qing*, Harvard University Press, 2010.

Honour, Hugh, *Chinoiserie: The Vision of Cathay*, Harper & Row, 1961.

St. Clair, Kassia, *The Golden Thread How Fabric Changed History*, John Murray, 2019.

Sand, Jordan, 'Was Meiji Taste in Interiors "Orientalist"?' *positions – asia critique*, vol. 8, issue 3, 2000, 637–73

Sandrock, John E, *The Foreign Banks in China, Part 1 Early Imperial Issues (1850–1900); Part II Imperial Chinese Issues (1900–1911)*, 1997: *thecurrencycollector.com*

Sassoon, Joseph, *The Global Merchants: The Enterprise and Extravagance of the Sassoon Dynasty*, Penguin Random House, 2022.

Schama, Simon, *The Embarrassment of Riches: An Interpretation of Dutch Culture in the Golden Age*, University of California Press, 1988.

Schell, Orville & Delury, John, *Wealth & Power: China's Long March to the Twenty-First Century*, Little Brown, 2013.

Schlegel, G, 'First Introduction of Tea into Holland', *T'oung Pao*, Second Series, 1:5, 1900, 468–72.

Schmid, Jon and Huang, Jonathan, 'State Adoption of Transformative Technology', *International Studies Quarterly*, vol. 61, no. 3, 2017, 570–583.

Schmidt, Nathan 'Voyage of the *Empress of China*: Private and National Interests toward Foreign Policy in the Early United States', *Western Illinois Historical Review*, vol. 8, 2017.

Schoff, Wilfred (trans.), *The Periplus of the Erythraean Sea: Travel and Trade in the Indian Ocean*, Longmans, Green, 1912.

Schottenhammer, Angela, 'Transfer of Xiangyao from Iran and Arabia to China: A Reinvestigation of Entries in the Youyang Zazu (863)', in Ralph Kauz (ed.), *Aspects of the Maritime Silk Road: From the Persian Gulf to the East China Sea*, Harrassowitz Verlag, 2010.

Schuman, Michael, *Superpower Interrupted: The Chinese History of the World*, Hachette, 2020.

See, Lisa, *Lady Tan's Circle of Women*, Scribner, 2023.

Severin, Tim, *The Sindbad Voyage*, Hutchinson & Co, 1982.
Shea, Eiren, *Mongol Court Dress, Identity Formation, and Global Exchange*, Taylor & Francis, 2020.
Seneca, *De Beneficiis*, *www.gutenberg.org*
Shore, Henry, *The Flight of Lapwing*, Longmans, Green, 1881.
Silbey, David J, *The Boxer Rebellion and the Great Game in China: A History*, Farrer, Straus & Giroux, 2012.
Siu, Yiu,'The Cessation of Zheng He's Voyages and the Beginning of Private Sailings: Fiscal Competition between Emperors and Bureaucrats', *Journal of Chinese History*, vol. 8, issue 1, 2024, 95–114.
Sleeswyk, Andre, 'The Liao and the Displacement of Ships in the Ming Navy', *The Mariner's Mirror*, vol. 82, no. 1, 1996, 3–13.
Smith, Adam, *Wealth of Nations*, Wordsworth Classics, 2012.
Spence, Jonathan, *God's Chinese Son: The Taiping Heavenly Kingdom of Hong Xiuquan*, W.W. Norton, 1996.
Spence, Jonathon, 'Opium Smoking in Ch'ing China', in F. Wakeman & C. Grant (eds), *Conflict and Control in Late Imperial China*, University of California Press, 1975, 143–173.
Spryou, Maria A. et al., 'The source of the Black Death in fourteenth-century central Eurasia', *Nature*, vol. 606, 2022, 718–724.
Steensgaard, Niels, *The Asian Trade Revolution: The East India Companies and the Decline of the Caravan Trade*, University of Chicago Press, 2017.
Steil, Ben, *The Battle of Bretton Woods*, Princeton University Press, 2013.
Stelle, Charles Clarkson, *Americans and the China Opium Trade*, Arno Press, 1981.
Stevens, Keith, 'The Han Lin Academy and a Chinese Deity', *Journal of the Hong Kong Branch of the Royal Asiatic Society*, 36, 1996, 231–33.
Stewart, Major-General Sir Norman, *My Service Days*, J. Ousley, London, 1908.
Subrahmanyam, Sanjay, 'Holding the World in Balance: The Connected Histories of the Iberian Overseas Empires, 1500–1640', *The American Historical Review*, vol. 112, issue 5, 2007, 1359–1385.
Szczesniak, Boleslaw B, 'Diplomatic Relations Between Emperor K'ang hsi and King John III of Poland', *Journal of the American Oriental Society*, vol. 89, no. 1, 1969, 157–61.

Tan, Andrew, *The Politics of Maritime Power*, Taylor & Francis, 2010.
Teng,YC, 'Reverend Issachar Jacox Roberts and the Taiping Rebellion', *The Journal of Asian Studies*, vol. 23, no. 1, 1963, 55–67.
Thomas, Greg M, 'The Looting of Yuanmingyuan and the Translation of Chinese Art in Europe', *Nineteenth-Century Art Worldwide* 7, no. 2, 2008, 23–56.
Thubron, Colin, 'Pleasure Domes and Postal Routes', *The New York Review*, 22 July 2021
Thubron, Colin, *Shadow of the Silk Road*, 2012, 305
Thurin, Susan, *Victorian Travellers and the Opening of China*, Ohio University Press, 1999.
Tichane, Robert, *Ching-te-chen: Views of a Porcelain City*, New York, 1983.
Tonti, Lucianne, *Sundressed: Natural Fibres and the Future of Fashion*, Black Inc, 2022.
Topik, Steven, Marichal, Carlos & Frank, Zephyr (eds), *From Silver to Cocaine*, Duke University Press, 2006.
Trocki, Carl A, *Opium, Empire and the Global Political Economy - A Study of the Asian Opium Trade 1750–1950*, Routledge, 1999.

Udias, Agustin, 'Jesuit Astronomers in Beijing, 1601–1805', *Quarterly Journal of the Royal Astronomical Society*, vol. 35, 1994, 463–478.
Urresti, Mariano F, *Colón y el Mapa Templario (Columbus and the Templar Map)*, Almuzara Publishing House, 2022.

Valder, Peter, *The Garden Plants of China*, George Weidenfeld and Nicolson, 1999.
Villiers, John, 'Silk and Silver: Macau, Manila and Trade in the China Seas in the Sixteenth Century', *Journal of the Hong Kong Branch of the Royal Asiatic Society*, vol. 20, 1980, pp. 66–80.
Vogel, Hans Ulrich (ed.), *Marco Polo Was in China: New Evidence from Currencies, Salts and Revenues*, Brill, 2013.
von Glahn, Richard, 'Myth and Reality of China's Seventeenth-Century Monetary Crisis', *The Journal of Economic History*, vol. 56, no. 2, 1996(a), 429–454.
von Glahn, Richard, *Fountain of Fortune: Money and Monetary Policy in China, 1000–1700*, University of California Press, 1996(b).

von Humboldt, Alexander, *Political Essay on the Kingdom of New Spain*, 1811, Longman, Hurst, Rees, Orme & Brown.

Wakeman, Frederic, *Telling Chinese History: A Selection of Essays*, Leah H. Wakeman (ed.), University of California Press, 2009.
Wakeman, Frederic, 'Voyages', Presidential Address, *American Historical Review*, 98, no. 1, 1993, 1–17
Wakeman, Frederic, *Strangers at the Gate: Social Disorder in South China, 1839–1861*, University of California Press, 1974.
Wakeman, Frederic and Grant, Carolyn (eds), *Conflict and Control in Late Imperial China*, University of California Press, 1975.
Waley, Arthur, *The Opium War Through Chinese Eyes*, Allen & Unwin, London, 1958.
Waley-Cohen, Joanna, *The Sextants of Beijing: Global Currents in Chinese History*, W.W. Norton, 2000.
Waley-Cohen, Joanna, 'Commemorating War in Eighteenth-Century China', in *Modern Asian Studies*, vol. 30, issue 4, 1996, 869–99.
Waley-Cohen, Joanna, 'China and Western Technology in the Late Eighteenth Century', *The American Historical Review*, vol. 98, no. 5, 1993, 1525–44.
Weatherford, Jack, *Genghis Khan and the Making of the Modern World*, Broadway Books, 2004.
Webster, Thomas, *Reports and Notes of Cases on Letters Patent for Inventions (1601–1843)*, vol. 1, T Blenkarn, London, 1844.
Westad, Odd Arne, *Restless Empire: China and the World Since 1750*, Random House, 2012.
Weststeijn, Thijs,'Cultural reflections on porcelain in 17th-century Netherlands', in J van Campen et al. (eds), *Chinese and Japanese Porcelain for the Dutch Golden Age*, Waanders Uitgevers, 2014,
Whitfield, Susan, *Life Along the Silk Road*, University of California Press, 1999.
Wills, John E Jnr, 'Introduction', in John E Wills Jnr (ed.), *China and Maritime Europe 1500–1800: Trade, Settlement, Diplomacy and Missions*, Cambridge University Press, 2011(a), 1–23.
Wills, John E Jnr, 'Maritime Europe and the Ming', in John E Wills (ed.), *op.cit.*, 2011(b), 24–77.
Wolseley, Garnet, *The Story of a Soldier's Life*, Legare Street Press, 2022, [1903].
Wolseley, Garnet, *Narrative of the War with China in 1860*, Elibron Classics, 2005 [1862].
Wong, JY, *Deadly Dreams Opium, Imperialism and the Arrow War (1856–60) in China*, Cambridge University Press, 1998.
Wood, Herbert J, 'England, China, and the Napoleonic Wars', *Pacific Historical Review*, 9, no. 2, 1940, 139–156.
Wood, Michael, *The Story of China: A Portrait of a Civilisation and its People*, Simon & Schuster, 2020.
Wyman, Patrick, *The Verge: Reformation, Renaissance, and Forty Years that Shook the World*, Grand Central Publishing, 2021.

Xu, Jin, *Empire of Silver A New Monetary History of China*, Yale University Press, 2017.

Yan, Xun, *In Search of Power and Credibility Essays on Chinese Monetary History (1851–1945)*, Dissertation, Department of Economic History, London School of Economics, 2015.
Yang, Lien-sheng, 'Economic Justification for Spending – An Uncommon Idea in Traditional China', *Harvard Journal of Asiatic Studies*, vol. 20, no. 1/2, June 1957, 36–52
Yang, Xiaoneng (ed.), *New Perspectives on China's Past: Chinese Archaeology in the Twentieth Century*, Yale University Press, 2001.
Yen-p'ing, Hao, *The Commercial Revolution in Nineteenth-Century China: the Rise of Sino-Western Mercantile Capitalism*, University of California Press, 1986.
Young, M.B., *The Rhetoric of Empire: American China Policy 1895–1901*, Harvard University Press, 1968.

Zhu, Ying, 'Evidence of Existing Knowledge of China and Its Influence on European Art and Architecture in the Sixteenth and Seventeenth Centuries', Ph.D. dissertation, Georgia Institute of Technology, December 2009.
Zong, Chuanming, 'The Journey of Euclid's Elements to China', *Notices of the American Mathematical Society*, vol. 70, no. 6, 2023, 953–961.

Acknowledgements

I AM INDEBTED TO the many specialists in various disciplines whose scholarly works I have studied and pored over during the last five years. Many are mentioned in the text; others in the Notes and Bibliography. Many others, too numerous to mention, were also consulted during the years of research, investigation, digression and writing. I was fortunate once again to have the indefatigable assistance of Dr. Joanna Penglase in my quest for material across the many topics that this book addresses. Joanna almost invariably managed to locate what I needed – frequently in little known journals, obscure publications and conference papers from all over the world. In the internet age it is no longer necessary to journey from one library to another in the search for source material.

Some others deserve special thanks for their advice, encouragement and conversation, including Kim Khong who continues to be a valued friend and occasional assistant; Dr. Rosalind Tan, whose enthusiasm for China was consistently informative and sparkling; Michael and Victoria Greene, whose deep knowledge of ceramics and wider knowledge of fine arts was always much appreciated; Kevin Tang, to whom I could turn for insights and suggestions; Major John Sutton, whose military and historical perspective was refreshingly atypical for his professional caste; Professor Dedee Murrell, whose knowledge of ancient Persia enthused me to follow paths that were ultimately limited by editing and publishing strictures;

Clara Leal Paz in Spain, who introduced me to Columbus' annotated copy of Marco Polo's Travels in the archives of Seville Cathedral; and finally, our charming and knowledgeable guides in China, above all Jane in Xiamen, who patiently answered my incessant questions and led me through Fujian's maritime and shipbuilding history.

My experienced and skilful agent Catherine Drayton from Inkwell Management, New York, brought me home to the publisher I knew the most, who understood me best and wanted the book more. This is the fourth book that Pam Brewster has published for me, and it has been the most wide-ranging, not to mention challenging. I am grateful for her commitment to this project and her ambitious vision. I am particularly thankful for the production and design team that Pam assembled around her led by Antonietta Anello, my meticulous project editor, who guided me through the twists and turns of the production process with calm assurance. Allison Hiew, my editor, deserves special thanks for her incisive challenges that contributed to a better book in every way. Nada Backovic excelled and delighted me with her cover design and Alex Hotchin instilled a charming and engaging artistic effect into my draft maps. The support team was large and it would be remiss of me not to mention also Neil Daly, indexer, Jasmin Chua, head of editorial, Kristin Thomas, design manager, Graeme Jones, typesetter, Todd Rechner head of production and Jessica Harvie production controller. I thank them all.

As always, my wife, Gillian Rose, was my lodestar. I owe her more than I can say. Our children, Olivia, Harriet, India and Nicholas were my inspiration.

Index

A

Acapulco: home port of the Manila galleons 135–6

Adams, John Quincy: supports war with China 188

Age of Discovery 37

de Albuquerque, Afonso: captures Goa 37

Alvarez, Jorge 40

Amherst, Lord: embassy to China (1816) 165–9

Amitav Ghosh *xxiv*, 180

de Andrade, Captain 41

de Andrade, Simao 42

Anson, Commodore George: and the Manila galleons 137

the Arrow 205

Astor, Jacob 109–10

Augustus, Roman emperor *xiii*

Augustus the Strong: first European-made porcelain 59–62

B

Bacon, Francis: on porcelain production 54

Baghdad: maritime trade with China 10

Balbuena (Spanish poet) 137

Banks, Sir Joseph 95

Baring, Francis: opposes reimbursement for seized opium 185

Baynes (Company taipan) 171–2

Beijing

  Boxers besiege the Legation Quarter (1900) 289

  falls (1858) 208

  founded by Emperor Yongle 27

  looting by Western forces after the Boxer Uprising 291–2

von Bell, Johann Adam Schall 76, 80

Benares (Varanasi): opium production centre 148

Benedict XII, Pope 83

Benoist, Michel 82

Binchun: first Chinese mission to the West 255

Bingham, Lieutenant 196

Boggs, Eli 249

Bonham, George 202

Böttger, Johann Freidrich: first European-made porcelain 59–62

Bowlby, Thomas

  captured and tortured 213, 216–17

  dies in captivity 217

Bowring, Sir John

  authorises the bombardment of Canton (1856) 206

  seeks a revision of the Treaty of Nanjing 203

  the seizure of the *Arrow* 205–6

Boxer Indemnity 295–6

  payments end in the mid20thC 298

Boxer Protocol terms and conditions 294–5

Boxer Uprising

  aftermath 294–6

  foreign reprisals, looting and atrocities 290–3

  hard line anti-foreign stance 289

  joint foreign forces crush the Boxers 289

  Legation Quarter in Beijing besieged 289

  rapid spread throughout N-E China 288–9

  Sichuan and Shaanxi neutrality 293

the *Bredenhoff* (Dutch ship) 119

Bridgman, Elijah: opposes the opium trade 228–9

British East India Company (*see* East India Company)

British Empire 164–5

British Peninsula and Orient Steam Navigation Company: participates in the opium trade 235

British Settlement 201

Bruce, Frederick (British ambassador) 210–11

  on China's new foreign policy office 252

  tries to force ratification of Tianjin Treaty 211

Brummell, Beau 98–9

bubonic plague (14thC) 23–4
Buddhism in China 21
Burke, Edmund: and the opium trade 154
Burlingame, Anson: leads a diplomatic mission to the West 256–7
Burlingame Treaty (1868) 256–7
Byron, Robert 8

C
Caesar, Julius 6
'Cambuluc' 23
Camellia sinensis 117–18 (*see also* tea)
Candliss, Henry: on opium and the Chinese people 244–5
Canton 40
  approach by sea 41
  bombarded (1841) 194
  bombarded (1856 & 1857) 206–7
  Bonham withdraws troops (1849) 202
  Mrs Baynes' visit 171
  Parkes' governorship 208
  Pearl River delta 40–1
Canton Regatta Club 109
Canton System 106–7
Caroline of Brunswick, Duchess 93
Carrhae battle (53 BCE) 5–6
Castiglione, Giuseppe 81–2
Catherine of Braganza
  brings tea to England 115–16
  marriage to Charles II 116
Central Asia: Silk Road route 8
centralised bureaucracy 4
Cerro Rico 312
Chambers, Sir William 94
  Chinese Pagoda at Kew Gardens 95–6
  handbooks of design 94–5
  impact on English gardens 94–5
Champion, Richard: royal patent for porcelain production 63–4
Chang'an (Xian) 7
  size and prosperity 9
China
  abandons paper money 126–7
  accumulation of silver 125
  ancient steel production 6
  annexes Taiwan (1683) 49
  canal and river transport 72–3
  centralised bureaucracy and government 4, 88–90
  'China's Catholic centuries' 75–83
  China's foreign policy office established 251
  Chinese coolie trade 245–8
  Christian converts (17thC) 79
  civil service examinations 90
  coal mining trial 260–1
  Confucian barriers to modernisation 252–3
  Confucian scorn for commerce 33
  copper currency 127
  decline and collapse (19thC-20thC) *xiv*, 238
  domestic unrest a perennial problem 201
  effects of silver-based economy 126–7
  El Nino events 17thC 140
  etymology of name 4–5
  European engagement strictly commercial 112
  generates a consumer revolution in Europe 142
  illicit trade in Japanese silver 130–1
  impacts of silver on Ming society 126
  'Incredible Famine' 1876-1879 272
  indemnity payments under the Treaty of Shimonoseki 279
  internal instability 17thC 140
  internal instability 19thC 164
  little knowledge of 18thC Europe 111–12
  manufacturing capacity (9thC) 10–11
  militarisation instead of industrialisation 252, 254
  military and naval weakness (19thC) 191, 195
  modernisation attempts 251, 252–4
  Mongol empire 21
  opium-addled image 158
  opium outlawed 154
  opium prohibition movement 245
  opium usage expands 156
  People's Republic established 1949 289–99
  population in 18thC 113
  porcelain mass production 65–74
  ports taken by the British (1841) 195
  Portuguese mariners arrive (1513) 40–4
  Portuguese resist expulsion (16thC) 43–4
  prejudices about foreigners 110–11
  Price Revolution 140–1
  Protestant missions 158
  railway construction opposed 254
  repeated invasions *xiv*
  Second Opium War penalties 209
  Self-Strengthening Movement 252
  silver ore reserves 130
  sovereignty eroded 249, 282
  telegraph installed 260
  treasure fleets 29–30
  treasure fleets reach the Americas 83
  treatment of Spanish priests 77
  war on drugs 176–80
  war with Japan (1894) 276
  world's largest economy 138–9
China Famine Relief Fund (London) 272
China Inland Mission: opposes opium use 244
Chinese coolie trade
  destinations 246–8
  indentured labourers as slaves 246
  recruitment and kidnapping 246
  replaces African slave trade 245
Chinese Pagoda at Kew Gardens 92, 95–6
chinoiserie in Europe 92–9
Chippendale, Thomas 97
Chongzhen emperor 47
Christian I, Elector of Saxony: porcelain collection 56

Christian mission: freedom of movement 220
Chun, Prince 260
  forced from office 260
  vendetta against Cixi and the West 258–9
Cixi 238
  becomes empress dowager 239
  builds her retirement home 274–5
  dies (1908) 296
  the empress dowagers adopt Chun's son as heir 259–60
  militarisation instead of industrialisation 252, 254
  moves against Kang Youwei 284–6
  organises Guangxu's heir 287
  plan to eradicate opium 245
  plans to modernise China 251
  resists railways 269–70
  retreats to Xian (1900) 289
  son becomes Xianfeng's successor 214
  supports the Boxers 289
  Tongzhi Restoration 252
Cleopatra 6
Cohong guild 109
Coleridge, Samuel Taylor 23, 157–8
Columbus, Christopher 36
Commissioner Lin 232
  banished 193
  confines the traders to the factory compound (1839) 178–80
  destroys seized opium 180
  moves to destroy the opium trade (1838) 177–80
'Complete Library in the Four Treasuries' 104
Confessions of an English Opium-Eater by Thomas De Quincey 157
Confucian mandarins
  conflict with eunuchs 28–9
  opposition to the treasure fleets 30
  scorn for trade and commerce 31–3
Confucianism 89
  in Europe 87
Confucius 23
Convention of Beijing 220
Cookworthy, William
  English porcelain production 62–4
  royal patent for porcelain production 63
Cushing, Caleb 234
  on American activities in China 232–3
Cushing, John Perkins 173
customs and tariffs
  Chinese officials 110
  corruption 110

D
Daoguang emperor
  appoints Commissioner Lin to destroy the opium trade (1838) 177–80
  on the growth of opium usage 170
  on losing the First Opium War 198
  quashes the opium trade 154
Davis, John: British representative in Canton 174–5
De Quincey, Thomas 157
Defoe, Daniel 59
Delano, Warren: opium smuggler 227
Delftware 96
d'Entrecolles, François Xavier 62, 69–70
  on Jingdezhen 66
Der Ling princess 283
Descartes, René 57
Designs of Chinese Buildings, Furniture, Dresses, Machines and Utensils by Sir William Chambers 94–5
Dias, Bartolomeu 36
Dickens, Charles: dismisses Chinese civilisation 199
van Diemen, Anthony 119–20
Disraeli, Benjamin: dislike of Jardine 155
Dissertations by Sir William Chambers 94–5
dragon kilns 66, 67–8
Drake, Francis 46, 56
  and the Manila galleons 137
Drury, Admiral: rebuffs Roberts' plans for Macau 163
Dutch chinoiserie 96
Dutch East India Company (*see* Verenigde Oostindische Compagnie (VOC))
Dutch Golden Age 57
Dutch traders
  arrive in China (1601) 45
  attack the *Santa Catarina* 45–6
  conflict with Portuguese traders 45–7
  expelled from Taiwan 49
  plunder Portuguese ship for porcelain 56
  raid Macau 46–7
  rebuffed by the Chinese 46–7
  retreat to Taiwan 47
Dzungar people 104

E
East India companies: stimulate Western commerce and fashion 57–8
East India Company 12
  as an opium drug cartel 152–4
  China trade profits 162
  concerns about Roberts' escapades 163–4
  established 1600 105
  establishes a tea industry in India 250
  first European 'factory' in Canton 105
  growth of silver exports 124
  increases opium production 154–5
  monopoly over China trade ends 174
  opium cultivation and processing 150–2
  Opium Department 150
  recalls Baynes 172
  steals tea plants and seeds 249
  tea trade beginnings 119
El Nino events
  17thC 140
  19thC 272
Elgin, Lord
  destroys the Old Summer Palace 217–18
  engineers the de facto legalisation of opium 236
  leads the British expedition in the Second Opium War 207

ratifies the Tianjin Treaty 219–20
returns to China (1860) 211
returns to England 210
Elizabeth I, Queen of England: porcelain collection 56
Elliot, Charles
British superintendent in Canton 176
dismissed and recalled 193
fails to convince Cabinet to end the First Opium War 195–6
guarantees reimbursement for seized opium 179
reaction to Lin's blockade 179
Emerson, Ralph Waldo: admiration for China 89
the Empress of China 225, 226
England (*see also* Great Britain)
cultural prejudice against China 120–1
English traders arrive in China *xiv*
growth of silver exports 123
growth of tea consumption 123
negative views of China 160
reaction to Amherst's embassy failure 168–9
tea trade growth 120
English Muscovy Company 12
eunuchs
conflict with scholar-officials 29
role in Chinese administration 28
Europe
China generates a consumer revolution 142
early admiration for China 88–9
evolving knowledge of China (14thC-16thC) 85–90
relationship strictly commercial 112
Evelyn, John 57
extraterritorial rights of foreign nations
description and implications 268–9
first granted under the Treaty of Nanjing (1842) 267
foreign banks and stock exchange 269
foreign courts and prisons 268–9
nations that were granted rights 268

F
factories in Canton 106
British factory 108–9
description and function 108–10
fanqui 110–11
Ferguson, Niall 139
First Emperor Qin 4
First Opium War 185–97
Fitzherbert, Maria 92–3
Flint, James 107–8
Fonthill Vase 55
Forbes, Paul S. 234
Forbes, Robert 227–8
criticism of British response to opium traders' petitions 173
on the traders' captivity in Canton (1839) 178
Forbidden City: built 27
Fortune, Robert: steals tea plants and seeds 249–50
1421: The Year China Discovered the World by Gavin Menzies 83
France
atrocities by troops in China 213
destroys Chinese fleet and shipyards 273
invasion of China (1857) *xiv*
joins Britain in the Second Opium War 207–8
launches the Tonkin War (1884) 271
leases Fort Bayard 282
porcelain production 62
preoccupied with the revolutionary wars 226
Treaty of Tianjin 209
free trade
opium economy of Great Britain 243
and the Treaty of Wangxia 234
Freedom of the seas 46
French chinoiserie
Masquerade of the King of China 96–7
masquerades and balls 96–7
Fuzhou Naval Shipyard
built under Prosper Giquel (1866) 254–5
destroyed by the French (1884) 271

G
da Gama, Vasco 36–7
brings porcelain to the Portuguese court 55
Gaozong emperor: on foreign trade 11
Garway, Thomas 117
Genghis Khan 17, 34
death 21
George, Prince of Wales: Royal Pavilion at Brighton 92–4
George III, King 93, 94
German chinoiserie 97
Giquel, Prosper
director of the new Fuzhou Naval Shipyard 254–5
led the Unvanquished Army against the Taipings 254
Gladstone, William: opposes Second Opium War 187–8
globalisation 138
Goa 39
Golden Lotus by Lanling Xiaoxiao Sheng *xxv*
Goldhaus (Dresden) 60
Gong, Prince
establishes China's first foreign policy office 251
releases Harry Parkes and others 216–17
supports the empress dowagers 239
Gordon, Major Charles: leads China's forces against the Taiping 253
Graham, Lord: critical of the opium traders' concerns 173
Grand Canal: restored in Yongle's rule 27
Great Britain (*See also* England)
assessment of Cixi 239

atrocities by troops in Second Opium War 195, 213
attempts to annex Macau 161–2
attempts to revise the Treaty of Nanjing 203
cabinet approves war with China (1839) 187
'Chinese election' 207
condemns and restricts opium trade 245
embassy to China (1816) 165–9
forces China to lease Port Edward (1898) 282
imperial development 19thC 159
invasion of China (1840) *xiv*
invasion of China (1857) *xiv*
leases the New Territories 282
manufacturers lobby against the Company's monopoly 173–4
Palmerston re-elected 207
public support for the First Opium War 198–9
Royal Navy's expansion 164
seeks inland trading concessions 203
Sinophobia 199
starts the Second Opium War 206–7
'Great Khanate' 17
Great Ming Precious Notes 126
Great Wall: rebuilt in Yongle's rule 27
Greater Bay Area 40
Grimm, Baron: on China 159–60
Grotius, Hugo 46, 56
Guangxu emperor 260
assumes power 275
becomes pro-Japanese 285
drought and famine 272
under house arrest 285–6
Hundred Days Reforms 283
influenced by Grand Tutor Weng 275
influenced by Kang Youwei 283
poisoned (1908) 296
retreats to Xian (1900) 289
Guangzhou (*see* Canton)
gunrunners and pirates 248–9
Guo Songtao
criticised for modernisation aims 261–2
first permanent ambassador to Britain 261
side-lined and forgotten 262
Gutzlaff, Karl: secret exploration of China's north coast 174
Güyük Khan 20

H
Hai Ling 196
Hakluyt, Richard 46
Han dynasty 3
silk as tribute and tax 9
Harry Parkes: captured and tortured 213, 216–17
Hart, Sir Robert 114
contribution to 'Make China Strong' 253–4
proposes expansion of foreign trade (1875) 260
Hayes, Captain Bully 249
van Heemskerck, Jacob 46
'High Qing' period 103
Hirobumi 277, 285
Holey Dollar 133
Hong Kong 40
Hong Kong and Shanghai Banking Corporation (HSBC) 269
Hong merchants: control of the factories 109–10
Hong Xiuquan 240–1
Hongwu emperor 25–6
Hongxi emperor 30
Hormuz 39
Hornby, Sir Edmund 273
'House of Confucius' 94
Howqua 109–10
Hume, David: on the consumption of Chinese goods 142
Hundred Days Reforms 283

I
Ibn Battuta 19
Imperial Customs Service
Sir Robert Hart 267
Western officials 267
'Incredible Famine' 1876-1879 272
Indonesian Moluccas 35
Industrial Revolution in Europe 114
Innocent IV, Pope 18
International Settlement 201
electric lighting arrives (1882) 269
Islam
commercial links to Venice 35
'gunpowder' empires 34–5

J
Japan
annexes Taiwan (1895) 49
annexes the Ryukyu Islands 271
dominates East Asia (late 19thC) 273
invades China (1859) *xiv*
invades Taiwan (1874) 271
navy modelled on the Royal Navy 275–6
silver deposits 130–1
war with China (1894) 276
Jardine, William
Baynes incident 171–2
campaigning for war with China 175–6
opium trading 155
opposes Chinese trade restrictions 170–1
opposes the East India Company monopoly 170
returns to England 177
role in the First Opium War 186–7
secret exploration of China's north coast 174
supports missionaries' cultural propaganda 229
wins Palmerston's support for war 189

Jardine Matheson & Co
  American competition for opium 226–7
  opium traders 155
  'Wusong Road Company' 270
Jefferson, Thomas 225
Jesuits in China 75–83
  contribution to Chinese science and culture 81–3
  problem of 'ancestor worship' 79–80
Jianjing emperor 70–1
Jiaqing emperor
  on Macartney's mission 165–7
  rebuffs Britain's attempt on Macau 161
  weak leadership 164
  writes to George III 168
Jingdezhen
  centre of porcelain production 32, 65–8
Jingtai emperor: abandons paper money 126–7
John II, king of Portugal 36
Johnson, Samuel: on Chinese architecture and design 90
Jordanus (Spanish missionary) 12
Jurchen tribes 103
Juvayni 19
Juvenal: on Rome's trade with China *xv*

K
Kang Youwei ('Wild Fox Kang')
  accomplices executed 286
  flees to Japan 286
  influence over Guangxu 283–5
  plans to kill Cixi 285
  proposes an imperial advisory board 283
Kangxi emperor 104
  bans Christian preaching in China 80–1
  Edict of Toleration 80
  embraces the Jesuits 76
  great leap forward (18thC) 141
  response to European approaches 105–6
'Kansu Braves' 289
kaolin 61, 62, 68, 69
Khanbaliq: Kublai Khan's new capital 23
Kipling, Rudyard: on China 165
Kowloon: ceded to Britain 220
Koxinga 48
Kubla Khan, Or A Vision in a Dream: A Fragment by Coleridge 157–8
Kublai Khan
  completes the subjugation of China 21
  employs Marco Polo 20
  four-tier social class structure 22–3
  re-unification of China 23
  religious tolerance 21–2

L
la maladie de porcelain 56
la ruta de la plata 136–7
Lady Tan's Circle of Women by Lisa See *xxiv*
Lanling Xiaoxiao Sheng *xxv*
de Legazpi, Miguel López
  discovers the *tornaviaje* 134
  founds Manila 134
Leibniz, Gottfried 60
  admiration for China 89
  on Confucianism 87
Leizu empress 5
Li Hongzhang
  on China's failure to modernise 277
  Grand Secretary 260
  promotes railways 271
  supports China's industrialisation 258
Liadong Peninsula 179
Limoges: porcelain production 62
Lin Yutang *xxiv*
Lin Zexu (*see* Commissioner Lin)
Lindsay, Hugh Hamilton
  secret exploration of China's north coast 174
  supports Jardine and Matheson's campaign 175–6
Lisbon: rivals Venice for commerce 39
Loch, Henry 220
Locke, John 11
  on English tea culture 119
Longyu empress 275
Longyu Empress Dowager 297
Louis IX, King of France 18
Louis XIV, King of France
  contribution to Chinese science 81
  enthusiasm for porcelain 58–9
Low, Miss Harriet 171
Lynch, George 292

M
Macartney, Halliday 254
Macartney, Lord
  mission to China 112–13, 159
Macau 40
  Jesuit missionary base 75
  leased by the Portuguese 44
the Macclesfield (British ship) 105, 120
MacDonald, Lady Claude 291
MacDonald, Sir Claude 286
Madison, James 225
Magellan 134
Mahan, General Alfred 229
Malacca 39
Manchuria
  China cedes half to Russia (1860) 220
  China cedes part to Japan (1860) 220
Manchus 103 (*see also* Qing dynasty)
  invade China 48
  relationship the Han Chinese 103–4
Mandate of Heaven 48
Mandeville, Sir john 85
Manila
  founded 1571 134
  nexus of trans-Pacific trade 137
Manila galleons
  construction 135–6
  trans-Pacific journey 134–5
  vulnerable to piracy 136–7
al-Mansur 10
Manuel I, king of Portugal 39

Map of the Ten Thousand Countries of the Earth 82–3
Mare Liberum by Hugo Grotius 46
marine insurance created 72
Martin, William: support for the Taipings 241
Mary II, Queen of England 119
Matheson, James
  Baynes incident 171–2
  campaigning for war with China 175–6
  opium trading 155
  opposes Chinese trade restrictions 170–1
  opposes the East India Company monopoly 170
  purchases the Isle of Lewis 155
  supports missionaries' cultural propaganda 229
Meadows, Thomas 111
  admiration for China 89
Medici family: porcelain collection 55–6
Meissen: birth place of European porcelain 61
Melbourne, Lord: opposes reimbursement for seized opium 185
Mencius 31
Mendoza, Juan 86
Menzies, Gavin 83
meritocratic selection system 4
Mexico City
  becomes an international 17thC city 137
  Camino del China 136
  a centre of trans-Pacific trade 136
M'Ghee: on the Old Summer Palace 215
Ming dynasty *xiii*
  collapse 140
  cultural impact of wealth and prosperity 128–9
  decline and fall 47–8
  end of sea-going navy and ship building 29–31
  the Forbidden City 23
  industry and agriculture expand 128
  isolationism 24, 29
  replaces the Mongols 24
  resistance to Qing take over 48–9
  role of eunuchs 28–9
  sea ban lifted (1567) 131
  trade and wealth 31–3
Ming porcelain 71
Mitford, Algernon 252
Mocatta, Moses 124
Moment in Peking by Lin Yutang *xxiv*
Mongols (*see also* Yuan dynasty)
  bubonic plague 23–4
  decline in China 23–4
  defeat the Song 12–13
  expansion across Eurasia 17
  oppression of the Han Chinese 22
  subjugation of China 21
Montesquieu: on silver-based Chinese commerce 126
Morris, Robert 225
Morrison, Robert
  embassy to China (1916) 165
  Protestant missionary 163
Morse, HB 280
Moule, Arthur 244
Mughal empire 34
Myanmar *xv*

N
Nanjing: Treaty of Nanjing (1842) 197
Napier, Lady
  response to the Chinese defeat 197
  supports Jardine and Matheson's campaign 175–6
Napier, Lord
  belligerent position 175
  British representative in Canton 174–5
Napoleon Bonaparte
  defeat frees British military resources 164
  supreme in Europe 162
  views on Amherst's failed mission 169
Needham, Joseph 75
Nemesis (iron-clad gunship) 190–1
Nestorian Christians in China 21
Netherlands: Dutch Golden Age 57
Newton, Sir Isaac: on the flow of silver to China *xiv*, 128
Nieuhof, Johan: illustrated book on China 87–8
Northern Chinese Famine (1876-1879) 272
Nugent, Thomas 62

O
Odoric of Pordenone 85
Ögödei: campaign in China 21
Old Summer Palace 82
  description and history 214–15
  destroyed 217–19
  looted 214–15, 218–19
On Friendship by Matteo Ricci 78
On the True Meaning of the Lord of Heaven by Matteo Ricci 79
opium 147
  British cultivation and smuggling *xiv*
  cultivation and production 150–2
  de facto legalisation in China 236
  domestic cultivation in China 243
  East India Company production 148–52
  expansion of trade after the Taiping Rebellion 242–3
  extensive use in China 244
  health effects 244
  history and usage 147–8
  opium economy of Great Britain 243
  outlawed in China 154
  smoking practice 157
  trade mechanism 149
  use in England 157
opium traders
  American trade expands 234
  British withdraw to Hong Kong 180
  building a pathway to war 173
  a Canton community 155

and Commissioner Lin 177–80
and the East India Company 152–3
growing Western opposition (late 19thC) 245
petition the British parliament 172–3
smuggling route 154
Opium Wars
First Opium War 185–97
Second Opium War 198–209
Ottoman empire 34–5
Outer Mongolia 104

P
Palmerston, Lord
becomes Prime Minister 203
on China's new foreign policy office 252
conceals the his support for the opium traders 188–9
opposes military action (1834) 186
proposes joint naval expedition with the French 204
supports military action (1839) 186
Papacy condemns ancestor worship 79–80
papal envoys to the Mongol court 20–1
papaver somniferum (*see* Opium)
Parkes, Harry
authorises the bombardment of Canton (1856) 206
outrage at the seizure of the *Arrow* 204–5
released 216
seeks a *casus belli* 204–5
unleashes undeclared war 206
'Warlord governor' of Canton 208
Parthia 5–6
Patna: opium production centre 148
Pearl (Guangxu's companion) 275
Pearl River: waterfront factories 108
Pearl River delta 40–1
People's Republic established 1949 289–99
Pepys, Samuel 117
Perkins, Thomas Handasyd 173
Persian empire (Safavids) 34
Peter the Great's enthusiasm for porcelain 58–9
Philip II, King of Sain and Portugal
porcelain collection 55
sends a fleet west across the Pacific 134
piculs 118
Piercy, Rev: supports the Opium Wars 230
Pinyin system of spelling *xxv*
pirates and gunrunners 248–9
Pires, Tomé 41, 42–3, 112
Polo, Maffeo 20
Polo, Marco 20
on China's maritime trade 19
introduces porcelain to the West 54
on Kublai Kahn's government 22
reception of his account of China 84–5
on the Song dynasty 12
Polo, Niccolò 20
porcelain
Chinese mass production 65–74
commonplace in Europe 57
constituent materials 68–9
early samples brought to Europe 55
first European manufacture 59–62
production secrets *xiii*
production (9thC CE) 10–11
properties 53
rapid spread across Europe 55–7
transportation 73
Port of London: tea transport 121
Portobelo 133
Portuguese
arrive in China (1513) *xiii–xiv*, 40–4
arrive in India 36–7
expansion in Asia 38–9
expelled from China (1521) 43–4
seeks a sea route to China 35–6
Potosi silver mines 131–2
Pottinger, Henry (Chief Superintendent): conduct of the First Opium War 194–5
Price Revolution 140–1
Protestant missionaries
follow traders into China 228
and the legalisation of opium 235–6
opium trade as God's will 235
opium trade condemned by Rev Bridgman 228–9
opium use condemned 244
some Western opposition to the Protestant missions 231
support the Opium Wars 230
and the Treaty of Wangxia 234
vision of opening China 229–30

Q
Qianlong emperor 103
achievements 104–5
economic prosperity 105
isolationism 114
Macartney's mission 112–13
military campaigns 104–5
restricts Europeans to Canton 106
suppresses Christian missions 81
Qin, First Emperor 4
Qin dynasty: achievements 4
Qing dynasty
the 'Great Clearance' 48–9
take over China 48
Qing Forever 255
Qishan (regional viceroy)
banished 193
negotiates with Elliot 192–3
Qiying (emperor's representative) 200
Quanzhou 12
Queen Mary of Orange: enthusiasm for porcelain 59
Quesnay, Francois: admiration for China 89

R
railways in China
first standard gauge track laid 270–1
resistance from government 269–70
'Wusong Road Company' 270

Raleigh, Walter 56, 164
captures the *Madre de Deus* 56
Reed, William
engineers a de facto legalisation of opium 236
seeks a revision of the Treaty of Tianjin 236
Reforms of 1898 283
Ricci, Matteo 28, 73, 82
on China's canal and river transport 73
on Confucianism and Christianity 78–9
journals 86–7
on porcelain 5
reports on China 77
translations of Chinese and Western classics 77–9
Rio de la Plata 133
Rites of Zhou by Confucius 23
Robert, Issachar: support for the Taipings 241
Robert, John 228
urges Britain to annex Macau 163
Roman Empire
cost of silk 8
early contact with China *xiii*
fiscal drain due to silk trade 7
silk arrives 3, 5–7
trade with China *xv*
Rome condemns ancestor worship 79–80
Russell, Samuel: opium smuggler 227–8
Russell & Co 226–8
briefly renounces opium trading 232
control of US consulates 234
Russia
forces China to lease Port Arthur (1898) 279
occupies Manchuria 279–80
occupies part of Xinjiang (1871) 271
Treaty of Tianjin 209
Rustichello 20, 84
Ryukyu Island *xv*

S
Santa Catarina: plundered by the Dutch 45, 56
Second Opium War 198–209
penalties 209
See, Lisa *xxiv*
self-strengthening movement
failure to develop Western military technology 273
funds defence, not famine relief 272
'Self-Strengthening Movement' 252
Seneca 6–7
Serica 4
sericulture 5
Seville: economic heart of Spain 133
Seymour, Admiral: bombards Canton (1856) 206
Shangdu 23
Shanghai Foreign Arms Corps 248–9
Shanghai Share Broker's Association 269
Shaw, Samuel 72, 225
Shen Kuo 11
Shunzhi emperor
embraces the Jesuits 76
rebuffs the Dutch 87
silk
adopted by the Mongols 18
adopted in Rome 5–7
as currency 8–9
impact on 17thC fashion 98–9
production 5
qualities *xiii*
Silk Road *xiii,* 2, 7–8
under the Mongol Empire 18–19
silver
basis of Chinese commerce 128
currency or commodity 128
deposits discovered on Honshu 130
enriches China *xiv*
Potosi mines 131–2
routes to China 132–3
Spanish colonial mines 131–2, 141
17thC oversupply 140
Zacatecas mines 141
Sima Qian *xv*
Simpson, Bertram: describes 'loot fever' 291
Sinae 4
Single Whip reform 126
'Six Gentlemen of the Hundred Days Reform' 286
Smith, Adam 141
China's canal and river transport 72
China's wealth 105
silver-based Chinese commerce 126
Society for the Diffusion of Useful Knowledge 229
Society for the Suppression of the Opium Trade 244
Society of Righteous and Harmonious Fists 288
Sogdiana 8
Song dynasty *xiii*
advanced economic management 11–12
expansion of ship building 12
introduces paper money 11–12, 19
South China Sea 39
European trade route *xv*
militarised by the Royal Navy (19thC) 161
Spain
colonial silver mines 131–2, 141
defaults on sovereign debt 139–40
founds Manila (1571) 45, 125–6
massive wealth from silver 138–9
Price Revolution 140–1
rejuvenated under the Bourbons 141
seeks a sea route to China 35–6
silver extraction rapidly increases (18thC) 141
17thC inflation 139–40
Spanish silver dollars: a global currency 133–4
Spanish silver pesos 127, 133

Spanish traders
  arrive in China (1598) 45
  arrive in the Philippines *xiv*
  conflict with Portuguese traders 45
  silver transport to China 136–7
Spice Islands 35
spice trade dominated by the Portuguese 39
Spoils of War by Hugo Grotius 46
Squiers, Herbert 291
Staunton, George 167
  opposes Jardine and Matheson's campaign 176
steel-making in ancient China 6
Steen, Jan 57
Stein, Aurel 8
Stevens, Edwin 240
Stoke-on-Trent: centre of English porcelain production 73–4
Strait of Malacca 39
Sulaiman's account of porcelain 53
Summer Palace 274
Supreme Court of China (Great Britain) 268
Sushun, prince: board of regents 238–9
sycee silver 127

T
taels 119
Taiping Heavenly Kingdom 240
Taiping Rebellion 239–42
  anti-Manchu stance 240, 241
  Ever-Victorious Army 242
  Gordon leads China's forces 253
  initial Western support 241
  Unvanquished Army 242
  Western powers arm the Qing government 242
Taiwan 47
  anti-Qing rebel stronghold *xv*
  ceded to Japan 279
  returned to China (1945) 49
Taklamakan Desert 7–8
Tamerlane 34
Tang dynasty *xiii*
  loss of Silk Road 9–10
  rise of maritime trade 10
  silk trade flourishes 9
tea
  cultivation and processing 117–18
  early shipments to Europe 115
  exchanged for silver 119
  health benefits 116–17
  high prices 117
  introduction to England 115
Temür emperor 83
'The Five Counter Measures Against Barbarians' 106–7
The Golden Lotus (1610) 129
The History of the Great and Mighty Kingdom of China by Juan Mendoza 86
The Road to Oxiana by Robert Byron 8
The Travels of Sir John Mandeville 85
Three Emperors of the Qing dynasty 103
Three Pillars of the Ming dynasty 79
Tibet
  annexed by Qianlong 104
  relationship with China *xv*
Tiger's Mouth 41
Toghon Temür: tolerance of Christian missionaries 20
Tongzhi emperor 238
  assumes power (1873) 259
  dies (1875) 259
Tongzhi Restoration 252
tornaviaje 134–5
Travels of Friar Odoric 85
treasure fleets 29–30, 83
Treaties of Tianjin 208–9
  ratified (Oct 1860) 220
  treaty participants 209
Treaty of Nanjing 197
  Britain attempts revision of the Treaty of Nanjing 203
  implementation difficulties 199–200
  interpretation differences 200–1
  terms 198
  trader disenchantment 202–3
Treaty of Nerchinsk 80
Treaty of Shimonoseki 278
Treaty of Tordesillas 38, 46
Treaty of Wangxia (1844) 233–4
treaty ports 201, 203, 233–4, 249, 267, 279
  new ports under the Treaty of Tianjin 209
Tregonning Hill 63
Trianon de Porcelaine 58–9, 92
Herr von Tschirnhaus: first European-made porcelain 60–1
Tumu Crisis 28–9
Tyler, US President: provides arms to China 233

U
United States of America
  benefits from the opium wars 225
  commences trade with China (1784) 122, 225
  doctrine of free trade in China 234
  government opposition to opium trade 232–3
  neutral during the Second Opium War 236–7
  opium profits fund development at home 227–8
  opium trade expands 235
  opium traders 226–8
  provides arms to China 233
  replaces French in Canton 226
  Treaty of Tianjin 209
de Urdaneta, Andrés: and the *tornaviaje* 134
Uyghurs 22
  support Qing genocide of the Dzungar 104

V
Valignano, Alessandro 77
Venice
rising trading power 19–20
silk trade with the Mongol Empire 18
Verbiest, Ferdinand 80
Verenigde Oostindische Compagnie (VOC)
dominance in the East 57
early tea trade 119–20
established (1602) 45
loss of the *Geldermalsen* 72
Vermeer, Johannes 57
Victoria, Queen: on the First Opium War 193–4
Vietnam *xv*
VOC (*see* Verenigde Oostindische Compagnie (VOC))
Voltaire: admiration for China 89

W
de Waal, Edmund 75
on the Jesuits in China 83
Waller, Edmund 116
Wang Zhen 28–9
Wanli emperor 47, 82
Ward, Frederick 248
Warring States Period 4
Wedgwood, Josiah
crushes Cookworthy's patent 63
porcelain production 64
Wei Yuan: on Chinese naval power 233
Wellington, Duke: supports the First Opium War 188
Weng, Grand Tutor 275
Western nations: invasion of China (1900) *xiv*
Whampoa 41
White, Thaddeus C. 283
White Porcelain Pagoda of Nanjing 87–8
built in Yongle's rule 27
Whitehead, William: admiration for China 90–1
Wilhelm II, Kaiser 279
forces China to lease Qingdao (1898) 279
Willow pattern 96
Wolseley, Garnet 220
on Chinese life (mid-19thC) 248

X
'Xanadu' by Samuel Taylor Coleridge 23
Xia Yuanji 30
Xianfeng emperor
delays the Tianjin Treaty ratification 210–11
flees to Chengde and dies (1861) 214, 238
repudiates the Tianjin treaties 211
resists the West's incursions 203
Treaty of Tianjin 208–9
Xinjiang *xv*, 104
Xu (emperor's representative) 200–2
Xu Jincheng 294
Xuande emperor 30
Xuantong emperor
abdicates 1912 297

Y
Ye, Canton Governor: seizes the *Arrow* 205
Yellow Emperor 5
'Yellow Peril' 279
Yongle, emperor 26–8
achievements 26–8
builds the 'treasure fleets' 27–8
treasure fleets 29–30
Yongle encyclopedia established 27
Yongzheng emperor: suppresses Christian missions 81
Yuan, General 285
Yuan dynasty *xiii*, 21–2 (*see also* Mongols)
decline 23–4
Yuan Shikai, General: 'Right Division' massacres 293
Yuqian, Confucian warrior 195

Z
Zacatecas silver mines 141
Zeng Guofan: assessment of Cixi 239
Zhang Tao: on China's cultural decay (1609) 129
Zhen, Empress Consort 214, 238
becomes empress dowager 239
the empress dowagers adopt Chun's son as heir 259–60
Zheng He 28, 83
Zheng (Qin First Emperor) 4
Zhengde emperor 42–3
Zhengtong emperor 28–9
bans naval expeditions 30
Zhenjiang: falls to the British (1842) 196
Zhigang 258
advocates China's industrialisation 257–8
report on the West 257
Zongli Yamen 251